The Legacy of Boethius in Medieval England: The *Consolation* and its Afterlives

MEDIEVAL AND RENAISSANCE
TEXTS AND STUDIES

VOLUME 525

The Legacy of Boethius in Medieval England: The *Consolation* and its Afterlives

Edited by

A. Joseph McMullen and Erica Weaver

ARIZONA CENTER FOR MEDIEVAL
ACMRS
AND RENAISSANCE STUDIES
Tempe, Arizona
2018

A generous contribution to support the publication of this volume was provided by The Pakis Family Foundation.

THE ARIZONA CENTER FOR
MEDIEVAL & RENAISSANCE
STUDIES

Published by ACMRS (Arizona Center for Medieval and Renaissance Studies)
Tempe, Arizona

Library of Congress Cataloging-in-Publication Data

Names: McMullen, A. Joseph, editor. | Weaver, Erica, 1990- editor.
Title: The legacy of Boethius in medieval England : the consolation and its afterlives / edited by A. Joseph McMullen and Erica Weaver.
Description: Tempe, Arizona : Published by ACMRS (Arizona Center for Medieval and Renaissance Studies), 2018. | Series: Medieval and renaissance texts and studies ; volume 525 | Includes bibliographical references and index.
Identifiers: LCCN 2018023350 | ISBN 9780866985819 (hardcover : alk. paper)
Subjects: LCSH: Boethius, -524--Influence. | Boethius, -524. De consolatione philosophiae. | English poetry--Middle English, 1100-1500--History and criticism.
Classification: LCC PA6231.C8+ 2018
LC record available at https://lccn.loc.gov/2018023350

Cover Illustration:
Bibliothèque nationale de France
Département des manuscrits, Français 1586, fol. 30v

∞
This book is made to last. It is set in Adobe Caslon Pro, smyth-sewn and printed on acid-free paper to library specifications.
Printed in the United States of America

Table of Contents

Acknowledgments vii

Reading Boethius in Medieval England: *The Consolation of Philosophy* from Alfred to Ashby ix
ERICA WEAVER AND A. JOSEPH MCMULLEN

Earlier Medieval England

The Protean Form of the Old English *Boethius* 1
SUSAN IRVINE, *University College London*

Knowledge and Rebellion in the Old English *Boethius* 19
NICOLE GUENTHER DISCENZA, *University of South Florida*

The Old English *Boethius* and Speculative Thought 35
PAUL E. SZARMACH, *University of California, Berkeley*

Purgatoria clementia: Philosophy and Principles of Pain in the Old English *Boethius* 53
HARUKO MOMMA, *University of Toronto*

An Ethical History for the Self: The Liberius *Exemplum* in the Old English *Boethius* 71
HILARY FOX, *Wayne State University*

Finding Consolation at the End of the Millennium 89
ERICA WEAVER, *University of California, Los Angeles*

Later Medieval England

Consolations of Friendship: The Augustinian Reception of Boethius in Twelfth-Century England 103
ANN W. ASTELL, *University of Notre Dame*

Sensible Prose and the Sense of Meter: Boethian Prosimetrics and the Fourteenth Century 125
ELEANOR JOHNSON, *Columbia University*

Nature, Astronomy, and Cosmology in Chaucer's *Boece* 143
A. JOSEPH MCMULLEN, *Centenary University*

Tragic Diction in Chaucer's *Boece*, the *Canterbury Tales*, and Hoccleve's *Series* 155
JONATHAN STAVSKY, *Tel Aviv University*

The Potages of Foryetfulness: Thomas Usk, Lady Love, and the Boethian Rhetoric of Personification 171
ANTHONY G. CIRILLA, *College of the Ozarks*

Translation for *Sentence* in Middle English Poetry: The Case of John Walton 193
TAYLOR COWDERY, *University of North Carolina at Chapel Hill*

Contributors 215

Acknowledgments

Like all books, this volume is the product of a great deal of good fortune and many wonderful interlocutors. Harvard University's Department of English, Standing Committee on Medieval Studies, Morton W. Bloomfield Fund, Provostial Fund Committee for the Arts and Humanities, Dumbarton Oaks Medieval Library, and *Sententiae: The Harvard Undergraduate Journal of Medieval Studies* were all invaluable, generously supporting the conference that first brought together this group of scholars in March 2014. We are grateful to the faculty, staff, and students of Harvard's English and Classics departments, the Medieval Studies program, and Houghton Library, especially Daniel Donoghue, Nicholas Watson, James Simpson, Jan Ziolkowski, Sean Gilsdorf, Peter Accardo, Gwen Urdang-Brown, Shayna Cummings, Case Kerns, and Anna McDonald, for their very kind assistance and eager attendance. Daniel and Nicholas, in particular, helped us to bring the conference to fruition and, later, to navigate the process of turning selected essays into a volume that, we hope, is greater than the sum of its parts. We are enormously thankful for their guidance.

The International Boethius Society was likewise a source of enthusiasm and support, providing a home for a selection of essays on Boethius's Continental legacy in a special issue of *Carmina Philosophiae: Journal of the International Boethius Society*. Susan Irvine, Ann W. Astell, and Eleanor Johnson were each model plenary speakers, and we are very appreciative. We thank also the conference attendees and speakers who do not appear in this volume but who nevertheless shaped it with their enthusiastic participation and comments: Gillian Adler, David Albertson, Jason Baxter, Alexis Becker, Margherita Belli, Stephen Blackwood, Kathryn Crowcroft, Brian FitzGerald, Jerold Frakes, Kara Gaston, Tony Harris, Kenneth Hawley, Bre Leake, Megan Murton, Alvaro Pires, Philip Phillips, Joel Relihan, Elaine Scarry, Anne Schindel, Eileen Sweeney, Fabio Troncarelli, Daniel Walden, Leah Whittington, and many others. We are likewise grateful to well-wishers, who were unable to attend but who nonetheless had a hand in shaping this volume by shaping one of its editors, and to Ian Cornelius who shared an advance copy of an essay with us, while we were finishing our introduction. Finally, we are grateful to our contributors, our two anonymous reviewers, and to the editorial staff at ACMRS for their careful attention to detail.

Reading Boethius in Medieval England: *The Consolation of Philosophy* from Alfred to Ashby

Erica Weaver and A. Joseph McMullen

Samuel Johnson once noted that "Chaucer, who is generally considered as the Father of our Poetry, has left a version of Boetius, on the *Comforts of Philosophy*; a book which seems to have been the favourite of the middle ages:—of so much celebrity, that it has been translated into Saxon by King Alfred, and illustrated with a copious comment ascribed to Aquinas."[1] As he rightly sensed, Anicius Manlius Severinus Boethius's *Consolation of Philosophy* (ca. 524) became one of the seminal texts of the Middle Ages, from its rise to popularity during the reign of Charlemagne (768–814) to its continued reworkings after the death of Chaucer (1400).[2] Written in prison, while Boethius awaited his execution after losing favor with the Gothic ruler of Italy, it recounts a philosophical awakening that influenced metaphysical thought and literary form for well over five hundred years. The Latin text is prosimetrical, staging a dialogue between the imprisoned Boethius and the larger-than-life Lady Philosophy in alternating prose and verse sections. Proceeding by way of a dazzling allegorical dialectic, Philosophy's teaching ultimately elicits self-knowledge and action: Fortune's wheel continually turns, so impermanent worldly riches—whether in the form of actual goods or prestigious positions—cannot be counted on for happiness. Boethius must instead reorient himself towards internal, inalienable truths.

---

[1] Samuel Johnson, *The Idler*, 69, in *The Idler and The Adventurer*, ed. W.J. Bate, John M. Mullitt, and L.F. Powell, *The Works of Samuel Johnson*, vol. 11 (New Haven: Yale University Press, 1963), 214.

[2] Boethius was not only known for the *Consolation*, however. During his time as a Roman statesman, he finished an impressive number of treatises, translations, and commentaries, including an influential theological tractate known as the *Opuscula sacra* and his *De institutione musica*, which shaped European musical thought for seven centuries and was at one time the most-copied treatise on music theory. And yet, the *Consolation* would surpass all of his other works, becoming a central school text and inspiring the translations and adaptations that form the core of our project here.

This message resonated strongly with medieval readers and thinkers, who debated Boethius's Neoplatonic ideals, experimented with his literary forms, and even cast themselves as Boethian interlocutors. Of all of the works of secular literature that survive from the European Middle Ages, the *Consolation* was the most widely copied, and the pervasiveness of its cultural influence is difficult to overstate. It was likely the most influential non-devotional text of the entire period, and, as C.S. Lewis once quipped, "[t]o acquire a taste for it is almost to become naturalised in the Middle Ages" as a whole.[3] In total, there are about four hundred extant manuscripts—many covered in glosses, commentary, and other *scholia*. Prompted by Boethius's allusions, medieval readers filled their margins with "contemporary explanations (and misunderstandings)" of a wide array of topics, ranging "from Sirens to Socrates and actresses to astronomy."[4] Had these annotated manuscripts only transmitted a wide body of classical learning, they would merit attention enough, but Boethius's speculative philosophy and prosimetrical form themselves fascinated later authors, who adapted Boethian dialectic to their own ends in a host of vernacular languages, including Old and Middle English, Old High German, and Old French, among others.[5] In the sixteenth century, the *Consolation* would be translated by Queen Elizabeth I, and, as Dr. Johnson's own interest suggests, it continued to exert an enormous influence on English literary culture well into the eighteenth century and beyond.[6] And yet, as Dr. Johnson might have predicted, the Alfredian and Chaucerian translations have served as the lodestones for each period's assessments of Boethius's impact on English arts and letters.

In medieval England, Boethius's *Consolation* exerted a strong pull elsewhere as well, however. John Walton's 1410 translation was almost twice as popular as Chaucer's, and influential figures such as Abbo of Fleury, Aelred of Rievaulx,

[3] C.S. Lewis, *The Discarded Image: An Introduction to Medieval and Renaissance Literature* (Cambridge: Cambridge University Press, 2012), 75.

[4] Malcolm Godden, Rohini Jayatilaka, and Rosalind Love, "Boethius in Early Medieval Europe: Commentary on *The Consolation of Philosophy* from the 9th to the 11th Centuries," Oxford University, Alfredian Boethius Project. <http://www.english.ox.ac.uk/boethius/>.

[5] For a general overview of Boethius's medieval reception, see *A Companion to Boethius in the Middle Ages*, ed. Noel Harold Kaylor, Jr., and Philip Edward Phillips (Boston: Brill, 2012); *The Cambridge Companion to Boethius*, ed. John Marenbon (Cambridge: Cambridge University Press, 2009); and Ian Cornelius, "Boethius' *Consolatio philosophiae*," in *The Oxford History of Classical Reception in English Literature, Vol. I: The Middle Ages*, ed. Rita Copeland (Oxford: Oxford University Press, 2016), 269–98, at 278. Our thanks are owed to Ian for sharing an advance proof with us.

[6] For further details, see Noel Harold Kaylor, Jr., and Philip Edward Phillips, eds., *The Consolation of Queen Elizabeth I: The Queen's Translation of Boethius's De Consolatione Philosophiae (Public Record Office Manuscript SP 12/289)* (Tempe: Arizona Center for Medieval and Renaissance Studies, 2009).

Thomas Usk, and Thomas Hoccleve reworked Boethian dialectic in interesting and important ways. But it is only occasionally that their works are taken into consideration at all. Indeed, they have been almost entirely overlooked in studies of Boethius's medieval legacy. Alastair J. Minnis's *Chaucer's Boece and the Medieval Tradition of Boethius*, for instance, mentions Usk only once—in a footnote, at that—and devotes only a handful of sentences to Walton.[7] This volume is the first to offer a holistic look at the place of the *Consolation* in medieval England.[8]

Moreover, the Old English *Boethius* has itself only been available in a representative edition since 2009, while the sources Chaucer consulted in translating his *Boece* have been recently edited for the first time.[9] As a result, the place of Boethius's *Consolation* in Anglo-Saxon and later medieval England has drawn the renewed interest of scholars and generated a number of recent studies on medieval philosophy, translation theory, and literary form with Boethius at their center. In the past decade, there has been continuous work on the late medieval Boethius and important new work on the early, with Boethian studies now emerging as a vibrant subfield among Anglo-Saxonists. These studies are always decidedly *early* or *late* medieval, however. Even as other figures are overlooked altogether, Boethius's English reception has fallen to two largely distinct camps, with Anglo-Saxonists working in isolation on the Old English *Boethius* and Chaucerians taking up with the *Boece* or, more often, with Boethian echoes in *Troilus and Criseyde*.

The time has come to rethink those divisions. To that end, we convened an international conference, "Revisiting the Legacy of Boethius in the Middle Ages," at Harvard University in 2014, featuring a range of voices from a variety of disciplinary perspectives and periods. In presenting selected essays here, we hope to spark a wider discussion of the shared methodologies, topics, and conclusions that emerge from reading the Old English *Boethius* and Chaucer's *Boece* together not only with each other but also with a host of other interlocutors from throughout the English Middle Ages. Indeed, in view both of these continuities and of gaps in contemporary scholarship, it seemed vital to us to make a particular point of reaching out into less familiar traditions where possible. So, this volume presents exciting new work on the Alfredian translations as well as an assessment of the Boethian readers and poets of later decades. It also takes note of Boethius's place in what can, for English departments, be a sort of no man's land, attending to the *Consolation*'s shaping of Anglo-Latin literature and

[7] Alastair J. Minnis, ed., *Chaucer's Boece and the Medieval Tradition of Boethius* (Cambridge: D.S. Brewer, 1993).

[8] See also Cornelius, "Boethius' *Consolatio philosophiae*," for an excellent condensed overview.

[9] These editions are Malcolm Godden and Susan Irvine, ed. and trans., *The Old English Boethius*, 2 vols. (Oxford: Oxford University Press, 2009); and Tim William Machan, ed., *Sources of the Boece* (Athens: University of Georgia Press, 2005).

twelfth-century ideals of friendship and monastic life. And, of course, the later essays look to and beyond Chaucer, so that his *Boece* can be understood in relation to the works of his contemporaries and followers and vice-versa. Crucially, Walton, Hoccleve, and Usk are also considered on their own and for their own merits.

While we considered arranging the essays in this volume thematically to further draw out transtemporal parallels, it seemed vital to maintain an essentially temporal arrangement, if only to challenge it by revising it in one crucial way: Hence, these essays relate to *earlier* and *later* medieval England. This is a subtle distinction, but we think it is an essential one. By arranging the essays in this way, we argue for a reassessment of the medieval English Boethian tradition as a 600-year continuum in reading and readership.

The Old English *Boethius* continued to circulate into the late eleventh or early twelfth century, so the Conquest did not rupture its circulation and transmission history. Moreover, interesting thematic overlaps emerge from reading across the centuries. Even though they encountered Boethius's Latin at different historic moments—and sometimes in different English versions—readers as distant as a late ninth- or early tenth-century translator and Geoffrey Chaucer responded to Boethian cosmology and formal hybridity in fascinatingly similar ways, highlighting its cosmological significance in both Old and Middle English, as temporally distant translators took similarly ecocritical approaches. Furthermore, just as the Old English *Boethius* took shape in two versions—one all-prose, one prosimetrical—so was Walton's translation conceived as the poetic counterpart to Chaucer's prose version. With this volume, we ask what might be gained from thinking about these and other similarities and continuities—not from searching for direct influence on the writing level, but from assembling early and late together for the first time to trace a nearly continuous vernacular reading tradition. The volume's two halves remind us that at its core this is a book about pairs: early and late, Latin and English, poetic and prosaic.

It provides a point of departure for new work on the *Consolation*'s *longue durée* in the English Middle Ages—something that we hope will only continue to come into sharper focus as the studies of the commentary tradition now underway continue to bear new fruit. Moreover, it takes stock of the emerging consensus that Boethius's *Consolation* had an enormous impact on formal experimentation in medieval British literature, from the Old English *Boethius*'s affiliations with the *opus geminatum* or "twinned work," proposed by Bill Griffiths, Erica Weaver, and Britt Mize,[10] and taken up here by Susan Irvine, to the hybrid

[10] Bill Griffiths first proposed the connection in his *Alfreds's Metres of Boethius* (Pinner: Anglo-Saxon Books, 1991), 12; and it has received an extended study in Erica Weaver, "Hybrid Forms: Translating Boethius in Anglo-Saxon England," *Anglo-Saxon England* 45 (2016): 213-38. Britt Mize likewise addressed the topic in his *Traditional Subjectivities: The Old English Poetics of Mentality* (Toronto: Toronto University Press,

forms and literary-theoretical experiments of the later Middle Ages discussed here by Eleanor Johnson and Anthony Cirilla.

Additional studies could no doubt explore the role of Boethius's music theory or theological tractates, but in order to keep this volume focused, we have elected for a cluster of essays on the *Consolation* alone. And, of course, we have limited our focus to England (though, indeed, it must be noted that one-third of *Consolation* manuscripts from the ninth century to the eleventh are of English origin or provenance, indicating a major Boethius "industry" north of the Channel).[11] By narrowing the book's scope this way, we have aimed for a cohesive collection of essays that are temporally and conceptually wide-ranging but geographically and textually focused. Within these limits we have also aimed for breadth, attending to vernacular translations and transformations as well as to the enduring Latin tradition. To this end, the essays that follow present new work on Boethius's Alfredian and Chaucerian receptions, as well as on the milieus surrounding the understudied figures mentioned above. Moreover, they range from explorations of Neoplatonism, speculative philosophy, cosmology, ethics, and literary self-fashioning to analyses of formal experiments with Boethian prosimetrum, dialectic, personification allegory, and translation theory.

The *Consolation* in Anglo-Saxon England

The earliest surviving manuscripts of the *Consolation* date to the beginning of the ninth century, once it had been brought to light in France—perhaps by Alcuin of York—after a gap of around three hundred years.[12] By ca. 900, Boethius's

2013), 161-3. See Susan Irvine's chapter for a full account of other scholars who have mentioned the subject in passing and for a new take on the topic.

[11] Malcolm Godden, "King Alfred and the Boethius Industry," in *Making Sense: Constructing Meaning in Early English*, ed. Antonette diPaolo Healey and Kevin Kiernan (Toronto: Pontifical Institute of Mediaeval Studies, 2007), 116–38, at 121.

[12] The rediscovery of the *Consolation* has long been associated with the Carolingian Renaissance, and the traditional view holds Alcuin responsible for finding the text, either in Italy or France in or after 790. For further details, see Pierre Courcelle, *La Consolation de Philosophie dans la tradition littéraire: Antécédents et postérité de Boèce* (Paris: Études Augustiniennes, 1967), 355; Diane K. Bolton, "The Study of the Consolation of Philosophy in Anglo-Saxon England," *Archives d'histoire doctrinale et littéraire du Moyen Âge* 44 (1977): 33–78, at 34; Margaret T. Gibson, "Boethius in the Carolingian Schools," *Transactions of the Royal Historical Society* 32 (1982): 43–56, at 45; and Malcolm Godden, "Alfred, Asser, and Boethius," in *Latin Learning and English Lore: Studies in Anglo-Saxon Literature for Michael Lapidge*, ed. Katherine O'Brien O'Keeffe and Andy Orchard (Toronto: University of Toronto Press, 2005), 326–48, at 327. More recently, Adrian Papahagi, "The Transmission of Boethius' *De consolatione philosophiae* in the Carolingian Age," *Medium Ævum* 78 (2009): 1–15, has suggested that Theodulf of

text had made its way across the Channel to England and would soon be widely read across the Continent.[13] The *Consolation* would become an essential work of reference over the course of the next one hundred years, when the English school system underwent repeated reformation, and Boethius's text was chosen to be translated among a series of books *niedbeðearfosta* [most necessary] for all people to know.[14] The Latin original continued to circulate, acquiring a growing

Orléans rediscovered and disseminated Boethius's *Consolation*. Orléans certainly proved influential in the text's transmission, and Orléans, Bibliothèque municipale, MS 270, dated to the first third of the ninth century, is believed to be the oldest extant copy.

[13] For further discussion of the text's subsequent circulation history in early medieval England and France, see Erica Weaver's essay in this volume. See also Bolton, "The Study of the Consolation of Philosophy in Anglo-Saxon England," 33–78.

[14] The translations are generally viewed as a broader part of the so-called Alfredian Revival (ca. 880–900) instituted by King Alfred in order to revive the state of learning in England after a host of Viking invasions. The king explains his motives in the Preface to the Old English *Pastoral Care*, noting, "Ða ic ða gemunde hu sio lar Lædengeðiodes ær ðissum afeallen wæs giond Angelcynn, ond ðeah monige cuðon Englisc gewrit arædan, ða ongan ic ongemang oðrum mislicum ond manigfealdum bisgum ðisses kynerices ða boc wendan on Englisc ðe is genemned on Læden Pastoralis ond on Englisc 'Hierdeboc,' hwilum word be worde, hwilum andgit of andgiete, swæ swæ ic hie geliornode" [When I remembered how the teaching of Latin decayed before this throughout England, and yet many could read English writings, then I began, among other various and manifold cares of this kingdom, to translate into English the book that is called *Pastoralis* in Latin, and *Pastoral Book* in English, sometimes word by word, sometimes sense for sense, just as I learned it]. *Sweet's Anglo-Saxon Reader in Prose and Verse*, rev. Dorothy Whitelock (Oxford: Clarendon Press, 1967) p. 7, ll. 66–72. For a good discussion of Alfred's translation theory and this Preface, see Robert Stanton, "King Alfred and Early English Translation," in *The Culture of Translation in Anglo-Saxon England* (Cambridge: D.S. Brewer, 2002), 55–100. For a good overview of the corpus of surviving vernacular works before 900, see Janet Bately, "Old English Prose before and during the Reign of Alfred," *Anglo-Saxon England* 17 (1988): 93–138; and Bately, "The Alfredian Canon Revisited: One Hundred Years On," in *Alfred the Great: Papers from the Eleventh-Centenary Conferences*, ed. Timothy Reuter (Burlington: Ashgate, 2003), 107–20. Malcolm Godden, "Did King Alfred Write Anything?" *Medium Ævum* 76 (2007): 1–23, has challenged the scholarly consensus that Alfred composed the extant translations of Gregory's *Pastoral Care*, Boethius's *Consolation of Philosophy*, Augustine's *Soliloquies*, and the first fifty Psalms and instigated the translations by others of Orosius's *History against the Pagans*, Gregory's *Dialogues*, and Bede's *Ecclesiastical History of the English People*. In response, Janet Bately, "Did King Alfred Actually Translate Anything?: The Integrity of the Alfredian Canon Revisited," *Medium Ævum* 78 (2009): 189–215, has maintained that one mind was behind the core translations and that it is reasonable to conclude that it was Alfred's. The question is still very much an open one, but for a recent overview of Alfredian prefaces and epilogues *in toto*, see Susan Irvine, "The Alfredian Prefaces and Epilogues," in *A Companion to Alfred the Great*, ed. Paul E. Szarmach and Nicole Guenther Discenza (Leiden: Brill, 2015), 143–70.

body of *interpretamenta*, forming a key part of the late Anglo-Saxon curriculum and influencing such authors as Byrhtferth of Ramsey,[15] but the translations of Boethius, Gregory, Augustine, and others instituted during Alfred's reign gave new prestige to the vernacular as a medium through which Latin learning could be not only transmitted but also adapted for an Anglo-Saxon audience.[16]

In this respect, the Old English *Boethius* is one of the most innovative of the Alfredian translations. Though the prose preface claims that the text is a somewhat faithful translation,[17] the *Boethius* omits substantial portions of the *Consolation* while doubling its length.[18] Boethius's interlocutors are also renamed, with Lady Philosophy debuting as the male figure Wisdom or *Gesceadwisnes* [reason]

[15] For an in-depth discussion of key curriculum authors, including Boethius, in Anglo-Saxon England, see Patrizia Lendinara, "The World of Anglo-Saxon Learning," in *The Cambridge Companion to Old English Literature*, ed. Malcolm Godden and Michael Lapidge (Cambridge: Cambridge University Press, 2013), 295–312; and Michael Lapidge, "The Study of Latin Texts in Late Anglo-Saxon England: The Evidence of Latin Glosses," in *Latin and the Vernacular Languages in Early Medieval Britain*, ed. Nicholas Brooks (Leicester: Leicester University Press, 1982), 99–140. For a list of the seventeen surviving pre-Conquest English manuscripts of the *Consolation*, see Lapidge, *The Anglo-Saxon Library* (Oxford: Oxford University Press, 2006), 293–94.

[16] Daniel Donoghue, *Old English Literature: A Short Introduction* (Malden: Blackwell, 2004), among others, notes that this assertion of the ability of Old English to accommodate the most sophisticated Latin from Late Antiquity is a statement of procedure that "carries a bold assumption for a ninth-century vernacular with virtually no literary tradition behind it" (108). See also Kathleen Davis, "The Performance of Translation Theory in King Alfred's National Literary Program," in *Manuscript, Narrative, Lexicon: Essays on Literary and Cultural Transmission in Honor of Whitney F. Bolton*, ed. Robert Boenig and Kathleen Davis (Lewisburg, PA: Bucknell University Press, 2000), 149–70. Davis notes that "Alfred's role as a translator is also a negotiation of his role as spiritual and secular leader, and English translation itself marks the emergence of the English people as a Christian political community" (149–50).

[17] For an edition of this preface along with its verse counterpart, see Godden and Irvine, ed. and trans., *The Old English Boethius*, 2 vols., edn. 1:239, trans. 2:1, hereafter cited parenthetically by volume and page. The two prefaces are thoroughly analyzed in Susan Irvine's essay in this volume. It must be noted that they were likely not written by Alfred but, rather, as Nicole Guenther Discenza "Alfred the Great and the Anonymous Prose Proem to the *Boethius*," *The Journal of English and Germanic Philology* 107.1 (2008): 57–76, argues, by "an associate or an admirer, working in Alfred's lifetime or shortly thereafter, with or without the knowledge and permission of Alfred" (60).

[18] For an in-depth introduction to the Old English *Boethius*, see Godden and Irvine, "Introduction," in *The Old English Boethius*, i.3–235, esp. 233–35, which includes a table of correspondences showing the relationship between each of the Old English versions and Boethius's Latin text. See also Nicole Guenther Discenza, "The Old English *Boethius*," in *A Companion to Alfred the Great*, ed. Paul E. Szarmach and Nicole Guenther Discenza (Leiden: Brill, 2015), 200–226.

and Boethius himself emerging as the disembodied *Mod* [mind]. As the essays in the first half of this volume explore, the translation challenges its source text on several points, augmenting rather than reproducing the wisdom of the past and retooling Boethius's logical vocabulary for an Anglo-Saxon audience.[19]

The *Boethius* seems to have undergone two stages of translation, first into prose and then into prosimetrum, and its surviving manuscript witnesses represent the distinct versions of the text. The twelfth-century Oxford, Bodleian Library, MS Bodley 180 (henceforth referred to as B) preserves the all-prose version, while the mid-tenth-century London, British Library, MS Cotton Otho A.vi (henceforth referred to as C) contains a prosimetrical translation, which is more formally similar to the Latin *Consolation*. Whereas Boethius's source text contains thirty-nine meters, however, the Old English *Boethius* has only thirty-one.[20] The prose version is generally considered to be the earlier of the two, with the versifier returning to the Old English prose text as an intermediary (rather than the Latin meters of the *Consolation*) for his retranslation of Boethius's poetic sections into Old English verse.[21] The all-prose version could have been an early

---

[19] For further discussion, see Nicole Guenther Discenza, "The Making of an English Dialogue," in *The King's English: Strategies of Translation in the Old English Boethius* (Albany: State University of New York Press, 2005), 57–86; Malcolm Godden, "The Translations of Alfred and His Circle, and the Misappropriation of the Past," H.M. Chadwick Memorial Lectures 14 (Cambridge: Department of Anglo-Saxon, Norse, and Celtic, 2004); and Ross Smythe, "King Alfred's Translations: Authorial Integrity and the Integrity of Authority," *Quaestio Insularis* 4 (2003): 98–114.

[20] The way in which these meters have been edited has influenced scholarship for the last century. W.J. Sedgefield's edition, *King Alfred's Old English Version of Boethius De Consolatione Philosophiae* (Oxford: Clarendon Press, 1899), does not print them in context. Instead, Sedgefield artificially separates them, so that the so-called "Meters of Boethius" appear as a collective body in the edition, even though we have no evidence that they ever circulated independently. For further details, see Paul E. Szarmach, "An Apologia for the *Meters of Boethius*," in *Naked Wordes in Englissh*, ed. Marcin Krygier and Liliana Sikorska (New York: Peter Lang, 2005), 107–36. On misleading editions (and the necessity for a new edition that would not only place the C manuscript's prose and verse together but also clearly differentiate between the B and C texts), see Malcolm Godden, "Editing Old English and the Problem of Alfred's *Boethius*," in *The Editing of Old English: Papers from the 1990 Manchester Conference*, ed. Donald G. Scragg and Paul E. Szarmach (Rochester: D.S. Brewer, 1994), 163–76; and Paul E. Szarmach, "Editions of Alfred: The Wages of Un-influence," in *Early Medieval English Texts and Interpretations: Studies Presented to Donald G. Scragg*, ed. Elaine Treharne and Susan Rosser (Tempe: Arizona Center for Medieval and Renaissance Studies, 2002), 135–49. The problem has since been solved by Godden and Irvine's magisterial 2009 edition, which supplies the Old English quotations throughout this volume.

[21] See Godden and Irvine, "Introduction," in *The Old English Boethius*, 1:44. For an alternate view, see Kevin S. Kiernan, "Alfred the Great's Burnt Boethius," in *The Iconic*

draft, still to undergo the versifying process,[22] or a final product that was used as the basis for a later revision in imitation of the Latin source text.[23] Either way, it continued to circulate long after its initial translation and was consulted by Ælfric of Eynsham at the end of the tenth century.[24] One of his patrons, the nobleman Æthelweard (d. 988?), also mentioned the translation in his *Chronicon*, which follows the Old English prefaces in ascribing the *Boethius* to King Alfred without differentiating between the all-prose and prosimetrical versions.[25]

Though addressed by the prefaces themselves, by Æthelweard, and by William of Malmesbury (ca. 1095–ca. 1143), the question of shared authorship remains unsettled, however. As Godden and Irvine have noted, both versions were "the work of an unknown writer of substantial learning, not necessarily connected with King Alfred or his court, but working some time in the period 890–930, probably in southern England."[26] While Kenneth Sisam, among others, argues that Alfred was responsible for the poetic translation as well as the prose,[27] Godden and Irvine present two problems with that position: 1) the versifier did not always know which parts of the prose version corresponded to Boethius's Latin meters; and 2) there are interpretive errors on several occasions, which suggest that the prose translator and the versifier were separate people.[28]

Page in Manuscript, Print, and Digital Culture, ed. George Bornstein and Theresa Tinkle (Ann Arbor: University of Michigan Press, 1998), 7–32.

22 See especially Kenneth Sisam, "The Authorship of the Verse Translation of Boethius's *Metra*," in *Studies in the History of Old English Literature* (Oxford: Clarendon Press, 1953), 293–97.

23 Godden and Irvine, "Introduction," in *The Old English Boethius*, 1:45.

24 For further details, see Malcolm Godden, "Ælfric and the Alfredian Precedents," in *A Companion to Ælfric*, ed. Hugh Magennis and Mary Swan (Boston: Brill, 2009), 139–63.

25 Æthelweard, *Chronicon*, iv.3, in *The Chronicle of Æthelweard*, ed. A. Campbell (London: Thomas Nelson & Sons, 1962), 50. For further context, see Paul E. Szarmach, "Boethius's Influence in Anglo-Saxon England: The Vernacular and the *De consolatione philosophiae*," in *A Companion to Boethius in the Middle Ages*, ed. Noel Harold Kaylor, Jr., and Philip Edward Phillips (Leiden: Brill, 2012), 221–54, esp. 221–23; and Malcolm Godden, "King and Counselor in the Alfredian Boethius," in *Intertexts: Studies in Anglo-Saxon Culture Presented to Paul E. Szarmach*, ed. V. Blanton and H. Scheck (Tempe: Arizona Center for Medieval and Renaissance Studies, 2008), 191–207. On the relationship between Ælfric and Æthelweard, see Mechthild Gretsch, "Historiography and Literary Patronage in Late Anglo-Saxon England: The Evidence of Æthelweard's Chronicon," *Anglo-Saxon England* 41 (2012): 205–48.

26 Godden and Irvine, *The Old English Boethius*, 1:146.

27 See Sisam, "The Authorship of the Verse Translation of Boethius's *Metra*,"; E.G. Stanley, "King Alfred's Prefaces," *The Review of English Studies* 39 (1988): 349–64; and Daniel Anlezark, "Three Notes on the Old English *Meters of Boethius*," *Notes & Queries* 51 (2004): 10–15.

28 Godden and Irvine, "Introduction," in *The Old English Boethius*, 1:146–51.

There are instances, however, where the versifier seems to draw on the Latin original to supplement the Old English prose and where he develops several significant additions such as the comparison of the Earth surrounded by the heavens to an egg surrounded by its shell.[29] Whether Alfred himself or a now-anonymous poet was responsible for the prosimetrical translation, "the way that [the versifier] rearranged the words of the prose offers a rare glimpse into the more elusive conventions of verse-making" in Anglo-Saxon England, as Daniel Donoghue has noted.[30]

The *Boethius* continues to provide an important lens into tenth-century poetic practice as well as into Anglo-Saxon learning and thought more broadly. Recent criticism asks what the translations' additions and adaptations reveal about Anglo-Saxon ontologies,[31] social practices,[32] and ideas about royal

---

[29] See Anlezark, "Three Notes on the Old English *Meters of Boethius*," for a discussion of three examples from the Meters which cannot be accounted for by the straightforward rendering of prose into verse. The egg motif is discussed in greater detail by Paul E. Szarmach and A. Joseph McMullen in their contributions to this volume.

[30] Daniel Donoghue, "Word Order and Poetic Style: Auxiliary and Verbal in the *Metres of Boethius*," *Anglo-Saxon England* 15 (1986): 167–96, at 167–68. M.S. Griffith, "Verses Quite Like *cwen to gebeddan* in *The Metres of Boethius*," *Anglo-Saxon England* 34 (2005): 145–67, concurs, arguing that the Meters offer a "unique opportunity to watch an Anglo-Saxon poet in the act of forging his word-hoard from the base metal of the non-poetic prose source" (146).

[31] On the threefold soul in Anglo-Saxon England, see Paul E. Szarmach, "Alfred, Alcuin, and the Soul," in *Manuscript, Narrative, Lexicon: Essays on Literary and Cultural Transmission in Honor of Whitney F. Bolton*, ed. Robert Boenig and Kathleen Davis (Lewisburg, PA: Bucknell University Press, 2000), 127–48. On the four cardinal virtues, see Szarmach, "Alfred's *Boethius* and the Four Cardinal Virtues," in *Alfred the Wise: Studies in Honour of Janet Bately on the Occasion of Her Sixty-Fifth Birthday*, ed. Jane Roberts, Janet L. Nelson, and Malcolm Godden (Rochester: D.S. Brewer, 1997), 223–35. On the connection between soul and mind, see Malcolm Godden, "Anglo-Saxons on the Mind," in *Learning and Literature in Anglo-Saxon England: Studies Presented to Peter Clemoes on the Occasion of his Sixty-Fifth Birthday*, ed. Michael Lapidge and Helmut Gneuss (Cambridge: Cambridge University Press, 1985), 271–98; Susan Irvine, "Ulysses and Circe in King Alfred's Boethius: A Classical Myth Transformed," in *Studies in English Language and Literature: 'Doubt Wisely': Papers in Honour of E.G. Stanley*, ed. M.J. Toswell and E.M. Tyler (New York: Routledge, 1996), 387–401; and Rūta Šileikytė, "In Search of the Inner Mind: Old English *gescead* and Other Lexemes for Human Cognition in King Alfred's *Boethius*," *Kalbotyra* 54 (2004): 94–102.

[32] The *Boethius* helps to contextualize Anglo-Saxon understandings of gender in Susan Irvine, "Rewriting Women in the Old English Boethius," in *New Windows on a Woman's World: Essays for Jocelyn Harris*, ed. Colin Gibson and Lisa Marr (Dunedin: Department of English, University of Otago, 2005), 488–501.

power,[33] to provide but a few examples of the exciting work now ongoing in the field. Nicole Guenther Discenza has suggested that the text was written not only as a "manual for the individual seeking transcendent truth" but also as a kind of *speculum principum* that teaches young aristocrats about the social responsibilities that their rank entails.[34] The free and divergent adaptation transforms much of Boethius's Neoplatonic thinking,[35] revising Boethius's original for an Anglo-Saxon worldview. As the essays in the first half of this volume demonstrate, this was not just a functional translation for those whose Latin was too poor to access the original. The *Boethius* was an imaginative literary project in its own right and has much to offer to anyone interested in pre-Conquest England.

The Commentary Tradition in England

Like the *Boethius*'s vernacular additions, early medieval copies of Boethius's original offer vast insights into Anglo-Saxon culture.[36] Comprising thousands of glosses tucked between the lines and in the margins of manuscripts housed across Europe, the vast commentary tradition is only now coming into focus, with a comprehensive study underway at Oxford University. Led by Malcolm Godden, Rohini Jayatilaka, Rosalind Love, and Paolo Vaciago, *Boethius in Early Medieval Europe: Commentary on The Consolation of Philosophy from the 9th to the 11th Centuries* has demonstrated that surviving glosses likely comprise "the contributions of many unknown commentators working in France, Germany,

[33] See Paul E. Szarmach, "Alfred's Nero," in *Source of Wisdom: Old English and Early Medieval Latin Studies in Honour of Thomas D. Hill*, ed. Charles D. Wright, Frederick M. Biggs, and Thomas N. Hall (Toronto: University of Toronto Press, 2007), 147–67. For an account of how Alfred adapts Hercules into a "prototype of himself," see Susan Irvine, "Wrestling with Hercules: King Alfred and the Classical Past," in *Court Culture in the Early Middle Ages: The Proceedings of the First Alcuin Conference*, ed. Catherine Cubitt (Turnhout: Brepols, 2003), 171–88, at 175. Nicole Guenther Discenza, *The King's English: Strategies of Translation in the Old English Boethius* (Albany: State University of New York Press, 2005), 58, has argued that the *Boethius* attempts to accomplish the goals of "increasing symbolic capital for Alfred and his language, granting cultural capital to his elite group of readers, and inculcating certain modes of discourse and values."

[34] Nicole Guenther Discenza, "Alfred the Great's *Boethius*," *Literature Compass* 3 (2006): 736–49, at 742.

[35] See Janet Bately, "Boethius and King Alfred," in *Platonism and the English Imagination*, ed. Anna Baldwin and Sarah Hutton (Cambridge: Cambridge University Press, 1994), 38–44.

[36] See footnote 15 above for a list of surviving manuscripts from Anglo-Saxon England.

England, Wales and Ireland."[37] Previously, scholars had long attributed glosses in pre-twelfth-century manuscripts to two early commentary traditions: 1) the "Remigian," attributed to Remigius of Auxerre (902–08); and 2) the "St. Gall," attributed to an anonymous scholar working in the abbey of St. Gall in the ninth century or early tenth.[38] When viewed more closely, however, the surviving *scholia* do not neatly divide into two distinct strands. As Love notes, "by the tenth century copies were being produced with such dense glossing that almost no vellum stayed empty," and these pages were filled with sometimes contradictory explanations and interpretations, testifying to the range of readers and thinkers at work.[39] Instead of having two discrete branches, then, Godden suggests that the commentary tradition should be imagined as "highly fluid compilations of glosses and scholia, continually supplemented and adapted over a long period."[40]

The question of whether the Old English *Boethius* was dependent on a commentary is a complicated one,[41] but it seems likely that the translator(s) took

---

[37] Godden, Jayatilaka, and Love, *Boethius in Early Medieval Europe*, <http://www.english.ox.ac.uk/boethius/>.

[38] For background on the commentary tradition, see H.F. Stewart, "A Commentary by Remigius Autissiodorensis on the *De Consolatione Philosophiae* of Boethius," *Journal of Theological Studies* 17 (1916): 22–42; Pierre Courcelle, "Étude critique sur les commentaires de la *Consolation* de Boèce," *Archives d'histoire doctrinale et littéraire du moyen âge* 14 (1939): 5–140; Courcelle, *La Consolation de Philosophie dans la tradition littéraire*; and Fabio Troncarelli, *Tradizione Perdute: La 'Consolatione Philosophiae' nell'Alto Medioevo* (Padua: Editrice Antenore, 1981).

[39] Rosalind Love, "Latin Commentaries on Boethius's *Consolation of Philosophy*," in *A Companion to Alfred the Great*, ed. Paul E. Szarmach and Nicole Guenther Discenza (Leiden: Brill, 2015), 83–111, at 83.

[40] Godden, "King Alfred and the Boethius Industry," 121. See also Joseph Wittig, "The Old English *Boethius*, the Latin Commentaries, and Bede," in *The Study of Medieval Manuscripts of England: Festschrift in Honor of Richard W. Pfaff*, ed. George Hardin Brown and Linda Ehrsam Voigts (Tempe: Arizona Center for Medieval and Renaissance Studies, 2010), 225–252, who argues that the manuscripts show evidence of gradually collected individual glosses that accrue into distinguishable clusters but were not from two original commentaries.

[41] Georg Schepss, "Zu König Alfreds Boethius," *Archiv für das Studium der neueren Sprachen und Literaturen* 94 (1895): 149–60, was one of the first to argue that Alfred used a commentary (later to be revealed from the Remigian tradition). Kurt Otten, *König Alfreds Boethius* (Tübingen: Max Niermeyer Verlag, 1964), built on Schepss's work. Brian S. Donaghey, "The Sources of King Alfred's Translation of Boethius's *De Consolatione Philosophiae*," *Anglia* 82 (1964): 23–57, argued that Alfred probably did not use the Remigian commentary but may have been influenced by the St. Gall commentary indirectly through a now-lost commentary written by Asser. Joseph S. Wittig, "King Alfred's *Boethius* and its Latin Sources: A Reconsideration," *Anglo-Saxon England* 11 (1983): 157–98, argued that Alfred did not depend on a Latin commentary but later ("The Old English *Boethius*, the Latin Commentaries, and Bede") revises his view slightly to ask

recourse to some kind of interpretive framework.[42] While the commentary tradition can account for some of Alfred's revisions, however, "the great majority of his additions and changes have no parallel in the commentaries."[43] In any case, the commentaries would not necessarily provide the cultural milieu that helped shape Alfred's thought. Whitney F. Bolton describes the two early scholarly theories, attempting to explain the differences between the *Consolation* and the *Boethius*: "One has made Alfred's learning, the Old English language, or Anglo-Saxon culture in general unequal to the task of translating the subtle Latin. The second, which has superseded the first, makes Alfred disagree with Boethius' world view and convert the Neoplatonism of the original to Christian existentialism."[44] Bolton, following Katherine Proppe,[45] argues that order is important for Alfred and, going further, concludes that the Alfredian alterations "embody the achievements of the Anglo-Saxon intelligentsia."[46] In many ways, the Old English additions and interpolations themselves form a vernacular commentary tradition, which complements the glosses then accreting in contemporary Latin copies of the *Consolation*. In this sense, the *Boethius* too can be read as an encyclopedia or reference book.[47]

Over the next few centuries, the *Consolation* would continue to inspire increasingly involved commentaries, beginning with French Scholastic William of Conches's widely circulated work, probably written in the 1120s.[48] As Ian

whether, instead of "sources," the glosses might instead be better regarded as "imperfect snapshots of interpretive activity" also reflected in the Old English adaptation (248). R.I. Page, "Recent Work on Old English Glosses: The Case of Boethius," in *Mittelalterliche volkssprachige Glossen: Internationale Fachkonferenz des Zentrums für Mittelalterstudien der Otto-Friedrich-Universität Bamberg 2. bis 4. August 1999*, ed. Rolf Bergmann, Elvira Glaser, and Claudine Moulin-Fankhänel (Heidelberg: Universitätsverlag C. Winter, 2001), 217–42, offers a substantial overview of the tradition while drawing attention to the practice of glossing.

42 Godden, "King Alfred and the Boethius Industry," 124–33, presents persuasive findings from his Alfredian *Boethius* project.

43 Discenza, *The King's English*, 134.

44 Whitney F. Bolton, "How Boethian is Alfred's *Boethius*?" in *Studies in Earlier Old English Prose*, ed. Paul E. Szarmach (Albany: State University of New York Press, 1986), 153–68, at 155. The first of these theories has been shown to be faulty by later scholarship.

45 Katherine Proppe, "King Alfred's Consolation of Philosophy," *Neuphilologische Mitteilungen* 74 (1973): 635–48.

46 Bolton, "How Boethian is Alfred's *Boethius*?" 163.

47 Paul E. Szarmach, "The Old English *Boethius* as a Book of Nature," in *Aspects of Anglo-Saxon and Medieval England*, ed. Michiko Ogura (Frankfurt am Main: Peter Lang, 2014), 69–93.

48 For an edition, see *Guillelmi de Conchis opera omnia*, vol. 2, *Glosae super Boetium*, ed. Lodi Nauta, CCCM 158 (Turnhout: Brepols, 1999). For further background, see Édouard

Cornelius helpfully summarizes, in the twelfth and thirteenth centuries especially, Boethian "commentary became a locus for original philosophical speculation on topics ranging from cosmology to anatomy to ethics," typically appearing independently rather than in the margins, as previous glosses predominantly had.[49] During this time there were also at least nine French translations of the *Consolation*, which survive in more than 150 manuscripts, though the vast majority of these never left the Continent.[50]

The text's English reception picks up again with what is perhaps the most influential and widely read commentary on the *Consolation*, the *Expositio super librum Boecii de consolatione*. Produced by the Dominican friar Nicholas Trevet around 1300, the *Expositio* is extant in more than one hundred manuscripts.[51] In it, Trevet carefully glosses Boethius's Latin, minutely explaining passages and building an encyclopedic compendium of medieval learning around the text. Throughout, he draws from a range of sources, the most important of which is William of Conches's commentary on the *Consolation*. While early scholarship accused Trevet of plagiarizing William's commentary (a complicated, possibly anachronistic, concept in the theory of medieval authorship),[52] Minnis and Lodi Nauta have persuasively shown that Trevet builds on William's discussion, at times tracing his sources and revising the interpretation accordingly.[53] Nauta argues that "Trevet was simply practicing what most of his predecessors had done: revising the commentary tradition and recasting it in the mould of his own age" and places his work firmly within the context of the Scholastic debates then

---

Jeauneau, "L'Usage de la notion d'integumentum à travers les gloses de Guillaume de Conches," *AHDLMA* 24 (1957): 35–100; and Nauta, "The Glosa as Instrument of the Development of Natural Philosophy: William of Conches' Commentary on Boethius," in *Boethius in the Middle Ages: Latin and Vernacular Traditions of the Consolatio Philosophiae*, ed. Lodi Nauta and Maarten J.F.M. Hoenen (New York: Brill, 1997), 3–39.

49 Cornelius, "Boethius' *Consolatio philosophiae*," 278.

50 For further discussion, see Cornelius, "Boethius' *Consolatio*," 277–79; Glynnis Cropp, "Boethius in Medieval France: Translations of the *De consolatione philosophiae* and Literary Influence," in *A Companion to Boethius in the Middle Ages*, ed. Noel Harold Kaylor, Jr., and Philip Edward Phillips (Leiden: Brill, 2012), 319–55; and Lodi Nauta, "The Consolation: The Latin Commentary Tradition, 800–1700," in *The Cambridge Companion to Boethius*, ed. John Marenbon (Cambridge: Cambridge University Press, 2009), 255–78.

51 For an edition, see Nicholas Trevet, *Expositio super Boetio de consolatione*, ed. E.T. Silk, accessible at <http://minnis.commons.yale.edu>.

52 See, for example, Courcelle, *La Consolation de Philosophie dans la tradition littéraire*, 319.

53 A.J. Minnis and Lodi Nauta, "*More Platonico loquitur*: What Nicholas Trevet really did to William of Conches," in *Chaucer's Boece and the Medieval Tradition of Boethius*, ed. A.J. Minnis (Cambridge: D.S. Brewer, 1993), 1–34.

unfolding.[54] By infusing the Boethian commentary tradition with more current theological and philosophical viewpoints, Trevet crafted an aid that would influence the way the *Consolation* would be read for the following two hundred years, most notably by Geoffrey Chaucer and John Walton, whose own translations were built upon the commentary tradition. Indeed, the prose commentary preserved in Copenhagen, Kongelige Bibliotek, MS Thott 304 2, a manuscript of Walton's translation, preserves the earliest extant English commentary on Boethius's text.[55]

Vernacular Adaptations in Later Medieval Britain

As a consequence of the thriving Boethian manuscript and commentary traditions in later medieval England, the *Consolation* would soon be translated into Middle English and serve as a foundational work for authors such as Geoffrey Chaucer, Thomas Hoccleve, Thomas Usk, and John Walton.[56] Indeed, it is out of this mass of commentary and glossing that Chaucer produced his *Boece*, the first Middle English translation of the text.[57] While the Old English *Boethius* was an imaginative adaptation, the aim of the all-prose *Boece* was much more practical: to open the *sentence* (meaning broadly, "sense" or "understanding") of the *Consolation* by being as faithful to the source text as possible and incorporating supplementary material to contextualize Boethius's argument for well-educated members of both the clergy and laity.[58] For Chaucer, translation and glossing were thought of as two sides of the same coin: his glossatorial additions are considered part of the canonical text, inserted into the body of his translation rather than written in the margins. As A.J. Minnis and Tim William Machan note:

---

[54] Lodi Nauta, "The Scholastic Context of the Boethius Commentary by Nicholas Trevet," in *A Companion to Boethius in the Middle Ages*, ed. Noel Harold Kaylor, Jr., and Philip Edward Phillips (Leiden: Brill, 2012), 41–67, at 42.

[55] A digital facsimile is available at <http://www.kb.dk/permalink/2006/manus/627/eng/>. For general background, see Brian Donaghey, Irma Taavitsainen, and Erik Miller, "Walton's Boethius: From Manuscript to Print," *English Studies* 80 (1999): 398–407, at 403–5; and A.J. Minnis, *Translations of Authority in Medieval English Literature: Valuing the Vernacular* (Cambridge: Cambridge University Press, 2009), 24.

[56] For a good introduction to this topic, see Ian Johnson, "Making the *Consolatio* in Middle English," in *A Companion to Boethius in the Middle Ages*, ed. Noel Harold Kaylor, Jr., and Philip Edward Phillips (Leiden: Brill, 2012), 413–46.

[57] Since Thomas Usk draws on the *Boece* in his *Testament of Love* (see below), Chaucer must have composed it by 1385. It is traditionally dated to ca. 1380.

[58] For an in-depth discussion of *sentence* and medieval translation theory, see Taylor Cowdery's essay in this volume.

> [T]his is translation of the type which routinely incorporates material from the glosses which were the stock-in-trade of the educational system, which had its lexical and semantic parameters largely defined by the grammatical definitions and assumptions which that system enshrined, and which reflects the theory of translation which was channeled by the schools and fed by their interest in semiotics and notions of textual explication (as applied in commentary on the classroom *auctores*).[59]

Beyond his text of the *Consolation*, the so-called "Vulgate" version common to fourteenth-century England,[60] which probably contained glosses from the Remigian commentary tradition,[61] Chaucer drew from two contemporary sources. He used Jean de Meun's translation, *Li Livres de confort*, for additions and as a reading aid for Boethius's most complicated Latin,[62] and he included material from Trevet's detailed commentary.[63] There is no particular pattern that the extrapolations, explanatory inserts, and general glossing in the *Boece* follow. Chaucer just as readily makes use of Jean as he does Trevet, combining and merging his sources to create a sort of amalgam text or "composite source,"[64] which "confers

[59] A.J. Minnis and Tim William Machan, "The *Boece* as a Late-Medieval Translation," in *Chaucer's Boece and the Medieval Tradition of Boethius*, ed. A.J. Minnis (Cambridge: D.S. Brewer, 1993), 167–88, at 168.

[60] Tim William Machan, *Textual Criticism and Middle English Texts* (Charlottesville: University Press of Virginia, 1994), explains that the Vulgate *Consolation* "is materially not very different from what Boethius probably wrote in the prison at Pavia, though there are pervasive (if minor) lexical differences: pronouns are inserted, syntax is modernized to that of late medieval Latin, unfamiliar idioms are normalized, and Greek quotations are almost uniformly translated into Latin or garbled beyond intelligibility" (158).

[61] Chaucer would draw from these glosses some twenty-six times. See A.J. Minnis, "'Glosynge is a glorious thyng': Chaucer at Work on the *Boece*," in *The Medieval Boethius: Studies in the Vernacular Translations of De Consolatione Philosophiae*, ed. A.J. Minnis (Woodbridge: Boydell and Brewer, 1987), 106–24, at 118; and Minnis, "Chaucer's Commentator: Nicholas Trevet and the *Boece*," in *Chaucer's Boece and the Medieval Tradition of Boethius*, ed. A.J. Minnis (Cambridge: D.S. Brewer, 1993), 83–166.

[62] For an edition of *Li Livres de confort*, see V.L. Dedeck-Héry, ed., "Boethius' *De Consolatione* by Jean de Meun," *Mediaeval Studies* 14 (1952): 165–275. See also *Sources of the Boece*, ed. Tim William Machan (Athens: University of Georgia Press, 2005), for a side-by-side edition of the Vulgate *Consolation* and *Li Livres de confort*.

[63] See Mark J. Gleason, "Clearing the Fields: Towards a Reassessment of Chaucer's Use of Trevet in the *Boece*," in *The Medieval Boethius: Studies in the Vernacular Translations of De Consolatione Philosophiae*, ed. A.J. Minnis (Woodbridge: Boydell and Brewer, 1987), 89–105; and Minnis, "Chaucer's Commentator," 83–166.

[64] Minnis and Machan, "The *Boece* as a Late-Medieval Translation," 181. See also Tim William Machan, *Techniques of Translation: Chaucer's Boece* (Norman, OK: Pilgrim Books, 1985).

a certain academic or critical authority on the English text," as Rita Copeland has noted.[65]

Chaucer seems to have held his translation in high esteem, and the influence of Boethius can be found widely throughout his corpus. This is, perhaps, no more apparent than in his *Retractions* at the end of the *Canterbury Tales*, in which he asks forgiveness for his "enditynges [compositions] of worldly vanities" (including *Troilus and Criseyde*, *The House of Fame*, *The Book of the Duchess*, *The Parliament of Fowls*, and parts of the *Canterbury Tales*, among others) but gives thanks for his other works (including the *Boece*), which should help save his soul.[66] In this volume, Eleanor Johnson argues that the *Retractions* must be read in the light of the *Consolation*—as Chaucer's "final Boethian turn," where he reveals the *Tales* as a "mixed-form work that, in the end, enables him to graduate to higher forms of contemplation." It is no wonder, then, that he cites the *Boece* first on his list of works of "moralitee, and devocioun."[67] Chaucer also mentions his translation of the *Consolation* in the *The Legend of Good Women* and his poem to his scribe, Adam Pinkhurst or "Adam Scriveyn."[68] He quotes the *Consolation* in *The House of Fame* and makes additional direct references to Boethius in the *Nun's Priest's Tale* and *Wife of Bath's Tale.*[69] In the latter, the knight's still-loathly wife lectures him on "gentillesse," or noble character, instructing him:

> Reedeth Senek, and redeth eek Boece;
> Ther shul ye seen expres that it no drede is,
> That he is gentil that dooth gentil dedis.[70]

Boethius proves fundamental elsewhere in the Chaucerian corpus. In the *Canterbury Tales*, Boethian themes have been found in the *Knight's Tale*, the *Tale of Sir Thopas*, and *Tale of Melibee* (which, Eleanor Johnson argues in this volume, are a Boethian dyad), the *Manciple's Tale*, the *Parson's Tale*, the *Monk's Tale*, and elsewhere.[71] A handful of shorter poems, known as the "Boethian Lyrics"

---

[65] Rita Copeland, *Rhetoric, Hermeneutics, and Translation in the Middle Ages* (Cambridge: Cambridge University Press, 1991), 143.

[66] Geoffrey Chaucer, *The Canterbury Tales*, in *The Riverside Chaucer*, ed. Larry D. Benson, 3rd edn. (Boston: Houghton Mifflin, 1987), X.1084–86. Citations to the *Canterbury Tales* are by fragment and line number.

[67] Chaucer, *The Canterbury Tales*, X.1087.

[68] Chaucer, *The Legend of Good Women*, in *The Riverside Chaucer*, ed. Benson, F 425; G 413. For the identification of "Adam Scriveyn" as Adam Pinkhurst, see Linne R. Mooney, "Chaucer's Scribe," *Speculum* 81 (2006): 97–138.

[69] Chaucer, *The House of Fame*, in *The Riverside Chaucer*, ed. Benson, ll. 972–978; *The Canterbury Tales*, VII.3242, 3294; III.1168–70.

[70] Chaucer, *The Canterbury Tales*, III.1168–70.

[71] See, for example, the essays by Eleanor Johnson and Jonathan Stavsky in this volume; William E. Coleman, "*The Knight's Tale*," in *Sources and Analogues for the*

(including "The Former Age," "Fortune," "Truth," "Gentilesse," and "Lak of Stedfastnesse") are likewise indebted to the *Consolation*.[72] So too is *Troilus and Criseyde*, in which Troilus muses on Boethian concepts of predestination, free will, and cosmic love.[73]

Chaucer's engagement with the *Consolation* would prove influential not only for his own writings but also for the work of his contemporaries and followers. The powerful influence of the *Boece* can be found most strikingly in Thomas Usk's *Testament of Love* (ca. 1385), as Anthony Cirilla notes in his contribution to this volume.[74] Like the *Consolation*, the *Testament* was written while Usk was unjustly imprisoned (and soon to be put to death) and presents an allegorical dialogue between the prisoner (Usk) and Lady Love, who is able help the prisoner overcome his depression by teaching him about the source of true happiness.[75] While the *Testament* reimagines the *Consolation* in order to reflect Usk's own imprisonment, much of the philosophizing (on free will, God's foreknowledge, etc.) is indebted to Boethius, possibly via Chaucer. Though parts of the *Testament* could be regarded as translation, Usk is able to put these themes to new use by crafting a text with its own political and aesthetic motivations.[76] Boethius and the *Consolation* also pervade Thomas Hoccleve's works. Ian Cornelius argues that Hoccleve channels the "grand pathos" of the *Consolation* while also subverting Philosophy's message in his *Regiment of Princes*,[77] possibly through the medi-

---

Canterbury Tales II, ed. Robert M. Correale and Mary Hamel (Suffolk: D.S. Brewer, 2009), 87–247; Jill Mann, "Chance and Destiny in *Troilus and Criseyde* and the *Knight's Tale*," in *The Cambridge Companion to Chaucer*, ed. Piero Boitani and Jill Mann (Cambridge: Cambridge University Press, 2003), 93–111; Thomas H. Bestul, "The Monk's Tale," in *Sources and Analogues of the Canterbury Tales I*, ed. Robert M. Correale and Mary Hamel (Suffolk: D.S. Brewer, 2002), 409–47; Vincent Dimarco, "The Squire's Tale," in *Sources and Analogues of the Canterbury Tales I*, 169–299; and Michael Masi, "Boethius, the Wife of Bath, and the Dialectic of Paradox," in *New Directions in Boethian Studies*, ed. Noel Harold Kaylor, Jr., and Philip Edward Phillips (Kalamazoo: Medieval Institute Publications, 2006), 143–54.

[72] See Cornelius, "Boethius' *De consolatione philosophiae*," 280–81 for a good overview.

[73] See Frank Grady, "The Boethian Reader of *Troilus and Criseyde*," *The Chaucer Review* 33.3 (1999): 230–51; and Megan Murton, "Praying with Boethius in *Troilus and Criseyde*," *The Chaucer Review* 49.3 (2015): 294–319.

[74] See Thomas Usk, *The Testament of Love*, ed. R. Allen Shoaf (Kalamazoo: Medieval Institute Publications, 1998).

[75] See Jennifer Arch, "The Boethian *Testament of Love*," *Studies in Philology* 105.4 (2008): 448–62.

[76] See Paul Strohm, "Politics and Poetics: Usk and Chaucer in the 1380s," in *Literary Practice and Social Change in Britain, 1380–1530*, ed. Lee Patterson (Berkeley: University of California Press, 1990), 103–12.

[77] Cornelius, "Boethius' *De consolatione philosophiae*," 269–70, 281.

ation of *Troilus and Criseyde*.[78] In this volume, Jonathan Stavsky traces Boethian influence and Chaucerian intertexts in Hoccleve's *Series*.[79]

Though Chaucer's translation is memorialized by Samuel Johnson in the opening quotation of this introduction, John Walton's 1410 verse translation of the *Consolation* seems to have been the more popular in later medieval England, with twenty extant manuscript witnesses compared to eleven of the *Boece*.[80] Walton, a Canon of Osney, had access to a Vulgate *Consolation* and also drew from Trevet's commentary. He replaces Jean de Meun with Chaucer, however, using the *Boece* as a third source to help craft his translation.[81] As Taylor Cowdery argues in this volume, Walton is preoccupied with "saving" the *sentence* of the *Consolation*'s "subtile matere" which he finds "so hard and curious":[82]

> As fro þe text þat I ne vary noght
> But kepe þe sentence in hys trewe entent,
> And wordes eke als neigh as may be broght
> Where lawe of metir is noght resistent[83]

Like Chaucer, Walton uses his sources to help clarify the sense of the Latin, expanding and interpreting Boethius's *sentence*. The most notable symptom of this expansion is a broader attempt to Christianize Boethius.[84] Ian Johnson observes:

---

[78] Nicholas Perkins, "Haunted Hoccleve? *The Regiment of Princes*, the Troilean Intertext, and Conversations with the Dead," *The Chaucer Review* 43 (2008): 103–39.

[79] See also Penelope B.R. Doob, *Nebuchadnezzar's Children: Conventions of Madness in Middle English Literature* (New Haven: Yale University Press, 1974), 208–31; and Eleanor Johnson, *Practicing Literary Theory in the Middle Ages: Ethics and the Mixed Form in Chaucer, Gower, Usk, and Hoccleve* (Chicago: University of Chicago Press, 2013), 202–31.

[80] Walton translates the first three books of the *Consolation* into octaves, the last two into rhyme royal. For an overview, see Brian Donaghey, Irma Taavitsainen, and Erik Miller, "Walton's Boethius: From Manuscript to Print," *English Studies* 80 (1999): 398–407.

[81] For a source discussion, see Ian Johnson, "Placing Walton's Boethius," in *Boethius in the Middle Ages: Latin and Vernacular Traditions*, ed. Lodi Nauta and Maarten J.F.M. Hoenen (New York: Brill, 1997), 217–42; and Johnson, "Walton's Sapient Orpheus," in *The Medieval Boethius: Studies in the Vernacular Translations of De Consolatione Philosophiae*, ed. A.J. Minnis (Cambridge: D.S. Brewer, 1987), 144–54.

[82] John Walton, trans., *De Consolatione Philosophiae*, ed. Mark Science, EETS o.s. 170 (London: Oxford University Press, 1927), 2.1, 3.

[83] Walton, trans., *De Consolatione Philosophiae*, 3.1–4.

[84] See Ian Johnson, "Walton's Heavenly *Boece* and the Devout Translation of Transcendence," in *The Medieval Mystical Tradition in England: Exeter Symposium VIII*, ed. E.A. Jones (Cambridge: D.S. Brewer, 2013), 162–75; see also Taylor Cowdery's contribution to this volume.

> Above all, then, his work is a translation, in the academic tradition, of a work of high authority more serious than nearly all that even a prestigious poet like Chaucer could offer. In this, Walton resembles such writers as Nicholas Love, whose works emanated from the commanding heights of cultural authority occupied by orthodox reworkings of the Bible and other authorities, glossed by layers of commentary, and taught in the educational system.[85]

Along these same functional lines, an anonymous Oxford cleric produced a partial translation of the *Consolation* called *The Boke of Coumfort of Bois* (Oxford, Bodleian Library, MS AUCT.F.3.5).[86] This translation, heavily reliant on the *Boece*, goes even further than Chaucer or Walton in supplementing the *Consolation* with encyclopedic information from a wider range of other works, probably "intended as a textbook for students in a monastic school."[87] As Cornelius notices, this practice proved "too onerous to be continued," and the amount of commentary is much reduced after Book 1, Prose 4 (1p4).[88] Johnson explains that "*The Boke of Coumfort* is another creative extension of the *Consolatio* tradition, for it repurposes Chaucer's words, brings further Latin commentary materials into expository vernacular play, and to a significant extent reslants the Boethian text devotionally," while also acknowledging that the text "revalorizes" Boethius, the original Latin *auctor*.[89]

Three final texts, written in the tradition of Usk and Hoccleve, must also be mentioned: James I's *Kingis Quair*, Robert Henryson's *Orpheus and Eurydice*, and George Ashby's *A Prisoner's Reflections*. Like Usk, James I of Scotland turned to Boethius's *Consolation* while imprisoned by the English, but he diverts greatly from the philosophy of the book that keeps him up all night reading.[90] Part autobiography, part musing on fortune and fate, *Kingis Quair* is an "inventively daring untranscendent unmaking of the *Consolatio*,"[91] in which the king turns to love and fortune in a "celebration of worldly felicity."[92] Henryson draws on Book

---

[85] Johnson, "Placing Walton's Boethius," 242.

[86] See "*The Boke of Coumfort of Bois* [Bodleian Library, Oxford Manuscript AUCT.F.3.5]: A Transcription with an Introduction," ed. Noel Harold Kaylor, Jr., and Philip Edward Phillips, in Kaylor and Phillips, *New Directions in Boethian Studies* (Kalamazoo, Medieval Institute Publications, 2007), 223–79. The editors date this text ca. 1380 × 1420.

[87] Philip Edward Phillips, "The English *Consolation of Philosophy*: Translation and Reception," *Carmina Philosphiae* 17 (2009): 97–126, at 102.

[88] Cornelius, "Boethius' *De consolatione philosophiae*," 287.

[89] Johnson, "Making the *Consolatio* in Middle English," 440–41.

[90] James I of Scotland, *The Kingis Quair*, ed. John Norton-Smith (Oxford: Clarendon Press, 1971).

[91] Johnson, "Making the *Consolatio* in Middle English," 442.

[92] Cornelius, "Boethius' *De consolatione philosophiae*," 290.

3, Meter 12 and Trevet's commentary (especially on *moralitas*) in his rewriting of the tale of Orpheus in his *Orpheus and Eurydice.*[93] After providing the Orpheus narrative, Henryson uses Trevet's commentary to make observations about morality. In *A Prisoner's Reflections* (1463), Ashby offers another autobiographical account of a bureaucrat's fall from fortune to imprisonment.[94] Cornelius explains that Ashby blends "Boethian language into a discursive matrix emphatically penitential and homiletic."[95] In this move, "The speaker offers himself to readers as a moral *exemplum* and urges readers to comprehend worldly adversity within an economy of sin and penitence"—ultimately championing patience.[96] These three texts reveal the scope of Boethius's legacy in later medieval Britain, where, following a flourishing commentary tradition and translations by Chaucer and Walton, the *Consolation* remained a widely popular text worthy of careful study and adaptation. Moreover, as Usk, James I, and Ashby's works attest, the *Consolation* holds an important place in the long history of prison narratives by such writers as Thomas More, John Bunyan, and Malcolm X.[97]

The Plan of the Book

As noted above, the time has come for a reassessment of the vernacular tradition. This volume is divided temporally in two, though we do not wish to position the halves too distantly and have cross-referenced the essays accordingly. The first, "Earlier Medieval England," examines the legacy of Boethius's *Consolation* in the Anglo-Saxon period, while the second, "Later Medieval England," traces its reception from the twelfth century through the fifteenth. Together, both halves form a continuous vernacular reading tradition, tracing Boethius's legacy in the English Middle Ages by attending not only to vernacular translations and transformations but also to Latin receptions and commentaries. Throughout, we have edited so that each essay can also stand alone and be read independently.

[93] See Robert Henryson, *The Poems of Robert Henryson*, ed. Denton Fox (New York: Oxford University Press, 1981). See also Kenneth R. Gros Louis, "Robert Henryson's *Orpheus and Eurydice* and the Orpheus Tradition of the Middle Ages," *Speculum* 41 (1966): 643–55; and John MacQueen, "Neoplatonism and Orphism in Fifteenth-Century Scotland," *Scottish Studies* 20 (1976): 69–89.

[94] George Ashby, *George Ashby's Poems*, ed. Mary Bateson, EETS e.s. 76 (London: K. Paul, Trench, Trübner & Co., 1899). See also John Scattergood, "George Ashby's *Prisoner's Reflections* and the Virtue of Patience," *Nottingham Medieval Studies* 37 (1993): 102–9.

[95] Cornelius, "Boethius' *De consolatione philosophiae*," 290.

[96] Cornelius, "Boethius' *De consolatione philosophiae*," 290.

[97] For an overview of this tradition, see Philip E. Phillips, ed., *Prison Narratives from Boethius to Zana* (New York: Palgrave MacMillan, 2014).

Earlier Medieval England

Five of the first six essays explore different aspects of the Old English translations of Boethius's *Consolation*, first into prose and then into prosimetrum. Susan Irvine's "The Protean Form of the Old English *Boethius*" introduces the two versions *en mouvance*, demonstrating that attention to their initial reception has as much to offer as a focus on their composition alone. In particular, she re-examines the two prefaces—one in prose and one in verse—to conclude that "the Old English *Boethius* underwent a formal relocation in the course of its transmission history."

Anglo-Saxon translations are often dismissed as secondhand rehearsals of earlier ideas. Three essays explore the philosophical departures and innovations of the Old English *Boethius*, especially as it expands on Boethius's exploratory psychology. Nicole Guenther Discenza directs our attention to the opposition of foreknowledge and free will in "Knowledge and Rebellion in the Old English *Boethius*." Examining the rebellious intent of readers who seek to know too much, she points to the translator's anxieties about his own speculative exploration. Discenza contends that the translator forgoes an extended discussion of God's providence in order to shift the reader's attention from divine to *human* knowledge, which threatens the divine order. In rerouting Boethius's anxieties, "The Old English text stands suspended in tension between obedience and knowledge," incorporating additional material about the giants' rebellion against Jove as well as an added allusion to the Tower of Babel.

Paul E. Szarmach further probes Anglo-Saxon epistemology in "The Old English *Boethius* and Speculative Thought," which situates the translation alongside Isidore of Seville's *Etymologies* and Augustine's *Soliloquies* to claim a place for speculative philosophy in Anglo-Saxon England. Szarmach makes a strong case for a speculative tradition in the vernacular, supported by an elegant reading of Meter 20, which recontextualizes Boethian Neoplatonism for a Christian audience by deftly answering to the hermeneutic difficulties of Book 3, Meter 9 (3m9). Szarmach concludes by examining a sophisticated analogy, unique to the Old English, which likens the relationship between stability and change to the axle and wheel of a cart. This image rewrites human morality in cosmological terms, with a person's proximity to God—at the hub of the wheel—determined by the nature of his or her actions.

Haruko Momma revisits this image as a site of particular philosophical intricacy in "*Purgatoria clementia*: Philosophy and Principles of Pain in the Old English *Boethius*," which examines alterations to Book 4 of the *Consolation* to argue for the importance of purgatory in the Old English. Her lucid analysis constellates divine judgment, the ethics of punishment, the arbitrary nature of human fate, and the pursuit of philosophy to argue for the *Boethius* as an internally cohesive translation that at times departs from its source text to further the translator's own ideals—namely that postmortem punishment is necessary to reconcile the fate of the "(redeemably) wicked."

Hilary Fox likewise turns to individual agency, subjectivity, and textual self-fashioning in her "An Ethical History for the Self: The Liberius *Exemplum* in the Old English *Boethius*," which argues that the *Boethius* encourages self-examination "through the deployment of exemplary historical narrative." Focusing on changes to the *exemplum* of Liberius, which opposes an upright counselor and a tyrant, Fox reconfigures Michel Foucault's "technologies of the self" to demonstrate that history formed a necessary component of Anglo-Saxon ethical education. Moreover, the Liberius *exemplum* cautions that virtue (and vice) require both interior and exterior action.

Looking beyond the *Boethius*, Erica Weaver's "Finding Consolation at the End of the Millennium" broadens outward "to demonstrate the resiliency of Boethius's dialectical original—and to claim another, more diffuse Boethian tradition for later Anglo-Saxon England." Drawing a connection between a fire, a letter, a manuscript, and a poem, Weaver reconstructs two potential trajectories of Boethius's text as it crossed and recrossed the Channel between Winchester, Fleury, and Ramsey in the decades on either side of the year 1000. She thus rounds out the first half of the volume with an essay on Boethius's legacy in the century after the *Consolation* was first translated into English, highlighting its reception amidst such luminaries as Dunstan, the Archbishop of Canterbury; Abbo of Fleury; and Byrhtferth of Ramsey; as well as lesser-known figures such as Lantfred of Winchester.

Later Medieval England

The second half of the volume traces similar diffusions across time and space. Continuing Weaver's focus on Anglo-Latin literary networks, Ann W. Astell casts light on "Consolations of Friendship: Boethius's Augustinian Reception in Twelfth-Century England." She examines the works of three monks—Lawrence of Durham, Lawrence's student Aelred of Rievaulx, and Aelred's scribe Walter Daniel—to locate a "pattern of bereavement and befriending" drawn from Boethius's *Consolation* and Augustine's *Soliloquies*.

Bridging the gap from the twelfth century to the fourteenth in her wide-ranging "Sensible Prose and the Sense of Meter: Boethian Prosimetrics and the Fourteenth Century," Eleanor Johnson notes that medieval commentators prioritized the ethical import of literary writing, leading late medieval writers to experiment with making their fictions ethically transformative. Boethian prosimetrum emerges as a vehicle for transmitting self-knowledge, providing what Johnson terms "a real-time spectacle of psychological transformation." Johnson traces this psychological transformation in Chaucer's *Troilus and Criseyde* before concluding with a prosimetrical reading of the *Canterbury Tales*.

The *Boece* itself is the subject of A. Joseph McMullen's "Nature, Astronomy, and Cosmology in Chaucer's *Boece*." Tracking Chaucer's additions, McMullen contends that his astronomical interests led him to expand on the cosmological sections of the *Consolation*. The *Boece*, then, was Chaucer's "first true foray into cosmological learning"—and the first display of the astronomical interests which would later be evident in his *Treatise on the Astrolabe*, in the *Miller's Tale*, and elsewhere throughout his works. Jonathan Stavsky then refracts the *Boece* through successive texts in "Tragic Diction in the *Boece*, the *Canterbury Tales*, and Hoccleve's *Series*." Beginning with Chaucer's departure from Trevet's commentary, Stavsky demonstrates that Chaucer remakes Boethian tragedy as a more flexible medium. He then examines divergences in the *Monk's Tale* and the *Boece*, which together generate a new sense of tragedy that, he argues, is also at work in Hoccleve's *Series*.

Anthony G. Cirilla focuses on another Boethian form in his "*The Potages of Foryetfulness*: Thomas Usk, Lady Love, and the Boethian Rhetoric of Personification," which re-examines Boethian personification allegory in terms of *ethopoeia*, or the making of a secondary *ethos*. Reading across Boethius and the much-less-studied Usk, Cirilla reminds us that personification is a powerful medium—not a mechanical narrative device—while making a strong case for Usk's literary-historical merit. Taylor Cowdery likewise attends to an understudied figure in "Translation for *Sentence* in Middle English Poetry: The Case of John Walton," whose fifteenth-century verse translation was fascinatingly conceived as a verse counterpart to Chaucer's all-prose *Boece*. Cowdery provides an overview of the project before moving to a broader study of late medieval translation theory, which, he argues, sought "to flesh out, as it were, the bones of the source with a new body of words."

We hope that this volume has done the same. Boethius's medieval legacy has received renewed attention in recent years with fresh editions, translations, and studies that place his profound influence in a new light. The Alfredian Boethius project of Oxford University, to pick just one example, has produced a critical edition of the Old English prose translation for the first time in more than one hundred years, and the project's growing database of early commentaries has already begun to reshape our understanding of the broader reception of the *Consolation* across medieval Europe, as mentioned above. We hope that this volume, too, will provide new directions for future work.

The Protean Form of the Old English *Boethius*

Susan Irvine

The existence of two versions of the Old English *Boethius*—one all in prose, the other in alternating verse and prose—makes this work exceptionally interesting from a formal point of view amongst vernacular compositions in Anglo-Saxon England. The nature of the relationship between the two versions has given rise to considerable debate amongst scholars, who disagree on such fundamental issues as which version was composed first and whether the same author was responsible for both.[1] Far from being the preserve of modern scholars, however, the interest in the existence of two versions, and in the relationship between them, was apparent already in the Anglo-Saxon period. The work is furnished with a prose preface that famously describes a two-stage process of composition:

> Ælfred kuning wæs wealhstod ðisse bec and hie of boclædene on Englisc wende swa hio nu is gedon . . . [Ð]a he þas boc hæfde geleornode and of

[1] Most scholars agree that (in line with the process described in the prose preface) the prose version was produced first and that the prosimetrical version represents a rendering into verse of those portions of the prose version which were meters in the Latin original. Kevin Kiernan, however, proposed that the prose version was derived from the prosimetrical one; see his "Alfred the Great's Burnt Boethius," in *The Iconic Page in Manuscript, Print, and Digital Culture*, ed. George Bornstein and Theresa Tinkle (Ann Arbor: University of Michigan Press, 1998), 7–32. There is more disagreement on authorship: on the basis of a detailed examination of the relationship between the corresponding prose and verse sections, Mark Griffith, "The Composition of the Metres," in *The Old English Boethius: An Edition of the Old English Versions of Boethius's De Consolatione Philosophiae*, ed. Malcolm Godden and Susan Irvine with a chapter on the Metres by Mark Griffith and contributions by Rohini Jayatilaka, 2 vols. (Oxford: Oxford University Press, 2009), 1:80–134, at 134, concludes that "such slight evidence as is provided by close comparison of the verse and the prose tends not to support the proposition that the versifier was also the translator."

> Lædene to Engliscum spelle gewende, þa geworhte he hi eft to leoðe swa swa heo nu gedon is.[2]
>
> [King Alfred was the translator of this book, and turned it from Latin into English, as it is now done . . . When he had learnt this book and turned it from Latin into English speech, he then produced it again as verse, as it is now done.]

It seems that for the Anglo-Saxons, as for modern scholars, the formal variation of the work warranted comment.[3] But what formal contexts did the Anglo-Saxons consider relevant to the *Boethius*? How was the relationship between the two versions interpreted from a formal perspective? This essay will argue that the prose and verse prefaces to the *Boethius* testify in important ways to the early reception of the work and to readers' attempts to place the text in the context of classical forms. Building on the suggestion of previous scholars that the composition of the *Boethius* may have been informed by the tradition of the *opus geminatum*, the essay will propose that the *Boethius*'s formal variation may be better understood in terms of reception and transmission than in terms of composition.

Boethius's *Consolation of Philosophy* was translated into English around the end of the ninth century, probably as part of the educational program instituted by King Alfred the Great that entailed the provision and dissemination of important works in the vernacular. The choice of this work for translation is in some respects puzzling, since although it was clearly circulating amongst the Carolingians throughout the ninth century, there is no explicit evidence that it was known in Anglo-Saxon England before the writing of the translation itself.[4] "Translation," incidentally, is somewhat of a misnomer, given that the Old English *Boethius* offers a substantially rewritten treatment of its Latin source, including extensive additions drawing on the various commentaries on *The Consolation of Philosophy* which were being produced on the Continent from the mid-ninth century onwards.[5]

The two versions of the *Boethius* were produced one from the other. It seems likely, given that the Latin meters are rendered much more closely in the Old English prose than in the verse, that the prose version was produced from the

[2] Godden and Irvine, *Old English Boethius*, prose preface, ll. 1–2, 7–9. Hereafter cited parenthetically by chapter from the B text or meter from the C text. Translations are my own unless otherwise stated. The textual problems of the preface are addressed below.

[3] On the reception of Boethius's form among later medieval readers, see Eleanor Johnson's essay in this volume, and, on late medieval translation strategies, see Taylor Cowdery's.

[4] Godden and Irvine, *Old English Boethius*, 1:4–5.

[5] Godden and Irvine, *Old English Boethius*, 1:5–8. An edition of these commentaries is currently in preparation by Malcolm Godden, Rohini Jayatilaka, and Rosalind Love as part of the *Boethius in Early Medieval Europe* project based at the University of Oxford.

Latin first, and that an alternating prose and verse (or prosimetrical) version, along the lines of the Latin but based on the Old English prose version, was then made.[6] Each version survives only in one manuscript. The prose version, though probably the earlier of the two versions in terms of composition, is preserved only in a late copy from around 1100, now Oxford, Bodleian Library, MS Bodley 180 (here cited as the B text). The other version, which consists of alternating verse and prose along the lines of *The Consolation of Philosophy* itself, survives (in a fire-damaged state) in London, British Library, MS Cotton Otho A.vi, written around the middle of the tenth century (here cited as the C text).[7] Despite the best efforts of Frederick Madden and Henry Gough, who restored the manuscript in the 1840s, a substantial proportion of it is still illegible or lost.[8] For these parts of its text, it is necessary to rely on the transcript made by Franciscus Junius in the seventeenth century: Junius transcribed the B text in the first instance, and then collated it with the C text, transcribing in full the verse sections unique to this manuscript.[9]

Both versions of the work seem to have circulated simultaneously: although the prosimetrical version was produced after the prose one, there is no evidence that it superseded its predecessor. The prose version was the one consulted by Ælfric, writing at the end of the tenth century, and the sole surviving copy of the prose version was, as noted above, made around 1100.[10] It seems likely that, far from being a draft for the prosimetrical version, the prose version was conceived as a final text and furnished with a chapter list (and perhaps a preface) before being circulated. Then, at some later stage, the prosimetrical version was conceived

---

[6] On the order of composition, see Godden and Irvine, *Old English Boethius*, 1:44 and 80–81. On the prosimetrical form, see Caroline D. Eckhardt, "The Medieval *Prosimetrum* Genre (from Boethius to *Boece*)," *Genre* 16 (1983): 21–38; and Jan Ziolkowski, "The Prosimetrum in the Classical Tradition," in *Prosimetrum: Crosscultural Perspectives on Narrative in Prose and Verse*, ed. Joseph Harris and Karl Reichl (Cambridge: D.S. Brewer, 1997), 45–65.

[7] On the fire of 1731 that destroyed so many of Robert Cotton's manuscripts, see Andrew Prescott, "'Their Present Miserable State of Cremation': The Restoration of the Cotton Library," in *Sir Robert Cotton as Collector*, ed. C.J. Wright (London: British Library Publications, 1997), 391–454.

[8] On the reconstruction of Cotton MS Otho A.vi, see further Susan Irvine, "Fragments of Boethius: The Reconstruction of the Cotton Manuscript of the Alfredian Text," *Anglo-Saxon England* 34 (2005): 169–81.

[9] Junius's transcript is preserved as Oxford, Bodleian Library, MS Junius 12. For a description of the manuscript, see Godden and Irvine, *Old English Boethius*, 1:24–34.

[10] For the relationships of the manuscripts and transmission of the text, see Godden and Irvine, *Old English Boethius*, 1:44–49. For Ælfric's use of the Old English *Boethius*, see Malcolm Godden, "Ælfric and the Alfredian Precedents," in *A Companion to Ælfric*, ed. Hugh Magennis and Mary Swan (Boston: Brill, 2009), 139–63.

and produced, with either the same author or a different one responsible for composing the Meters.

The fact that both versions continued to circulate simultaneously has led some scholars, most recently Britt Mize and Erica Weaver,[11] to suggest that they should be seen as a pair of texts belonging to the tradition of the *opus geminatum*, or "twinned work."[12] According to this view, the Latin tradition of combining a prose and a verse text on a single subject is here represented by the provision of a prose and a prosimetrical text. "Perhaps what we have in the double text of the Old English *Boethius*, or in the production of the Metres that created that bifurcation," writes Mize, "is an imitation of not just the mixed form of the *Consolation*, but the dual form of the *opera geminata* of past Anglo-Saxon luminaries."[13] In this paper I will argue that the relationship between the two versions of the *Boethius* and the *opus geminatum* form is more complex than has previously been acknowledged. It is my contention that the evidence, far from suggesting that the *Boethius* was produced in imitation of the dual form of the *opus geminatum*, indicates rather that it was interpreted as such from an early stage in its reception. Before turning to the prefaces, which provide important evidence of how readers tried to place the work, I will briefly consider the translation techniques of

[11] Britt Mize, *Traditional Subjectivities: The Old English Poetics of Mentality* (Toronto: University of Toronto Press, 2013), 161–63; Erica Weaver, "Latin Learning and the Vernacular: Translating Boethius in Anglo-Saxon England," paper delivered at the International Congress on Medieval Studies, Western Michigan University, Kalamazoo, May 2013. Other scholars who have in passing linked the *Boethius* to the *opus geminatum* tradition include Bill Griffiths, ed., *Alfred's Metres of Boethius*, rev. ed. (Pinner: Anglo-Saxon Books, 1994), 12; Daniel Anlezark, "Three Notes on the Old English *Meters of Boethius*," *Notes and Queries* 51 (2004): 10–15, at 10, fn. 4; and Paul E. Szarmach, "An Apologia for the *Meters of Boethius*," in *Naked Wordes in Englissh*, ed. Marcin Krygier and Liliana Sikorska (Frankfurt: Peter Lang, 2005), 107–36, at 119.

[12] This tradition is characterized by "a pair of texts, one in verse and one in prose, which ostensibly treat the same subject"; see Bill Friesen, "The *Opus Geminatum* and Anglo-Saxon Literature," *Neophilogus* (2011): 123–44, at 124. See also Peter Godman, "The Anglo-Latin *Opus Geminatum*: From Aldhelm to Alcuin," *Medium Ævum* 50 (1981): 215–29; Patrizia Lendinara, "The World of Anglo-Saxon Learning," in *The Cambridge Companion to Old English Literature*, ed. Malcolm Godden and Michael Lapidge, 2nd edn. (Cambridge: Cambridge University Press, 2013), 295–312, at 304; and Gernot Wieland, "*Geminus Stilus*: Studies in Anglo-Latin Hagiography," in *Insular Latin Studies: Papers on Latin Texts and Manuscripts of the British Isles: 550–1066*, ed. Michael W. Herren (Toronto: Pontifical Institute of Mediaeval Studies, 1981), 113–33.

[13] Mize, *Traditional Subjectivities*, 162. Examples of Anglo-Saxon *opera geminata* (written in Anglo-Latin) include Aldhelm's *De virginitate* (late seventh century), Bede's *Vita Sancti Cuthberti* (early eighth century), and Alcuin's *Vita S. Willibrordi* (late eighth century).

the prose author and versifier in order to assess whether these point towards two projects intended to stand independently of each other or a unified one.

The motivations and interests of the author(s) of the two versions were clearly very distinct.[14] The prose translation gives little evidence that its author was attaching much importance to the distinction between poetry and prose. The focus throughout is on conveying the argument of the original. Thus the Latin prose sections are translated more fully than the verse ones, and some of the Latin poems are not recorded as poems in the Old English.[15] The prose author is not averse to using stylistic techniques more commonly associated with poetry, such as alliteration and two-stress phrases. In this he is far from unique amongst other writers of Old English prose.[16] But it is worth noting that he uses these techniques in translating the prose as well as the verse of his Latin source. In Chapter 5 of the B text, for example, rendering Book 1, Prose 6 (1p6) of *The Consolation of Philosophy*, Philosophia's words are put in the mouth of Wisdom as follows:

> Þær þu cyðdest eac þæt þu nystest mid hwilcan gerece God wylt þisse worulde, oððe hu he wolde þæt heo wære, þa þu sædest þæt þu wendest þæt þios sliðne wyrd þas woruld wende butan Godes geþeahte. Ac þæt wæs swiðe micel pleoh þæt þu swa wenan sceoldest. (5.81–85)
>
> [When you acknowledged that you did not know with what rule God controls this world, or how he wanted it to be, you said that you thought that this cruel fate moved this world without God's design. But it was very perilous that you should think so.]

Here the word *sliðen*, normally used only in poetry, is used within a two-stress phrase, "þios sliðne wyrd" [this cruel fate]. The phrase connects alliteratively in its use of "s" and "w" with the preceding phrase "þa þu sædest þæt þu wendest" [when you said that you thought] and with the subsequent phrase, which itself alliterates and has two stressed syllables, "þas woruld wende" [moved this world]. This combination of poetic diction, alliteration, and two-stress phrases produces a rhetorical effect that relies on techniques more akin to poetry than to prose.

The prose author's use of diction and techniques characteristic of vernacular verse, when he is translating the Latin prose as well as the meters, suggests that in using them he is not so much attentive to whether his Latin source is in a prosaic or poetic form but, rather, is acknowledging the movement of the Latin itself between elevated and less elevated styles throughout, within prose sections

[14] The evidence points marginally towards a separate translator and versifier; see fn. 1 above.

[15] Godden and Irvine, *Old English Boethius*, 1:45.

[16] See Roberta Frank, "Poetic Words in Late Old English Prose," in *From Anglo-Saxon to Early Middle English: Studies Presented to E.G. Stanley*, ed. Malcolm Godden, Douglas Gray, and Terry Hoad (Oxford: Clarendon Press, 1994), 87–107.

as well as between verse and prose. The lack of attention this author pays to the different forms of prose and verse in his own stylistic techniques, combined with his inconsistent practice in recording where verse switches to prose and back again and his omission of some meters altogether, make it unlikely that the idea of producing a prosimetrical version from the prose version as a twin was envisaged from the outset. The prose version seems to have been conceived by its author as an independent project.

The prosimetrical version, unlike the prose one, was primarily conceived with a literary imitation of the form of the original in mind. The versifier, or whoever commissioned the new version, aimed to reproduce the formal mixture of prose and verse that characterized the Latin source. Notwithstanding a few slips in carrying out this exercise (Meter 23, for example, offers only a partial versification of the material corresponding to *Consolation* Book 3, Meter 12 (3m12), and the Old English equivalent of *Consolation* 4m7 is not versified at all), the prosimetrical version represents a determined and highly skillful attempt to reproduce in the vernacular the form of the Latin original.

The Meters themselves, it should be noted, while deftly deploying the techniques of Old English poetic composition, are markedly different in style from that of traditional Old English poetry. This can be attributed in particular to the versifier's use of features normally confined to Old English prose. The prosodic systems of the Meters, as Mark Griffith argues, have apparently been "reshaped by constant contact with the prose source."[17] Although such reshaping has commonly been attributed to an unconscious dilution of the poetic ideal, Emily V. Thornbury has recently suggested that it may be part of a wider movement away from the classical Old English tradition and towards a new mode of verse, which "enabled readers to enjoy the illusion that they were themselves reading an important and difficult work of Latin literature."[18] The curiously un-poetic features of the poetry, in other words, might represent an attempt to move an audience out of its vernacular comfort zone, allowing them to feel that they are engaging directly with Latin texts, even as they read them in English. This would fit well with the production of an Old English prosimetrical version, which, in replicating the Latin's alternation between verse and prose, allows readers "to forget that they are reading a translation."[19]

The prosimetrical version, in replicating the form as well as conveying the argument of the Latin original, seems to me to demonstrate a more sophisticated aesthetic than the prose version, possibly to appeal to a different type of reader. In speculating on whether the prosimetrical version was produced to serve as an independent work or as the second part of an *opus geminatum*, it is important to

[17] Mark Griffith, "The Composition of the Metres," 130.

[18] Emily V. Thornbury, *Becoming a Poet in Anglo-Saxon England* (Cambridge: Cambridge University Press, 2014), 235.

[19] Thornbury, *Becoming a Poet*, 234.

acknowledge that there is no extant evidence that the two versions ever circulated together. Since, however, the alternative versions of the Anglo-Latin *opera geminata* themselves often circulated separately,[20] no definitive conclusions can be drawn from this. Perhaps more tellingly, the substantial amount of overlap between the two versions—the prose sections are near-identical in both—is quite uncharacteristic of the *opus geminatum* tradition and may make it unlikely that whoever produced the prosimetrical version had that model in mind.

The question of whether the prosimetrical version might have been intended as an independent project rather than as a twin to the prose version is complicated further by the prefaces to the work, and it is to these that I shall now turn to probe more fully the formal interest of the *Boethius*. The prefaces, I shall argue, indicate that the connection between the *Boethius* and the *opus geminatum* may have developed in the context of the early reception of the work rather than in the context of its composition.

The verse preface to the prosimetrical version focuses exclusively on the composition and function of its poetic sections:

> Ðus Ælfred us ealdspell reahte,
> cyning Westsexna, cræft meldode,
> leoðwyrhta list. Him wæs lust micel
> ðæt he ðiossum leodum leoð spellode,
> monnum myrgen, mislice cwidas,
> þy læs ælinge ut adrife
> selflicne secg, þonne he swelces lyt
> gymð for his gilpe. Ic sceal giet sprecan,
> fon on fitte, folccuðne ræd
> hæleðum secgean. Hliste se þe wille. (verse preface, ll. 1–10)

> [Thus Alfred, king of the West Saxons, maker of verse, told us old stories, revealed his craft, his skill. He greatly desired to tell verse to this people, various discourses, as a joy to men, lest weariness drive away the self-regarding man, when he little cares for this because of his pride. I shall speak further, put well-known advice into poetry, say it to men. Listen he who will!]

The poem is notoriously intriguing, not least because it is so hard to identify the referents of the first-person pronouns: *us* in the first line is probably the voice of a reader, but is the *ic* in line 8 the voice of the supposed author Alfred, or an imagined performer reciting the text, or perhaps the voice of the book itself? What the preface undoubtedly does do, however, is bring Alfred's role as poet ("leoðwyrhta," l. 3) to the fore. Its primary interest is in poetry, and it strongly

[20] See Mize, *Traditional Subjectivities*, 161 and fn. 25, citing Godman, "Anglo-Latin *Opus Geminatum*," and Wieland, "*Geminus Stilus*."

implies that it introduces a work composed in verse. If it hints at the alternating discourses of prose and verse in the work that follows—as in, for example, the verb *spellode* (l. 4) or the phrase *mislice cwidas* (l. 5)—it does so very obliquely indeed.[21]

The underlying conceit of this preface, however, relies on a contrast between poetry and prose. Poetry, the preface tells us, induces pleasure and therefore means that those who find the matter (the "ræd") itself tedious might be persuaded to keep listening. It seems unlikely, given that imitation of the form of the Latin original is so clearly the overriding motive here, that the production of the prosimetrical version of the *Boethius* was actually prompted by Alfred's, or anyone else's, desire to prevent the less attentive members of his audience from becoming bored.[22] The notion that the Meters were composed to appeal to the more easily distracted members of an audience is likely instead to reflect a well-established literary *topos*. The idea that teaching can be made more palatable through the pleasure of poetry recalls the contrast in *The Consolation of Philosophy* itself between the weighty and lengthy prose argument and the sweetness of the

[21] In Susan Irvine, "The Alfredian Prefaces and Epilogues," in *A Companion to Alfred the Great*, ed. Nicole Guenther Discenza and Paul E. Szarmach (Boston: Brill, 2015), 143–70, at 163, I suggest that the collocation of *spellian* with *leoð* in line 4b of the verse preface may "reflect the juxtaposition of verse and prose in the work itself," on the grounds that elsewhere in the OE *Boethius* the author "takes care to distinguish semantically between reciting verse (for which the verb 'singan' is used) and speaking prose (for which the verb 'spellian' is used)." This distinction, however, may have been the prose author's and not one the versifier (assuming the latter was a different person) was aware of or concerned about. For other comments on *spellian*, see David Pratt, *The Political Thought of King Alfred the Great* (Cambridge: Cambridge University Press, 2007), 281; and Tiffany Beechy, *The Poetics of Old English* (Aldershot: Ashgate, 2010), 35. On *mislice cwidas*, see, for example, Allen J. Frantzen, "The Form and Function of the Preface in the Poetry and Prose of Alfred's Reign," in *Alfred the Great: Papers from the Eleventh-Centenary Conferences*, ed. Timothy Reuter (Aldershot: Ashgate, 2003), 121–36, at 134; the fact that the phrase qualifies *leoð* in the previous line, however, and the lack of any evidence elsewhere in Old English that *cwide* means "discourse" in this sense, may make it more plausible to interpret it here as "various [poetic] utterances." Compare "song soðcwida sumne þa geta" [sang one more true utterance] (Meter 7, l. 3) and "singan soðcwidas" [sang true utterances] (Meter 8, l. 3). For the meanings of *cwide* across the Old English corpus, see s.v. *cwide* in *Dictionary of Old English: A to H*, online, ed. Angus Cameron, Ashley Crandell Amos, Antonette diPaolo Healey et al. (Toronto: Dictionary of Old English Project, 2016).

[22] See also Malcolm Godden, "King Alfred and the *Boethius* Industry," in *Making Sense: Constructing Meaning in Early English*, ed. Antonette diPaolo Healey and Kevin Kiernan (Toronto: Pontifical Institute of Mediaeval Studies, 2007), 116–38, at 138. Notwithstanding its metrical interludes, the prosimetrical *Boethius* contains some lengthy and difficult prose passages, undoubtedly carrying little appeal for the restless audience members imagined in its verse preface.

poetry. The *Consolation*, writes Eleanor Johnson, "treats prose as the form that embodies rational thought and meter as the form that embodies sensuality and pleasure," with both forms working "in a productive synergy" with each other.[23] The idea is carried over from the Latin to the Old English version: Mod, for example, speaking to Wisdom, remarks on the distinction between "þinre smealican spræce" [your penetrating speech, 22.6] and "þinre wynsumnesse ðines sanges" [your sweetness of your song, 22.6–7],[24] and Wisdom, speaking to Mod, acknowledges that Mod has been tired by "þis langan spelle" [this long argument, 39.328] and offers "se læcedom and se drenc" [the medicine and drink, 39.329] of songs.[25] For Boethius, both in his own words and in their vernacular equivalent, poetry is a source of refreshment and pleasure which ultimately enhances the didactic aims of the work.

The *topos* of the sweetness of poetry and its ability to manipulate is not of course Boethius's own. It has a long classical tradition, with Homer, Plato, Cicero, and Horace among its best known proponents.[26] In his use of this *topos*, Boethius may also have had in mind his specifically prosimetrical models, such as Martianus Capella's fifth-century *De nuptiis Philologiae et Mercurii* [*The Marriage of Philology and Mercury*]. As Gerard O'Daly notes, Capella explicitly acknowledges that the "tediousness" ("taedium") of his subject may best be relieved by the "pleasantness" and "wit" ("lepor" and "iocus") of verse.[27] The dichotomy between the usefulness of prose and the pleasure of verse underlies the form of the *prosimetrum*.

The verse preface to the *Boethius* can therefore be situated within a well-established Latin tradition, associated with the *prosimetrum*, which sees the pleasures of poetry as an antidote to the tedium of prose. In exploiting this tradition, the versifier implicitly aligns Alfred with Boethius himself. This is just one of a number of ways in which the identities of Alfred and Boethius merge

---

23 Eleanor Johnson, *Practicing Literary Theory in the Middle Ages: Ethics and the Mixed Form in Chaucer, Gower, Usk, and Hoccleve* (Chicago: University of Chicago Press, 2013), 19. See also her essay in this volume.

24 For the Latin source, see *Anicii Manlii Severini Boethii Philosophiae Consolatio*, ed. Ludwig Bieler, CCSL 94 (Turnhout: Brepols, 1957), 3p1.2. For the translation, see Boethius, *The Consolation of Philosophy*, trans. S.J. Tester, Loeb Classical Library 74 (Cambridge, MA: Harvard University Press, 1973): "quam tu me uel sententiarum pondere uel canendi etiam iucunditate refouisti" [how well you have revived me with the weight of your arguments and also with the delight of your songs].

25 See *Anicii Manlii Severini Boethii Philosophiae Consolatio*, 4p6.57. See also Godden and Irvine, *Old English Boethius*, 39.105–11; cf. *Anicii Manlii Severini Boethii Philosophiae Consolatio*, 4p6.6.

26 See, for example, Gerard O'Daly, *The Poetry of Boethius* (Chapel Hill: University of North Carolina Press, 1991), 30–73.

27 O'Daly, *Poetry of Boethius*, 19. See *Martianus Capella: De nuptiis Philologiae et Mercurii*, ed. James Willis (Leipzig: B.G. Teubner, 1983), 307 (8.809).

in the preface. Like Alfred, Boethius was a maker of verse who interpreted "ealdspell" [old stories, l. 1], revealed "cræft" [skill, l. 2], spoke various "cwidas" [utterances/discourses, l. 5], and put "folccuðne ræd" [well known advice, l. 9] into poetry. The contrast in the preface between Alfred the skillful poet and the unnamed self-regarding man may also reflect the contrast between the author Boethius and his persona within the work who self-indulgently revels in his misery before eventually achieving philosophical enlightenment.[28]

In the verse preface to the *Boethius*, then, Alfred is implicitly likened to Boethius, investing the king, and the vernacular translation itself, with all of Boethius's literary, religious, and political authority. Just as Boethius exploited the pleasures of Latin poetry to further his didactic aims, so too, it is suggested, does Alfred craft vernacular verse to similar effect. The composition of the verse preface clearly has its precedent within the tradition of Boethius and his prosimetrical models.

For those who received and transmitted the work, however, the dichotomy between the usefulness of prose and the pleasure of verse may have prompted associations with a different tradition, that of the *opus geminatum*. We might look, for example, at the first epistle to Macedonius by the fifth-century author Caelius Sedulius, which commonly acted as a prefatory letter to his *Carmen paschale*,[29] the verse work that he combined with his corresponding prose version the *Opus paschale* to produce the earliest example of the *opus geminatum*. Here we find a number of similarities to the verse preface to the *Boethius*:

> Cur autem metrica uoluerim haec ratione conponere, non differam breuiter expedire . . . Multi sunt quos studiorum saecularium disciplina per poeticas magis delicias et carminum uoluptates oblectat. Hi quicquid rhetoricae facundiae perlegunt, neglegentius adsequuntur, quoniam illud haud diligunt . . . Horum itaque mores non repudiandos aestimo sed pro insita consuetudine uel natura tractandos, ut quisque suo magis ingenio uoluntarius adquiratur Deo.[30]

---

[28] Other Alfredian prefatory material also elides the figures of Alfred and the Latin source author. For a discussion of the link established between Alfred and Gregory in the prose preface to the Old English *Dialogues*, see Irvine, "The Alfredian Prefaces and Epilogues," 149.

[29] Carl P.E. Springer, *The Manuscripts of Sedulius: A Provisional Handlist* (Philadelphia: American Philosophical Society, 1995), 10 and fn. 27.

[30] "Epistola ad Macedonium," in *Sedulii Opera Omnia*, ed. Iohannes Huemer, CSEL 10 (Vienna: Gerould, 1885), 1–13, at 4–5. The text has been recently printed, with a translation (on which mine is based), in Sedulius, *The Paschal Song and Hymns*, trans. with an introduction and notes by Carl P.E. Springer (Atlanta: Society of Biblical Literature, 2013), 213.

> [But I will not delay in explaining briefly why I chose to compose this work in metrical form . . . There are many for whom instruction in worldly letters is all the more attractive because of the delights of poetry and the pleasures of verse. These readers are more inattentive to whatever they read in the way of rhetorical prose, since they take hardly any pleasure in it . . . So I think that these readers' habits should not be disregarded but handled in accordance with their established customs and nature, so that each should be won for God of his own will in greater accord with his own disposition.]

Both this passage and the *Boethius* verse preface state that their author wanted to compose in verse and offer an explanation. Both focus on the pleasure offered by poetry. Both present a picture of an inattentive reader or listener who finds prose tedious. Both end by accepting that the best way to teach such a person is to cater to their needs with the provision of poetry.

Although there is no reason to think that this particular passage influenced the verse preface, it usefully demonstrates the association between the *opus geminatum* tradition and the *topos* of the pleasures of poetry. Sedulius offers just one example of a number of uses made of this *topos* within the *opus geminatum* tradition.[31] But even from consideration of the example of Sedulius alone, it is clear how familiar this tradition must have been to Anglo-Saxon audiences. Sedulius's writings are known to have enjoyed wide circulation in the early medieval period, both on the continent and in England.[32] As Michael Lapidge has shown, a number of surviving manuscripts of the *Carmen paschale* can be attributed to Anglo-Saxon England, the earliest of which was written in the eighth century, and the work was clearly one of the staple texts of the typical Anglo-Saxon library.[33] The study it received is attested not only by the precedent it set for the composition of works in the *opus geminatum* form (such as those by Aldhelm, Bede, and Alcuin mentioned above) but also by citations and paraphrases in the works of Anglo-Saxon authors such as Aldhelm and Bede, and by the glosses accompanying the text (perhaps linked to classroom use) in surviving copies.[34] Aldhelm and Bede quote frequently and at some length from Sedulius's *opus geminatum*.[35] Bede,

---

31 See further Friesen, "The *opus geminatum* and Anglo-Saxon Literature," 132–42.

32 See Springer, *The Manuscripts of Sedulius*.

33 Michael Lapidge, *The Anglo-Saxon Library* (Oxford: Oxford University Press, 2006), 127.

34 See Michael Lapidge, "The Study of Latin Texts in Late Anglo-Saxon England: The Evidence of Latin Glosses," in *Latin and the Vernacular Languages in Early Medieval Britain*, ed. Nicholas Brooks (Leicester: Leicester University Press, 1982), 99–140, at 113–16; repr. in *Anglo-Latin Literature 600–899* (London: Hambledon Press, 1996), 455–98, at 481–83 (cited hereafter from the latter), and Gernot R. Wieland, "The Glossed Manuscript: Classbook or Library Book?" *Anglo-Saxon England* 14 (1985): 153–73.

35 For Aldhelm's debt to Sedulius, see Andy Orchard, *The Poetic Art of Aldhelm* (Cambridge: Cambridge University Press, 1994), 164–66 and 233–35.

in his *Historia Ecclesiastica*, explicitly mentions Sedulius's *opus geminatum* as the inspiration for Aldhelm's *De Virginitate*.[36] Bede's Old English translator apparently coins a vernacular term for this form, the *twifeald weorc* [twofold work]:

> Wrat he [Aldhelm] eac heah boc 7 weorðlice *de uirginitate*, 7 þa on bysene Sedulius twifealde weorce meterfersum asang 7 geradre spræce gesette.
>
> [Aldhelm also wrote a noble and distinguished book *De virginitate*, and following the example of Sedulius's double work he composed it in verse and also set it down in suitable speech.][37]

There is evidence too that Sedulius was being read in the late ninth century within the Alfredian circle, and thus perhaps close to the milieu in which the *Boethius* was composed. In Asser's Life of King Alfred, Asser quotes in error from the first book of the *Carmen paschale*, having mistaken Geta in that poem for an ancestor of Alfred's.[38] His citation offers clear evidence, however, of the work's availability at the time he was writing. Manuscript evidence for the availability of the *Carmen paschale* and the first epistle to Macedonius around this time is similarly intriguing. The earliest extant copy of these works written in Anglo-Saxon England, made in the eighth century, occurs in what is now the fifth and last booklet of Cambridge, Corpus Christi College, MS 173, otherwise known as the Parker Manuscript, which also contains the A Text of the Anglo-Saxon Chronicle and the Laws of Alfred.[39] The manuscript therefore offers a copy of Sedulius's works alongside vernacular works of Alfredian origin. Unfortunately, the date when this booklet was added to the manuscript is not known. Malcolm Parkes has suggested that the inscription *FRIÐESTAN diacon* written over an erasure on the first leaf of this booklet might be a significant detail in terms of identifying when the booklet and manuscript came together, and he proposes that the person responsible for this inscription is perhaps the tenth-century annotator of the Parker Chronicle who marked "in unmistakable fashion" an entry in the first booklet recording the accession of Frithestan to the see of Winchester

---

36 *Bede's Ecclesiastical History of the English People*, ed. Bertram Colgrave and R.A.B. Mynors (Oxford: Clarendon Press, 1969), 514.

37 *The Old English Version of Bede's Ecclesiastical History of the English People*, ed. Thomas Miller, 2 vols. (London: Trübner & Co., 1890–98), 1:448.

38 *Asser's Life of King Alfred, together with the Annals of St. Neots, erroneously ascribed to Asser*, ed. William Henry Stevenson (1904; repr. with article by Dorothy Whitelock, Oxford: Clarendon Press, 1959), 3. See *Alfred the Great: Asser's Life of King Alfred and Other Contemporary Sources*, ed. and trans. Simon Keynes and Michael Lapidge (Harmondsworth: Penguin, 1983), 229.

39 N.R. Ker, *Catalogue of Manuscripts Containing Anglo-Saxon* (Oxford: Clarendon Press, 1957), 57–59 (nos. 39/40).

in AD 909.[40] As Parkes notes, however, it is not ultimately possible to determine whether the Sedulius booklet was part of the manuscript throughout the Middle Ages or was, rather, brought together with the rest of the manuscript at a later date "by a sharp-eyed antiquary who recognized a connection between the Frithestan whose name appeared in the first booklet and the Frithestan whose name appeared in the fifth."[41]

We have moved some distance from the *Boethius* itself and its verse preface. But the evidence presented here for the association between the pleasures-of-poetry *topos* and the *opus geminatum* tradition, and for the Anglo-Saxons' familiarity with the *opus geminatum* form, perhaps in a classroom context, provides an important context for my consideration of the other preface with which the *Boethius* was furnished, this time in prose. The prose preface was attached to both the prose and prosimetrical versions of the *Boethius*. But it is ostensibly out of place as an introduction to the prose version of the work, since it refers to the composition not just of this version but also of the prosimetrical one. The preface, briefly alluded to in my opening paragraph, is cited here in full (from the B text):

> Ælfred kuning wæs wealhstod ðisse bec and hie of boclædene on Englisc wende swa hio nu is gedon. Hwilum he sette word be worde, hwilum andgit of andgite, swa swa he hit þa sweotolost and andgitfullicast gereccan mihte for þam mistlicum and manigfealdum woruldbisgum þe hine oft ægðer ge on mode ge on lichoman bisgodan. Đa bisgu us sint swiþe earfoþrime þe on his dagum on þa ricu becoman þe he underfangen hæfde, and þeah ða he þas boc hæfde geleornode and of Lædene to Engliscum spelle gewende, þa geworhte he hi eft to leoðe swa swa heo nu gedon is; and nu bit and for Godes naman he halsað ælcne þara þe þas boc rædan lyste þæt he for hine gebidde, and him ne wite gif he hit rihtlicor ongite þonne he mihte, forþam þe ælc mon sceal be his andgites mæðe and be his æmettan sprecan þæt he sprecð and don þæt þæt he deþ. (prose preface, ll. 1–13)
>
> [King Alfred was the translator of this book, and turned it from Latin into English, as it is now done. Sometimes he set it down word for word, sometimes sense for sense, in whatever way he could most clearly and intelligibly explain it, on account of the various and multiple worldly cares which often busied him in mind and body. It is hard for us to count the troubles which in his time came upon the kingdoms which he had received, and yet when he had learnt this book and turned it from Latin into English speech, he then produced it again as verse, as it is now done; and now he

[40] Malcolm Parkes, "The Palaeography of the Parker Manuscript of the *Chronicle*, Laws and Sedulius and Historiography at Winchester in the Late Ninth and Tenth Centuries," *Anglo-Saxon England* 5 (1976): 149–71, at 168–69. See also *MS A*, ed. Janet M. Bately, vol. 3 of *The Anglo-Saxon Chronicle: A Collaborative Edition*, ed. David Dumville and Simon Keynes (Cambridge: D.S. Brewer, 1986), xix.

[41] Parkes, "Palaeography," 170.

> prays and beseeches in God's name everyone who takes pleasure in reading this book to pray for him, and not to blame him if they understand it more correctly than he was able to, for everyone must speak what he speaks and do what he does according to the power of his understanding and his leisure.]

The preface is almost certainly not original in its current form. The allusion to the poetic version, along with the clumsy repetition of "as it is now done," is most convincingly explained as an interpolation, whether it be part of a longer interpolation ("Ða bisgu . . . gedon is"), as Godden and Irvine have argued, or a "light modification" as proposed more recently by David Pratt.[42] If we accept the preface's status as a revised text, two anomalies remain, not unconnected with one another. The first is that its allusion to verse seems to make it out of place in a manuscript containing only the prose version. The second is the odd description of the prosimetrical version as "poetry."

One possible explanation for the first is confusion in transmission: the revised preface, designed for the prosimetrical version, somehow became attached to a copy of the prose version.[43] But if, as Nicole Guenther Discenza has suggested, the preface in its current form was designed to fit both versions at once,[44] then perhaps such an explanation is unnecessary. If the writer who adapted the preface had in mind the availability of two different versions, then the adaptation might have been made so that the preface could accompany either of them (or indeed both). The preface explains that two versions were made, irrespective of any specific manuscript context.

The second anomaly, the description of the prosimetrical version as "poetry," poses more of a problem. One possible answer lies in the interpretation of *leoðe*. In his use of this word, the reviser of the prose preface may perhaps reflect a tendency in the Middle Ages to give priority to the poetry when describing the form.[45] In a ninth-century *Vita Boethii* [Life of Boethius], the author describes the *Consolation* as a poem, comparing it in this respect to Martianus Capella's *De nuptiis*, also a prosimetrical work:

> In quo repositus hos libros per satiram edidit imitatus uidelicet marcianum felicem capellam qui prius libros de nuptiis philologiae et mercurii eadem specie poematis conscripserat.

---

[42] Godden and Irvine, *Old English Boethius*, 2:242–44; David Pratt, "The Voice of the King in 'King Edgar's Establishment of Monasteries,'" *Anglo-Saxon England* 41 (2012): 145–204, at 204.

[43] See Godden and Irvine, *Old English Boethius*, 2:243.

[44] Nicole Guenther Discenza, "Alfred the Great and the Anonymous Prose Proem to the *Boethius*," *Journal of English and Germanic Philology* 107 (2008): 57–76, at 60.

[45] Ziolkowski, "The Prosimetrum in the Classical Tradition," 46–47.

> [When he had been put in that place (prison), he produced these books as a satire, in clear imitation of Martianus Felix Capella who had previously written the books *De nuptiis Philologiae et Mercurii* in the same form of a poem.][46]

Just as the author of this *Vita* applied the term *poem* to the prosimetrical works by Boethius and Martianus Capella, so too the reviser of the prose preface may have distinguished the prosimetrical version of the *Boethius* from the prose one by defining it as "leoðe."

Although it is possible that when the reviser wrote *leoðe*, he had in mind prioritizing the poetry of a prosimetrical text, it is perhaps unlikely given that the context here is the actual process of versification. More likely, I suggest, is the possibility that the reviser was drawing on the information provided by the verse preface. Just as the verse preface ascribes the composition of the poetry to Alfred, so too does the prose preface. Just as the verse preface alludes only to the composition of poetry, so too does the prose preface. It is perhaps the precedent of the verse preface that leads the reviser of the prose preface to refer to the second version as "poetry."

The reviser of the prose preface, then, was apparently attempting to place the two versions of the *Boethius* in the context of the *opus geminatum*. The verse preface may well have steered him in that direction, albeit inadvertently. The pairing of prose and "verse" texts, and the context of the *topos* of poetry and its pleasures—which, as we have seen, was firmly associated with the *opus geminatum* tradition—may explain why the prose preface, in its adapted form, focuses on the production of two different versions of the work, one in prose and one in verse.

Tantalizingly, the prose preface to the *Boethius* seems briefly to echo a preface by the Carolingian commentator Remigius of Auxerre (ca. 840–908) to Sedulius's *Carmen paschale*. Just as the reviser of the preface outlines the twofold process of composition which underlay the *Boethius*, so too Remigius explains how Sedulius's work was composed first in prose and then afterwards in verse: "Et sciendum, quia prius prosaice fecit, postea metrice composuit" [And being well acquainted with it, because he first did it in prose, he afterwards composed it in verse].[47] As it happens, Remigius was confused about the ordering: Sedulius first

[46] *Anicii Manlii Severini Boetii Philosophiae consolationis libri quinque: accedunt eiusdem atque incertorum opusculum sacra*, ed. Rudolf Peiper (Leipzig: B.G. Teubner, 1871), xxxi (cited by Ziokowski, "The Prosimetrum in the Classical Tradition," 46) The texts of this *Vita* will be published in the edition of Boethian commentaries currently in preparation as part of the *Boethius in Early Medieval Europe* project.

[47] "Excerpta ex Remigii expositione in paschale carmen," in *Sedulii Opera Omnia*, ed. Huemer, 316–59, at 316. For the correct order of composition (verse followed by prose), see Sedulius's second epistle to Macedonius, *Sedulii Opera Omnia*, ed. Huemer, 171-4.

wrote a verse work and produced the prose version afterwards. It is intriguing to think that Remigius's mistake might have led readers of Sedulius's work to assume (wrongly) that the prose version preceded the verse one, given that, as Michael Lapidge notes, the *Carmen paschale* seems mainly to have been studied in Anglo-Saxon England by means of Remigius's commentary.[48] In any case, the Remigius preface offers a further slight—admittedly speculative—link between the *Boethius* and Sedulius's *opus geminatum*.

The evidence presented here for the impact of the tradition of the *opus geminatum* on the *Boethius* after the production of either of the two versions suggests that its form may have been reinterpreted in the course of its transmission. There is no firm evidence that the author(s) of the prose or the prosimetrical version of the work had in mind the *opus geminatum* tradition. As we have seen, the prose author seems to have been interested primarily in conveying the argument of the original, with relatively little attention paid to its form. The prosimetrical version was presumably produced because the versifier, or whoever commissioned it, was interested in a literary imitation of the mixture of prose and verse that characterized the Latin original. Although an interest in form is undoubtedly demonstrated here, the focus of that interest is on the production of a *prosimetrum* in the vernacular. The *Boethius* prose preface, in its adapted form, seems to represent an attempt to steer readers of the work toward thinking of it within the context of the *opus geminatum*. The formal interest of the work shifts away from the *prosimetrum* of the Latin original, reflected in the production of the Old English prosimetrical version itself, and towards the *opus geminatum* tradition, within which the two different versions can coexist. The change of perspective strongly suggests that the prose preface as it stands was produced later than either version of the work, and by a different writer.

This essay has proposed that any interpretation of the formal variation of the *Boethius* has to take fully into account the work's reception and transmission. The prefaces, I have argued, offer important evidence for the early reception of the *Boethius*, indicating that its Anglo-Saxon readers were interested in placing it in the context of the Latin genre of *opus geminatum*.[49] This conception of the work may have been an afterthought, perhaps in the same way that the claims of King Alfred's authorship for both versions of the work may have been an afterthought.[50] Although the idea of the *opus geminatum* undoubtedly acts as a

---

[48] See Lapidge, "The Study of Latin Texts," 482–83. Remigius's confusion about the order in which the two versions were composed is noted by Godman, "Anglo-Latin *Opus Geminatum*," 219 and fn. 35.

[49] For another approach to translations of Boethius as they intersect with contemporary ideas of genre, see Jonathan Stavsky's essay in this volume, which attends to the *Consolation's* formal permutations around the nascent genre of "tragedy."

[50] See Malcolm R. Godden, "Did King Alfred Write Anything?" *Medium Ævum* 76 (2007): 1–23; for a different view, see Janet M. Bately, "Did King Alfred Actually

useful context for thinking about the *Boethius*, it is more relevant perhaps to the reception and transmission of the text than to its composition. The two versions of the *Boethius* show what a protean vehicle translation could be, and how the notionally separate forms of prose and poetry gained energy from their various combinations and juxtapositions. In seeking to adapt classical learning for a contemporary audience, writers and readers were also grappling with the formal varieties from different Latin literary traditions and negotiating their reshaping in a vernacular cast. The *Boethius*, in its remarkable formal layering, offers a fine testament to the efforts made by Anglo-Saxon writers and readers to adapt the wisdom of the old world to the intellectual context of the new.[51]

Translate Anything? The Integrity of the Alfredian Canon Revisited," *Medium Ævum* 78 (2009): 189–215.

[51] I would like to thank Malcolm Godden and the volume's two anonymous readers for their very helpful comments on an earlier draft of this essay. I submitted the essay to the editors of this volume in October 2014. It was discussed and cited in advance of publication (with my permission) by Erica Weaver in her article "Hybrid Forms: Translating Boethius in Anglo-Saxon England," whose publication in *Anglo-Saxon England* preceded that of this essay.

Knowledge and Rebellion in the Old English *Boethius*

Nicole Guenther Discenza

Boethius's *De consolatione philosophiae* asks enduring questions: Why do the good suffer while the bad thrive? What is the true good? How can one be happy? Do we really control our own lives, or do outside forces determine what we do and what happens to us? The ongoing vitality of the questions that the imprisoned Boethius debates with Philosophy, and the answers that their dialogue suggests, impelled readers, commentators, and translators for nearly a millennium and a half now. The Old English *Boethius* engages all of these key issues, though it modifies some of the Latin text's arguments, changing emphasis, partially redeeming worldly goods, and at times relying more on authority and less on rigorous logic to support its points.[1] For the most part, the *Boethius* arrives at the same major conclusions: God himself is the true good, and happiness comes from conforming oneself to God; both the suffering of the good and the success of the wicked are temporary; God carefully orders the cosmos in ways that discourage

[1] The Old English *Boethius* dates to the late ninth century or the first quarter of the tenth and offers a very free translation of the Latin text. See my book *The King's English: Strategies of Translation in the Old English Boethius* (Albany: State University of New York Press, 2005); and my chapter "The Old English *Boethius*," in *A Companion to Alfred the Great*, ed. Nicole Guenther Discenza and Paul E. Szarmach (Leiden: Brill, 2015), 200–228. On all these issues, see also Kurt Otten, *König Alfreds Boethius*, Studien zur englischen Philologie, neue Folge no. 3 (Tübingen: Max Niemeyer, 1964); F. Anne Payne, *King Alfred and Boethius: An Analysis of the Old English Version of the Consolation of Philosophy* (Madison: University of Wisconsin Press, 1968); and David Pratt, *The Political Thought of King Alfred the Great* (Cambridge: Cambridge University Press, 2007), especially chap. 13, "The Search for a Satisfactory Consolation," 264–307. Not all agree that earthly goods are partly redeemed: for instance, Malcolm Godden and Susan Irvine, eds., *The Old English Boethius: An Edition of the Old English Versions of Boethius's De Consolatione Philosophiae*, 2 vols. (Oxford: Oxford University Press, 2009), 2:336–41, comment on Chapter 24 of the B text and argue that the Old English makes a *stronger* contrast between worldly goods and real goods than the Latin does.

and punish evil and encourage and reward virtue; and human free will exists and has significance.[2]

On this last point, however, the two texts differ significantly in their handling. In the final book of the *Consolation*, the narrator expresses grave concern that God's providence and foreknowledge leave no room for human free will, making reward and punishment arbitrary and prayer and the pursuit of virtue meaningless. Philosophy argues there that God's will and foreknowledge do not negate human free will. Foreknowledge, she teaches, is really a misnomer.[3] Philosophy explains God's nature as eternal so that his knowledge is not really *fore*knowledge but knowledge of any time as if it were knowledge of the present. God no more causes us to make the choices he knows that we will than my knowledge that everyone in the audience at a conference presentation is sitting forces them all to sit.[4] Philosophy spends most of the 171 lines of Latin in Book 5, Prose 6 (5p6), the final section of the text, explaining the nature of eternity and how God's knowledge operates in relation to it. God experiences what we would call past, present, and future as we experience the present. Only God possesses this pure intellection, encompassing everything at once and knowing each thing truly as it is. Human beings must live in time and perceive through limited senses, not truly and fully knowing anything.[5] Philosophy then closes with an exhortation to join with God in prayer, seeking unity with that sole stable and

[2] Though I take these points to be conclusions, I acknowledge that they are not fully satisfactory. For a discussion of the internal contradictions and problems raised by the *Consolation*, see John Marenbon, *Boethius*, Great Medieval Thinkers (Oxford: Oxford University Press, 2003), especially chaps. 6–8. Joel C. Relihan, with William E. Heise, *The Prisoner's Philosophy: Life and Death in Boethius's Consolation* (Notre Dame, IN: University of Notre Dame Press, 2007), argues that the whole *Consolation* is a satire revealing the limits of Philosophy and the need for the prisoner to turn to a different path, the way of Christian wisdom, so that most apparent conclusions remain very much in question.

[3] The problem exists in English as much as in Latin, in *foreknow* and *foreknowledge* as much as in *praenoscere* and *praenotio*. Both languages have prefixes that signify temporal priority and no easy way to refer to anything not experiencing sequential time as people do. For further discussion, see also Paul E. Szarmach's essay in this volume.

[4] For Boethius's handling of God's experience with regard to time, see Marenbon, *Boethius*, 135–44. Marenbon rejects the idea that Boethius conceived of God as simply atemporal, the reading of a number of other scholars; for my purposes here, God's exact relationship to time does not matter.

[5] As both Marenbon and Relihan note, the argument is neither wholly consistent nor wholly satisfactory, for Philosophy then, in the closing section of the *Consolation*, seems to accept that God's knowledge *does* indeed cause everything because he knows everything according to himself: see Marenbon, *Boethius*, 144–45; and Relihan, *The Prisoner's Philosophy*, 30–32.

perfect good. This solution answers the narrator's last fear, that God's order limits human freedom, bringing the text to a close with an exhortation to prayer.[6]

The Old English *Boethius*, however, shows less concern about God's providence and prescience, and less interest in eternity. Where the Latin Book 5 is about 16% of the whole *Consolation*, the Old English spends a mere 7% of its length on the equivalent sections. Some scholars have argued that the translator, be he Alfred or an anonymous scholar, does not fully understand the idea of eternity, which would explain why the *Boethius* disposes of the problems of eternity and the nature of God's knowledge so quickly.[7] Whether the translator understands the concept of eternity or not, the *Boethius* simply does not share the Latin text's depth of concern about a too-rigid divine order. Instead, the *Boethius* reveals a greater anxiety that human knowledge, and human and angelic free will, threaten divine order and result in ruin on earth. That fear works counter

---

[6] Relihan, *The Prisoner's Philosophy*, presents order as a more pervasive problem in the Latin text than I do; he writes, "The obsession with asserting the order of the world is the hub of the discussion in the final books" (165, note 10).

[7] I argue for the translator's understanding of eternity in *The King's English*, esp. 25–28. So do Otten, *König Alfreds Boethius*, 78–80; Katherine Proppe, "King Alfred's Consolation of Philosophy," *Neuphilologische Mitteilungen* 74 (1973): 635–48, at 640; and W.F. Bolton, "How Boethian is Alfred's *Boethius*?" in *Studies in Earlier Old English Prose*, ed. Paul E. Szarmach (Albany: State University of New York Press, 1986), 153–68, at 162. J.M. Wallace-Hadrill, *Early Germanic Kingship in England and on the Continent* (Oxford: Clarendon Press, 1971), 147, is not sure whether Alfred misunderstood the distinction between time and eternity or recognized it and chose to reject it. Payne, *King Alfred's Boethius*, 18–21, writes that rejecting the distinction is fundamental to Alfred's translation. Questions of authorship do not affect my argument here but may hold interest nonetheless. Three major positions have been staked out recently: in favor of Alfred as author, see Janet L. Bately, "Alfred as Author and Translator," in *A Companion to Alfred the Great*, ed. Nicole Guenther Discenza and Paul E. Szarmach (Boston: Brill, 2015), 113–42; and "Did King Alfred Actually Translate Anything? The Integrity of the Alfredian Canon Revisited," *Medium Ævum* 78 (2009): 189–215. Against Alfred's authorship, see Malcolm R. Godden, "Did King Alfred Write Anything?" *Medium Ævum* 76 (2007): 1–23; and "The Player King: Identification and Self-Representation in King Alfred's Writings," in *Alfred the Great: Papers from the Eleventh-Centenary Conferences*, ed. Timothy Reuter (Aldershot: Ashgate, 2003), 137–50. For the argument that one person (who may or may not have been Alfred) did three of the four translations attributed to him but another did the Prose Psalms, see Paramjit S. Gill, Tim B. Swartz, and Michael Treschow, "A Stylometric Analysis of King Alfred's Literary Works," *Journal of Applied Statistics* 34.10 (2007): 1251–58; and Michael Treschow, Paramjit Gill, and Tim B. Swartz, "King Alfred's Scholarly Writings and the Authorship of the First Fifty Prose Psalms," *Heroic Age* 12 (May 2009), <http://www.heroicage.org/issues/12/treschowgillswartz.php>. For more detailed bibliography, see my "Appendix: Annotated Bibliography on the Authorship Issue" in *A Companion to Alfred the Great*, ed. Nicole Guenther Discenza and Paul E. Szarmach (Boston: Brill, 2015), 397–415.

to a major thread of the Latin text and leads to the much-abridged ending in the Old English, where the workings of God are not examined too closely. These apprehensions appear in the *Boethius*'s repeated declarations that men and angels do not obey God, in the anecdotes offered in Chapter 35, and in the close of the text. The Old English text moves from an emphasis on divine order and a concern that humans undermine it to a more specific anxiety that searching for knowledge itself constitutes a form of rebellion. The *Boethius* never fully resolves the tension between its drive to know God and its fear that such knowledge runs contrary to God's order and thereby causes chaos and destruction. Thus the text simultaneously probes the workings of God and shies away from doing so.

The Old English text follows most of the Latin text's arguments, and, conversely, most of its arguments originate in the Latin, including discussions of order and disorder. The *Boethius*'s apprehensions about unruly humans have roots in the Latin *Consolation*. The narrator sings in an apostrophe to God in Book 1, Meter 5 (1m5):

> nihil antiqua lege solutum
> linquit propriae stationis opus.
> Omnia certo fine gubernans
> hominum solos respuis actus
> merito rector cohibere modo.[8]
>
> [By ancient law, nothing abandons its work nor is freed from its proper station. Governing all things towards a particular end, Ruler, you refuse to constrain only human acts with your deserved measure.]

Here human disobedience is the sole exception to divine order, emphasized by the absolutes "nihil," "omnia," and "solos." God *chooses* to allow human freedom, and the narrator even suggests that God should *not* allow quite so much freedom but that He as Ruler *should* restrain ("cohibere") it, in a deserved measure ("merito modo"). The verb *respuo*, literally "to spit out," invests God's exclusion of human acts from divine harmony with a visceral quality.[9] The Latin narrator spends the rest of 1m5 remonstrating with Fortune over her abuse of human beings before returning in the last three lines to an appeal to the "rector" [ruler, 1m5.46] that he quickly seize control and stabilize the situation. The Latin *Consolation* then develops the allegorical character of Fortune as a woman who has a personal relationship with the narrator. The narrator feels betrayed by Fortune,

---

[8] All quotations from the Latin, hereafter cited parenthetically, are taken from Boethius, *De consolatione philosophiae*, in *Opuscula theologica*, ed. Claudio Moreschini, 2nd edn. (Munich: K.G. Saur, 2005); all translations are my own. Here, 1m5.23–27.

[9] For *respuo*, see Charlton T. Lewis and Charles Short, *A Latin Dictionary* (Oxford: Clarendon Press, 1879), 1582, also available online at <http://www.perseus.tufts.edu/hopper/resolveform?redirect=true&lang=Latin>.

but Philosophy explains that Fortune did not betray him; instead, she remained true to her own nature, which is to be changeable. The narrator criticizes God's failure to enforce upon humanity the laws that the rest of the universe follows, but the force of that criticism is blunted as the work progresses and Philosophy corrects the narrator's perspective: God no more fails than Fortune betrays. Though God and Fortune are stable, God allows human beings to introduce disorder into his cosmos.

Both texts question why God allows humans such latitude. The Boethius character in the Old English work, like the Latin narrator, asserts, "Hwæt þe ealle gesceafta heorsumiað and þa gesetnessa þinra beboda healdað butan men anum se þe oferheorð" [Indeed, all creatures obey you and hold the order of your commands, except humanity alone, who disregard you].[10] The *Boethius* never really constructs Fortune as an independent entity, and so the lament that follows omits the Latin's address to Fortune. Instead it speaks solely to God and asks why he allows *wyrd* [fate or fortune] to behave thus.[11] God's decision here is presented as a choice to allow *wyrd* rather than human beings to run wild; the Old English does not at this point emphasize human disobedience as the source of disorder, although the passage suggests that possibility.[12] Later the *Boethius* shifts more emphasis to the rebels as it develops its own concerns, but those concerns stem from early portions of the Latin text.

This passage comes in Book 1 of the Latin text, and the narrator at this stage is distraught, as Philosophy and Wisdom respectively note: each tells the narrator that his emotional outbursts reveal him to be quite far from his homeland (1p5.2–3 and 5.4–10). Wisdom explicitly adds that he is wrong to think that the world runs "buton Godes geþeahte and his þafunge and monna gewyrhtum" [without the counsel of God and his consent and the works of humanity, 5.8–9]. Thus both texts show God consenting to human free will, and both stress the uniqueness of humanity in its disobedience to God, but the *Boethius* adds a little emphasis here to the role of humanity in the affairs of the world. Later Philosophy raises the issue of human disobedience when she sings:

---

[10] All quotations from the Old English *Boethius*, hereafter cited parenthetically, are from Godden and Irvine, *Old English Boethius*; all translations are my own. I quote the all-prose B text, and in all the quotations used in this chapter, the prosimetrical C version is substantially the same. Here, 4.13–14.

[11] The Old English term *wyrd* sometimes translates Latin *fortuna* [fortune] and sometimes *fatum* [fate], but as Pratt argues, it always results from God's forethought and remains "flexible . . . dynamically responding to human actions" (300); see *The Political Thought*, esp. 295–302.

[12] "Hwy þu la drihten æfre woldest þæt seo wyrd swa hwyrfan sceolde?" [Why, O Lord, did you ever want fate to go in this way? 4.16–17].

O felix hominum genus,
si vestros animos amor
quo caelum regitur regat! (2m8.28–30)

[O happy humankind, if the love that rules the heavens ruled your souls!]

Love clearly does *not* rule human souls. Wisdom's version of the meter does not refer to love, however: "Eala þætte þis moncyn wære gesælig gif heora mod wære swa riht and swa gestaðelod and swa geendebyrd swa swa þa oðre gesceafta sindon" [Oh, how happy would humanity be if their minds were as right and as stable and as ordered as those of other creatures are, 21.44–47]. Where *amor* [love] should govern in the Latin, in the English the emphasis is on order, on a mind "riht" and "gestaðelod" and "geendebyrd."

Tellingly, the Latin *Consolation* does not repeat its early concern about human disorder and disobedience in the same ways that the Old English *Boethius* does. The issue remains a major concern into the fourth book, for the foundational problem, according to the narrator, is that he suffers for following philosophy and protecting the Roman Senate (see especially 1p4). Yet Philosophy insists repeatedly on divine order. Twice in the text, where Philosophy emphasizes order, the Old English Wisdom qualifies the statements, showing less certainty that order prevails. Philosophy sings,

Quantas rerum flectat habenas
natura potens, quibus immensum
legibus orbem provida servet
stringatque ligans inresoluto
singula nexu (3m2.1–5)

[What reins powerful Nature directs over things; by what laws provident [Nature] protects the great cosmos and binds each individual thing together, tying them with an indissoluble knot.][13]

Thus everything obeys Nature, with no exceptions, unlike Philosophy's earlier presentation of humanity as disobedient. The Latin speaks of perfect order undisturbed by any errant creation; human disorder at best appears by implication in Philosophy's words here. Wisdom expands on the concise Latin and adds explicit exceptions:

hu wundorlice drihten welt eallra gesceafta mid þam bridlum his anwealdes, and mid hwilcere endebyrdnesse he gestaðolað and gemetgað ealle gescefta, and hu he hi hæfð geheaðorade and gehæfte mid his unanbindendlicum

[13] Thanks to Rosalind Love, Thomas Williams, and Dominic Mark Holtz for help with this passage.

> racentum, þæt ælc gesceaft bið heald [onloten] wið hire gecynde, þære gecynde þe heo to gesceapen wes, buton monnum and sumum englum þa weorðað hwilum of hiora gecynde. (25.2–8)
>
> [how wonderfully the Lord directs all creations with the bridles of his power, and with what order he establishes and regulates all creatures, and how he has restrained them and bound them with his unbreakable chains, that each creation is held inclined to its nature, that nature for which it was created, except humanity and some angels who sometimes become opposed to their own natures.]

The Old English version removes Nature as an intermediary force and describes God directly ordering the universe; the only nature here is the individual nature with which God has endowed each creation. At the same time, Wisdom specifies a human exception where Philosophy does not, and the Old English adds angels where the Latin has none.[14] The *Boethius* continues to display concern about disorder and disobedience after the Latin has moved past the topic.

In the next instance, Philosophy and the narrator have a simple exchange: "—Nihil est igitur, quod naturam servans deo contra ire conetur?—Nihil, inquam" ["Therefore there is nothing that seeks to act against God while preserving its own nature?" "Nothing," I said, 3p12.19]. They then agree two sentences later that nothing wants or is able to oppose the highest good (3p12.21). The Old English again qualifies the conclusion: "Ða cwæð he: 'Nis nan gesceaft þe tiohhige þæt hio scyole winnan wið hire scippendes willan gif hio hire gecynd healdan wile?' Ða cwæð ic: 'Nis nan gesceaft þe wið hire scipendes willan winne buton disig mon oððe eft þa wiðerwierdan englas'" [Then [Wisdom] said: "Is there no creation that ordains that it must fight against its creator's will if it wants to retain its nature?" Then I said: "There is no creation which fights its creator's will except foolish humanity or again the contrary angels," 35.102–105]. The added concession is not even needed: both texts already except beings not holding to their natures, with the clear implication that most human beings work against their own natures when they mistakenly pursue good in partial goods. The *Boethius* goes out of its way to remind its audience that people defy God's order, and here it specifies that the "disig," the foolish, are the ones who oppose God. This qualification might seem reassuring but for the additional stipulation of "wiðerwierdan englas." The Latin *Consolation* virtually never treats angels and shows no concern for their disobedience. The Old English seems fraught, lessening the power of human disobedience by finding it only in the foolish, but adding angelic disobedience as a force against God's will.

[14] At least two Latin glosses add the exception for humans, but they do not mention angels (although Godden and Irvine note that the devil appears in glosses to the start of the meter); see Godden and Irvine, *Old English Boethius*, 2:342.

The final explicit reference to human and angelic free will in the Old English contradicts its own previous references, as if to reassure the audience — or the translator. In the midst of constructing a hierarchy of kinds of sense and knowledge, the Old English *Boethius* states, "Forþam sint ðas sceafta þus gesceapene þæt ða unstyriendan hi ne ahebben ofer þa styriendan ne him wið ne winnan, ne þa styriendan ofer þa men, ne þa men ofer þa englas, ne þa englas wið God" [For these creatures are made so that the motionless do not elevate themselves over those that move nor contend against them, nor the moving ones over humanity, nor humanity over the angels, nor the angels against God, 41.140–143]. This paean to order echoes earlier passages in the Latin that it has already translated: the end of 3m2 proclaims that all creations match their ends and their beginnings in stable orbits (3m2.34–38), and the Old English rendering captures the idea fairly faithfully (25.27–29) before making more explicit the end of all creations in God (25.29–34). This passage near the end of the *Boethius* is also reminiscent of 3m9 with its insistence on divine order, translated and expanded in the Old English (33.142–251). Yet all of these passages contradict the *Boethius*'s own insistence quoted above (25.2–8 and 35.102–105) that humans and rebel angels revolt against the divine hierarchy. The Old English text offers reassurance about cosmic order after it has repeatedly shown that the two creations closest to God, angels and humans, violate that order.

Those demonstrations of disobedience occur not only in relatively abstract arguments but also memorably in concrete anecdotes. Two narratives dramatize the Old English *Boethius*'s concern about human and angelic disobedience well beyond anything in the Latin text and give a specific cause for disobedience: a desire for knowledge. After that above exchange in 3p12, equivalent to Old English Chapter 35.29–194, where Philosophy and the narrator agreed that nothing can oppose the highest good while remaining true to its nature, Philosophy obliquely alludes to the giants' rebellion against Jove: "'Accepisti,' inquit, 'in fabulis lacessentes caelum Gigantas; sed illos quoque, uti condignum fuit, benigna fortitudo disposuit'" ["You have learned in myths," she said, "of the giants who attacked heaven; but also a benevolent strength disposed them properly, as was right," 3p12.24]. The Latin line seems obscure; why refer to giants at all here?[15] At the same time, the statement makes verbal connections to what came before and what comes after: the word *lacessentes* picks up the narrator's "stultitiam magna *lacerantem*" [stupidity that rips apart great things, 3p12.23, emphasis

[15] See Relihan's commentary to his translation, *Boethius: Consolation of Philosophy* (Indianapolis: Hackett, 2001), 179. Relihan elsewhere notes that the prisoner has just praised Philosophy's quotation from the biblical Book of Wisdom, but "Philosophy hardly follows up on it" (28); he argues that Philosophy deliberately, teasingly defies the prisoner's expectations here, *The Prisoner's Philosophy*, 28. See also Hilary Fox's essay in this volume, which examines the use of exemplary narratives in ethical self-formation.

added] from the previous sentence.[16] In the sentence after her allusion to the giants, Philosophy refers to smashing arguments together: "rationes ipsas invicem collidamus" [dash these arguments into one another, 3p12.25]. This imagery may in turn look back to the giants' attack, the divine strength that disposed of that rebellion, or the clash of the two.[17] Whatever work this reference to the giants does, it does so briefly and suggestively, not explicitly. In the allusion, the giants' rebellion ends four words after it has begun, and more words are spent on the outcome than the revolt. Order is re-established, and readers are assured of the justness of the rebellion's quelling after the brief moment of disruption.

The Old English *Boethius* develops the allusion dramatically. The *Consolation* sketches the rebellion and its handling in a mere dozen words of Latin; the Old English *Boethius* takes 125 words (35.116–128). Some of the extra verbiage serves to establish the tale as a falsehood: the Latin *fabulis* becomes "ealdum leasum spellum" [old false tales, 35.117], and the falsity of the story is reiterated ten lines later. Even more obviously, Wisdom uses the verb *sculan* repeatedly to remind audiences at every step that these things did not happen but only supposedly happened, or must have happened according to false myths. The *Boethius* tells us first:

> Iob Saturnes sunu **sceolde** beon se hehsta god ofer ealle oðre godas, and he **scelde** bion þæs heofenes sunu and **scolde** ricsian on heofenum. And **scoldon** gigantas bion eorþan suna, and þa **sceoldon** ricsian ofer eorðan. And þa **sceoldan** hi beon swilce hy wæron geswystrena bearn, forþam þe he **sceolde** beon hefones sunu and hi eorðan. Þa **sceolde** þam gigantum ofþincan þæt he hæfde hire rice, woldon ða tobrecan þone hefon under him. (35.117–124; emphasis added)
>
> [Jove, Saturn's son, **was supposed** to be the highest god over all other gods, and he **would** be the son of heaven and **would** rule in heaven. And the giants **were supposed** to be the sons of earth, and they **would** rule over the earth. And then they **were supposed** to be sisters' sons, because he [Jove] **would** be the son of heaven and they of earth. Then **supposedly** the giants took offense that he had their kingdom, and they wanted to ravage heaven under him.]

A form of *sculan* appears before almost every lexical verb in the classical story to stress its falsity: *sceolde* and *sceoldon* appear nine times in ten lines in the edition.[18]

---

16 Godden and Irvine note the verbal echo, *Old English Boethius*, 2:407.

17 Relihan suggests that the clashing *rationes* are "philosophy and revelation," *The Prisoner's Philosophy*, 82.

18 See 35.118, twice in 119, twice in 120, 121, 122, 123, 124; the latter is after the quotation above ends.

Only three verbs in the story are declined instead of depending on *sculan*, making it impossible for readers or hearers to forget that the tale is false.[19]

Not only is the tale false but the expanded version does not even make good sense. Much of the addition in the Old English treats the reasons for the rebellion, which the Latin text does not even mention. Yet this account seems self-contradictory: if the giants ruled the earth, then how does Jove have their kingdom two sentences later? Why destroy heaven instead of taking it for themselves, or just taking back earth?[20] The rebellion seems ill-conceived—or the story so flawed as to discourage readers from accepting its truth as the repetition of *sculan* does.

What emerges clearly in the Old English is that giants rebelled against a god, and he destroyed them: "Þa **sceolde** he sendan þunras and lygetu and windas, and towyrpan eall hira geweorc mid, and hi selfe ofslean" [Then he **supposedly** sent thunder and lightning and winds, and obliterated all their work with them, and killed the giants themselves, 35.124–126, emphasis added]. The Old English does not offer the Latin's simple reassurance that "a benevolent strength disposed them properly"; this force does not seem benevolent at all. The use of Jove here offers some distance from the Christian God and may underscore the false belief underlying the tale. The translator need not reassure readers as to the intentions of a pagan god in "leasunga" [lies, 35.127]. He also adds that Jove destroyed all their work, an important detail not present in the Latin.[21] The disorder is obliterated: neither the rebels nor their works remain to threaten order again. The Old English develops a brief, perplexing Latin allusion to make it into a memorable if still perplexing tale at whose climax the giants and their work are destroyed for disobedience.

Why does the Old English tell the tale at all, when the text insists so strenuously on its falsity? First, the story vividly illustrates the translator's concern with disobedience to God and its effects; second, it leads neatly into another story that exemplifies the same lesson even better. The translator turns from the destruction of the classical giants' work to a biblical story about a rebellious giant and the destruction of his and his people's work. Wisdom declares of the tale he has just told, "Ðyllice leasunga hi worhton, and mihton eaðe secgan soðspell gif him þa leasunga næron swetran, and þeah swiðe gelic þisum" [Such lies they made, and they could easily have told true stories if the lies had not been sweeter to them, and yet very like [the true tales], 35.126–127]. He distances himself from

[19] The conjugated verbs are *wæron*, 35.121, and *hæfde*, 35.123, both in dependent clauses where the main clause uses *scylan*; and *woldon*, 35.124.

[20] See Godden and Irvine, *Old English Boethius*, 2:409.

[21] John Brinegar, "'Books Most Necessary': The Literary and Cultural Contexts of Alfred's *Boethius*" (Ph.D. diss., University of North Carolina at Chapel Hill, 2000), 82–83, suggests that the translator takes this detail from the account of the giants' death in Ovid, *Metamorphoses* Book 1 (1.152–55), where the giants pile mountains on top of each other to reach heaven and where that mass of mountains is then destroyed by Jove's lightning.

the account while preserving its benefits: that he retold the tale at some length suggests that the tale of the giants and Jove may indeed be more entertaining to audiences than the true tale he is about to tell. The translator then carefully constructs the story of the Tower of Babel to parallel the account of the giants and Jove and thus to replace it, substituting a true tale for a false one, or at least using the false to reinforce the true. Structural similarities make the Tower of Babel story conform to the outlines of the story of Jove and the giants.

Wisdom begins his second account by contrasting the falsity of the previous tale of disobedience to the divine ("leasunga," 35.126 and 127) with what the tellers *could* have said: "Hi mihton secgan" (35.128). Where *sculan* dominated the classical account, all of the verbs in the Tower of Babel story appear in the simple past, subtly emphasizing its factuality in contrast with the previous tale. Both stories begin with genealogy: Job was said to be the son of Saturn (35.117–118) and of heaven (35.119), and giants were said to be the sons of earth (35.120). Nimrod was the son of Chus, Chus the son of Ham, and Ham the son of Noah (35.129–130). The Old English calls Nimrod (OE *Nefrod*) "se gigant" [the giant, 35.129], as the rebels against Jove were "gigantas" [giants, 35.120]. Nimrod is singular, and the singular verb *het* describes his orders to build the tower (130). Yet the next sentence contains a plural, "Þæt hi dydon" [They did that, 35.132]. Nimrod and his people are united in their desires, as the giants were. The translator also explains both sets of builders' motives: the giants of the classical account wish to rule earth and are offended that Jove rules, and they want to ravage heaven. Their desire springs from jealousy and seems purely destructive. The similarities to this point highlight the contrast here: Nimrod and his people desire to *know* heaven—how high and how thick and how strong it is, and what lies above it (35.132–134). They do not seek to destroy anything. Yet their search for knowledge is itself destructive. As at the end of the previous tale (see 35.124–126), God utterly destroys the work, "towearp þone torr" [demolished the tower, 35.136]. He kills many but not all, scattering the rest. This episode of destruction carries with it the additional comment "swa hit cynn wæs" [as it was fitting, 35.135]. The translator further adds, lest anyone miss the point: "Swa gebyreð ælcum þara ðe winð wið þam godcundan anwealde. Ne gewexð him nan weorðscipe on þam, ac wyrð se gewanod þe hi ær hæfdon" [So it happens to each of those who struggle against the divine rule. Nor does glory increase for them in that way, but instead what they had before is diminished, 35.138–140]. These two dozen lines pack in two sobering accounts of disobedience causing destruction—and the second of them equates excessive curiosity to disobedience. Both cause ruin.

Curiosity about God and heaven thus appears to pose a problem for the translator, who both embraces and shies away from it. Godden and Irvine note that the *Boethius*'s identification of "intellectual curiosity" as the problem runs contrary to the giants' motivation in the classical story; they also remark that the sin at the Tower of Babel is usually understood as pride, and indeed they find no parallels to the *Boethius*'s interpretation.[22] In the Vulgate Genesis, at best God links their abilities to their thought: "et dixit [Dominus] ecce unus est populus et unum labium omnibus coeperuntque hoc facere nec desistent a cogitationibus suis donec eas opere conpleant" [And he said: Behold, it is one people, and all have one tongue: and they have begun to do this, neither will they leave off from their designs, till they accomplish them in deed, Genesis 11:6].[23] The Old English *Heptateuch* renders the sentence fairly closely in one manuscript, using *geþohta* for *cogitationibus*: "Ne hi ne geswicað heora geþohta ær þan þe hi mid weorce hi gefyllan" [Nor will they stop their plans until they have fulfilled them all in deed, 11.6].[24] Two other manuscripts omit the reference to thoughts entirely, reading simply, "Ne geswicað hig ær þan þe hit gearu sig" [Nor will they stop until it is complete, 11.6].[25] In one text, the people's thoughts do not seem to be a problem except insofar as they will not abandon them; the other does not even mention their thoughts. These texts do not say what became of the unfinished tower. The Old English poem *Genesis* also gives the story (ll. 1661–1701) and spells out the builders' motivation: "for wlence and for wonhygdum" [for pride and for recklessness, l. 1673]. The poem further says that they left the tower and its accompanying city or fortification unfinished (ll. 1699–1701). All versions have the dispersal of a once united people and language, but the *Boethius* stands alone in telling the story as curiosity leading to full-scale destruction where other tellings emphasize pride and stubbornness.

The translator's handling of curiosity about God elsewhere in the *Boethius* also suggests discomfort. The Latin narrator asks several pointed rhetorical questions before he reminds Philosophy of his devotion to her (1p4.2–4). He recalls "cum tecum naturae secreta rimarer, cum mihi siderum vias radio describeres" [when I scrutinized the secrets of nature with you, when with your rod you measured for me the paths of the stars, 1p4.4]. The Old English narrator begins his speech with a general question about the rewards of his obedience to Wisdom, replacing the specific questions in the Latin. His memories of exploring the mysteries of creation do not appear in the Old English. The translator follows the sentence after the omitted one more closely, citing Plato as the Latin text does

[22] Godden and Irvine, *Old English Boethius*, 2:411.

[23] *Biblia sacra iuxta vulgatam versionem*, ed. Bonifatius Fischer et al., 3rd edn. (Stuttgart: Deutsche Bibelgesellschaft, 1983); translation from *The Bible* II IntraText Edition CT, ETML tagging by Èulogos, *The Challoner Revision of the Douay-Rheims Bible* (Baltimore, MD: John Murphy Co., 1899), <http://www.intratext.com/IXT/ENG0011/>.

[24] *The Old English Heptateuch and Ælfric's Libellus de Veteri Testamento et Novo*, ed. Richard Marsden, vol. 1: Introduction and Text, EETS OS 330 (Oxford: Oxford University Press, 2008), manuscript C.

[25] Marsden, *Heptateuch*, manuscript L; manuscript B is identical except for minor spelling differences.

(1p4.5 and 3.33–35). The translator seems reluctant to ascribe probing the mysteries of nature to the narrator here as well as in the second meter (3.21–26), where he again omits mention of the narrator's past explorations of nature's secrets (1m2.6–23). Yet even without these passages, the Old English *Boethius* is filled with mentions of the mysteries of nature and the heavens. The sun's hidden path appears in both texts ("secreto tramite," 3m2.32; "dæglan wegas," 25.25). The Old English Chapter 4 addresses God's control of the cosmos, the stars, and the seasons. Chapter 21 again treats God's control, his actions like a bridle reining in the elements and the seasons (21.12); if he failed to rein them in, disorder would result (21.36–37). The image of the bridle is repeated at the start of Chapter 25, where God's control is described as worthy of awe or wonder ("wundorlice," 25.2) before the section describes how various creations remain true to the natures with which God has endowed them even though they have been captured or compelled in other ways by humans. Then, 33.142–251 (translating 3m9) details the bonds and tensions among the elements—God's very construction of the universe. The same text that warns against the destructive power of curiosity at other moments searches the heights of God's creation. The fact that the builders of the Tower were disobedient without defying any specific commandment suggests that seeking knowledge can itself violate God's will—and that no clear demarcation exists to distinguish acceptable and unacceptable curiosity.

Thus implicit tensions about knowledge and curiosity run throughout the Old English *Boethius*. How much do Nimrod's investigations of heaven really differ from the text's own? The Tower of Babel attempted to reach the heavens physically; the *Consolation* and the *Boethius* attempt to reach God intellectually. That attempt peaks in the Latin Book 5, which examines different forms of cognition and time. As the *Boethius* nears the experiences peculiar to God, the translator abridges more and more, significantly diminishing the treatment of God. It would make a tidy conclusion to say that as the builders of the Tower of Babel could not be permitted to reach heaven, so the writer and readers of the *Boethius* cannot be permitted to reach full understanding of God, but that would be an overstatement. The Old English text stands suspended in tension between obedience and order on the one hand and knowledge on the other.

Sometimes the *Boethius* veers towards knowledge, potentially disturbing order. As Godden and Irvine have observed, the *Boethius* is not always a cautious work. Indeed, Godden has described the *Boethius* and the Old English *Soliloquies* together as "bold rewritings of texts known at the time to be difficult, dangerous, and distinctly heterodox."[26] In the most theologically problematic point in the text, Philosophy sings that the soul must remember truths but is hindered by the body's heaviness, suggesting a Platonic pre-existence of the soul and a

[26] Godden, "The Alfredian Project and its Aftermath: Rethinking the Literary History of the Ninth and Tenth Centuries," Sir Israel Gollancz Memorial Lecture, 15 January 2009, *Proceedings of the British Academy* 162 (2009): 93–122, at 107.

dualism verging on heterodoxy (3m11). The corresponding portion of the *Boethius*, Chapter 35, leavens the dualism a little by adding a reference to vices ("unþeawas," 35.14), but it makes two references to the body's heaviness ("swærnes," 35.14, and "hefignesse," 35.27). More importantly, the section still describes a pre-existent mind working to recall what it once knew. Glossators were quick to point out that Augustine had first accepted but later rejected the idea of a pre-existent soul.[27] Yet in the *Boethius*, Wisdom seems to add authority to the notion of the pre-existent soul enfleshed in a heavier body by declaring the idea true as he cites Plato: "hit is swiðe ryht spell þæt Plato se uðwita sæde" [it is a very just account that Plato the philosopher said, 35.24]. The narrator reinforces Wisdom's statement: "Ic eom geðafa þæt þæt was soð spell þæt Plato sæde" [I agree that that was a true tale that Plato said, 35.29].[28] These statements show little of the caution one might expect from the writer who expanded on the giants' rebellion against Jove and added the story of the Tower of Babel. The *Boethius* also shares the challenging idea that fate works through the motions of the stars and through demons (4p6.13, rendered in the *Boethius* 39.144–147). This passage upset commentators: "The glosses note that Boethius speaks more as philosopher than as orthodox believer (*catholice*) here and that some have criticized him as a heretic for following astrologers and teaching that all things are governed by the decree of the stars."[29] The *Boethius* simply makes the statement without hedging or noting disagreement.

The *Boethius* never resolves the apparent conflict between its repeated cautions against disobedience and specifically seeking knowledge not meant for people with its own inquiries into the nature of creation, humanity, and God himself. At the end of the text, the translator becomes more cautious. In rendering Book 5, he downplays human knowledge of God and emphasizes God's authority. Where the Latin treats at length the apparent logical contradiction between divine foreknowledge and human free will in 5p3, the Old English replaces an argument from logic with an analogy: just as a king could not rightly have a kingdom with no free men, so too God could not have a universe with no free subjects. Instead, "he gesceop twa gescedwisan gesceafta frio, englas and men" [he created two rational, free creatures: angels and human beings, 41.25–26]. The translator skips more than half of this Latin prose, in which the Latin narrator suggests that foreknowledge means that human actions are necessitated (5p3.5–28), though the Old English keeps and develops the idea that if free will did not

[27] See Godden and Irvine, *Old English Boethius*, 2:403.

[28] On this passage, see Godden and Irvine, *Old English Boethius*, 2:401–3; and Godden, "The Alfredian Project and its Aftermath," 113–14.

[29] Godden and Irvine, *Old English Boethius*, 2:465; see also Godden's "Alfredian Project and its Aftermath," 113.

exist, reward and punishment would be unjust.[30] The translator then drastically shortens the second half of the Latin Book 5. He condenses the idea that knowledge is according to the capacity of the knower, not of the object known.[31] He sharply curtails discussion of the substantive differences between living in time and living in eternity, essentially removing the Latin's glimpses into the mind of God.[32] He omits altogether treatment of simple and conditional necessity (5p6). The translator does treat differences in perception and knowledge between animals and humans, and he takes up a suggestion of angels ("intelligentia sola divini" [pure intelligence belongs to divinity alone], 5p5.4) to describe differences between human and angelic knowledge. He keeps the idea that free will is needed for reward and punishment to be just and the closing exhortation to pray and to embrace virtue.[33] The Old English *Boethius* drastically reduces consideration of how God knows, instead accentuating God's role as a just king and how humans perceive and know. Our perception and knowledge are compared to and contrasted with the angels' more than directly with God's.[34] Human knowledge, its workings, and its limits are fit subjects for exploration; God's knowledge may not be suitable for too much human prying.

Here the text seems to suggest that obedient human beings must accept limits on their knowledge to keep their proper place in God's order. Fuller participation in the divine may be understood to come after life ends; it is, after all, an eternal reward for one's goodness ("ecu edlean hiora godes," 37.68).[35] After that passage, the *Boethius* begins to abridge more. By the very end of the text, it jettisons Latin sentences right and left. At the end, Philosophy urges the narrator, and presumably the reader as well, to pray and turn away from vice (5p6.46–48). The Old English does likewise (42.46–55). A scribe or two has enacted these prayers for us, closing the book with an "AMEN" and then an additional prayer not attributed to the translator that invokes not only God but also Saint Mary, Saint Michael, and all the saints in a very orthodox affirmation of belief.[36]

---

30 For further discussion of human agency and divine punishment, see Haruko Momma's essay in this volume.

31 See 5p3, 5p4, 5m4; compare 41.10–19, 105–16, and 138–43.

32 See 5p6; compare 42.1–20.

33 See 5p4.24–27/41.105–131, 5p5.1–4/41.131–143, 5p3.28–32/41.40–49, 5p6.45/42.44–47, and 5p6.46–48/42.47–54, respectively.

34 See 41.143–148, where wise men may even know as angels do.

35 Relihan argues in *The Prisoner's Philosophy* that the *Consolation* turns from philosophy and towards wisdom at last; the Old English translator might agree with this reading, but he uses significantly different means to achieve his end. Relihan finds Philosophy contradicting herself on the matter of necessity at the end of the *Consolation* (30–32). The *Boethius* avoids contradiction by transforming or cutting most of the arguments here.

36 The prayer is not in Godden and Irvine's edition of the *Boethius* but appears in *King Alfred's Old English Version of Boethius De Consolatione Philosophiae*, ed. Walter John

The Old English *Boethius* cannot fully reconcile the tensions between its own aspirations towards knowledge of God and his works with its anxieties that such knowledge is bound to rebellion and consequently to death. It insists that only humans and angels revolt against the divine, and it sometimes emphasizes order where the Latin emphasizes love. These anxieties crystallize in two anecdotes: though the Old English omits a number of allusions and myths, it expands the story of the giants rebelling against Jove and adds the story of Nimrod and the Tower of Babel. Finally, the translator shrinks from fully delineating the differences between perpetuity and eternity and between kinds of necessity. While Godden and Irvine have rightly called our attention to how daring the Old English *Boethius* is in its explorations of philosophy and the universe, the text reveals some discomfort with its own probings into the workings of God. Presumably, unlike the giants or Nimrod, the translator has no rebellious intent, yet the traces of taboo linger here—not enough to prevent the translation, but perhaps enough to shape and curb it in places, particularly as the work closes. The resulting text leaves its readers to extend their own knowledge of God and simply to pray at the end, perhaps with the prayer helpfully supplied by a scribe. Despite his own cautions against wanting to know too much about God and heaven, the translator, copyists, and generations of readers have continued to explore those mysteries.

Sedgefield (Oxford: Clarendon Press, 1899), 149, ll. 11–26. A few Latin manuscripts incorporate brief prayers at the end of the *Consolation* such as "Deo gratias" [Thanks be to God] or "Amen" but nothing on the scale of what appears at the end of the Old English; see Moreschini's edition, apparatus to 5p6.48.

The Old English *Boethius* and Speculative Thought

Paul E. Szarmach

The publication of a new edition of the Old English translation of *The Consolation of Philosophy* has created authorship controversies in the field of Anglo-Saxon studies, but it has also begun to cast a new light on ways of looking at the "Alfredian" rendition beyond authorship questions.[1] My aim here is not to choose sides in the authorship question or to propose a cunning solution between competing interpretations. The new edition—offering a text deriving from a fresh study of the manuscript evidence of various versions and containing as well an authoritative translation, informed commentary adumbrating a forthcoming edition of the Latin glosses, discussions of language and meter, and consideration of special issues such as relationships with other Old English texts—presents a solid platform for advanced research. I seek to call attention to the Old English *Boethius* and its efforts to engage speculative thought. As will be seen from evidence brought forward below, some scholars had already begun to encounter the *Boethius* on different terms. Kurt Otten and F. Anne Payne were pioneers in their respective approaches to sources and interpretations; one may consider them ahead of their time.[2] Malcolm Godden and Ronald J. Ganze have separately argued for the philosophical temper of the Old English adaptation of

[1] Malcolm Godden and Susan Irvine, eds., *The Old English Boethius: An Edition of the Old English Versions of Boethius's De Consolatione Philosophiae*, 2 vols. (Oxford: Oxford University Press, 2009). The work continues. The full corpus of glosses is forthcoming: Malcolm Godden, Rohini Jayatilaka, Rosalind C. Love, and P. Vaciago, eds., *Glosae super Boetii De Consolatione Philosophiae, saeculorum IX-XI*, CCCM (Turnhout: Brepols). The "select" edition is also forthcoming: Malcolm Godden, Rohini Jayatilaka, and Rosalind C. Love, eds. and trans., *The Reception of Boethius's Consolation of Philosophy in Anglo-Saxon England*, Anglo-Saxon Texts (Woodbridge: Boydell and Brewer).

[2] Kurt Otten, *König Alfreds Boethius*, Studien zur englischen Philologie, neue Folge no. 3 (Tübingen: Max Niemeyer, 1964); F. Anne Payne, *King Alfred and Boethius* (Madison: University of Wisconsin Press, 1968). But of course one need not agree with everything they say: thus Otten feels obliged to deal with Germanic mythology and Payne with Christian existentialism.

Augustine's *Soliloquies*, which is a mate to the *Boethius*.[3] The connection between the Old English *Boethius* and the Old English *Soliloquies* will be an important theme in the prelude to new directions of research. The description and analysis of the philosophical temper of the *Boethius* must be the starting point.

Preliminaries

There are difficulties in seeking to describe the engagement with speculative thought in this cultural period that can only receive an introductory mention here. Janet M. Bately has exhaustively studied terminology in the choice between *uþwita* and *philosophus* with reference to word frequency in Alfredian texts and in the Old English *Orosius*.[4] The matter admits of some complexity in a broad field of choice where Old English gives the opportunity to select several words with overlapping shades of meaning. The relevance of her study for this essay is her careful conclusion that the term *uþwita* was of "some considerable antiquity" perhaps before the idea of *philosophus* was known to the Anglo-Saxons.[5] Alfred chose the imprecise *uþwita*, which is characteristic of his methods, and the *Orosius*-translator chose the Latin terminology, *philosophus*.[6]

The central question is what could or what did Anglo-Saxon England know about speculative thought? In his *Etymologies*, a work well known in Anglo-Saxon England, Isidore of Seville transmits an outline of late classical thinking through division of the subject and through definition of its key elements.[7] There he defines philosophy as "rerum humanarum diuinarumque cognitio cum studio bene uiuendi coniuncta" [the understanding of human and divine things

---

[3] Ronald J. Ganze, "The Individual in the Afterlife: Theological and Sociopolitical Concerns in King Alfred's Translation of Augustine's *Soliloquies*," *Studia Neophilologica* 83 (2011): 21–40; Malcolm Godden, "Text and Eschatology in Book III of the Old English *Soliloquies*," *Anglia* 121 (2003): 79–188.

[4] Janet Bately, "*Uþwita/Philosophus* Revisited: A Reflexion on Old English Usage," in *Essays on Anglo-Saxon and Related Themes in Memory of Lynne Grundy*, ed. Jane Roberts and Janet Nelson, King's College London Medieval Studies 17 (London: King's College London, Centre for Late Antique & Medieval Studies, 2000), 15–36.

[5] Bately, "*Uþwita/Philosophus* Revisited," 35–36.

[6] Bately, "*Uþwita/Philosophus* Revisited."

[7] W.M. Lindsay, ed., *Isidori Hispalensis Episcopi Etymologiarum sive Originum Libri XX* (Oxford: Clarendon Press, 1911), II.xxiv.1. I quote the translation of Steven A. Barney, W.J. Lewis, J.A. Beach, and Oliver Berghof, with Muriel Hall, trans., *The Etymologies of Isidore of Seville* (Cambridge: Cambridge University Press, 2006), 79. See also Isidore of Seville, *Etymologies: Book II, Rhetoric*, ed. and trans. Peter K. Marshall (Paris: Auteurs Latins du Moyen Âge, 1983).

joined with the pursuit of living well].[8] Isidore goes on to present the three kinds of philosophy: the natural (i.e., physics), the moral (i.e., ethics), and the rational (i.e., logic). In another place, Isidore calls philosophy "ars artium et disciplina disciplinarum" [the art of arts and the discipline of disciplines].[9] Isidore offers another subject division when he distinguishes between speculative and practical philosophy. On speculative philosophy, he explains:

> Inspectiua dicitur, qua supergressi uisibilia, de diuinis aliquid et caelestibus contemplamur, eaque mente solummodo inspicimus, quoniam corporeum supergrediuntur obtutum.
>
> [That branch of philosophy is called speculative (*inspectivus*) by which, having passed beyond visible things, we contemplate in some measure concerning divine and heavenly things, and we investigate those things by the mind alone because they pass beyond the corporeal gaze.][10]

Isidore supplements his etymological methods with an informative review of the pagan philosophers, their schools, their ideas, and their (foolish) beliefs and practices (VIII.vi). The many distinctions and sub-classifications suggest an awareness of speculative thinking still possible, if rather abstract, in the seventh century. One can argue for a breaking point in the cultural system and backward look of Isidore's overview, but one can also see what awaited tenth- and eleventh-century *uþwitan* to study and understand. The threefold division of philosophy, viz., the natural (physics), the moral (ethics), and the rational (logic), is general enough to serve as a broad description of the *Consolation* where the natural world, ethics, and logic are evident themes and concerns. In wrestling with the Latin *Consolation*, I argue that the Old English translator was engaging in the kind of speculative philosophy that Isidore describes—explaining things that passed "beyond the corporeal gaze." His method was metaphorical argument.

Nevertheless, there are major caveats. There is the broad, contextual disciplinary issue involving Latinity. The Latin language as a vehicle for philosophical communication was in its beginning, revised stages. Old English lacked a suitable technical lexicon. Ælfric of Eynsham had a stake in the Eucharistic controversy of his time, but later writers could understand the issues better, thanks to Scholastic vocabulary absent in his time. It was still a distance to Scholasticism and its marble surface, although few would go as far as Bertrand Russell in his dismissal of medieval philosophy.[11] There are as well difficulties generated by

---

[8] Isidore, *Etymologies*, II.xxiv.1. Marshall, *Etymologies: Book II, Rhetoric*, cites Cassiodorus, *Institutes* 2, 3, and 5 as the source for Isidore (106, n. 231).

[9] Isidore, *Etymologies*, II.xxiv.9.

[10] Isidore, *Etymologies*, II.xxiv.11. Barney et al., *Etymologies*, 80.

[11] See Bertrand Russell, *History of Western Philosophy* (London: Routledge, 1946): "There is little of the true philosophic spirit in Aquinas. He does not like the Platonic

(early) medieval philosophy (and admittedly by other fields as well) within their own disciplinary boundaries. John Marenbon makes a plea to scholars and generalists that Boethius should be read "whole" so as to overturn specialization and to see that Boethius is "original in a complex rather than a simple sense."[12] The plea does not quite extend to specialists and generalists working in the vernacular, which one might admit is another major difficulty. The great body of vernacular literature in Old English, duly noted and acknowledged, is something of an achievement, but there has been no significant attempt to link speculative thought to the vernacular. For the Anglo-Saxonist there is no established method to engage the texts beyond literary modes. The interpretive stance adopted here is essentially descriptive or perhaps empirical—even a kind of close reading—that follows the Old English translator in his mistakes and struggles between the two languages.

Meter 20

With this background and within this approach, Meter 20 offers the most significant example of speculative thought in the *Boethius*[13] and provides the starting point for discussion.[14] Meter 20 is one of thirty-one Old English meters, so num-

---

Socrates, set out to follow wherever the argument may lead." If the leading light of the schoolmen does not pass muster, Boethius does better: "During the two centuries before his time and the ten centuries after it I cannot think of any European man of learning so free from superstition and fanaticism … his survey is lofty, disinterested, and sublime" (453). For a more recent, positive overview of medieval philosophy, see Steven P. Marrone, "Medieval Philosophy in Context," in *The Cambridge Companion to Boethius*, ed. John Marenbon (Cambridge: Cambridge University Press, 2009), 10–50.

[12] John Marenbon, "Introduction: Reading Boethius Whole," in *The Cambridge Companion to Boethius*, ed. John Marenbon (Cambridge: Cambridge University Press, 2009), 1–10, at 1–2.

[13] See Paul E. Szarmach, "The *Timaeus* in Old English," in *Lexis and Texts in Early English: Studies Presented to Jane Roberts*, ed. Christian J. Kay and Louis M. Sylvester (Atlanta: Rodopi, 2001), 255–67; "Boethius's Influence in Anglo-Saxon England: The Vernacular and the *De Consolatione Philosophiae*," in *A Companion to Boethius in the Middle Ages*, ed. Noel Harold Kaylor, Jr., and Philip Edward Phillips (Boston: Brill, 2012), 221–54, esp. 230–34; and "The Old English *Boethius* as a Book of Nature," in *Aspects of Anglo-Saxon and Medieval England*, ed. Michiko Ogura (Frankfurt am Main: Peter Lang, 2014), 69–92, esp. 5–19. See now also Nicole Guenther Discenza, "The Old English *Boethius*," in *A Companion to Alfred the Great*, ed. Nicole Guenther Discenza and Paul E. Szarmach (Boston: Brill, 2015), 200–226.

[14] The relationship between 3m9 and the Old English *Boethius* awaits elucidation. See R.B.C. Huygens, ed., *Serta Mediaevalia: Textus varii saeculorum x–xiii*, CCSL 171 (Turnhout: Brepols, 2000); and Susanna E. Fischer, "*Boethius Christanus sive Platonicus*:

bered, but the count must be explained, since the Latin numbers thirty-nine meters. In the Old English, Meter 1 is the "back story" of sorts or simply an introduction, not part of the Boethian text. The Latin Book 3, Meter 9 (3m9) is the source text for Meter 20. It contains twenty-eight hexameter lines drawing on Plato's *Timaeus* and Proclus's commentary. As Joachim Gruber has observed,[15] 3m9 stands in the middle of the work, occupying a significant place in the overall poetic structure of the *Consolation*. Other scholars join in the praise and appreciation of 3m9. Henry Chadwick offers a powerful reading of the poem, emphasizing that the ideas of the poem are derived from Plato and from Proclus's commentary.[16] Stephen Gersh shows how the ideas of 3m9 reflect characteristic Boethian concerns.[17] Gerard O'Daly connects the poem to the theme of nature operating throughout the *Consolation*.[18] Seth Lerer emphasizes the functionality of the poem, placing it as self-reflexive of the wider aims of the work and no mere Platonic set-piece.[19] Marenbon places Boethius and the *Consolation* in context in *Early Medieval Philosophy: An Introduction*.[20] The foregoing is but a brief list of the scholars who find the Boethian text to be without parallel and brilliant in execution.[21]

Yet 3m9, for all its transcendent beauty, did not win universal approval from its early medieval readers. When 3m9 waxes lyrical over the "world soul," Christian exegetes had to explain it by glossing it as "sol" or Christ, which was

Frühe mittelalterliche Kommentare zu *O qui perpetua, mundum ratione gubernas*," in *Boethius Christianus?: Transformationen der* Consolatione Philosophiae *im Mittlealter und Früher Neuzeit*, ed. Reinhold Glei, Nicola Kaminski, and Franz Lebsanft (New York: Walter de Gruyter, 2009), 157–77, for a brief summary (157). See also the review by Erica Weaver in *Carmina Philosophiae* 22 (2013): 133–35.

[15] Joachim Gruber, *Kommentar zu Boethius,* De Consolatione Philosophiae, *Texte und Kommentare* (New York: Walter de Gruyter, 1978), 277.

[16] Henry Chadwick, *Boethius: The Consolations of Music, Logic, Theology, and Philosophy* (Oxford: Oxford University Press, 1981).

[17] Stephen Gersh, *Middle Platonism and Neoplatonism: The Latin Tradition*, vol. 2 (Notre Dame, IN: University of Notre Dame Press, 1986), 647–718, esp. 671–75 and 711–14.

[18] Gerard J.P. O'Daly, "Nature in the Poetry of the *Consolation*," in *The Poetry of Boethius* (Chapel Hill: University of North Carolina Press, 1991), 104–77.

[19] Seth Lerer, *Boethius and Dialogue: Literary Method in the Consolation of Philosophy* (Princeton: Princeton University Press, 1985).

[20] John Marenbon, *Boethius* (Oxford: Oxford University Press, 2003), offers an overview of Boethius's entire oeuvre with special reference to the *Consolation* and edits a collection of essays that fulfills the mandate of the distinguished series: *The Cambridge Companion to Boethius*. Marenbon's study considers the "incoherence" of Boethius's arguments (158–59). Noel Harold Kaylor, Jr., and Philip Edward Phillips gather fifteen essays in *A Companion to Boethius in the Middle Ages* (Boston: Brill, 2012). The editors take a comprehensive view of their subject.

[21] See Szarmach, "The *Timaeus* in Old English." My treatment here develops further the analysis in that article.

something of an interpretive leap. Marenbon describes the dual challenge faced by Christian thinkers: to explain the Neoplatonic allusions and to consider the extent to which they were acceptable for a Christian.[22] Bovo II of Corvey (d. 916) gives vent to the Christian problem in a slam against "philosophicum ... uenenum" [the poison of the philosophers].[23] Other commentators were perhaps less florid than Bovo II, but the Neoplatonic response to 3m9 made it a text in its own right, inspiring a commentary with its own textual tradition. Current research has not yet determined whether the Old English writer rendered his version from a self-standing text of 3m9 or from a section of a complete Latin text.

A closer look at 3m9 will disclose further important characteristics.[24] The twenty-eight lines are cast in the form of a hymn, and Gruber offers Norden's three-part outline of the structure:

I. *epiclesis*, lines 1–5, opening in praise
II. *aretalogy*, lines 6–21, regarding the work of the Creator
  1. the universe: lines 6–9
  2. the elements: lines 10–12
  3. the world soul: lines 13–17
  4. the kinds of souls: lines 18–21
III. *euksai*, lines 22–28, closing in praise[25]

Marenbon stresses the explicit announcement of 3m9 as a prayer and "a hymn to God as the Platonists understood him."[26] The versecraft further tightens the structure. The Latin hexameters—described by Joel C. Relihan as "the meter that we have been anticipating since [1m1]"—place 3m9 in the tradition of didactic poetry with the "most grand and respectful treatment."[27] The poetic voice addresses God in the second person singular (*tu*), becoming a section marker at lines 10, 13, and 18; giving emphasis at lines 6, 26, and 27; and, changing form, as an imperative singular, at lines 7, 22, 23 (2x), and 25. As the poem ends, the petitions to God become increasingly stronger and more effective. The imagery or figurative language tends towards the abstract, or philosophical. The speaker of 3m9 merits

---

22 John Marenbon, *Early Medieval Philosophy, 480–1150: An Introduction* (London: Routledge, 1983), 85–88, at 85.

23 R.B.C. Huygens, ed., "Mittelalterliche Kommentare zum 'O qui perpetua . . .,'" *Sacris Erudiri* 6 (1954): 373–427, at 398. Quoted and discussed by Rosalind Love, "The Latin Commentaries on Boethius's *De Consolatione Philosophiae* from the 9th to the 11th Centuries," in Kaylor and Phillips, *A Companion to Boethius in the Middle Ages*, 111–13, at 112.

24 See Szarmach, "The *Timaeus* in Old English."

25 Gruber, *Kommentar zu Boethius*, 277–90. See also Eduard Norden, *Agnostos Theos. Untersuchungen zur Formgeschichte religiöser Rede* (Leipzig: B.G. Teubner, 1913).

26 Marenbon, *Boethius*, 150–53, at 153.

27 *Boethius: Consolation of Philosophy*, ed. and trans. Joel C. Relihan (Indianapolis: Hackett Publishing, 2001), 176.

a special note. Philosophy says the prayer on behalf of herself and the character Boethius. This identification is a rhetorical convenience, perhaps, but more importantly it underlines the fact that Philosophy is not a Christian figure as such. As Marenbon puts it, she is a "human searcher," and 3m9 is a prayer to God offered for herself and for Boethius.[28] As a poem, 3m9 exhibits a deep philosophical texture and a challenging resonance. It is, in a sense, finally untranslatable. Why, then, did the Old English translator not simply omit a rendition as he omitted others?

One may entertain the possibility that the translator was aware of "the poison of the philosophers" and sought to eliminate it with his own treatment of God's creative powers as a substitute. Most interpreters would agree that the Old English rendition of 3m9 is rather free-wheeling and that such a substitution would be within the poet's poetic range. Even without external pressures from other interpreters or interpretations, the poem as a poem would make severe demands on any poet. The power of Latin hexameters, for example, disappears as the Old English alliterative line, trailing its origins in oral poetry and with filler lines, is pressed into service to explain and describe Neoplatonic mysteries. There is also an apparent deficit of diction or terminology, about which I will provide more later. The significant feature of the Old English rendition, however, is the tendency to amplify whatever ideas are stated or derived from the Latin; thus the twenty-eight lines of the Latin stand in relation to the 281 lines of Meter 20 (as compared to 191 lines in the all-prose B text). These amplifications show the translator attempting to engage the Latin's speculative thought or to work around it.

Godden and Irvine note that the Old English author follows the Latin meter "at the beginning and end but in the long central section, especially on the elements, spins freely and sometimes repetitively."[29] It is this central section that showcases the translator's rendering of speculative thought in his vernacular text. Essentially, the beginning and endpoint are the prayerful envelope for both the Latin and vernacular. While 3m9 describes God's creative powers, the Old English Meter 20 gives further information and launches sub-themes not hinted at in the Latin. In the Old English translation, God, to use other terminology, is the unmoved mover who puts all things in motion; he creates according to his image and likeness; he is self-sufficient, needing nothing; God is Great; he is the highest good. These praising prayers lead to a lengthy discussion of the makeup of the world conceived of as the four elements: earth, water, fire, and air.[30] In so

---

28 Marenbon, *Boethius*, 154.

29 Godden and Irvine, *The Old English Boethius*, 2:378.

30 Godden and Irvine, *The Old English Boethius*, cite generally Ambrose's *Hexameron*, Isidore's *De natura rerum*, and Bede's *De natura rerum* as among several possible sources. For editions and translations, see: Ambrose, *Hexameron*, in *Sancti Ambrosii Opera*, ed. C. Schenkl, CSEL 32.1 (Vienna: F. Tempsky, 1896), 3–261; *Hexameron, Paradise, and Cain and Abel*, trans. John J. Savage (New York: Fathers of the Church, 1961), 3–283,

doing, the translator takes Boethius's argument about the unseen and renders it in terms of the sensible and the visible. The analysis here has a certain intricacy as the Old English author describes the interaction of the elements. One learns, for example, that the homeland of fire is properly above all other creatures visible across the spacious earth; or that the cold earth produces many marvelous fruits.[31] Then too, the elements have to be restrained and kept under control. Whatever the pedigree of the theme of the four elements, the treatment in Meter 20 is a cosmology quite different from the Neoplatonic outline found in 3m9.

The rest of the central section is noteworthy for its imagery and anthropology. A brief summary analysis will highlight the relevant points. The discussion of the soul and its activities occupies a major part of 3m9. Wisdom describes a soul operating much as the world-soul would, but of course does not call it such. In Meter 20, the soul has other attributes that occupy attention, namely, the threefold soul that contains the irascible, the concupiscible, and the rational.[32] The discussion moves into detail, indicating that the rational is the best aspect because no animal possesses it except mankind. The God of Nations has given mankind a soul so that there is no less of it in the little finger than there is of it in the whole body. This last detail is the sort of analogy that a classroom master might use to make his point about the insubstantiality of the soul. The most startling image, however, is the world as egg. The Old English versifier cites God's power as the cause that established the earth so firmly that it does not go side to side, nor does it sink any more than it always did, and

> is þeah efneðe   up and ofdune
> to feallanne   foldan ðisse,
> þæm anlicost   þe on æge bið
> gioleca on middan,   glideð hwæðre
> æg ymbutan. (Meter 20, ll. 167–171a)

> [it is as easy for this earth to fall up as down, very much like what the yolk is in the middle of the egg, and the egg however glides about.]

---

at 19; Bede, *De Natura Rerum*, in *Opera Didascalica*, vol. 1, ed. C.W. Jones, CCSL 123A (Turnhout: Brepols, 1975), 173–234; and *Bede: On the Nature of Things and On Times*, trans. Calvin B. Kendall and Faith Wallis (Liverpool: Liverpool University Press, 2010), 71–105, at 75–76.

[31] Godden and Irvine, *The Old English Boethius*, Meter 20. Hereafter cited parenthetically by chapter from the B text or meter from the C text. All translations are taken from Godden and Irvine.

[32] See Paul E. Szarmach, "Alcuin, Alfred and the Soul," in *Manuscript, Narrative, and Lexicon: Essays on Literary and Cultural Transmission in Honor of Whitney F. Bolton*, ed. Robert Boenig and Kathleen Davis (Lewisburg, PA: Bucknell University Press, 2000), 127–48.

The earth as egg is a metaphor added to the Latin text by the translator as he works to explain Boethius's speculative thought to his own culture. In so doing, the translator draws on a commonplace: Godden and Irvine cite three Latin manuscripts (Einsiedeln, Stiftsbibliothek, MS 179; Gotha, Forschungsbibliothek, MS M. II 103; and Paris, Bibliothèque nationale de France, MS lat. 13953); Daniel Anlezark cites the Old English *Soliloquies* and the Old English *Martyrology*; J.E. Cross the Hiberno-Latin *Liber De Ordine Creaturarum*; and Peter Dronke a long tradition of the image throughout Europe.[33] Once again the image is a homely one, which may have proven successful as part of an introduction to cosmology. The egg image explains how the earth has both movement and stasis as it glides about. The forces of the world—water, air, stars—stand still, and the bright shell turns around every day as it always has. The image is ingenious and, given its long popularity—Dronke lists some thirty-two instances through about 1300—is a serious attempt to explain the world outside of the Neoplatonic context established by Boethius. The versifier also has within his repertory the capacity to offer a less startling image, which he shows when he likens the soul in its mobility to a wheel revolving around itself.

The argument here is more than an exercise in source criticism. In fact, Meter 20 is not so much a translation as a substitution. The Old English author takes the text he has received and invests it with his own meaning. The use of metaphor or arresting similitude is the signature of the versifier. The free-wheeling precedent that the Old English author has initiated should serve as a warning to interpreters that consideration of the vernacular must yield space to a translator who does not fetishize the text.

Fate and *Wyrd*[34]

"Gæð a wyrd swa hio scel"

[33] Godden and Irvine, *The Old English Boethius*, 2:511–12; Daniel Anlezark, "Three Notes on the Old English *Meters of Boethius*," *Notes and Queries* 51 (2004): 10–15; J.E. Cross, "*De Ordine Creaturarum Liber* in Old English Prose," *Anglia* 90 (1972): 132–40; and Peter Dronke, *Fabula: Explorations into the Uses of Myth in Medieval Platonism*, Mittellateinische Studien und Texte 9 (Leiden and Cologne: Brill, 1974), Appendix A, 154–66.

[34] Godden and Irvine, *The Old English Boethius*, observe that *wyrd* is used to represent both *fortuna* and *fatum*. Their important discussion of terminology ends by holding that the Old English author sets up *wyrd* "as the apparently irrational power that distributes prosperity and adversity in the early part [of the *Consolation*] and then demonstrating that *wyrd* is under the control of a benign and just providence" (1:79).

[Fate goes on ever as it must!][35]

So spoke Beowulf. But what did he mean by "wyrd"? Early in the history of the subject, the word *wyrd* was heavily freighted with Germanic mythology by scholars who participated in the *furor Teutonicus*.[36] Presumably the literary scholars and the source critics found embedded in the literature and myth they studied a cosmology that would suit the fruits of their research, particularly as unconscious enthusiasts for the pagan. Opinions were strong on either side of the Christian vs. pagan divide. Jerold C. Frakes's exposition of the situation is masterful, noting that the "traditional interpretation of *wyrd*, as a proto-Germanic goddess of fate, who controls all human affairs, lives on in the secondary literature dealing with Alfred's use of the term."[37] Such an Old English poem as *Deor*, with its reference to Germanic heroes, served for some as partial proof of the presence of the lingering goddess. The poem *The Wanderer* mentions *wyrd* four times, once in a cosmological mode—"wyrd bið ful aræd!" [fate is fully decided!]—and once generally descriptive—"wyrd seo mære" [fate the famous].[38] Frakes further argues:

> When one approaches the Alfredian text without an *a priori* definition of *wyrd*, it becomes clear, however, that *wyrd* is neither a controlling power which rivals God, nor does the concept exist at all, except as an integral element in the divine system, subject to God.[39]

On the assumption that he would be a proper Alfredian Boethian, Beowulf would be affirming *wyrd* as a dispenser equally of the good and the bad, all within the divine plan, as it is in the world. In *Klaeber's Beowulf*, the editors give their authority in asserting that *wyrd* refers only to the passage of events and not to a personified force.[40] Yet Beowulf's half-line requires some explanation because

---

[35] R.D. Fulk, Robert E. Bjork, and John D. Niles, eds., *Klaeber's Beowulf*, 4th edn. (Toronto: University of Toronto Press, 2008), l. 455b.

[36] Jerold C. Frakes, *The Fate of Fortune in the Early Middle Ages: The Boethian Tradition* (New York: Brill, 1988), traces the search for Germania through the early research with special focus on *wyrd*. See also Otten, *König Alfreds Boethius*, 60–70.

[37] Frakes, *The Fate of Fortune in the Early Middle Ages*, 90.

[38] George Philip Krapp and Elliott Van Kirk Dobbie, eds., *The Exeter Book*, Anglo-Saxon Poetic Records 3 (New York: Columbia University Press, 1936), 134–37, at 134 and 136, ll. 5b and 100b. See also Roy F. Leslie, ed., *The Wanderer*, Exeter Medieval English Texts and Studies (Exeter: Exeter University Press, 1988), 88.

[39] Frakes, *The Fate of Fortune*, 90.

[40] Fulk, Bjork, and Niles, *Klaeber's Beowulf*, 144, note to 455b. In his classic *The Search for Anglo-Saxon Paganism* (Cambridge: D.S. Brewer, 1975), 92–94, E.G. Stanley discerns five uses of *wyrd* as a scholarly construct: 1) as the translation of *Parcae*; 2) as the translation of *fatum*; 3) in connection with the poetic word *frage*, signifying "final fate,

of the ambiguity of terminology and the presence of the translator's perennial problem—that is, one word may have various meanings and connotations over a given text, and the appearance of *wyrd* some eleven times in *Beowulf* is an invitation to speculate. Some steps towards Beowulf's possible meaning(s) and that of the writer of the *Boethius* now follow. There is no similar text to 3m9 existing independently that could have in turn inspired the Old English writers in their renderings.[41] Allowing the Old English writer to make adjustments or changes or to choose to depart from Boethius to establish his own understanding of the discussion points at hand, Godden and Irvine amass a wealth of information about the Old English variances, the relevant Latin, and the commentary tradition. Chapter 39 of the B text (Prose 29 in the C text) is a major treatment of fate and providence.[42] As is common enough in the whole work, the major theme running through the chapter is "how God runs things" or, in contemporary discourse, "What did God know, and when did He know it?" After Wisdom finishes singing, Boethius (the character) asks for further clarification of a bothersome problem, which inspires a simile (suggesting that Wisdom was thinking of ducking the question) and this more direct response: "Þu spenst me on ða mæstan spræce on þa earfoðestan to gerecenne" [You entice me into the biggest discussion and the most difficult to explain, 39.85–86]. Wisdom temporizes with a story of Hercules and the nine-headed hydra, which actually functions as an anecdote to characterize the Old English author's continued pestering of Wisdom with his questions (one question is answered, but another pops up) but then moves on to give descriptions of fate and providence. Providence is the divine intelligence foreknowing all, while fate delivers to all creatures appearance and places and times and orderings. Divine Providence is single, unchangeable, and rules everything by order. God is like a craftsman who considers and designs his work before he carries it out. This mutable fate is called *wyrd*. Wisdom has, in effect, given the Old English author the explanation that he has been seeking in shorthand.

Wisdom offers an analogy to assist understanding which men are subject to fate and which are not. The analogy, originating with the Old English author, is to a cart, its wheels, and its axles, drawn out to a level of specific detail

doom, death"; 4) signifying the working out of God's will; and 5) signifying "that which happens or has happened, an event, occurrence, incident, fact" and thus connected with the verb *weorðan* [to become].

[41] Huygens, *Serta Mediaevalia*. The commentators are Bovo of Corvey, Anonymous of Einsied, and Adalbold of Utrecht. See also Fischer, "*Boethius Christanus sive Platonicus*."

[42] Richard Marsden offers an extract from Chapter 39 of the B text in his *The Cambridge Old English Reader* (Cambridge: Cambridge University Press, 2004), 37–42. His title for the selection is "The Wagonwheel of Fate." Perhaps "The Wagonwheel of God" might be preferable.

that is remarkable.[43] The Old English author retains his fondness for an image that approaches, even exceeds, the demands of the English metaphysical poets. It recalls as well the opening of the Old English *Soliloquies* and its emphasis on woodcraft. The Latin prosa seeks to distance God from the real world and from the muck of reality, as any good Neoplatonic explanation would do. Its abstract description of concentric circles offers a mathematical clarity. In the Old English, Wisdom introduces his "analogy" ("bispell," 39.153) to make the *Boethius*'s speculation understandable to his audience. This "bispell" is a self-conscious aid to understanding which men are subject to fate and which are not. The analogy requires a knowledge of cart mechanics, which Godden and Irvine admirably draw out in their translation, followed here.[44] The main point of the analogy is the relationship between stability and change. God is the axle, who is stable and unchanging. As the eye of the observer moves from the axle down to the rims (the eye is implied in such a movement, not stated), the various moral states are seen or disclosed. The best men are next to God, as the hub goes next to the axle, and the middle-most men are like the spokes. At one end, the spoke is attached to hub, at the other to the rim. The Old English writer changes the focus of the analogy by citing a middleman who looks to heaven with one eye and to the earth with the other. The middle has a range of men: the better ones are closer to the hub and the weaker ones closer to the rim pieces. The rim pieces are furthest from the axle. The best place their affection closer to God. The Old English writer concludes his analogy with a summary of the principle involved:

> Be þy þu miht ongitan þæt se wæn bið micle leng gesund þe læs bið todæled from þære eaxe; swa bioð þa men eallra orsorgoste aegðer ge þises andweardan lifes earfoða ge þæs toweardan, þa ðe fæste bioð on Gode. Ac swa hi swiðor asyndrode bioð fram Gode, swa hi swiðor bioð gedrefde and geswencte ægþer ge on mode ge on lichoman. (39.188–193)
>
> [From that you can see that the less the cart is separated from the axle the longer it is sound; so those men are most secure of all, from the hardships of both this life and the next, who are fixed to God. But the more they are separated from God, the more they are troubled and harassed both in mind and in body.]

[43] As Brian Donaghey has shown, the analogy of the cart survived until about 1300 in Nicholas Trevet's Latin commentary. See his "Nicholas Trevet's Use of King Alfred's Translation of Boethius, and the Dating of his Commentary," in *The Medieval Boethius: Studies in the Vernacular Translations of De Consolatione Philosophiae*, ed. A.J. Minnis (Cambridge: D. S. Brewer, 1987), 1–31. See also Haruko Momma's extended treatment of the cart metaphor in her essay in this volume.

[44] See also Meter 28. I present an abbreviated version of the image of the cart.

By linking cosmology to the personal moral life, the Old English writer gives his analogy a dimension that Boethius could not. The cost of this rhetorical move is clarity, which is lost because of the intricacies of cart engineering and also because the connections of the argument can be confusing.

Chapter 39 of the B text picks up on various themes embedded in the cart analogy but also finds others to discuss. Wisdom thus refutes philosophers ("uðwitan") who hold that fate ("wyrd") controls the good and the bad fortunes of every man, saying: "Ic þonne secge, swa swa ealle cristene men secgað, þæt sio godcunde foretiohhung his wealde, næs sio wyrd, and ic wat þæt hio demð eal ðing swiðe rihte, þeah ungesceadwisum monnum swa ne þince" [I then say, as all Christians say, the divine providence controls him, not fate, and I know that it judges all things very justly, though it may not seem to unreasoning men, 39.206–9].[45] Here Wisdom simply asserts or states what must be the case, invoking the standard of Christian belief.

Wisdom then opens a discussion of "mixed good and evil," explaining that men cannot know God's view of things and that this lack of knowledge about men or about situations can account for what seems to be the moral ambiguities or apparent inconsistencies in God's actions. Wisdom goes through a number of theoretical situations where the gap between human knowledge or understanding and God's divine view of matters is apparent: "Þæt we þonne hatað wyrd, þonne se gesceadwisa God, þe aelces monnes þearfe wat, hwæt wyrcð oððe geþafað þæs þe we ne wenað" [We call that fate then when the reasoning God who knows the need of every man does or permits something that we do not expect, 39.244–45]. Wisdom ends Chapter 39 by acknowledging the length of his speech and suggesting that the Old English author look to the stars of the high heavens that stay loyal to God. Chapter 39 has a certain formlessness about it. The by-play of the dialogue genre—complaints about length, about fatigue, about points made not clear enough, etc.—can be read as mere rhetoric, but a close reading lends accuracy to such observations. The discussion points do not come forward as part of a sharp or coherent plan of exposition at this point.

Chapter 40 of the B text, however, opens in an admirable way with a topic sentence. Wisdom says: "Hweþer þu nu ongite hwider þios spræce wille. Þa cwæð ic. Sege me hwider hio wille. Þa cwæð he. Ic wille secgan þæt ælc wyrd bio god, sam hio monnum god þince, sam hio him yfel þince" ["Do you now understand where this discussion is going?" Then I said: "Tell me where it is going." Then he said: "I want to say that all fate is good, whether men think it good or evil," 40.1–3]. The discussion that follows faces the apparent paradox that a bad fate is not a bad thing. Every wise man must contend against adverse fate and despair, and avoid (moral) overconfidence against a pleasant fate. In the discussion, which proceeds cleanly and clearly, there is a sub-theme involving the think-

[45] Note the translation "fate" for *wyrd*, as is the practice in their translation.

ing of the people. Wisdom cautions against the views of "common people" who might think that the more unpleasant fate is evil—lest "we" forsake all reason and justice. The point thus circles back to the initial exchange in this chapter between Wisdom and the Old English author.

The author of the *Boethius* next brings up two major themes that complete Chapter 40. Almost casually he asks about chance and its role in human affairs. Wisdom dismisses chance by citing Aristotle's *Physics* and the anecdote of buried gold. Divine Providence led the one who hid the gold and the one who found it. Godden and Irvine note that Lady Philosophy says nothing about providence here but later does indicate the role of providence.[46] One might have wished for a more extended discussion of chance. The final major topic in Chapter 40 is the question of human freedom. The Old English author asks whether "we" have freedom or power to do or not do, or whether providence or fate (*wyrd*) compels "us" to what they want. In a series of brief exchanges where the Old English author is a cardboard character asking questions which are a reflex of previous passages on providence and fate, Wisdom asserts that rational creatures—men and angels—have freedom. Men have more freedom when they set their minds nearer divine things, less when they turn from God and become blinded by folly.

Mixed good and evil, chance, and human freedom are not the only by-products stemming from the image of the cart. The Old English author is troubled by Wisdom's granting of freedom to everyone to do whatever they wish when God knows that they want to do evil. The Old English author is unhappy with the moral situation, and Wisdom constructs another analogy of sorts, though he does not call it that. Wisdom points out how unnatural it is when a king should rule a kingdom entirely of slaves. God is not such a king, for he gives freedom to men and to angels who can do whatever they wish. Though they cannot forestall death, men can defer it with good deeds.

Yet the Old English author has further anxieties over God's foreordaining. The central question is, can God change what he has foreordained? Wisdom makes a double move in response. The first move is historical: Wisdom cites Cicero who, along with others, could not find an answer because of a preoccupation with "desire" for the world. The second move is something of a feint in that Wisdom chides the Old English author for forgetting all that they had already covered, which he then proceeds to reprise. It is the standard message of human freedom with the possibility of repentance for moral failure. There is no proof, of course, but reiteration. The Old English author would appear to continue with doubts about change. His concern would be a matter of future contingents and multiple possibilities of an action, all of which are answered (in theory) by the image of God as a pilot who anticipates a great wind and a rough sea before it happens.

---

[46] Godden and Irvine, *The Old English Boethius*, 2:484, note to 40.98–99.

Wisdom now pursues a different line of exposition with a discussion resembling audience response criticism. To the Old English author's astonishment that so many wise men struggled with the issue of change, Wisdom observes that there are different levels of understanding. Wisdom says: "Hu ne wast þu þæt manig þincg ne bið no ongiten swa swa hit bið ac swa swa þæs andgites mæð bið þe þæræfter [spirað]?" [Do you not know that many a thing is understood not as it is but as the ability of the sense that enquires after it is? 41.106–108]. Continuing, Wisdom offers an analogy involving the senses. He says (for example) that sight, hearing, and touch perceive the body of a man, but differently. Then too, an individual perceives what he perceives in another "synderlice" [in various different ways, 41.128]. Wisdom draws a comparison with angels in the matter of understanding: angelic understanding is better than human reason. Wisdom rises to an exhortation: "Ac uton nu habban ure mod up swa swa we yfemest mægen wið þæs hean hrofes þæs hehstan andgites, þæt ðu mæge hrædlicost cumon and eðelicost to þinre agenre cyððe þonan þe ðu ær come" [But let us now raise our minds as high as we can towards the high roof of the highest understanding so that you can most quickly and easily come to your own homeland from which you came before, 41.155–58]. At this point, Wisdom concludes the dialogue, indicating that doubts about everything will be resolved at the homeland and urging that "we" should know more about God. Wisdom ends with a celebration of God's attributes culminating in direct exhortation: "Hatiað yfel and flioð swa ge swiðost magon. Lufiað cræftas and folgiað þam. Ge habbað micle þearfe þæt ge simle wel don forþam ge simle beforan þam ecan and þam ælmehtigan Gode doð eall þæt þæt ge doð. Eall he hit gesihð and eall he hit forgilt. AMEN. FINIT." [Hate evil and flee it as much as you [plural] can. Love virtues and follow them. You men have great need that you always do well for you always do all that you do in the presence of the eternal and almighty God. He sees all and He repays it all. [Amen. The end.], 42.51–55]. The B version, as has been increasingly apparent, has developed into a moral tract.

The *Boethius* and the *Soliloquies*

"It is impossible to resist the conclusion that the two works [the *Boethius* and *Soliloquies*] are by the same author, as indeed most scholars have long believed."[47] Godden and Irvine are endorsing the common belief that begins with Frank Hubbard, continues with Henry L. Hargrove, and still resides with the modern

[47] Godden and Irvine, *The Old English Boethius*, 1:136. For a more comprehensive discussion of the OE *Soliloquies*, see my "Augustine's *Soliloquia* in Old English" in *A Companion to Alfred the Great*, ed. Nicole Guenther Discenza and Paul E. Szarmach (Leiden: Brill, 2015), 227–55. See also Haruko Momma and Ann W. Astell's essays in this volume.

editor Thomas A. Carnicelli.[48] They give a brief summary of the evidence, citing among other things the "many close parallels in ideas and treatment with parts of the OE Soliloquies that are not from its Latin source."[49] They further hold that the *Soliloquies*, in its Latin and Old English forms, was a source for both of the Old English texts. In his edition Carnicelli gives eight pages of detailed discussion. There he has the scope to make extended comparisons between the two works.[50] Just to cite one particular example: Carnicelli compares translation passages in the Old English *Soliloquies* and the *Boethius* that "correspond closely in phrasing despite the fact that the Latin sources are entirely different."[51] His discussion acknowledges that such a correspondence is a strong argument for common authorship. Yet Carnicelli is willing to consider the possibility that the correspondence is a function of unconscious borrowing, either by the translator himself from his own previous work or by a second translator who borrows from the *Boethius*. Not all correspondences are of equal value, of course. The handling of dialogue is similar in the two works. Carnicelli amasses many examples but is quick to relegate them to secondary or tertiary proof; "Ac sege me nu" [But tell me now] is what one might expect in any dialogue exchange. One could become fussier in weighing other correspondences. Thus, comparing the souls of angels and of men as eternal creations might be more of a Christian commonplace than independent proof. How to determine the commonplace nature of any correspondence has its ambiguities, which would require deep research. Behind the discussion of correspondences are the metaphysical questions: When is a source a source? When does an apparent source have probative value? There is no attempt here to overturn the opinion of Godden and Irvine and others who might see a close relationship between the *Soliloquies* and the *Boethius*. Rather, there is the hope for nuance and judgment in weighing possibilities.

---

48 Frank G. Hubbard, "The Relation of 'The *Blooms* of Alfred' to the Anglo-Saxon Translations of Boethius," *Modern Language Notes* 9 (1894): 161–71; Henry Lee Hargrove, ed., *King Alfred's Old English Version of St. Augustine's Soliloquies*, Yale Studies in English 13 (New York: H. Holt, 1902); Thomas A. Carnicelli, ed., *King Alfred's Version of St. Augustine's Soliloquies* (Cambridge, MA: Harvard University Press, 1969). Hargrove offers a translation of the *Soliloquies* in *King Alfred's Old English Version of St. Augustine's Soliloquies, turned into Modern English*, Yale Studies in English 22 (New York: H. Holt, 1904). Carnicelli compares Hubbard and his analyses in a discussion of translation issues. Hargrove concentrates on translation methods in Book 1 (xl–xlvi). He observes: "In Book I, we may say [Alfred] was a translator; in Book II he was an adapter; in Book III he was an author, as far as Augustine is concerned" (xl). Dorothy Whitelock gives a translation of the Preface in *English Historical Documents, Volume I, 500–1041*, 2nd edn. (New York: Oxford University Press, 1979), 917–18, item 237.

49 Godden and Irvine, *The Old English Boethius*, 1:135.

50 Carnicelli, *King Alfred's Version of St. Augustine's Soliloquies*, 29–37.

51 Carnicelli, *King Alfred's Version of St. Augustine's Soliloquies*, 29.

Perhaps it is time to disengage the *Soliloquies* from its Latin source and consider it as a text in its own right rather than a point of comparison with the *Boethius*. One tone and thematic that might be released from source work would be the personalist dimension. The *Soliloquies*, especially in the first two books, presents a tone and a voice—a persona, of course—that is engaging and rhetorically successful. The primary theme is friends and friendship, discussed in a speaking voice.[52] Reason and "Augustine" have a friendly match about the soul and friends:

R. Non igitur amas amicos tuos?
A. Quo pacto eos possum, amans animam, non amare?
R. Hoc modo ergo et pulices et cimices amas?
A. Animam me amare dixi, non animalia.
R. Aut homines non sunt amici tui, aut eos non amas: omnis enim homo est animal, et animalia te non amare dixisti.

[R. Do you not love your friends, then?
A. How can I not love them and love the soul?
R. Do you love fleas and insects in this same way?
A. I said I love the soul—the *anima*—not animals.
R. Either men are not your friends or you do not love them, for, every man is an animal, and you said you do not love animals.][53]

One can hardly imagine Boethius engaging in such humorous wordplay as he discusses the five goods or contemplates his unfortunate situation, alternatively, sharing the discomfort of a toothache. These human moments in the *Soliloquies* contrast with the high seriousness of the main narrative and hint at the further range that Old English prose, had there been more witnesses, would have provided.

More important for this essay is the suggestion to assess the literary impact or meaning of the *Boethus* and the *Soliloquies*. Assuming that there is only one translator, the burden of understanding is more limited than if there were two. One translator could mean one remarkable individual, perhaps trained at a continental center, who took inspiration from the ninth-century rage for Boethius and his *Consolation*. In these speculations the name of John the Scot often emerges, his *floruit* coming to an end perhaps in 877, which would strain chronology. If there were two translators, one for each work, several persons might

[52] For more on the theme of friendship drawn from Boethius's *Consolation* and Augustine's *Soliloquies*, see Ann W. Astell's essay in this volume.

[53] Augustine, *Soliloquia*, in *Sancti Aurelii Augustini Opera*, ed. Wolfgang Hörmann, CSEL 89 (Vienna: Hoelder-Pichler-Tempsky, 1986), II.7; Thomas F. Gilligan, trans., *The Happy Life, Answer to the Skeptics, Divine Providence and the Problem of Evil, Soliloquies*, The Fathers of the Church 5 (New York: Cima, 1948), 333–426, at 351.

finally emerge from Alfred and his circle, headed by Asser. The Alfredian roster would also include John the Old Saxon, Grimbald of St. Bertin, and Wærferth of Worcester, possibly among others. Dividing up the work—if that is how it was done—would assume that a foreign scholar would be able to deal with the vernacular, and all scholars would have to manage Latin capably. But a (court) school would have implications for the existence of literary history. Is it possible to construct a literary history based on comparatively scarce evidence? The relationship between the *Boethius* and the *Soliloquies* would not mean more source work but, rather, would be an attempt to go beyond these two works, which would serve as benchmarks for a comprehensive appraisal of literary evidence. The *Boethius* would be a link to the vibrant Latin tradition of the ninth century, developed from the Carolingians. This link would be the legacy of Boethius in both the vernacular and Latin. The *Soliloquies* would define the literary history from a different perspective as a unique achievement or masterpiece. Together the *Boethius* and the *Soliloquies* would redefine the subject.

In this essay I have sought to follow the translator of Boethius's *Consolation of Philosophy* as he engaged the difficult speculative thought of a Latin philosophical text. As I hope to have shown, the Old English translator understood speculative philosophy in the tradition of Isidore, who explained such thinking as an engagement with things that "pass beyond the corporeal gaze." Whatever his training, he had neither the vernacular lexicon available to him nor the philosophical schooling to cope with Boethius's more rarified speculations. His methods, as we have seen, involved drawing on metaphor and analogy to bring the invisible into the sensible realm for explanation. However much he endeavored to follow his Latin author, he nonetheless created another work, one framed to the sensibilities of his ninth-century Anglo-Saxon audience.[54]

[54] I should like to thank Katherine O'Brien O'Keeffe for her many useful suggestions.

Purgatoria clementia: Philosophy and Principles of Pain in the Old English *Boethius*

Haruko Momma

In his Sir Israel Gollancz Memorial Lecture "The Alfredian Project and its Aftermath," Malcolm Godden invited us to take a second look at some of the accepted opinions about the history of Old English literature in the ninth and tenth centuries. To take as an example Alfred's preface to his translation of Gregory's *Pastoral Care*, we may re-examine the king's claim that the reason for his use of the vernacular for literary purposes was to make available "some books that are most necessary for all men to know" ("suma bec, ða þe nidbeðyrfesta sien eallum monnum to witanne").[1] It is true that some of the Latin texts translated into English during this period, and most typically Gregory's *Pastoral Care* and *Dialogues*, are mainstream religious texts orthodox enough to be assigned to this category. But what about Augustine's *Soliloquies* and Boethius's *Consolation of Philosophy*? The former is Augustine's early work, written prior to his baptism and containing a theory of the immortality of the soul that Augustine himself later retracted as "totally unacceptable and unorthodox."[2] The latter was read widely enough in ninth-century Europe, and yet it contains some problematic concepts (often Platonic or Neoplatonic), including the pre-existence of the soul and anamnesis.[3] In other words, the *Consolation* may not exactly be considered a book that needs to be read by all men; if anything, it is, to use Godden's expression, "quite dangerous for ordinary people to know."[4] Furthermore, the Old English

[1] *King Alfred's West-Saxon Version of Gregory's Pastoral Care*, ed. Henry Sweet, 2 vols. (London: Published for the Early English Text Society by N. Trübner & Co., 1871–72), 1:6.

[2] Malcolm Godden, "The Alfredian Project and its Aftermath: Rethinking the Literary History of the Ninth and Tenth Centuries," *Proceedings of the British Academy* 162 (2009): 93–122, at 107, 115.

[3] For the Old English *Boethius*'s approach to Platonic and Neoplatonic ideas, see Janet Bately, "Boethius and King Alfred," in *Platonism and the English Imagination*, ed. Anna Baldwin and Sarah Hutton (Cambridge: Cambridge University Press, 1994), 38–44.

[4] Godden, "Alfredian Project," 114.

Boethius and the Old English *Soliloquies* may not be dismissed as peripheral to the Alfredian literary project, because both of them are attributed to the king himself. Since only four Old English translations are traditionally believed to be his, the *Boethius* and the *Soliloquies* may even be considered central to his vernacular enterprise.

In recognizing the possibility that Alfred's translation project may not have exclusively aimed to disseminate standard texts for pastoral or devotional purposes, we may be inclined to reconsider the equally famous claim made in Alfred's "Preface," that his promotion of the literary use of the vernacular has resulted from the decline of learning in England to such an extent that literacy in Latin was no longer common among its inhabitants. This "over-familiar story," as Godden puts it, may well have been given to support the claim made in the king's literary manifesto: namely, that the great majority of the "English people" ("angelcynn") had to be edified with the help of vernacular translations as necessary, if inferior, substitutes. Despite the sorry picture that Alfred paints in his "Preface" (which is "in many ways a founding document for the modern narrative of Anglo-Saxon cultural history"),[5] his lament over the decline and loss may have been, to a degree, a literary topos, since some of the products of his workshop seem to be addressed to a learned readership, for which the vernacular was probably an expedient medium for the discussion of certain issues. By questioning some of the assumptions about Alfredian texts, therefore,

> we allow ourselves to see them in a very different light: as intellectually ambitious and learned enterprises and, in the case of the *Boethius* and *Soliloquies* at least, enterprises aiming, however hubristically, to go well beyond the range of their Latin predecessors and to attempt something remarkably adventurous—and creating in the process the first English works of philosophy.[6]

This essay will take as its starting point Godden's claim that the Old English *Boethius* is one of the "first English works of philosophy" so that we may explore some of the ideas developed in this ambitious text that freely combines translation, commentary, adaptation, and original composition.

In the rest of this essay, I will focus on the section corresponding with Book 4 of *The Consolation of Philosophy*. This section has generally been considered a more "faithful" rendition of the original Latin than other parts of the text: unlike the section corresponding with Book 5, for instance, it has no major omissions; most additions made are relatively short; and alterations are minor or at least minor enough for us to recognize the corresponding passages in the Latin, even

[5] Godden, "Alfredian Project," 94.

[6] Godden, "Alfredian Project," 122. On the Old English *Boethius* and *Soliloquies* as works of speculative philosophy, see also Paul E. Szarmach's essay in this volume.

when they are used in different contexts.[7] There are, however, some exceptions. Of these, by far the most notable is the Old English author's transformation of the abstract image of concentric circles in Book 4, Prose 6 (4p6) of the original into a more concrete image of a cartwheel. Furthermore, the Old English text omits most of the concluding meter of Book 4, in which Philosophy sings of the exploits of Hercules and other classical heroes. These and other changes made to Book 4 are typically seen as separate phenomena: after all, what could the insertion of the image of a cartwheel possibly have to do with the omission of a narrative about Hercules? But such an episodic reading would only enhance the general impression that the Old English *Boethius* is a protean translation at best and, at worst, the product of a translator who was unable to comprehend the intricate philosophical debate sustained in the Latin. In the discussion that follows, I will propose that the section corresponding with Book 4 not only gives an internally cohesive argument but also presents the author's own view on the ethics of punishment, man and his fate, and the pursuit of philosophy and that these topics, despite the apparent lack of mutual connection, contribute to the development of the section's overarching theme of judgment.

The Ternary Hereafter

In order for us to discern the intricate pattern on the textural fabric wrought by the author of the Old English *Boethius* for the section corresponding with Book 4 of the *Consolation*, I will first direct our attention to his treatment of a brief dialogue that takes place in 4p4, where the prisoner asks Philosophy a question that seems tangentially related to their ongoing debate on the merit of punishment:

> sed quaeso, inquam, te, nullane animarum supplicia post defunctum morte corpus relinquis? Et magna quidem, inquit, quorum alia poenali acerbitate, alia uero purgatoria clementia exerceri puto; sed nunc de his disserere consilium non est.
>
> ["But the question I pose to you is this: Do you not leave room for any punishments of souls after the death of the body?" "Yes, indeed. There will be considerable punishments, some of which I believe are imposed with punitive harshness, but others with a kindly process of cleansing. But I have no intention of discussing these now."][8]

---

[7] For the Old English *Boethius*'s departure from its original, see, for example, W.F. Bolton, "How Boethian is Alfred's *Boethius*?" in *Studies in Earlier Old English Prose: Sixteen Original Contributions*, ed. Paul E. Szarmach (Albany: State University of New York Press, 1986), 153–68.

[8] See 4p4.22–23. Quotations from *The Consolation of Philosophy* are taken from *Anicii Manlii Severini Boethii Philosophiae consolatio*, ed. Ludwig Bieler, CCSL 94 (Turnhout:

Philosophy's response to the prisoner's query is in the affirmative: There will be punishments for the souls of evil-doers after their deaths. But she forecloses this line of investigation by adding a rather brusque disclaimer. In the Old English *Boethius*, the corresponding portion of this exchange seems fairly close to the Latin original, if somewhat longer:

> Ac ic þe halsige get þæt þu me segge hwæþer þu wene þæt ða yfelan habban ænig wite æfter þisse worulde, oððe þa godan ænig edlean heora godes. Hu ne sæde ic þe ær þæt ða godan habbað edlean hiora godes ægþer ge [her ge] on ecnesse, and þa yfelan eac habbað edlean heora yfeles ægþer ge her ge eft on ecnesse? Ac ic wille dælan þa yfelan nu on twa, forþam ðe oðer dæl þara yfelena hæfð ece wite, forþam hi nane mildheortnesse ne geearnodon, oðer dæl sceal beon geclænsod and amered on þam heofonlicon fyre swa her bið sylfor, forþam he hæfð sume geearnunga sumere mildheortnesse. Forþam he mot cuman æfter þam earfoðum to ecre are.[9]
>
> ["But I beg you still to tell me whether you think that the evil have any punishment after this world, or the good any reward for their goodness." Then he said: "Did I not tell you before that the good have reward for their goodness both here and in eternity, and the wicked also have reward for their evil both here and again in eternity? But I want to divide the wicked into two, for one part of the wicked have eternal punishment, because they earned no mercy, and the other part must be cleansed and purified in the heavenly fire as here silver is, because it has somewhat earned some mercy. And so it is allowed to come after those hardships to eternal favour."]

At first the Old English author seems to have simply embellished the Latin with explanatory notes. Upon closer look, however, we realize that he has made a subtle but significant change. To begin with, the Old English text introduces a new category when the *I*-narrator, who is identified as Boethius or Boethius's "mod" [mind] in the opening of the text, asks about the fates not only of the evil but also of the good.[10] This added category is duly acknowledged by Wisdom, Philoso-

Brepols, 1984). The translation of the text comes from Boethius, *The Consolation of Philosophy*, trans. P.G. Walsh (Oxford: Oxford University Press, 1999).

[9] Malcolm Godden and Susan Irvine, eds., *The Old English Boethius: An Edition of the Old English Versions of Boethius's De Consolatione Philosophiae*, 2 vols. (Oxford: Oxford University Press, 2009), 38.142–52, hereafter cited parenthetically by chapter and line number. Translations of the Old English are also drawn from Godden and Irvine. Nicole Marafioti, "Earthly Justice and Spiritual Consequences: Judging and Punishing in the Old English *Consolation of Philosophy*," in *Capital and Corporal Punishment in Anglo-Saxon England*, ed. Jay Paul Gates and Nicole Marafioti (Woodbridge: Boydell, 2014), 113–30, at 122–23, discusses this passage in the light of penitential literature.

[10] See further Godden and Irvine's commentary on this passage in their *Old English Boethius*, 2:450–51. On *mod* in the Old English *Boethius* and elsewhere in Anglo-Saxon

phy's transgender avatar: The good shall have their reward for their goodness, just as the wicked will have their punishment for their wickedness. The addition of the new category gives rise to a tripartite classification for postmortem souls: namely, good, wicked, and what might be called somewhat wicked. We also notice that Wisdom creates this classification by using two binaries: first the entire assemblage of disembodied souls is divided into two groups, that is, good and wicked; and then the latter is divided further into two groups, that is, completely wicked and somewhat wicked. Yet the fates of these three groups of postmortem souls hinge on a single criterion, which is the amount of "mildheortnes" [mercy] they have earned in this world. The good have amassed enough mercy to win eternal favor presumably without any trial; the wicked have earned no mercy so that they receive eternal punishment presumably without any further consideration; and the somewhat wicked have gained some mercy so that they shall be granted eternal favor but only after their souls are "geclænsod and amered on þam heofonlicon fyre" [cleansed and purified in the heavenly fire, 28.149–150].

The Old English author gives a ternary organization of postmortem souls in which those belonging to the middle group must undergo a purgatorial process before being allowed to share the reward of the good. Wisdom's idea of the cleansing of the souls of the somewhat wicked seems to have its kernel in Philosophy's use of the phrase "purgatoria clementia" [mercy of cleansing] in the corresponding passage, but the Old English author literally centralizes it by placing it between the fates of the good and the wicked. He even gives weightiness to this middle category by introducing a simile of precious metal, comparing the process of cleansing souls to that of purifying silver. This trope, combined with the reference to heavenly fire (which is also an addition made by the Old English author), may have reminded his readers of the passage in the First Epistle to the Corinthians, where Paul exposits upon the fate of blessed people on the day of reckoning:

> Si quis autem superaedificat supra fundamentum hoc—aurum, argentum, lapides pretiosos, ligna, faenum, stipulam—uniuscujusque opus manifestum erit. Dies enim Domini declarabit, quia in igne revelabitur, et uniuscuiusque opus, quale sit, ignis probabit. Si cujus opus manserit quod superaedificavit,

literature, see M.R. Godden, "Anglo-Saxons on the Mind," in *Learning and Literature in Anglo-Saxon England: Studies Presented to Peter Clemoes on the Occasion of His Sixty-Fifth Birthday*, ed. Michael Lapidge and Helmut Gneuss (Cambridge: Cambridge University Press, 1985), 271–98, esp. 274–77 and 287–91. For the function of the first-person speaker in the Old English *Boethius*, see Malcolm Godden, "The Player King: Identification and Self-Representation in King Alfred's Writings," in *Alfred the Great: Papers from the Eleventh-Centenary Conferences*, ed. Timothy Reuter (Burlington, VT: Ashgate, 2003), 137–50, esp. 138–46.

> mercedem accipiet. Si cuius opus arserit, detrimentum patietur, ipse autem salvus erit, sic tamen quasi per ignem.
>
> [Now if any man build upon this foundation (i.e., of Christ)—gold, silver, precious stones, wood, hay, stubble—every man's work shall be manifest. For the day of the Lord shall declare it, because it shall be revealed in fire, and the fire shall try every man's work, of what sort it is. If any man's work abide which he hath built thereupon, he shall receive a reward. If any man's work burn, he shall suffer loss, but he himself shall be saved, yet so as by fire.][11]

Ethics of Punishment

I believe that the Old English author's transformation of Philosophy's brief reference to the postmortem punishment of the wicked casts a long shadow (or, perhaps, illuminating light) on the rest of the section corresponding with Book 4 of *The Consolation of Philosophy*. In this section of the essay I will examine the Old English author's treatment of 4p4 as a whole (which comprises the majority of Chapter 38 of the B Text) by paying particular attention to his treatment of the original text before and after the dialogue on the punishment of postmortem souls.[12] Generally speaking, the translator makes greater alterations on the portion of 4p4 leading up to this point than the portion following it. Arguably the most significant alteration is the addition of several negative remarks that the *I*-narrator makes on God's role as a judge. In fact, the section corresponding with 4p4 opens with one such remark: "gif ic hæfde swilcne anweald swylce se ælmihtega God hæfð, þonne ne lete ic no þa yfelan derian þam godum swa swiðe swa hi nu doð" [if I had such power as almighty God has then I would not let the wicked harm the good as much as they now do, 38.53–54]. Wisdom responds to the *I*-narrator's protest by insisting that the wicked can practice evil only for a short while and vouchsafing, in another added passage, that "God hæfð getiohhod to sellenne witu and ermþa þam yfelum monnum [for] hiora yflum weorcum" [God is determined to give punishments and miseries to the wicked men for their evil works, 38.67–69]. A longer addition of this type occurs immediately before the dialogue on the punishment of postmortem souls:

---

[11] 1 Corinthians 3:12–15; *The Vulgate Bible*, ed. Angela M. Kinney (Cambridge, MA: Harvard University Press, 2013), 874–75; this parallel edition consists of the Vulgate Bible and the Douay-Rheims Version. On the connection between this passage and the Bible, see Godden and Irvine, *Old English Boethius*, 2:451. See further Jacques Le Goff's comment on this "very difficult passage" in his *The Birth of Purgatory*, trans. Arthur Goldhammer (Chicago: University of Chicago Press, 1984), 43.

[12] On the B text of the Old English *Boethius*, see Godden and Irvine, *Old English Boethius*, 1:9–18.

> Ða cwæð ic. Ic eom swiðe gedrefed mid þisse spræce, and wundrige forhwi swa ryhtwis dema ænige unrihte gife wille forgifan. Ða cwæð he. Be hwam cwest þu þæt? Ða cwæð ic. Forþam ðe ðu ær cwæde þæt he unriht dyde þæt he lete unwytnod þa yfelan. Ða cwæð he. Þæt is his weorðscipe þæt he swa gifol is, and swa rumedlice gifð. Þæt is micel gifu þæt he gebit oððæt þa yfelan ongitað hyra yfel and gecyrrað to gode. Ða cwæð ic. Nu ic ongite þæt hit nis ece gifu þæt he gifð þam yflum, ac is hwæthwegu eldung and anbid ðæs hehstan deman. For þam anbide and for þam geðylde me þyncð þæt he sie ðe swiðor forsewen. (38.130–140)
>
> [Then I said: "I am very troubled by this speech, and wonder why such a just judge will award any unjust gift." Then he said: "What are you referring to?" Then I said: "Because you said before that he did injustice in that he left the evil unpunished." Then he said: "That is his honour, that he is so generous, and gives so fully. That is a great gift that he waits until the wicked perceive their evil and turn to good." Then I said: "Now I understand that it is not an eternal gift that he gives the wicked but is a partial delay and abiding of the highest judge. Because of that abiding and that patience I think that he is the more despised."][13]

Here the *I*-narrator seems as discontented as ever. The eruption of his indignation is so sudden that Wisdom needs to ask for clarification. Once being told that by "unrihte gife" [unjust gifts] his interlocutor meant God's leniency towards the evil, he explains that the highest judge is so magnanimous as to give them chances to repent on their own. This exposition, which cannot be found in the corresponding portion of the Latin, seems nonetheless to echo a later passage, in 4p6, where Philosophy lists different strategies that Providence takes to induce amelioration in the wicked: Sometimes he puts them through hardships, and sometimes he gives them seemingly unwarranted blessings (4p6.43–47). But unlike the prisoner, who tacitly approves Philosophy's argument through his attentive audience, the Old English *I*-narrator demonstrates his skepticism by criticizing the ways of the highest judge to men. Even though he is glad to learn that God's patience towards the wicked will not be eternal, he nonetheless believes that this misplaced generosity would only promote contemptuous feelings, presumably among the rest of the population. We might be startled by the *I*-narrator's wording here, but I believe that the increasingly strong tone with which he airs his dissatisfaction towards God's seeming injustice paves the way to the dialogue on the fates of postmortem souls. Once hearing Wisdom's explanation on the system of judgment in the hereafter, the *I*-narrator suspends his concern about the highest judge's treatment of people in this world and pursues other issues in the rest of the section corresponding with 4p4.

---

[13] See further Godden and Irvine's comment on this extended addition, *Old English Boethius*, 2:450.

But why should Wisdom's exposition on the punishment of postmortem souls be so effective? Was it not literally a moment earlier that the *I*-narrator dismissed God's "abiding and patience" towards the wicked as nothing more than a cause of negative emotions among others? His change of mind does not seem to be caused by Wisdom's acknowledgement of salvation history, for the Old English author places Boethius's philosophical dialogue in a Christian framework from very early on.[14] In the section corresponding with Book 1, for example, Wisdom tells his interlocutor that "þu eart an þara rihtwisena and þara ryhtwillendra. Þa beoð þære heofencundan Ierusalem burgware" [you are one of the righteous and well-intentioned. Those are the citizens of the heavenly Jerusalem, 5.17–19]. In Chapter 37, which includes the section corresponding with 4p3, he asserts that "ne þearf nænne wisne mon tweogan þæt þa yfelan nabban eac ece edlean heora yfeles, þæt bið ece wite" [no wise person need doubt that the evil do not also have eternal reward for their evil, that is eternal punishment, 37.68–70].

If, then, the *I*-narrator has already been informed about the salvation of the righteous and the damnation of the wicked, why should he complain about the highest judge's treatment of people in this world? I believe that his concern here is less about the fate of the good or the evil than about the fate of those who are neither indisputably good nor incontestably evil, that is, people who might be saved if they could make up for their earlier misdeeds through proper punishment. Left to their own devices, they may never repent by themselves; and even if they did, the moment might not be soon enough for them to attain salvation; the highest judge would not be doing them any favor by being patient with them. But the *I*-narrator's dilemma evaporates when Wisdom finally gives the answer for which he has been looking: Such individuals will still have a chance at salvation thanks to the mechanism of cleansing with heavenly fire. To put it another way, the fire of purgation in the hereafter justifies the highest judge's treatment of the (redeemably) wicked in this world: He will complete any task that he has left unfinished for them by submitting their disembodied souls to purgatorial sufferings.

The fire of purgation passage marks a turning point for the Old English author's treatment of 4p4, in that he makes far fewer alterations on the text after this passage. There is, however, one notable exception. He omits a certain passage that is essential for the understanding of Philosophy's view on external punishment:

> Vide autem quid aeterna lex sanciat. Melioribus animum conformaueris; nihil opus est iudice praemium deferente, tu te ipse excellentioribus ad-

---

[14] See, for example, Bolton, "How Boethian is Alfred's *Boethius*?" esp. 154–55; and Nicole Guenther Discenza, *The King's English: Strategies of Translation in the Old English* Boethius (Albany: State University of New York Press, 2005), esp. 37–43.

> didisti; studium ad peiora deflexeris: extra ne quaesieris ultorem, tu te ipse in deteriora trusisti. (4p4.28–29)
>
> [Note what the immortal law ordains: shape your mind to better things, and you will not need a judge to bestow a reward, for you set yourself among the more outstanding features of creation; turn your affections towards the worse, and you need to look for no outsider to impose retribution, for you have relegated yourself to the region of baser things.]

Noting the Old English author's treatment of this passage, Malcolm Godden and Susan Irvine write: "What is strikingly omitted from [the Old English *Boethius*'s] adaptation is Philosophia's two emphatic statements that there is no need for an external judge or avenger, since virtue and vice (or contemplation and abasement) are their own reward and punishment."[15] Because the Old English author passes over Philosophy's reference to the immortal law ("aeterna lex"), which renders judges' decrees ultimately irrelevant to one's own happiness, and yet translates the rest of 4p4 more or less faithfully, the resulting effect is the emphasis that the Old English text places on the importance of external punishment. In the following passage, for instance, Wisdom extols the virtue of suffering to be inflicted on criminals by earthly authorities:

> gif þa scyldigan ænigne spearcan wisdomes hæfdon and be ængum dæle ongitan þæt hi mihtan hiora scylda þurh wite gebetan þe him her on worulde on become, þonne noldan hi na cweþan þæt hit wære wite, ac woldon cweþan þæt hit wære hiora clænsung and heora betrung, and noldon nænne þingere secan, ac lustlice hi woldon lætan þa rican hie tucian æfter hiora agnum willan. (38.242–248)[16]
>
> [if the guilty had any spark of wisdom and understood to any degree that they could amend their crimes through punishment which fell upon them here in this world, then they would not say that it was punishment, but would say that it was their cleansing and their amendment, and they would not seek an advocate but would gladly let the authorities afflict them according to their own desire.]

When read in isolation, Wisdom's insistence on the uselessness of a "þingere" [advocate] who tries to reduce the sentence for the guilty, like its counterpart in the Latin, would seem rather counter-intuitive, at least for uninitiated readers.[17] But the Old English author attempts a cohesive development of the argument by not only placing this passage shortly after the dialogue on the purgation of postmortem souls but also replacing Philosophy's idea of punishments as a use-

---

[15] Godden and Irvine, *Old English Boethius*, 2:452–53.

[16] This corresponds to Boethius, *Consolation*, 4p4.38–40.

[17] See, for example, Marafioti, "Earthly Justice and Spiritual Consequences," 122.

ful measure for balancing out the criminals' guilt with Wisdom's claim that the pain of punishment effects the "clænsung" [cleansing] and "betrung" [bettering] of the guilty. In so doing, the Old English author makes a connection between the earthly system of punishment for the (redeemably) guilty and the divine system of punishment for the souls of the (somewhat) wicked: The affliction imposed upon the former by earthly authority is analogous to the pain inflicted on the latter by the highest judge. And if we remember the general nature of the purgatorial fire of the hereafter, that it will be, to use Augustine's expression, "grauior . . . quam quidquid potest homo pati in hac uita" [more painful . . . than anything that a person can endure in this life],[18] physical pains inflicted on the guilty by earthly authority should be far preferable to the torment brought upon disembodied souls by the divine judge. Because the earthly and heavenly systems of justice operate on similar principles and yet the former causes far less pain than the latter, the guilty should seek speedy justice while they still have time to cleanse themselves. Failure to do so would result in a far worse situation, for, as Wisdom puts it in another added passage, "swa he lengra bið swa hi bioð ungesæligran . . . [ond] him wære ealra mæst unsælð þæt se fyrst wære oð domes dæg" [the longer it is the more unfortunate they will be . . . [and] the greatest misfortune of all for them would be that the time was until doomsday, 38.163–164]. The logical consequence of this reversed correlation between time to punishment and the degree of happiness is that earthly judges have a moral obligation to punish the guilty. The Old English author concludes the section corresponding with 4p4 with a reformulation of the ethics of punishment from the perspective of the guilty: "Þæt is þonne hiora mildsung þæt mon wrece hiora unþeawas be hiora gewyrhtum" [This then is their mercy, that one punishes their vices according to their merits, 38.251–252].[19]

A Tripartite Cartwheel of Fate

The previous two sections of this essay considered how the author of the Old English *Boethius* develops his own theory of punishment by altering some of the material in 4p4 of the Latin original: first, by introducing a tripartite system of punishment in the hereafter, which administers purgation of souls for the somewhat wicked; and second, by using this system to define the primary function of earthly punishments as the cleansing and bettering of the (redeemably) guilty. In this section I will consider the influence of the tripartite classification of souls on the Old English author's treatment of the rest of Book 4 in general and 4p6

---

[18] *Sancti avrelii Augustini, enarrationes in Psalmos I–L* (Turnhout: Brepols, 1961), 384.

[19] Marafioti, "Earthly Justice and Spiritual Consequences," suggests that "the argument presented in Chapter 38 is very much in line with the judicial priorities of the king's later reign" (129).

in particular. Special attention will be paid to Wisdom's "bispell" [parable] of a cartwheel, which, as mentioned at the beginning of this essay, is based on Philosophy's more abstract metaphor of concentric circles:

> Nam ut orbium circa eundem cardinem sese uertentium qui est intimus ad simplicitatem medietatis accedit ceterorumque extra locatorum ueluti cardo quidam circa quem uersentur exsistit, extimus uero maiore ambitu rotatus quanto a puncti media indiuiduitate discedit tanto amplioribus spatiis explicatur, si quid uero illi se medio conectat et societ in simplicitatem cogitur diffundique ac diffluere cessat. (4p6.65-73)
>
> [Imagine a series of concentric circles revolving round the same axis; the innermost one lies closest to the single nature of the central point, and itself acts as a sort of axis round which the other circles lying outside it can turn. The outermost circle travels round in a wider circle, and the further it departs from the undivided middle point, the more widespread is the area over which it extends.]

Despite its multiple circles, Philosophy's mandala presented here essentially shows a contrast between Fate and Providence. The former exerts influence on all of the rotating circles, whereas the latter can be found only in one place, namely, the unmoving center. Philosophy's geometrical image fundamentally teaches a lesson in binarism: "uti est ad intellectum ratiocinatio, ad id quod est id quod gignitur, ad aeternitatem tempus, ad punctum medium circulus, ita est fati series mobilis ad prouidentiae stabilem simplicitatem" [As the power of reasoning relates to the intellect, as becoming is to being, as time is to eternity, as a circle is to its mid-point, so is the shifting chain of Fate related to the unchanging oneness of Providence, 4p6.15–17].

It is not difficult to see how the Old English author has used Philosophy's allegory to create a metaphor of his own: Wisdom's cartwheel, like Philosophy's concentric circles, is a round object turning on an axle located at the center, and it is designed to explain "hwylce men bioð underþied þære wyrde, [hwylce] ne bioð" [which men are subject to fate, [which] are not, 391.54]. But the similarities between the two may not go much further. Wisdom's circular object is an artifact made up of diverse parts, such as a hub and rim pieces. He still considers the unmoving center of this moving circle to be a representation of "þæt hehste god þe we nemnað God" [the highest good which we call God] and, accordingly, treats the hub, being adjacent to the stationary axle, as a place reserved specifically for "þa selestan men" [the best men, 39.162]. But he has divided the rest of this circular object into two portions: the rim and the spokes. The former belongs to "þa [mætestan] men" [the weakest men, 39.175], who, because of their attachment to the rim, "eallunga wealwigen on þære eorþan" [wallow wholly in the earth, 39.174-75]. People on the rim are therefore the opposite of those who are stationed on the hub:

> Þeah þa [mætestan] ealle hiora lufe wenden to þisse worulde, hi ne magon þæron wunigan ne to nauhte ne weorðað, gif hi be nanum dæle ne bioð gefæstnode to Gode, þon ma þe ðæs hweohles felga magon bion [on] þam færelde gif hi ne bioð fæste on þam spacum and þa spacan on þære eaxe. Ða felga bioð fyrrest þære eaxe; forþam hi farað ungerydelicost. (39.176-82)
>
> [Though the weakest turn all their affection to this world, they cannot remain in it, nor come to anything if they are in no way fastened to God, any more than the wheel's rim-pieces can be in that movement if they are not fixed to the spokes and the spokes to the axle. The rim-pieces are furthest from the axle; therefore they move most roughly.]

The spokes, which comprise the intermediary portion of the cartwheel, are reserved for "þa midmestan men" [the middle-most men]. They are different from both the best men on the hub and the weakest men on the rim, in that they do not have a fixed distance to the axle. Just as the spokes run the full length of the wheel's radius, the middle-most men may either come closer to the central point or move further away from it. The middle-most men nonetheless share qualities with both the best men and the weakest men: some are more like people on the hub, and others are more like people on the rim, just as some parts of the spoke are closer to the hub, while others are closer to the rim. Though belonging neither to the hub nor to the rim, the middle-most man may understand the way of life in either extreme. His mixed nature is such that "oðre hwile [he] smeað on his mode ymb þis eorðlice lif, oðre hwile ymb þæt godcundlice" [sometimes he thinks in his mind about this earthly life, sometimes about the divine life, 39.166–67].[20]

We may note that the configuration of Wisdom's cartwheel is homologous to his classificatory system of postmortem souls. In Chapter 38 he takes issue with the fates of the individuals after their departure from this world. In Chapter 39 (which contains the section corresponding with 4p6) he discusses the fates of people who journey through this world on the cartwheel, as it were, of life. Each of these two passages, as we recall, is a creative adaptation of the Latin original where Philosophy presents a binary system. And in each case, the Old English author has transformed it into a ternary one. The fate of postmortem souls depends on their nature as being good, wicked, or somewhat wicked; the cartwheel of fate is divided into a hub, a rim, and spokes, accommodating the best, weakest, and mid-most people, respectively. There seems to be a further correlation

[20] F. Anne Payne, *King Alfred and Boethius: An Analysis of the Old English Version of the Consolation of Philosophy* (Madison: University of Wisconsin Press, 1968), points out that "the wheel is seen to embrace society as a whole, as well as the single individual," so that "men . . ., whatever their decisions, are nevertheless bound to other men and to God" (97–98). See also Paul E. Szarmach's essay in this volume for another reading of the cartwheel metaphor.

between these two ternary systems. Just as souls of the good have "edlean hiora godes ægþer ge [her ge] on ecnesse" [reward for their goodness both here and in eternity, 38.145], the best people clinging to the hub are said to be the "eallra orsorgoste ægðer ge þises andweardan lifes earfoða ge þæs toweardan" [most secure of all, from the hardships of both this life and next, 39.189–191]. While souls of the wicked shall have "ece wite" [eternal punishment, 38.148], the weakest people on the rim, who "hiora lufe wenden to þisse worulde" [turn their affection to this world, 39.177], shall come to naught, so Wisdom claims, "gif hi be nanum dæle ne bioð gefæstnode to Gode" [if they are in no way fastened to God, 39.178–179]. The mid-most people on the spokes, not unlike the middle group of souls, are characterized by their place in between the other two; they are neither completely good nor utterly weak, but they have some attributes of goodness and weakness.

We may note that the mid-most people who occupy the spokes of Wisdom's cartwheel have no counterpart in Philosophy's binary metaphor of rotating circles, whereas Wisdom's exposition that the souls of the somewhat wicked shall undergo a cleansing process in the hereafter seems to correspond with Philosophy's remark that some of the wicked will be subjected to the "clementia purgatoria" [clemency of purgation] after their separation from their bodies. We may therefore infer that the Old English author has created the mid-most men on the spokes as a category comparable with the middle category of postmortem souls so that there may be a parallel between the classificatory system of people in this world and the classificatory system of souls in the next. The mid-most man, in other words, is a figure unique to the philosophical world of the Old English author.

The Mid-Most Man as a Philosopher

But what do we know about the mid-most man? If we assume that there is a correlation between the middle part of the cartwheel and the middle group of souls in the hereafter, he should ultimately be a happy figure, just as the soul of a somewhat wicked person shall receive eternal favor after having endured the heavenly fire of purgation. Because of his interest, at least in part, in the divine life, the mid-most man will likely "hæfð sume geearnunga sumere mildheortnesse" [have somewhat earned some mercy, 38.150–151] prior to his departure from this world. In Chapter 39, Wisdom uses an interesting simile to describe the divided interest of the mid-most man on the spoke: It is "swelce he locie mid oðre eagan to heofonum, mid oðre to eorþan" [as if he looked with one eye to heaven and with the other to earth, 39.167–168]. The Old English author probably did not conjure up the image of a person with such a Janus-like gaze out of thin air, for a similar idea occurs in 4p4 of the Latin: "ueluti, si uicibus sordidam humum caelumque respicias, cunctis extra cessantibus ipsa cernendi ratione nunc caeno nunc sideribus interesse uidearis" [It is as though your gaze were trained alternately on the filthy earth and the sky, with nothing else in sight; on the evidence of your eyes alone, you would appear at one moment to be down in the filth, and at the next among the stars, 4p4.29]. The person described here is reminiscent of the mid-most man on the spoke, who may turn either to the axle of the highest good or to the rim soiled with filthy earth. Philosophy seems to use the simile in a positive way here, for she continues: "At uulgus ista non respicit. Quid igitur, hisne accedamus quos beluis similes esse monstrauimus?" [But the common herd does not gaze at the stars above. So what are we to do? Should we join those whom we have shown to be brute beasts? 4p4.29–30].[21] Philosophy's simile of a two-way gaze is particularly important for our consideration of the Old English author's idea of judgment, since it occurs immediately after her reference to the "immortal law," which, as we have seen, is omitted from the rendition of the passage in the Old English *Boethius*. Given the proximity of Philosophy's reference to the immortal law and her use of the simile of a gaze, a man who follows the immortal law in judging himself (as well as others) may well be capable of directing his gaze to both the filthy earth and the glorious stars.

This is admittedly one of the several possible interpretations of the difficult passage surrounding Philosophy's simile of a gaze, and it was probably not the most widely accepted interpretation in the early medieval tradition.[22] But such a reading of the passage seems to be reflected in the Old English author's treatment of the middle portion of Book 4: while he omits Philosophy's reference to the immortal law in 4p4, he uses some of the omitted material to create a speech for Wisdom to explain his opinion to his interlocutor:

> Ðy ic nat hu nyta þu me tæhst to þam dysegum monnum, þa næfre æfter me ne spyriað. Ic ne sprece næfre to þam, ac ic sprece to þe forþam ðu teohhast þæt ðu spyrige æfter me and swiðor swincst on þam spore þonne hi don. Ne recce ic hwæt hi deman. Ic læte nu to þinum dome ma þonne to hiora, forþam hi ealle lociað mid bam eagum on þas eorðlican þing, and hi him liciað eallunga ægþer ge on þæs modes eagum ge on þæs lichoman. Ac þu ana hwilum bescylst mid oðre eagan on þa hiofenlican þing, [mid oðre] þu locast nu get on þas eorðlican. (38.185–193)
>
> [So I do not know for what purpose you show me to the foolish men, who never seek after me. I never speak to them, but I speak to you, since you intend to seek after me and toil more on the track than they do. I do not

[21] See also Karmen Lenz, "The Star-like Soul in the *Metra* of the Old English *Boethius*," *Anglo-Saxon England* 39 (2010): 139–62, at 158–61. For the idea of "elite audience" in the *Consolation*, see, for example, Seth Lerer, *Boethius and Dialogue: Literary Method in the Consolation of Philosophy* (Princeton: Princeton University Press, 1985), 179–80.

[22] See Godden and Irvine, *Old English Boethius*, 2:452.

> care what opinions they have. I concern myself with your opinion more than theirs, for they all look with both eyes at these earthly things, and those please them totally, both in the mind's eyes and in the body's. But you alone sometimes look with one eye to heavenly things, with the other you look now still on these earthly things.]

In this passage, the Janus-like gaze is unambiguously attributed to the *I*-narrator so as to distinguish him from "þam dysegum monnum" [those foolish people] who turn both eyes to earthly things and nothing else.[23] The difference between such foolish people and the *I*-narrator is manifold: the former consider the source of happiness to be freedom from punishment, whereas the latter believes punishment to be a necessary process for gaining happiness; the former have no desire to attain wisdom, while the latter would seek wisdom even in the face of hardships. When it comes to their fundamental nature, however, the *I*-narrator and the foolish people are not diametrically opposed to each other, as good is to evil, because they are both interested in earthly things. Their relationship is analogous, instead, to the relationship between the rim pieces and the spokes of the cartwheel. The foolish people are similar to the weakest people on the rim, since they "all look with both eyes at these earthly things"; the *I*-narrator is not unlike the people on the spokes, in that he sometimes looks to heavenly things and sometimes observes earthly matter. In fact, he may even be considered an exemplary mid-most man because of his unflagging desire to reach the highest good.

Conclusion: The Birth of a New Philosopher Hero

I will conclude this essay with a brief discussion on the Old English author's treatment of the last Meter of Book 4 of the *Consolation*. Modern readers are often puzzled by his omission of most of this Meter, because the exploits of the classical heroes mentioned therein, and Hercules's fight with monsters in particular, would not have rung unfamiliar to the Anglo-Saxon ear. As Susan Irvine has pointed out, the Old English author was not programmatically opposed to deeds of valor, for he has earlier added a reference to Hercules as a champion who killed the hydra or, as he puts it, a "nædre . . . þe hæfde nigan heafdu" [serpent which had nine heads, 39.90].[24] The Old English author's suppression of the references to Hercules in the Meter in question may therefore imply that he has found the very nature of Hercules, the patron saint of the Stoics, to be incompatible with his conclusion on the section corresponding with Book 4. In the *Conso-*

[23] See also, Godden and Irvine, *Old English Boethius*, 2:452–53.

[24] Susan Irvine, "Wrestling with Hercules: King Alfred and the Classical Past," in *Court Culture in the Early Middle Ages: The Proceedings of the First Alcuin Conference*, ed. Catherine Cubitt (Turnhout: Brepols, 2003), 171–88, esp. 174–76.

lation, Philosophy at length explains how Hercules has won his fame through his labors, conquering not only the Hydra but also Centaurs, Cerberus, Achelous, and so on. The moral lesson that she encourages her addressees—identified as "fortes" [intrepid ones]—to draw from this conspicuous example is to maintain "firmis medium uiribus" [the middle ground with steadfast strength]. In order to gain the gods' favor and win a place among the stars, Hercules had to have his shoulders befouled with the Erymanthian boar's saliva before using them to sustain the sphere of heaven. The meter concludes with Philosophy's admonition to follow the hero on his lofty path.[25] The exhortation inspires the prisoner so much that he becomes (more than) ready for Philosophy's rigorous exposition on God's foreknowledge and man's free will in Book 5.

The Old English author's decision to omit the Herculean meter is a highly calculated one. For one thing, Wisdom's interlocutor does not need the same level of preparation as Philosophy's, since the Old English *Boethius* drastically truncates Book 5. Even more important, a Herculean hero would not have been entirely in line with the figure of a philosopher that the Old English author carefully constructs over the course of the section corresponding with Book 4. Unlike Philosophy, therefore, Wisdom does not admonish his addressees—identified as wise men—to conquer the earth with superhuman exploits and reach the stars. Instead, he urges each of them to follow "þone midmestan weg" [the middle way] to attain a seemingly less ambitious goal:

> ælc wis mon scyle a winnan ægþer ge wið þæ reþan wyrde ge wið þa winsuman, þy læs he hine for þære wynsuman wyrde fortruwige oððe [for] þære reðan forþence. Ac him is þearf þæt he aredige þone midmestan weg betwyhs þære reþan wyrde and þære liþan, þæt he ne wilnige wynsumran wyrde and maran orsorhnesse þonne hit gemetlic sie, [ne] eft reðre, forþam he ne mæg naðres ungemet adriohan. (40.49–55)
>
> [every wise man must always contend both against adverse fate and against the pleasant fate, lest he become overconfident because of the pleasant fate or despair because of the adverse. But it is necessary for him to follow the middle way between the adverse fate and the mild, so that he does not desire more pleasant fate and greater freedom from care than is moderate, nor again more adverse, for he cannot endure excess of either.]

Wise men must shun both extremely difficult and extremely pleasant fates, because they are, so Wisdom insists, incapable of handling either. Even when they tread the mid-most way, their journey will likely be fraught with hardships. But if they are willing to bear them with patience, "gemetgað him God þa reþan

[25] This passage spans 4p7.19–4m7. For Boethius's use of the literary tradition concerning Hercules and other classical characters, see, for example, Lerer, *Boethius and Dialogue*, 183–201.

wyrde ge on þisse worulde ge on þære toweardan, swa swa [hi eaðe] adrygan magan" [God will moderate the adverse fate both in this world and in the one to come, such as they can easily endure, 40.58–60]. The reward may at first seem modest, but as long as they face their adverse and yet tempered fate with determination, God will eventually reward them with "ecre eadignesse" [eternal bliss, 40.70–71] and lift them "ofer ðæm tunglum" [above the stars, 40.70]. Wisdom's addressees are not heroic achievers of the golden mean but, rather, steadfast followers of the middle way. The Old English *I*-narrator was chosen as Wisdom's interlocutor precisely because he will ever tread the mid-most way, mediating the extremes that envelope the world of man: pleasure and care, wickedness and goodness, motion and stillness, the earthly and the divine. In the end, the seeker of wisdom in the Old English *Boethius* is charged with a goal far greater than what Hercules has accomplished through his extraordinary labors. And the only way for him to achieve this goal is to be aware of his weakness as well as his potential goodness—that is, to recognize his human nature—and to be ever willing to endure pain in following the mid-most path, until it at length takes him to a place that lies beyond the realm of stars.

An Ethical History for the Self: The Liberius *Exemplum* in the Old English *Boethius*

Hilary Fox

In the opening of the Old English *Boethius*, Wisdom (Philosophia) instructs the ailing Mod (Boethius) to say whether it knows "hwæt þu self wære" [what you yourself are, 5.71].[1] Mod does not know—or, at least, remember—the whole answer; Wisdom finds what Mod knows about himself, "þæt ic on libbendum men and on gesceadwisum eom and þeah on deadlicum" [that I am in a living and rational, and yet mortal, man, 5.72–73], to be insufficient. To correct this forgetfulness, Wisdom and Mod pursue questions that involve identity in problems of fate and fortune and in the relationship of the human to the true good and the divine. Wisdom argues that Mod will find the answers to these questions within his own self, which is an inalienable property and not subject to the whims of fortune: "Ic wat gif þu nu [hæfdest] fullne anweald þines selfes," Wisdom tells Mod, "þonne hæfdest þu hwæthwega on þe selfum þæs þe þu næfre þinum willum alætan woldest, ne seo wyrd þe on geniman ne mihte" [I know, if you had full power over yourself, then you would have something in yourself which you would never lose by your own will, and which fortune could never take from you, 11.62–65]. The acquisition of this power comes through the labor of self-recovery, which takes place within oneself and with one's own proper faculties; this labor is self-contemplative, reflexive, a turn inward to a "oneself" to make oneself—whatever that is—an object of examination and cultivation. Moreover, this contemplative process, however laborious, is an ethical impera-

[1] All quotations from the Old English *Boethius* (hereafter cited parenthetically by chapter and line number from the B text) are from Malcolm Godden and Susan Irvine, eds., *The Old English Boethius: An Edition of the Old English Versions of Boethius's De Consolatione Philosophiae*, 2 vols. (Oxford: Oxford University Press, 2009). The Latin text of *The Consolation of Philosophy* is from *Anicii Manlii Severini Boethii Philosophiae Consolatio*, ed. Ludwig Bieler, CCSL 94 (Turnhout: Brepols, 1957); references to the *Consolation* are by book, prose or meter, and line number. All translations from Old English and Latin are my own, unless otherwise noted.

tive placed upon the individual, as an obligation that cannot be transferred or delegated to others. As such, methods or strategies that enable self-examination—propaedeutics to self-study—play a crucial role in the *Boethius*'s goal of self-recovery and formation.[2]

This essay discusses how the *Boethius* enables self-examination through the deployment of exemplary historical narrative. In it, I investigate the *Boethius*'s modifications to the *exemplum* of Liberius in Chapter 16 of the B-text to explore how the narratives and reading strategies in the text participate in the Boethian legacy of preoccupation with self-care and self-knowledge. By examining its participation in the post-Augustinian tradition of engaging with literary and historical texts, I seek to reconfigure what Michel Foucault's *Technologies of the Self* argues is an essential split between the "technologies of the self" that predominated in Greco-Roman philosophies and those of early Christianity.[3] Namely, while Foucault sees the latter, through its embrace of confession, as one of self-publication and consequent self-abnegation and the former as self-construction and citizen-construction, the *Boethius* seems to participate simultaneously in both ways of self-reading and self-writing. Its ethical enjoinments, while calling for abstention from and renunciation of sin, also deal with the necessity of understanding one's particularity as a social being in need of proper ethical equipment. After two necessary caveats regarding the historicity and framing of this social being, I will continue to discuss the use and study of history as a component of ethical education and then turn to consideration of the *exemplum* of Liberius itself.

Inevitably, any discussion of the *Boethius* must contend not only with *The Consolation of Philosophy* but also with the question of the commentary tradition and, more significantly, with the figure of Alfred the Great of Wessex (r. 871–99), to whose hand or authority the *Boethius* has been attributed. In an effort to dodge this inevitability, the present essay does not interrogate the relationship between the *Boethius* and its possible antecedents in the body of early medieval commentaries on the *Consolation*, nor does it operate under the assumption that the mind or authorizing hand behind the *Boethius* is either Alfred's or that of a scholar working under his patronage or direction. Rather, it takes Malcolm Godden at his word when he suggests that reading the Alfredian canon as exercises in the royal authoring of its own authority "makes us too inclined to interpret everything in terms of a royalist, authority-centred position

[2] For an account of Boethian formal experimentation and ethical work in the later Middle Ages, see Eleanor Johnson's essay in this volume.

[3] Michel Foucault, *Technologies of the Self: A Seminar with Michel Foucault*, ed. Luther H. Martin, Huck Gutman, and Patrick H. Hutton (Amherst: University of Massachusetts Press, 1988).

and to miss much that is critical and subversive of authority."[4] Perhaps dangerously for someone considering questions of history and the use of history, I look at the *Boethius* not with only Alfred's goals in mind; given the presence of the *Boethius* beyond Alfred's reign, I am also interested in receptions and audiences who would not necessarily have been subjects of Alfred's direct political or intellectual authority.

Another caveat regards my use of the word *self.* In constructing a working definition of a self in the *Boethius*, I draw on contemporary theories of the political subject, particularly those of Foucault and Peter Haidu, as well as recent scholarship on self and identity in Anglo-Saxon England. Haidu juxtaposes two forms of subjectivity in the early Middle Ages: 1) "what is often designated as the 'medieval' subject, committed to the subjection of complete abnegation"; and 2) "the model of the 'modern' subject: a specifically political subject, negotiating the fundamental loyalty to the governor and his rule."[5] In his reading of the Oaths of Strasbourg (written in 842), Haidu points to how the injunction the Oaths placed upon the retainers of Louis the German and Charles the Bald—that they refuse to follow their respective lords if Louis or Charles violate the terms of their oath—thrust the kings' men into "the unaccustomed autonomy of ideological choice" between loyalty to the king and loyalty to truth.[6] The politicized subject stands in contrast to the abnegated early Christian subject of Foucault's *Technologies of the Self*, which sees in the self-care of early Christianity the ultimate renunciation of the self, either through ascetic practice or through confession, in which disclosure of the self—one's sins, vagaries, and misdeeds—is a simultaneous disavowal of the self, the culmination of a process of ruthless self-examination and self-publication.[7] More broadly, however, Foucault asserts, "technologies of the self" are practices or methods that:

> permit individuals to effect by their own means or with the help of others a certain number of operations on their own bodies and souls, thoughts,

[4] Malcolm Godden, "Did King Alfred Write Anything?" *Medium Ævum* 76 (2007): 1–23, at 18. Godden also explores the problematic shift in the attitudes toward kingship and thegnship expressed by the first-person figures in the *Boethius* and *Soliloquies*, which to him suggests not a royal mind behind the text but a noble one that is attempting to come to grips with its position in the natural and political order; see his "The Player King: Identification and Self-Representation in Alfred's Writings," in *Alfred the Great: Papers from the Eleventh-Centenary Conference*, ed. Timothy Reuter (Burlington, VT: Ashgate, 2003), 137–50.

[5] Peter Haidu, *The Subject Medieval/Modern: Text and Governance in the Middle Ages* (Stanford, CA: Stanford University Press, 2004), 9 and 11.

[6] Haidu, *Text and Governance*, 11.

[7] Foucault, *Technologies of the Self*, 43 and 48.

> conduct and way of being, so as to transform themselves in order to attain a certain state of happiness, purity, wisdom, perfection, or immortality.[8]

This broader formulation of self-care includes not only confessional or ascetic practice but, as I hope to suggest, also includes the kinds of self-reflective practices encouraged by the *Boethius*—practices that result in the production of an ethical political and social actor.

In recent years, questions of self, identity, and agency have been a focus of study for Anglo-Saxonists, who have further complicated the medieval/modern bifurcation criticized by Haidu and elucidated Anglo-Saxon attempts to come to grips with what "the self" might be.[9] Michael Matto's study of technologies of the self in *The Seafarer*—a study to which the present essay owes a significant debt—rejects a subjectivity grounded purely in the body or in the mind/soul, and thus in particularity, in favor of seeking an understanding of self through "the production of wisdom, confessional technologies of personal salvation, the heroic and elegiac ethic of constraining the impulses of the inner mind, and public rituals of communal integration."[10] The ambivalence confronted by the self of *The Seafarer*—whether it is located in the body or in the mind—remains unresolved; it dramatizes a moment, Matto says, a "difficult stage of the process of conceiving the Christian self, one in which the state of earthly life itself remains a hindrance to imagining the self as dependent on but ultimately not tied to the body."[11] Similarly, Ronald Ganze has suggested that "an essential self that transcends the material world and the forces which have shaped it, yet appears to bring along with it all those elements of its identity which social and material forces contributed in constructing" is present in the Old English *Soliloquies*, a text often seen as a companion to the *Boethius*.[12] Ganze's dissertation anticipates Leslie Lockett's arguments on the doctrine of the unitary *sawol* in the Old English *Soliloquies*, which represents a progression from the still-bifurcated *sawol*

---

[8] Foucault, *Technologies of the Self*, 18.

[9] See, *inter alia*, Antonina Harbus, *The Life of the Mind in Old English Poetry* (New York: Rodopi Press, 2001); Michael Matto, "True Confessions: *The Seafarer* and Technologies of the *Sylf*," *JEGP* 103 (2004): 157–79; Ronald Ganze, "Conceptions of the Self in Augustine, King Alfred, and Anglo-Saxon England" (Ph.D diss., University of Oregon, 2004); Leslie Lockett, *Anglo-Saxon Psychologies in the Vernacular and Latin Traditions* (Toronto: University of Toronto Press, 2011); Britt Mize, *Traditional Subjectivities: The Old English Poetics of Mentality* (Toronto: University of Toronto Press, 2013), esp. 155–235 for discussion of Meter 1 of the prosimetrical *Boethius* and its refiguring of the prose; and Benjamin A. Saltzman, "The Mind, Perception, and the Reflexivity of Forgetting in Alfred's *Pastoral Care*," *ASE* 42 (2013): 147–82.

[10] Matto, "Technologies of the *Sylf*," 178.

[11] Matto, "Technologies of the *Sylf*," 171.

[12] Ganze, "Conceptions of the Self," 140–41. For the relationship between the *Boethius* and *Soliloquies*, see Godden and Irvine, *Old English Boethius*, 1:136.

and *mod* of the *Boethius*.[13] The tension between the forgetful mind and the eternal soul forms a running concern in the *Boethius*, as the translator moves from division to unity, coaxing Mod to remember its own eternality rather than its temporality. The anxiety expressed at numerous points in the *Boethius* regarding what can be affected by external forces and what can be affected only by oneself becomes, in the end, one of Wisdom's reassurances: There are parts of oneself that *cannot* be touched, altered, or alienated by external forces.

My working definition of the self in the *Boethius* is, therefore, something of a hybrid. For the purposes of this essay, I define a self as an individual entity: a soul-mind-body totality that does not presuppose stability, permanence, immutability, or complete privacy. This individual being is oriented in multiple ways: towards itself, its exterior environment (the natural world and human society), and its creator, and it bears primary responsibility for its own care and cultivation. It is *how* this self is oriented towards these things, and how it exercises its responsibilities, that are the concern of the *Boethius*. Furthermore, the self in the *Boethius* is conceptualized as a thing that has exclusive agency or responsibility for itself, and thus the primary obligation to care for itself and its moral life. It is, as Paul Ricoeur writes, the "kind of being which is characterized by the capacity to question itself and relate itself to its own being."[14] Moreover, the self does not only possess this capacity for self-questioning, it is required to exercise that capacity in the service of its own care and the practice of virtue. As such, to Matto, Ganze, and Lockett I add Katherine O'Brien O'Keeffe's discussion of agency and identity, particularly her analysis of agent action and responsibility in Ælfric of Eynsham, in which moral responsibility is a result of human freedom.[15]

Consequently, the social aspect of the *Boethius* insists on a connection between the *theory* of philosophy and the *ethic* of it: the latter without the former was impossible, but the former without the latter was empty. As such, the community that gathered around philosophy—that learned it, was formed by it, and taught it in turn—was a community devoted to an interpretive practice that was both theoretical and practical. As Brian Stock argues in *Augustine the Reader*, the "charitable trust" that obtains between author and audience in Augustine's confessional literature "can be described as a community around a text: it is interpretive in formation and behavioural in possibilities."[16] The concern of the *Confessiones* in particular, Stock writes, "was ethical before it was literary, and

---

[13] Lockett, *Anglo-Saxon Psychologies*, 318–25.

[14] Paul Ricoeur, *Oneself as Another*, trans. Kathleen Blamey (Chicago: University of Chicago Press, 1992), 199.

[15] Katherine O'Brien O'Keeffe, *Stealing Obedience: Narratives of Agency and Identity in Later Anglo-Saxon England* (Toronto: University of Toronto Press, 2012), 21–25.

[16] Brian Stock, *Augustine the Reader: Meditation, Self-Knowledge, and the Ethics of Interpretation* (Cambridge, MA: Harvard University Press, 1996), 215.

it was literary only in combination with ethics."[17] Compositional and interpretive communities were, for Augustine, organized along ethical lines; the writing of texts and their reception brought together teachers and learners, the latter of whom could become teachers in their turn; the community's goal was learning the proper way to read texts and, by learning to read properly, learning to live properly as well.[18] Such an understanding of the relationship between text, community, and ethics was not limited to the circles of Augustinian influence; the application of textual lessons to ideas of the self forms the intellectual and psychological core of Alfred's translation program, and Asser's *Vita* depicts Alfred's behavior as "quite simply, governed by texts. They orient, by providing a structure for, his actions."[19] The text is to be read and understood and then have its lessons put into practice, a demonstration of the *cræft*, skill, or virtue of the reader; the labor of reading becomes the labor of performance, without which virtue is nonexistent.[20] This labor lies at the heart of the *Boethius*, its exemplarity, and its concern with self-care.

The *exemplum*—a (usually) short narrative told to illustrate a moral or ethical point—had a well-established history in the Christian West by the Anglo-Saxon period, and saw consistent use throughout the Middle Ages. *Exempla* were not static narratives; rather, they were almost infinitely flexible, able to stretch to accommodate nearly any meaning with which a writer or reader wished to invest them. Such flexibility allowed the creation of a corpus of "moralized" or moralizing literature that embraced commentaries on classical poetry, bestiaries, homilies, and incidental incorporations of illustrative tales in longer works such as the *Consolation*. Although modern readers take a dim view of such literature, these works were composed not necessarily for preaching but as part of a hermeneutic exercise that began in analysis of the text and concluded in analysis the

[17] Stock, *Augustine the Reader*, 17.

[18] Augustine, *De doctrina Christiana*, ed. J. Martin, CCSL 32 (Turnhout: Brepols, 1962). "Porro si et credit et diligit, bene agendo et praeceptis morum bonorum obtemperando efficit, ut etiam speret se ad id quod diligit esse uenturum. Itaque tria haec sunt, quibus et scientia omnis et prophetia militat, fides, spes, caritas" [If he both believes and loves, then through good words and close attention to the precepts of good morals, he then hopes that he may attain that which he loves. And thus these are the three things which all knowledge and all prophecy must serve: faith, hope, and love, 1.37].

[19] Scott DeGregorio, "Texts, Topoi, and the Self: A Reading of Alfredian Spirituality," *Early Medieval Europe* 13 (2005): 79–96, at 93–94.

[20] For the use of *cræft* in the *Boethius*, see Peter Clemoes, "King Alfred's Debt to Vernacular Poetry: The Evidence of *ellen* and *cræft*," in *Words, Texts and Manuscripts: Studies in Anglo-Saxon Culture Presented to Helmut Gneuss on the Occasion of His Sixty-Fifth Birthday*, ed. Michael Korhammer (Cambridge: D.S. Brewer, 1992), 213–38; and especially Nicole Guenther Discenza, "Power, Skill, and Virtue in the Old English *Boethius*," *ASE* 26 (1997): 81–108, esp. 100–7.

self.[21] Ideally, this self-transformation would be both intellectual and ethical: the reader would enact the lessons of the text in his life by reforming his behavior. As such, the exemplary narrative takes its strength and authority from its expectation that readers can be persuaded to act according to its prescripts, to "emulate the protagonist's moral success, or avoid his or her moral failure. It persuades by conveying a sense of communal identity with its moral lesson."[22] As a story, the *exemplum* is intimately related to the premise behind Walter Benjamin's "The Storyteller," in which all stories bear the trace of earlier communicative goals, and the art of storytelling is "the art of exchanging experience," the "popular exercise of practical wisdom."[23] The *exemplum* is, as Ricoeur argues of narrative in general, "the first laboratory of moral judgment," where the "reciprocal constitution of action and self" is played out and made available for assessment.[24] Because of this, Ricoeur writes, "there is no ethically neutral narrative. Literature is a vast laboratory in which we experiment with estimations, evaluations, and judgments of approval and condemnation through which narrativity serves as a propaedeutic to ethics."[25] That is, because the ethical freight of the text had to be picked up by the reader—interpreted and then enacted—the *exemplum* is free to assume different meanings, depending on the needs of the text employing it. In the Liberius *exemplum* discussed below, the ethical thrust of the narrative focuses on self-governance and its relationship to ethical behavior, as well as to virtuous self-formation. I look at the historical *exemplum* for its opposition of the virtuous counselor and the wicked tyrant in order to elucidate the simultaneously interior and exterior nature of vice and virtue, as well as to provide an example of how narrative condenses the vast body of knowledge and philosophical demands of the *Boethius* at large.

Classical History in Anglo-Saxon England

In *Solomon and Saturn I*, Saturn boasts to Solomon that he has "boca onbyrged þurh gebregdstafas / larcræftas onlocen Libia and Greca, / swylce eac istoriam Indea rices" [tasted books through the literary arts and unlocked the lore of Libya and Greece, and also the history of the Indian realm, ll. 3–5]. Saturn's breadth of

[21] For an extensive discussion of memory, ethics, and medieval reading practices, see Mary J. Carruthers, *The Book of Memory: A Study of Memory in Medieval Culture* (Cambridge: Cambridge University Press, 1990), esp. 156–88.

[22] Larry Scanlon, *Narrative, Authority, and Power: The Medieval Exemplum and the Chaucerian Tradition* (Cambridge: Cambridge University Press, 1994), 35.

[23] Walter Benjamin, "The Storyteller," in *Illuminations*, trans. Harry Zohn (New York: Schocken Books, 1969), 89–103.

[24] Ricoeur, *Oneself as Another*, 118.

[25] Ricoeur, *Oneself as Another*, 118.

reading, for what it's worth, has exposed him to books from all the lands across the sea—that is to "ıglanda eallra . . . boca" [the books of all the islands, ll. 2–3], including those of the ancient seats of learning, Libya and Greece, and those even further afield, from India.[26] This breadth, nevertheless, may lack depth; Saturn's use of *onbyrged* [tasted] points to a superficiality of knowledge, an inability (or unwillingness) to engage in proper interpretive practice.[27] In terms of subject, Saturn's taste in genre runs toward the secular and the ancient; the Latin word [*h*]*istoria* links Saturn explicitly with knowledge of a classical, long-distant past. And yet, Saturn admits, for all his reading, "Swylce ic næfre on eallum þam fyrngewrytum findan ne mihte / soðe samnode" [I could never find, in all these ancient writings, truth gathered together, ll. 8–9a].

Saturn's dilemma perhaps reflects the fact that in Anglo-Saxon England, classical history was not studied for its own sake, if it was studied at all; like Saturn, an Anglo-Saxon scholar might aspire to only a taste of classical sources—and not from the smorgasbord-like excess to which Saturn had access.[28] Still, while Anglo-Saxons were not actively engaged in the reproduction of classical texts, the histories of the pagans (like their literature) were ripe for reinterpretation and reappropriation when Anglo-Saxons could get hold of them. Rather than being studied for its own sake, history was instead harnessed to grammar, rhetoric, and ultimately the interpretation of Scripture; as such, it was subordinated to the liberal arts proper and to the histories of the Scriptures and Christianity in the writings of patristic authors who helped shape Anglo-Saxon intellectual traditions. In *De doctrina Christiana*, Augustine permits the study of the classics, including history, "even the kind that is learned apart from the Church at school"; nevertheless, the "faithful and useful narration" of historical

---

[26] Elliott van Kirk Dobbie, ed., *The Anglo-Saxon Minor Poems*, ASPR 6 (New York: Columbia University Press, 1942), 31.

[27] Jonathan Wilcox, "Eating Books: The Consumption of Learning in the Old English Poetic *Solomon and Saturn*," *ANQ* 4 (1991): 115–18.

[28] See Michael Lapidge, "The Study of Latin Texts in Late Anglo-Saxon England (I): The Evidence of Latin Glosses," in *Latin and the Vernacular Languages in Anglo-Saxon England*, ed. Nicholas Brooks (Leicester: University of Leicester Press, 1982), 99–140. In *The Anglo-Saxon Library* (Oxford: Oxford University Press, 2006), Lapidge finds no evidence for important prose historians such as Caesar, Livy, or Tacitus, and he believes that the lack of manuscript evidence, in conjunction with the lack of citation, quotation, or significant reference, bears out the absence of these authors from the holdings of Anglo-Saxon libraries (68). In her source study of the Old English *Orosius*, Janet M. Bately suggests that the translator may have acquired his information through additions to the manuscript used for the translation; she details the translator's apparent ignorance of some portions of the texts from which he quotes, as reflected in his occasionally awkward use of material and his interpretations of some events that indicate independence from the original sources; see *The Old English Orosius*, EETS s.s. 6 (Oxford: Oxford University Press, 1980), lxi–lxii.

writing was ancillary to the proper study of Scripture and the pursuit of higher truth.[29] The value of classical history is also apparent in Isidore of Seville's *Etymologiae*: although it is subordinated to grammar, history is that which is "worthy of remembrance," and histories are called *monumenta* "because they grant a remembrance (*memoria*) of deeds that have been done."[30] Moreover, the relationship between historical narrative and memory is individual and collective, with history linking contemporary readers to their own collective past and to larger histories of Christian salvation—links that could be both genealogical and spiritual.[31] In the dedicatory preface of the *Historia Ecclesiastica*, Bede claimed that he wrote the history of the English church for history's sake and for the edification of Ceolwulf of Northumbria and his subjects:

> Siue enim historia de bonis bona referat, ad imitandum bonum auditor sollicitus instigatur; seu mala commemoret de prauis, nihilominus religiosus ac pius auditor siue lector deuitando quod noxium est ac peruersum, ipse sollertius ad exsequenda ea quae bona ac Deo digna esse cognouerit, accenditur.[32]
>
> [Should history tell of good men and their good estate, the thoughtful listener is spurred on to imitate the good; should it record the evil ends of wicked men, no less effectually the devout and earnest listener or reader is kindled to eschew what is harmful and perverse, and himself with greater

---

[29] Augustine, *De doctrina Christiana*, 2.28.42-44. For the translation, see *Teaching Christianity*, trans. Edmund Hill, OSB (Hyde Park, NY: New City Press, 1996).

[30] In full, the corresponding Latin reads "Haec disciplina ad Grammaticam pertinent, quia quidquid dignum memoria est litteris mandatur. Historiae autem ideo monumenta dicuntur, eo quod memoriam tribuant rerum gestarum," as edited in Isidore of Seville, *Etymologiarum siue originum libri xx*, ed. W.M. Lindsay, 2 vols. (Oxford: Clarendon Press, 1911; repr. 1989), 1.41.2; the translation is from Stephen A. Barney, W.J. Lewis, J.A. Beach, and Oliver Berghof, *The Etymologies of Isidore of Sevilee* (Cambridge: Cambridge University Press, 2006), 67.

[31] See, e.g., Daniel Anlezark, "Sceaf, Japheth, and the Origins of the Anglo-Saxons," *ASE* 31 (2002): 13–46, at 15. Anlezark also points out that texts such as the West-Saxon royal genealogy locate and legitimize mythical heroes and euhemerized gods within divine history. The Anglo-Saxons had a keen interest in correspondences between biblical history and their own; see Nicholas Howe, "The Landscape of Anglo-Saxon England: Inherited, Invented, Imagined," in *Inventing Medieval Landscapes: Sense of Place in Western Europe*, ed. John Howe and Michael Wolfe (Gainesville: University of Florida Press, 2002), 91–112, at 92–93.

[32] Bede, *Historia ecclesiastica gentis Anglorum*, ed. and trans. André Crépin, Michael Lapidge, Pierre Monat, and Philippe Robin, 3 vols., Sources chrétiennes 489 (Paris: Cerf, 2005), 1:94–96. The translation is taken from Bede, *The Ecclesiastical History of the English People*, ed. and trans. Bertram Colgrave and R.A.B. Mynors (Oxford: Clarendon Press, 1969), 3.

> care to pursue those things which he has learned to be good and pleasing in the sight of God.]

The exemplary possibilities of historical figures, although in this case applied to the history of the Northumbrians and the English church, extended to revisions of classical history. As Rita Copeland writes, *enarratio*, the study of and commentary on text, "revalorizes a world of ancient literature and learning" from which medieval intellectual traditions had become estranged and "comes to represent a dynamic, re-creative engagement with the language of tradition."[33] Like rhetoric, which was itself linked to ethics by early medieval thinkers, history provided both a model for and impetus to living a righteous life.[34] The reinterpretation of classical history and its reinscription with Christian ethics was not meant purely for the acquisition of knowledge but also for the acquisition of proper behavior and, ultimately, salvation.[35] In the same way that genealogies or national histories allowed their readers to acquire a sense of familial or group identity linked to blood or affinity, the "moral utility of history"[36] allowed readers to acquire a sort of ethical history or genealogy—a past full of philosophical forebears whose actions could be learned from and imitated, or avoided. In the *Boethius*, one such example is the figure of Liberius in Chapter 16.

Explicating the Liberius *Exemplum*

Philosophia's inclusion of the philosopher Zeno's defiance of Nearchus (or Diomedon) in Book 2, Prose 6 (2p6) provides a fitting parallel to Boethius's own situation. Like Boethius, Zeno of Elea failed in his attempt to bring down a tyrant; unlike Boethius, Zeno used his capture and interrogation to thwart his captor's attempts to force him into capitulation:

> Cum liberum quendam uirum suppliciis se tyrannus adacturum putaret ut aduersum se factae coniurationis conscios proderet, linguam ille momordit

---

[33] Rita Copeland, *Rhetoric, Hermeneutics, and Translation in the Middle Ages: Academic Traditions and Vernacular Texts* (Cambridge: Cambridge University Press, 1991), 61. For examples of "rewritten" history in the *Boethius*, see Malcolm Godden, "The Anglo-Saxons and the Goths: Rewriting the Sack of Rome," *ASE* 31 (2002): 47–68; and Paul E. Szarmach, "Alfred's Nero," in *Source of Wisdom: Old English and Early Medieval Latin Studies in Honour of Thomas D. Hill*, ed. Charles Wright, Frederick M. Biggs, and Thomas N. Hall (Toronto: University of Toronto Press, 2007), 47–67.

[34] Copeland, *Rhetoric, Hermeneutics, and Translation*, 59.

[35] Rosamond McKitterick, *History and Memory in the Carolingian World* (Cambridge: Cambridge University Press, 2004), 276. See also Nicole Guenther Discenza's essay in this volume.

[36] Roger Ray, "Bede's *vera lex historiae*," *Speculum* 55 (1980): 1–21, at 11.

> atque abscidit et in os tyranni saeuientis abiecit; ita cruciatus, quos putabat tyrannus materiam crudelitatis, uir sapiens fecit esse uirtutis. (2p6.23–28)
>
> [When the tyrant [Nearchus] thought to force a certain free man [Zeno], by tortures, into revealing his co-conspirators in a plot against him, he [Zeno] bit through his tongue and tore it off and threw it in the face of the cruel tyrant; these torments, which the tyrant thought an opportunity for cruelty, the wise man turned into an opportunity for courage.]

Boethius elides the account of Zeno's bravery in Diogenes Laertius's *Lives of Eminent Philosophers*. Of special note is his omission of Diogenes's assertion that the philosopher's defiance roused the citizens of Elea to stone Nearchus to death.[37] Instead, the *exemplum* is couched within Philosophia's discourse on the inherent freedom of the rational mind and the inability of outside forces to affect it: "Num quicquam libero imperabis animo?" Philosophia asks, "Num mentem firma sibi ratione cohaerentem de statu propriae quietis amouebis?" [Can you impose anything on a free mind? Can you sway a mind united in itself by firm reason from its place of tranquility?]. Her answer—composed of the serial *exempla* of Zeno, Busiris (put to death by Hercules), and the Roman commander Regulus (put in chains by a Carthaginian general)—argues that the only power that can be exercised by one person over another is that exercised either on the body ("in solum corpus") or its possessions ("fortuna," both at 2p6.6). As such, Philosophia concludes, how can political power—and the attendant force it can exercise on the bodies involved in it—be considered true power "when a man cannot guarantee that another does not force on him what he can force on others?" (2p6.12). The conclusion of 2p6 leads into Philosophia's further disquisition on the attraction political power holds for evil men and the inability of political power to confer happiness. The cruelty of the tyrant, representing the oppressiveness of the state, is a reiteration of the cruelty of Theodoric, further advancing Philosophia's argument that good is found in the individual, rather than in kingdoms at large.[38]

Unlike Boethius, the Anglo-Saxon translator was not writing from prison; he was writing for a group of people who were ostensibly very much involved (perhaps, in his view, over-involved) in the vagaries of political life, and his modifications to the Latin suggest that he executed the translation for the edification of royal counselors or students who aspired to high secular office—individuals who had little interest in the abandonment of the world.[39] Such divergence from

---

[37] Diogenes Laertius, *Lives of Eminent Philosophers*, ed. and trans. R.A. Hicks, 2 vols. (Cambridge, MA: Harvard University Press, 1925), 9.5.27. Diogenes provides varying accounts of Zeno's actions: in one, he bites off Nearchus's ear; in another, Nearchus's nose; the version inherited by later writers, including Plutarch and eventually Boethius, is, according to Diogenes, the most widely accepted version.

[38] For more background on this, see Godden, "Rewriting the Sack of Rome," 64.

[39] Godden, "The Player-King," 137–50.

Boethius's fatalistic disinterest is evident in Wisdom's handling of the Zeno/Liberius *exemplum*. As in the *Consolation*, the story comes up as part of Wisdom's discussion of the weakness of the body compared to the mind and the (relatively feeble) ability of one man to harm another in his body, while the mind remains invulnerable. However, the exemplum reads somewhat differently in the *Boethius*:

> Ne nan mon ne mæg þam gesceadwisan mode gederian, ne him gedon þæt hit ne sie þæt þæt hit bið. Þæt is swiðe sweotol to ongitanne be sumum Romaniscum æþelinge se wæs haten [Liberius], se was to manegum witum geworht forþam þe he nolde meldian on his geferan þe mid him sieredon ymbe þone cyning þe hie ær mid unrihte gewunnen [hæfde]. Þa he þa beforan þone graman cyning gelæd wæs and he hine het secgan hwæt his geferan wæron þe mid him ymbe sieredon, þa forceaw he his tungan and wearp hine þærmid on þæt neb foran. Forþam hit geweарð þæt þam wisan men com to lofe and to wyrðscipe þæt se unrihtwisa cyning him teohhode to wite. (16.58–68)

> [No man can harm the rational mind, nor cause it not to be what it is. This can be understood very clearly [in the example of] a certain Roman nobleman who was called Liberius, who was condemned to many torments because he refused to give up his companions who were conspiring with him against the king who had unjustly opposed them. Then, when he was led before the king, and he [the king] ordered him to say who his allies were, the ones who were in league with him, he bit off his tongue and threw it at the king's face. Because of this the wise man acquired praise and honor, such that the wicked king dragged him off to torture.]

The passage does not expand significantly on the Latin; much of the additional length is accounted for by the translator's decision to repeat the mention of the co-conspirators. There are two differences, however, that I would like to draw out a little more: the Old English's specific interest in the rational mind; and the lesson the translator draws from the *exemplum*. Whereas Boethius uses Zeno as the model philosopher, who turns his torment into an "opportunity for courage," the Anglo-Saxon translator gives Liberius the chance to exercise virtue and win fame and honor for doing it.[40] In a text meant for the secular elite, the mention

[40] The two versions of the *Boethius* diverge here. Godden and Irvine emend the B-manuscript, Oxford, Bodleian Library, MS Bodley 180's reading of the name *tiberius* to *Liberius*, which is given in the C-text, London, British Library MS Cotton Otho A.vi; see the apparatus for the B-text in their edition, *Old English Boethius* 1:273. In their commentary on the passage, Godden and Irvine suggest that the translator was working from a Latin copy of the *Consolation* in which the adjective *liberum* was corrupted to *liberium*, or that "the author may have decided to use his imagination, and some license, and to recast the story to fit the context of Boethius's own supposed situation and the

of *lof*, praise or honor, may have been meant as the carrot, the bribe to convince skeptical young noblemen that virtue had rewards other than itself. However, it also emphasizes the public nature of the virtuous act; whereas Philosophia's Zeno is presumably satisfied with the virtue of biting off his tongue rather than ratting out his colleagues, Wisdom's Liberius has the additional satisfaction of knowing that his virtuous act will redound to his greater glory.

The Old English supplies the name Liberius, possibly a result of the translator's misunderstanding of the adjective *liberum* to be a proper name. Then again, the translator may have been reading the passage allegorically, which would have given him the idea to name his hero "the free man," whose virtue, in allowing him access to power, is opposed to—and conquers—the anonymous tyrant who is enslaved to vice. As such, referring to the protagonist as Liberius could be, rather than a mistake, a deliberate interpretive move. The *Consolation* refers to its hero as a "free man" but does not otherwise indicate his status; it is possible that, in the *Boethius*, the designation of Liberius as *æþeling* is both a clarification of his social position and a further gloss on *liberum quendam*, although only one late gloss suggests a possible equivalence between *liber* and *æþel*.[41] More importantly, naming Liberius—which the *Consolation* does not do—gives the character a particularity, a form of quasi-historical detail; he is not the nameless *liber quidam* of the *Consolation* but a named figure, one whose name (as will be seen) is remembered not because of his hunger for glory but because of the courage that comes from a mind in full possession of itself—a courage that will be rewarded with the fame it does not seek.

The rational and inviolate mind that cannot be harmed and the public nature of virtue bookend the Anglo-Saxon *exemplum* as two unified halves of a wholly realized human being. Behind these two images—the mind that thinks and the body that acts—lies one of the objectives of the *Boethius*, which is geared toward the recovery of that rational mind and, consequently, the recovery of the individual's ability to act virtuously. I want first to discuss the nature of the *gescead-wis mod*, the rational mind, by discussing what sorts of things are found in the interior and what parts of "inwardness" were important to the *Boethius*-translator's conception of what constituted fully realized selfhood. I will then turn to a consideration of how virtuous behavior is cultivated and how the publication of

preceding references to the resistance of the Roman kings" (*Old English Boethius* 2:311). I have adopted their emendation, but see further discussion below for the translator's interpretation of the character.

[41] In his edition of the Antwerp-London glossaries, Lowell Kindschi gives "freobearn [uel] æþelborene cild" as a gloss for *liberi*; see "The Latin-Old English Glossaries in Plantin-Moretus MS. 32 and British Museum MS. Additional 32246" (Ph.D. diss., Stanford University, 1955), l. 185. The glossary dates from the late eleventh century. Godden and Irvine, *Old English Boethius*, 2:311, also note that "several [medieval copies of the DCP] gloss *liberum* as *nobilem, generosum*."

one's interiority is a necessary corollary to virtuous interiority. Last I will discuss how the example of Liberius is an instance of textual transformation—that is, the deliberate alteration of narrative and ethical aim—in service of the *Boethius*-translator's larger interest in radically transforming and reorienting the interiority of his readers.

The lessons of the *Boethius* begin on the inside. Reflexivity in the *Boethius* consists in recovering truths of Mod's existence: namely, properties that allow it to be a discerning and aware entity. This reflexivity is what allows the mind to become an agent, and it is that transformation to which the second half of the Liberius *exemplum* attends. Wisdom's urgings of self-scrutiny all have as their goal the recovery of innate properties; answers are found within a deeper, more stable self, an inalienable property not subject to the whims of fate or fortune. The self is not the body, which can be harmed, become ill, and otherwise be subject to the various cruelties of the world. Rather, it is partially constituted by a set of internal possessions of which one can never be deprived except through one's own forgetfulness. Such properties are not only permanent; they are also divine. Whoever exercises the faculties of perception, memory, and rational desire also possesses the *similitudo Dei* that Wisdom tells Mod is the closest a created thing can come to being like its creator:

> Hwæt, ge þonne þeah hwæthwega godcundlices on eowerre saule habbað, þæt is andgit and gemynd and se gesceadwislica willa . . . Se þe þonne þas ðreo hæfð, þonne hæfð he his sceoppendes onlicnesse, swa forð swa swa ænegu gesceaft furemest mæg hiere sceppendes onlicnesse habban. (14.76–80)
>
> [Indeed, you have something divine in your soul, that is perception and memory and rational will . . . He who has these three things has his creator's likeness, as much as any creature can have its creator's likeness.]

Behind the *gesceadwislic mod* of Liberius, then, lies a set of assumptions about what the mind is and how the mind is best actualized. The rational mind is the mind that has reflected on itself, that knows what it is and knows that it is autonomous in the sense that it cannot be made subject to the power of others. Wisdom's numerous disquisitions on the nature of *anweald*, and who possesses the earthly semblance of it and who possesses the truth of it, make that clear. Liberius, as a wise man and philosopher—and as a free man—stands as the embodiment of such rationality.

The reflexivity of the *Boethius* is, on one hand, a natural operation of the soul; on the other, it is a learned and difficult process. The natural impulse of the soul is toward contemplation and self-involvement: like a wheel, the soul turns or revolves within itself, contemplating its own nature, a movement that is as natural and perpetual as the orbit of heaven (33.225–228). Despite this apparent instinctiveness, such contemplation does not seem to be wholly involuntary;

self-reflection necessitates the rejection of the external world and its preoccupations: one has to *want* to do it. By actively rejecting external distractions and the "uselessness" that has preoccupied him—a rejection that must be willed—the individual can perceive his own *ingeþanc*—his own interiority, the disposition of his thoughts, the divinity that his mind resembles. The self is never automatically or fully aware of either itself or the full potential of its faculties; instead, these potentialities must be brought out by the exercise of reflection and memory. The soul has the "kernel (*corn*) of righteousness in it," something that inheres in every individual, but the seed is latent; it requires reflection and study in order to grow (35.16–22). The seed of memory has the potential to flower into virtue, as the self begins to recover knowledge of the things that make it human—not biographical knowledge, or knowledge of its own particularity, but the tools of reason, perception, and memory that allow it to evaluate itself insofar as it is able to do so.

The second part of the *exemplum* of Liberius has to do with the worldly life, concerned as it is with the acquisition of praise—or, specifically, the virtuous behavior for which Liberius earns praise and honor. Acting virtuously involved not only the simple fact of action but included the motivations that lay behind the performance, and motivations were necessarily open to scrutiny. As mentioned earlier, it is possible that the *Boethius*-translator's modification to the Latin to have Liberius earn "praise and honor" instead of merely using his self-mutilation as "an occasion for virtue" was meant to appeal to secular readers who would either be unimpressed by virtue for its own sake or who would have appreciated Liberius' willingness to embrace pain in the face of overwhelming odds. Alongside the more immediate appeal to the sensibilities of its readers, the *exemplum* of Liberius also seeks to render the reader "benivolum, attentum, et docilem" to additional instruction, namely, the possibility that truly praiseworthy action is driven by motivations that are properly oriented.[42]

[42] Making readers "willing, attentive, and docile" before they receive instruction was one of the purposes of narrative in classical and medieval rhetoric. The Latin phrase is Cicero's, from his *De inventione* I.15.20, although Cicero uses it to describe the purpose of the *exordium* rather than *narratio*. Elsewhere in the *Boethius*, Wisdom points to the need for examples and narrative in conveying difficult lessons, e.g., in the discussion of the utility of the *ealde lease spell*, the "old lying tale" of myths and fables: "Þeah we nu scylon manega and mistlice bisna and bispell reccan, þeah hangað ure mod ealne weg on þam ðe we æfterspiriað. Ne fo we na on þa bisena and on bispell for þara leasana spella lufan, ac forþam þe we woldan mid gebeacnian þa soðfæstnesse, and woldon þæt hit wurde to nytte þam geherendon" [Although we must now include many and various examples and parables, nevertheless our mind always remains fixed on the [topics] which we pursue. We do not include these examples and parables out of love for these fables, but because we wish to point to the truth with them, and want it to become useful to those who hear it, 35.185–89]. For further discussion of the rhetorical ends of the *Boethius*'s old lying fables, see Nicole Guenther Discenza's essay in this volume.

The Liberius *exemplum* and its immediate context point to the *Boethius*'s association of self-awareness with self-care, the obligation incumbent on each individual to decipher his inner thoughts. This approach to self-examination was first advanced by John Cassian in the fifth century and by Gregory the Great in the sixth; their hermeneutics of the self takes the shape of the decipherment of inner thoughts, driven by the understanding that "there is something hidden in ourselves and that we are always in a self-illusion which hides the secret."[43] Such fragmentation lies at the heart of the *Boethius*, in which the mind is first estranged from itself—ignorant of what it is—and can only gradually come to a fuller understanding of itself. The Liberius *exemplum* is particularly appropriate to Mod's own circumstances and biography; indeed, it anticipates Mod's failed attempt to make an *exemplum* of himself, which comes about one hundred lines later.

Unlike the philosopher, who attains *anweald* without looking for it, Mod seems to have wanted authority for the sole purpose of not being forgotten:

> þæt mine cræftas and anweald ne wurde [forgiten] and forholen, forþam ælc cræft and ælc anweald bið sona forealdod and forswugod, gif he bið buton wisdome . . . Þæt is nu hraþost to secganne þæt ic wilnode weorðfullice to libbanne þa hwile þe ic lifede, and æfter minum life þam monnum to læfanne [þe] æfter me wæren [min] gemynd on godum weorccum
>
> [so that my virtues and authority should not be forgotten and concealed, because every virtue and power is soon diminished and silenced, if it is without wisdom . . . To say it briefly, I desired to live honorably while I lived, and after my life leave my memory in good works to the men who came after me, 17.21-23 and 17.26-28]

Wisdom asserts that Mod's motivations are problematic because, in his drive for praise, he has abandoned "the virtues of your *ingeðonc* and your perception and your reason"—the interior properties that make self-reflection possible.[44] Unlike Liberius, whose fame is a sort of bonus over and above virtue, Mod is guilty of making fame the primary motivator of his actions. Virtue may be its own reward, but fame (in Mod's opinion) pays better. The correction of this misapprehension has to come through rigorous self-examination, the excavation of the drives and impulses that lie deep beneath the shell of his justification. Instead of chasing after good repute, Mod must learn to look for his reward in himself and in God.

Wisdom's disquisition on the questionable good of praise is rather lengthy. By the end of it, however, Mod is ready to hear more. Wisdom remarks, "Ic ongeat sona, þa ðu swa wel geswugodest and swa lustlice geherdest mine lare, þæt ðu woldest mid inneweardan mode hi ongiton and smeagean" [I quickly perceived, when you kept silent and heard my teaching so happily, that you desired

[43] Foucault, *Technologies of the Self*, 46.

[44] Translating 2p7.19: "conscientiae uirtutisque."

to perceive and contemplate it with your inward mind, 22.17–19]. Wisdom's use of the *inneweard mod* suggests that Wisdom's words are acting at that deep level, down beneath the surface, where technologies or hermeneutics of the self must dig. Rigorous self-examination in this context, however, does not seem to lead to the self-abnegation Foucault associates with early Christian monastic or confessional practices—that is, the equation of disclosing the self with the self's simultaneous dissolution—but, rather, leads to a transformation that is closer to the Stoic antecedents which shaped much of the *Consolation*'s own philosophy. That is, Stoic self-examination and judgment were part of a mental and physical discipline that showed the way to self-knowledge by superimposing truth about the self through memory, through memorization of codes of conduct.[45] In the case of misdirected Mod, the way to self-knowledge has to be repaved with *better* intentions, to be guided by his effort to know himself.

The example of Liberius contains, in miniature, the larger philosophical and ethical issues of the *Boethius*, as well as an illustration of how philosophy had deeply practical and immediate concerns; it was as much *praxis* as *theoria*, if not more so. In Liberius, Wisdom finds a figure who is grounded within himself and whose very name demonstrates the freedom associated with the liberation of the mind from the vice that restrains it from pursuing virtue. Moreover, the infliction of pain on Liberius's body—pain inflicted by Liberius himself—demonstrates the extent to which the rational mind disregards the pain of the flesh and knows it to be secondary to its own integrity. The praise Liberius achieves is not the goal toward which he strives but, rather, the result of his being an *exemplum* of probity in the face of tyranny, the man who (as Louis and Charles vow to do) places truth above loyalty to a despot. Mod, who still misunderstands himself, is clearly meant to take Liberius as his example, to recognize that praise should be considered a secondary good, contingent upon actions that arise from a mind that is driven first (and only) by the pursuit of virtue. There may also be a subtle reminder not to go down the paths of Nearchus, Bosiris, and Regulus. The *exempla* of the latter two tyrants—Bosiris is drowned in the Nile by Hercules (the translator adds "swiðe ryhte be Godes dome," suggesting that Bosiris's punishment is divinely appointed) and Regulus is captured by the Africans he has only just finished slaughtering—further demonstrate the uselessness of possessing power that does not have a firm foundation in virtue and wisdom. Taken together, the *exempla* of Liberius and the humiliated Bosiris and Regulus serve to introduce—perhaps to sweeten—the next part of Wisdom's lesson, on the fickleness of power and praise, and later, the questionable good of wealth.

---

[45] Foucault, *Technologies of the Self*, 32–35. In the *Boethius*, the ethical *exempla* may also be geared toward forcing Mod to reconsider his motivations, which are admittedly murky; along with providing codes of behavior, they provide Mod the opportunity to assess himself and his motives, insofar as is possible.

The history of opposition to tyrants, grounded in the named (if pseudonymous) figure of Liberius, provides a pattern of action for Mod—a pattern that, like the Strasbourg Oaths, propels him into a subjectivity formed, relentlessly, by questions of politics and loyalty, where the rational self stands opposed, not subordinate, to the ruler and the power the ruler wields over politically subject bodies. It is, in part, the beginnings of understanding a self not rooted in the body—or a self that is not dependent on the body but is defined by its ability to exercise actions upon itself when no other agent can—that makes such a gesture possible in the *Boethius*. This self is not transcendent; like *The Seafarer*, which resolves the crisis of selfhood in the transcendence of the afterlife,[46] the *Boethius* seems to make the same promise—even as it, like *The Seafarer*, defers fulfillment: Wisdom informs Mod that he must, after rising high above the tempests of the world with Wisdom's help, return again "for godra manna þearfe" [for the need of good men, 7.100–105].

The translator's reinterpretation of the Liberius/Zeno *exemplum*—like Boethius's own reinterpretation—serves not only as "a simple propaedeutic . . . but a comprehensive, recuperative inquiry" into classical writing.[47] It also functions as an enjoinment to self-correction and to action, an enjoinment articulated most emphatically by Wisdom in the closing chapters of the *Boethius* when he commands *wisan menn* [wise men] to follow in the footsteps of their predecessors and exhorts the lazy to inquire, learn, and emulate: "gað ealle on þone weg þe eow lærað þa foremæran bisna þara godena gumena and þæra weorðgeornena wera þe ar eow wæron" [stay on the path which the famous examples of good men and of those men eager for honor, those who were before you, have shown to you, 40.61–63].[48] The good examples left by Mod's ethical ancestors provide him, and the reader, with an ethical history and ethical lineage that demand both self-scrutiny and performance of virtue—the creation of one's own *exempla*—in the reformation and care of the self.

---

46 Matto, "Technologies of the *Sylf*," 166.

47 Copeland, *Rhetoric, Hermeneutics, and Translation in the Middle Ages*, 57.

48 The *Boethius*, 40.61–71, amplifies on the last four lines of 4m7; instead of attempting to pick its way through a host of mythological references—Agamemnon, Odysseus, and Hercules—the translator expatiates on the necessity of following the good examples (*bisna*) set by virtuous (and unnamed) historical figures who, because they strove after honor and attained it, "wuniað nu ofer þam tunglum on ecre eadignesse for heora godum weorcum" [now dwell beyond the stars in eternal blessedness because of their good works, 40.70–71]. For further discussion of this passage, see Paul E. Szarmach's essay in this volume.

Finding Consolation at the End of the Millennium

Erica Weaver

On August 10, 974, a group of craftsmen put aside the new bell they had been casting for the church tower at Fleury, finished their work for the day, and went to bed.[1] Over the door, they left a candle burning, giving in to their tired limbs and forgetting to extinguish the flame, which consumed the remaining wax, sputtered, and caught the nearby beds on fire. Soon the monastery was ablaze, the wind threatening to spread the conflagration to the nearby granary. Monks hurried into the church of St. Benedict, wrapped the relics in the altar cloth, and ran out again. And then the wind died. The ash settled. And the church, guesthouse, kitchen, and bakery emerged unsinged.

Other buildings had not been so lucky.[2] Aimoin, a monk of Fleury and chronicler of the *Miracula Sancti Benedicti*, recorded his horror at the massive destruction, describing how "totus ignium globus . . . cælum versus cacumen extendit" [the entire ball of flames . . . stretched from the grass to the sky].[3] Throughout his account he notes his subsequent wonder at the astonishing survival of certain monastic buildings, observing, "Non solum autem illa, quæ sexaginta et non multo amplius ab ipsa distabat passibus, verum universa intra ambitum castri admodum arctum constructa ædificia . . . horreo . . . incorrupta mansere ab ignibus" [I tremble that . . . not only that one, which was standing no more than

[1] A nearly contemporary account is preserved in *Miracula Sancti Benedicti* [hereafter *MSB*] II.9, edited by Eugène de Certain in *Les miracles de Saint-Benoît écrits par Adrevald, Aimoin, André, Raoul Tortaire et Hugues de Sainte Marie* (Paris: Renouard, 1858), 110–12, from which I derive my summary of the night's events. All translations of the *MSB* are my own. Whereas Book I of the *MSB* had been written by Adrevald, Books II and III were written by Aimoin. Both were monks at Fleury. For a general overview of the text, see Alexandre Vidier, *L'historiographie à Saint-Benoît-sur-Loire et les Miracles de Saint Benoît* (Paris: Picard, 1965).

[2] For further information about the fire, see Jean Mabillon, *Annales Ordinis Sancti Benedicti*, 6 vols. (Paris, 1703–39), 3:632.

[3] *MSB* II.9.

sixty paces from there, but truly all the buildings arranged in the exceedingly contracted orbit of the monastery, remained intact from the flames].[4] This miraculous intervention befits an account of Saint Benedict's miracles, but Aimoin's version of the fire elides the devastating reality of the events: certain key buildings left in rubble and the objects inside of them destroyed. In a more personal account in a letter to Dunstan (Archbishop of Canterbury, 970-78), Lantfred of Fleury describes "hoc coenobium Floriacense quo nunc degit—utpote igne consumptum" [the monastery of Fleury where he now lives, having been destroyed by fire], suggesting that the ravages of the fire were much more extensive than Aimoin let on.[5] But what were these buildings, which had been reduced to ashes, and what was lost along with them?

Drawing from the accounts of various fires in the *Miracula*, Elizabeth Dachowski provides an overview of the layout of late tenth-century Fleury, which helps in reconstructing exactly what was lost when the monastery burned:

> The monastic complex was enclosed by a wall and included two churches: Notre Dame, which held the relics of St. Benedict, and Saint-Pierre. Buildings serving the needs of the monks crowded together within the enclosure: a dormitory, a kitchen, a bake house, a guesthouse, and several granaries. Other passages in the *Miracula* mention a sacristy, a library, a treasury, an infirmary, and various other buildings.[6]

These were cramped quarters, connected by narrow passageways that made fires both quick to spread and difficult to stop in the "ambitum castri admodum arctum" [exceedingly contracted orbit of the monastery], as Aimoin described the

---

4 *MSB* II.9.

5 The letter is edited and translated by Michael Lapidge in his *The Cult of St. Swithun*, Winchester Studies 4.ii (Oxford: Clarendon Press, 2003), 220–21.

6 Elizabeth Dachowski, *First Among Abbots: The Career of Abbo of Fleury* (Washington: Catholic University of America Press, 2008), 42. For more on the layout of the monastery at this time, see Robert-Henri Bautier, "Le monastère et les églises de Fleury-sur-Loire sous les abbatiats d'Abbon, de Gauzlin et d'Arnaud (988–1032)," *Mémoires de la Société nationale des antiquaires de France* 9.4 (1968): 71–156, at 87–88. The treasury, at least, largely postdates the 974 fire. In fact, a fireproof treasury chamber was built by Abbo's treasurer, Gauzfred, toward the end of the century, as recorded by Aimoin in his *Vita sancti Abbonis*, ed. and trans. Robert-Henri Bautier and Gillette Labory, in *L'Abbaye de Fleury en l'an mil* (Paris: Centre national de la recherche scientifique, 2004), chap. 15. For an in-depth discussion of Carolingian monastic architecture and the famous Plan of St. Gall, see Walter Horn and Ernest Born, *The Plant of St-Gall: A Study of the Architecture and Economy of, and Life in, a Paradigmatic Carolingian Monastery*, 3 vols. (Berkeley: University of California Press, 1982); and Werner Jacobsen, *Der Klosterplan von St. Gallen und die Karolingische Architektur: Entwicklung und Wandel von Form und Bedeutung im fränkischen Kirchenbau zwischen 751 und 840* (Berlin: Deutscher Verlag für Kunstwissenschaft, 1992).

arrangement of the buildings. Indeed, flames would also ravage Fleury in 1002, 1005, and 1026.[7] In 974, the church of Saint-Pierre was incinerated, along with at least a part of Fleury's prized monastic library.

Founded ca. 640, Fleury—or Saint-Benoît-sur-Loire, as it is sometimes called—flourished in the ninth and tenth centuries, exerting a strong influence on Anglo-Saxon England.[8] As Marco Mostert has rightly observed, "the intellectual riches of the abbey, its library and scriptorium were bound to attract almost as much as the treasure which rested in its crypt": the translated bones of Saint Benedict himself, the father of Western monasticism, brought to Fleury from the ruins of Monte Cassino.[9] Fleury became a hotbed of intellectual activity during the Carolingian Renaissance, and D.A. Bullough notes that "[e]nough books, orthodox or unusual, survived the sacking of the monastery by Northmen in 865 or were acquired in the next seventy years to give it an enviable reputation as a centre of learning" during the tenth-century Benedictine revival movements, which sought to renew—and standardize—monastic life in England and on the Continent.[10]

---

[7] Thomas Head outlines the successive responses in his *Hagiography and the Cult of Saints: The Diocese of Orléans, 800–1200* (Cambridge: Cambridge University Press, 1990), 158–60.

[8] For a general history, see G. Chenesseau, *L'abbaye de Fleury à Saint-Benoît-sur-Loire: Son histoire – ses institutions – ses églises* (Paris: Beauchesne, 1931); and J. Laporte, "Fleury," in *Dictionnaire d'Histoire et de Géographie Ecclésiastiques* 17 (Paris: Letouzey et Ané, 1969), cols. 441–76. On the cross-Channel culture, see Marco Mostert, "Relations between Fleury and England," in *England and the Continent in the Tenth Century: Studies in Honor of Wilhelm Levison (1876–1947)*, ed. David Rollason, Conrad Leyser, and Hannah Williams (Turnhout: Brepols, 2010), 185–208; and Stéphane Lebecq and Alban Gautier, "Routeways Between England and the Continent in the Tenth Century," in the same volume, 17–34.

[9] Marco Mostert, *The Political Theology of Abbo of Fleury: A Study of the Ideas about Society and Law of the Tenth-Century Monastic Reform Movement* (Hilversum: Uitgeverij Verloren, 1987), 23. In his survey of the extant manuscripts, Mostert has noted that 634 manuscripts still survive from Fleury—currently housed in more than sixty-one libraries in nine countries. For the full catalog, see his *The Library of Fleury: A Provisional List of Manuscripts* (Hilversum: Verloren Publishers, 1989). For an account of the later fates of the books in Fleury's library, see Frère Denis, "Les anciens manuscrits de Fleury," *Bulletin trimestriel de la Société archéologique et historique de l'Orléanais* 2 (1962): 266–81, esp. 267–70. See also Bernhard Bischoff, *Manuscripts and Libraries in the Age of Charlemagne*, trans. Michael M. Gorman (Cambridge: Cambridge University Press, 2007); and Élisabeth Pellegrin, "La tradition des textes classiques latins à l'abbaye de Fleury-sur-Loire," *Revue d'histoire des textes* 14 (1986): 155–67.

[10] D.A. Bullough, "The Continental Background of the Reform," in *Tenth-Century Studies: Essays in Commemoration of the Millennium of the Council of Winchester and Regularis Concordia*, ed. David Parsons (London: Phillimore & Co., 1975), 20–36. Fleury had been reformed by Odo of Cluny ca. 930 and forged close ties with Winchester

In deference to Fleury's importance as a Benedictine monastery, books were sent as gifts from English houses. As Adrian Papahagi has noted, these bookish tributes included the Winchester Benedictional (Paris, Bibliothèque nationale de France, MS lat. 987), the Winchcombe Sacramentary (Orléans, Bibliothèque municipale, MS 127 (105)), and an elaborate copy of Boethius's *Consolation of Philosophy* (Paris, Bibliothèque nationale de France, MS lat. 6401), which was produced at the very end of the tenth century at Christ Church, Canterbury.[11] These books and other productions and acquisitions enlarged Fleury's library, increasing its renown as an expansive collection, stocked with classical and contemporary texts alike. Unfortunately, however, when the bell-makers left their candle burning in 974, some of those holdings were lost to the flames.

This essay explores the possibility that one of the burned books was a copy of Boethius's *Consolation*. In the previous centuries, Fleury's famed library and scriptorium had served as a fount of Boethian knowledge. Four early manuscripts of the *Consolation* have been ascribed to the Fleury scriptorium.[12] Moreover, Papahagi has demonstrated that the *Consolation* seems to have been completely unknown or, at least, unread until the late eighth or early ninth century, when it resurfaced, likely in the vicinity of Fleury.[13] Indeed, Papahagi argues that

in the following decades, influencing certain customs in the *Regularis concordia*. Indeed, monks from Fleury were present when the *Regularis concordia* was drafted at the Council of Winchester (ca. 970). For an overview of what the Council of Winchester and related efforts sought to accomplish, see Christopher A. Jones, "Ælfric and the Limits of 'Benedictine Reform,'" in *A Companion to Ælfric*, ed. Hugh Magennis and Mary Swan (Leiden: Brill, 2009), 67-108.

[11] Papahagi, "An Anglo-Saxon Palimpsest from Fleury: Orléans, Bibliothèque Municipale, MS 342 (290)," in *Palimpsests and the Literary Imagination of Medieval England: Collected Essays*, ed. Leo Carruthers, Raeleen Chai-Elsholz, and Tatjana Silec (New York: Palgrave MacMillan, 2011), 21–34, at 24.

[12] These manuscripts are Orleans, Bibliothèque Municipale (Médiathèque), MS 270; [Rome], Città del Vaticano, Biblioteca Apostolica Vaticana, MS Vat. lat. 3363; Bern, Burgerbibliothek, MS 179; and Florence, Biblioteca Laurenziana Medicea, MS Pluteo XIV.15. All date to the late ninth or early tenth century. For further details, see Fabio Troncarelli, *Boethiana Aetas: Modelli grafici e fortuna manoscritta della "Consolatio philosophiae" tra IX e XII secolo* (Alessandria: Edizioni dell'Orso, 1987); and Mostert, *The Library of Fleury*. By the ninth century, MS Pluteo XIV.15 had traveled to Fulda, where it was in the possession of Lupus of Ferrières. MS Vat. lat. 3363 had made its way to England by the late ninth or early tenth century.

[13] Adrian Papahagi, "The Transmission of Boethius' *De Consolatione Philosophiae* in the Carolingian Age," *Medium Ævum* 78.1 (2009): 1–15, repr. in his *Boethiana Medievala: A Collection of Studies on the Early Medieval Fortune of Boethius' Consolation of Philosophy* (Bucharest: Zeta Books, 2010), 15–36. Papahagi has also proposed Fleury as a potential point of origin for Christianizing commentary on the *Consolation* in "Destin et providence (*Consolatio Philosophiae* IV.pr.6): la réception du néoplatonisme Boécien

Theodulf of Orléans (ca. 750/60–821), rather than Alcuin of York, revived and disseminated the *Consolation* in the Carolingian era, shifting the initial center of interest from Aachen to Orléans, roughly eighty-five miles south of Paris.[14] From the Loire valley—and specifically Fleury—Papahagi speculates that the text "may have been transmitted first to the other monastic centres in the area (Tours, Ferrières, Auxerre), then to other continental centres (Laon, Reims, Corbie, Aachen, Cologne, and especially St. Gall and Reichenau). Some time around 900, the *Consolation* reached Anglo-Saxon England."[15] Papahagi has suggested that Fleury remains an essential starting point for understanding the reception of Boethius in England. In this essay, I suggest that England, too, could have offered Boethius back to Fleury.

Tracing a path between the *Carmen de libero arbitrio* [Poem about free will] (a Boethian poem written at Winchester in 971–72) and a copy of the *Consolation* produced at Fleury in the last quarter of the tenth century (now known as Paris, Bibliothèque nationale de France, MS lat. 6401), this essay proposes that a manuscript of Boethius's *Consolation* made the return journey from England to Fleury at the end of the millennium. Boethius's Anglo-Saxon reception usually centers on the translation of the *Consolation* into English in the beginning of the tenth century.[16] In turning instead to the end of the century and to the beginning of the next, this essay demonstrates the resiliency of Boethius's dialectical

---

à l'époque carolingienne," *Académie des Inscriptions de Belles-lettres: Comptes rendus des séances de l'année* (2006): 671–711, at 700–702.

[14] The rediscovery of the *Consolation* has been traditionally attributed to Alcuin of York, who became a leading scholar in the Carolingian Renaissance. See, for instance, Courcelle, *La Consolation de Philosophie dans la tradition littéraire: Antécedents et posterité de Boèce* (Paris: Études Augustiniennes, 1967), 335: "A la fin du VIIIe siècle, Alcuin semble avoir découvert la *Consolation*" [At the end of the eighth century, Alcuin seems to have discovered the *Consolation*]. See also: Diane Bolton, "The Study of the *Consolation of Philosophy* in Anglo-Saxon England," *Archives d'histoire doctrinale et littéraire du Moyen Âge* 44 (1977): 22–78, at 34; M.T. Gibson, "Boethius in the Carolingian schools," *TRHS* (1982): 43–56, at 45; and Malcolm Godden, "Alfred, Asser, and Boethius," in *Latin Learning and English Lore: Studies in Anglo-Saxon Literature for Michael Lapidge*, ed. Katherine O'Brien O'Keefe and Andy Orchard (Toronto: University of Toronto Press, 2005), 326–48, at 327. See also Godden, "King Alfred and the Boethius Industry," in *Making Sense: Constructing Meaning in Early English*, ed. Antonette diPaulo Healey and Kevin Kiernan, Publications of the Dictionary of Old English 7 (Toronto: University of Toronto Press, 2007), 116–38.

[15] Adrian Papahagi, *Boethiana Medievala*, 36.

[16] For an overview of this translation project, see the first five essays in this volume. The translation project is usually dated to 890-930. For further details, see Malcolm Godden and Susan Irvine, ed. and trans., *The Old English Boethius*, 2 vols. (Oxford: Oxford University Press, 2009), 1:146.

original—and claims another, more diffuse Boethian tradition for later Anglo-Saxon England.

Accounts of Boethius's *Consolation* at the end of the millenium are often no more than passing references to Ælfric of Eynsham's perusal of the all-prose *Boethius* or to his patron, the nobleman Æthelweard ("the Fat"), who ascribed the Old English translation to King Alfred in his *Chronicon*, a dense Latin rendition of the Anglo-Saxon *Chronicle*. Even here, Æthelweard's allusion to the *Consolation* consists of only three words, as he slips "Boetii lachrymosus . . . motus" [the tearful passion of Boethius] into a speedy commendation of Alfred's broader translation program.[17] However, Rosalind C. Love notes that "[f]ourteen complete or fragmentary copies of the *Consolation* survive which were certainly written or annotated in southern England in the late tenth and early eleventh centuries," testifying to the scholarly energy dedicated to Boethius's original long after it had been translated into English.[18] Moreover, ties between England and Francia remained strong, with manuscripts and readers crisscrossing the Channel.

There has been a lot of recent interest in the Continental background to the English monastic reforms of the tenth century, but comparatively little work has been done on the cross-Channel exchanges of the following decades. Scholars lament the incursions of ransacking Norsemen throughout the period and the devastating arrival of the Normans in 1066, but Anglo-Saxon literary culture is typically understood to be almost entirely Insular. It may and frequently *does* incorporate Norse elements, but only in those places where Vikings had settled or when a Danish king ascended to the throne—or so the usual narrative goes. And yet, letters, books, and readers moved back and forth between England and greater Europe, not only in the international circles of Boniface (ca. 675–754) and Alcuin (ca. 735–804) but also to and from Alfred's court (r. 871–899) and the courts of his successors. Elizabeth Tyler and Thomas O'Donnell have begun to trace some of the networks tying regional centers in southern England to those in Lotharingia and Francia in the first half of the eleventh century, but the broader field is only just emerging and remains a promising area for further inquiry.[19] I retrace one speculative cross-Channel network here.

---

[17] Æthelweard, *Chronicon*, iv. 3, in *The Chronicle of Æthelweard*, ed. A. Campbell (London, 1962), p. 50.

[18] Rosalind C. Love, "Latin Commentaries on Boethius's *Consolation of Philosophy*," in *A Companion to Alfred the Great*, ed. Paul Szarmach and Nicole Guenther Discenza (Leiden: Brill, 2015), 83–111, at 95.

[19] Thomas O'Donnell, "Some Unexamined Geographies and Social Networks of English Literary Culture," paper co-authored with Elizabeth M. Tyler and delivered at the Harvard University English Medieval Colloquium (Cambridge, MA, Feb. 2015). See also Tyler's *England in Europe: English Royal Women and Literary Patronage, c. 1000-c. 1150* (Toronto: University of Toronto Press, 2017). I have begun mapping similarly transnational networks of exchange in a social network analysis of late Anglo-Saxon letters.

Though other English scribes seem to have been active in the Loire valley,[20] this story begins and ends with one Lantfred, a Frankish monk, who trained at and later returned to Fleury but who acquired English scribal skills during a stint at Old Minster, Winchester.[21] Michael Lapidge summarizes his career as follows:

> As a monk of Fleury he was probably invited to Winchester by Æthelwold [Bishop of Winchester, 963–84]. While at Winchester he advised Æthelwold on the monastic customs of Fleury (advice which Æthelwold incorporated in the *Regularis Concordia*), composed his *Translatio et miracula S. Swithuni*, and composed a small corpus of Latin poetry as well. He was on intimate terms with Archbishop Dunstan as well as with Osgar [Abbot of Abingdon], whom he had perhaps met on an earlier occasion while Osgar was studying at Fleury. He was in the habit of making periodic trips to the Continent, and on one of these trips he decided to remain at Fleury. Whether he ever returned to England, or when or where he died, is unknown.[22]

Just as Fleury had been a Carolingian center of learning and monastic reform, so was Winchester "the supreme intellectual center in late Anglo-Saxon England," as Mechthild Gretsch has observed—and a likely site of Boethian interest.[23]

The city had provided a sort of headquarters for King Alfred's program of translation and textual transmission at the end of the ninth century and, as a leading center of book production, remained at the heart of political and intellectual life into the eleventh.[24] Unsurprisingly, Winchester and Fleury maintained

Early iterations of this project, provisionally entitled *Mapping Anglo-Saxon Letters*, have been presented at Digital Britain: New Approaches to the Early Middle Ages (Harvard University, March 2016) and Seafaring: An Early Medieval Conference on the Islands of the North Atlantic (University of Denver, Nov. 2016).

[20] Jean Vezin has identified an English scribe named Leofnoth who was active at Fleury during the later tenth century in "Leofnoth: un scribe anglais à Saint-Benoît-sur-Loire," in *Codices Manuscripti* 4 (1977): 109–20. Malcolm Parkes has also proposed an Anglo-Saxon scribe active at Fleury at this time in "An Anglo-Saxon Text at Fleury: The Manuscript of the Leiden Riddle," in his *Scribes, Scripts and Readers: Studies in the Communication, Presentation, and Dissemination of Medieval Texts* (London: Hambledon Press, 1991), 263–74.

[21] For more on the localization of Lantfred to Fleury, see Lapidge, *Cult of St. Swithun*, 218–24.

[22] Lapdige, *Cult of St. Swithun*, 224.

[23] Mechthild Gretsch, "Late Old English (899–1066)," in *A Companion to the History of the English Language*, ed. Haruko Momma and Michael Matto (Chichester: Wiley-Blackwell, 2008), 165–71, at 169.

[24] A copy of *Bald's Leechbook* remained in Winchester, as did the Old English *Orosius*; the *Pastoral Care*; and, potentially, both the *Boethius* and the *Bede*.

close ties throughout the period.[25] Æthelwold himself had wished to study there, but King Edgar (r. 959–75) prevented him from going abroad, prompting the future Bishop of Winchester to send his pupil Osgar to the Continent in his stead. Fueled in part by the subsequent influx of books and scholars from Fleury and from Corbie, whence Æthelwold invited monks to teach plainchant, under Æthelwold's bishopric Winchester boasted a famous cathedral school—one that would give rise to two of late Anglo-Saxon England's most important authors: Ælfric of Eynsham in prose and Wulfstan Cantor in poetry.[26]

In the midst of this vibrant textual community, at Winchester in 972–74, Lantfred wrote the *Translatio et miracula Sancti Swithuni*, the first account of Saint Swithun's life and miracles, which would be subsequently reworked as the cult grew around Winchester's new patron saint, a theretofore little-known ninth-century bishop.[27] Sometime between 975 and 984 (after the death of Edgar and before the death of Æthelwold), Lantfred then penned a Latin poem in elegiac couplets, which Michael Lapidge has titled the *Carmen de libero arbitrio*.[28]

---

[25] For further information on the close ties between reformed monasteries in England and Fleury, see Dachowski, *First Among Abbots*, 39; Papahagi, *Boethiana Medievalia*, 28; Jean-Marie Berland, "L'influence de l'abbaye de Fleury-sur-Loire en Bretagne et dans les Îles Britanniques du Xe au XIIe siècle," in *Questions d'histoire de Bretagne*, vol. 2 of *Actes du 107e Congrès National des Sociétés Savantes: Brest, 1982, Section de Philologie et d'Histoire jusqu'à 1610* (Brest: C.T.H.S., 1984), 275–99; and Mostert, "Relations between Fleury and England."

[26] By some estimates, one-sixth of all surviving Old English literature may be ascribed to Ælfric. Though less prolific than his partner in prose, Wulfstan Cantor penned some shorter works along with the *Narratio metrica de Sancti Swithuno*, which is itself the longest surviving Anglo-Latin poem from before the Conquest and a *tour de force* of poetic virtuosity and political negotiation. It may be found in Lapidge, *Cult of St. Swithun*, 335–549. For further background on Wulfstan's career and surviving works, see the introduction in Michael Lapidge and Michael Winterbottom, eds. and trans., *Wulfstan of Winchester: The Life of St. Aethelwold* (Oxford: Clarendon Press, 1991).

[27] Lantfred of Winchester, *Translatio et miracula S. Swithuni*, in *The Cult of St. Swithun*, 252–333. Together, the early lives of Swithun constitute an *opus geminatum*. For a reading of these lives as a possible parallel to the two versions of the Old English *Boethius*, see my "Hybrid Forms: Translating Boethius in Anglo-Saxon England," *Anglo-Saxon England* 45 (2016): 213-38, esp. 227-28. On the *opus geminatum*, see also Susan Irvine's essay in this volume. For a new account of the later development of the Winchester Lives of Swithun, see Jennifer A. Lorden, "Landscapes of Devotion: The Settings of St Swithun's Early *Vitae*," *Anglo-Saxon England* 45 (2016): 285-309.

[28] For further details and an edition and translation of the poem, see Michael Lapidge, "Three Latin Poems from Æthelwold's School at Winchester," *Anglo-Saxon England* 1 (1972): 85–137; repr. in his *Anglo-Latin Literature, 900–1066* (London: Hambledon Press, 1993), 225–78, from which I quote here. The poem is contained in a late tenth-century Winchester manuscript (Cambridge, University Library, MS Kk. 5. 34, fols. 75v–80r) along with two other poems, all headed by an intriguing rubric:

This poem comprises a philosophical exploration of free will and divine foreknowledge, providence and predestination.[29] At the center is Boethius's famous image of the man on the watchtower: "Rex sapiens residet specula sublimis in alta / providus ac pugnax, praepete mente sagax" [A wise king sits elevated on a high watch-tower, / provident and militant, sagacious because of his alert mind, ll. 69–70].[30] This vision of God looking down from above as a spectator who assigns rewards and punishments according to our merits closely resembles Boethius's king on a watchtower from Book 4, Prose 6 (4p6).[31] Indeed, as Lapidge argues, "a reading of the *de consolatione philosophiae* was the inspiration of the questioning of the *de libero arbitrio*," and "much of the vocabulary used in Boethius's discussion of providence is also found in the Anglo-Latin poem."[32] Soon after completing this work, Lantfred re-crossed the Channel and returned to Fleury.

Feeling the lack of some books destroyed in the 974 fire, Lantfred then wrote to Dunstan, requesting that some manuscripts previously in his possession at Winchester might be returned to him at Fleury:

"versus .L. de quodam superbo" [verses of Lantfred about a certain proud person], which speaks more to the content of the first poem, a lively debate between a schoolmaster and his student. Building on a suggestion made by Henry Bradshaw, Michael Lapidge, "Three Latin Poems," has demonstrated that this "L" may be reasonably identified with Lantfred. Lantfred likewise signs himself as ".L." in his letter to Dunstan. For a more recent treatment of the poem, see Aaron J. Kleist's chapter on "Lantfred of Winchester and the *Carmen de libero arbitrio*," in his *Striving with Grace: Views of Free Will in Anglo-Saxon England* (Toronto: University of Toronto Press, 2008), 121–44. See also James P. Carley, "Two Pre-Conquest Manuscripts from Glastonbury Abbey," *Anglo-Saxon England* 16 (1987): 197–212, esp. 204–12. For further discussion of the manuscript, see Helmut Gneuss and Michael Lapidge, *Anglo-Saxon Manuscripts: A Bibliographical Handlist of Manuscripts and Manuscript Fragments Written or Owned in England up to 1100* (Toronto: University of Toronto Press, 2014), 41–42, at 28.

[29] Though Katherine O'Brien O'Keeffe does not treat the *Carmen de libero arbitrio* specifically, her masterful discussion of the tensions inherent in expressions of individual agency in late Anglo-Saxon monastic contexts provides a helpful backdrop for Lantfred's Boethian verses. See her *Stealing Obedience: Narratives of Agency and Identity in Later Anglo-Saxon England* (Toronto: University of Toronto Press, 2012). See also Hilary Fox's essay in this volume on free will and self-formation in the Old English *Boethius*.

[30] *Carmen de libero arbitrio*, ed. and trans. Lapidge, "Three Latin Poems," 266–77, at 270.

[31] Lapidge even notes a possible verbal echo of Boethius's God "qui cum ex alta providentiae specula respexit, quid unicuique conveniat agnoscit et quod convenire novit accomodat" [who looks forth from the high watchtower of providence, recognizes what is suited to each, and assigns what he knows to be fitting, 4p6] in Lantfred's metaphor of "quos novit iustos convocat ad superos" [[God] summons those whom he knows to be just to him on high, l. 18]. Lapidge, "Three Latin Poems," 244.

[32] Lapidge, "Three Latin Poems," 243.

> Dein vestrum flagitat benivolentiam ut commentum Flori quod habet domnus abbas Oscarus, et alios libellos qui habentur Wintonie quique conda[m] sui fuerunt, [nunc] pro Christi nomine illi reddere faciatis, quoniam qui[dem] hoc coenobium Floriacense quo nunc degit—utpote igne [consumptum]—his caret codicellis.
>
> [Furthermore, he entreats your good will in asking that you arrange to have returned to him the commentary of Florus which Abbot Osgar now has, as well as other books which are at Winchester and which formerly belonged to him, since in fact the monastery of Fleury where he now lives, having been destroyed by fire, lacks these manuscripts.][33]

Though it now survives only in London, British Library, MS Cotton Tiberius A. xv (s. xi^1), the letter has been dated to 974 × 984—and thus to roughly the same window as the *Carmen de libero arbitrio*.[34] This was clearly a period of Boethian interest for Lantfred, but why should we presume that one of the books he entreated Dunstan to send might have been a copy of Boethius's *Consolation*?

Other copies may have been closer at hand, but Lantfred and Dunstan were friends, and he may have regretted leaving his personal copy behind. Both the *Carmen de libero arbitrio* and the *Translatio et miracula* had testified to his intense interest and strong familiarity with Boethius's prosimetrum. In the *Translatio et miracula*, for instance, Lantfred quotes from 2p1, 3p9, 5p3, and 5p6.[35] I propose that he had brought a favored copy of the *Consolation* with him to Winchester, left it there on the assumption that the text would be available to him at Fleury, and then requested its return after the 974 fire destroyed the Fleurisian copy—or copies—of Boethius's work.

A potential candidate survives for this Wintonian *Consolation*: Paris, Bibliothèque nationale de France, MS lat. 6401, produced in the last quarter of the tenth century.[36] Its provenance has not previously been wholly understood. Rosalind Love notes that the manuscript was either "taken from England to Fleury,

33 Lapidge, *Cult of St. Swithun*, 220–21.

34 For more details, see Lapidge, *Cult of St. Swithun*, 220–22. Likely copied at Canterbury, this manuscript preserves a notable collection of early correspondence, including many of Alcuin's letters. See Gneuss and Lapidge, *Anglo-Saxon Manuscripts*, 293–94 (MS 368).

35 For verbal echoes, see Lapidge, *Cult of St. Swithun*, 252–333, notes 17, 140, 180, 203, and 268.

36 This manuscript is Gneuss and Lapidge, *Anglo-Saxon Manuscripts*, 639–40 (MS 886). In addition to Boethius's *Consolation* and *De institutione arithmetica*, it also includes copies of Radulf of Liège and Ragimbold of Cologne's letters on geometry, the *Epitaphium Gauzlini*, and an incomplete copy of *Oratio animae poenitentis*.

or more likely written at Fleury by an English scribe."[37] Both possibilities seem tenable here. MS lat. 6401 could be one of the missing books Lantfred wanted back—either after he himself had brought it to England from Fleury ca. 970 or after he had copied or else newly acquired it during his stay in Winchester. It could similarly be a copy, which Lantfred made soon after his return from England and the subsequent return of his books. Either way, MS lat. 6401 was at Fleury by the beginning of the eleventh century.

The manuscript has puzzled art historians, since it seems to have been produced by one person who was both Frankish and English. Paleographically, it must have been copied by someone trained on the Continent. Nevertheless, MS lat. 6401 contains three miniatures in the same hand, which must have been drawn by an Englishman—and, in particular, an Englishman trained at one of the early Benedictine Reform monasteries that practiced the bold style of drawing now known as the trademark mode of the Winchester School.[38] Lantfred himself provides a likely contender: a French monk who first took orders at Fleury, later studied under Æthelwold at Winchester, and finally returned to his own monastery, bringing with him the Winchester style and demonstrating just how far-reaching Winchester's mode of artistic production really was. Furthermore, MS lat. 6401 was copied (possibly at Fleury) in the last quarter of the tenth century—either just before Lantfred left for England, during his time at Winchester, or just when he would have completed his stint with Æthelwold's *familia* and returned to his home monastery.

There are other surviving manuscripts of mixed Fleurisian and English provenance. To provide but one example with striking similarities to MS lat. 6401, Michael Lapidge notes that London, British Library, MS Harley 2506 "was evidently written at Fleury, but . . . was decorated by a late tenth-century English illustrator, either at Fleury or in England"—perhaps providing another

[37] Rosalind C. Love, "The Latin Commentaries on Boethius's *De consolatione philosophiae* from the 9th to the 11th Centuries," in *A Companion to Boethius in the Middle Ages*, ed. Noel Harold Kaylor, Jr., and Philip Edward Phillips (Leiden: Brill, 2012), 75–134, at 93.

[38] See, for instance, Francis Wormald, *English Drawings of the Tenth and Eleventh Centuries* (London: Faber and Faber, 1952), 70, 73–74, and plates 13 and 14; and her "The 'Winchester School' before St. Æthelwold," in *England before the Conquest: Studies in Primary Sources Presented to Dorothy Whitelock*, ed. Peter Clemoes and Katherine Hughes (London: Cambridge University Press, 1971), 305–13, at 311–12. The heavy borders and rich ornamentation of Æthelwold's Benedictional (London, British Library, Add. MS 49598) are striking examples of the Winchester style. For further details, see Robert Deshman, *The Benedictional of Æthelwold* (Princeton: Princeton University Press, 1995); and *The Benedictional of St. Æthelwold: A Masterpiece of Anglo-Saxon Art, A Facsimile*, ed. Andrew Prescott (London: British Library, 2002).

example of a Lantfredian cross-Channel production.[39] In his illuminating study of Fleurisian palimpsests, Papahagi notes that "the exchanges of books and the circulation of scribes and illuminators between English centers and Fleury were so multifarious that it is not uncommon to find drawings by English masters in books copied at Fleury by local monks."[40] But Lantfred himself bears witness to at least one scribe-cum-illustrator who was *both* English master and local monk, suggesting a cross-Channel intelligentsia who deftly blended English and Frankish styles in their pursuit of beautiful books.

Furthermore, Lantfred had written the *Carmen de libero arbitrio* between 975 and 984, so the poem and the letter requesting the return of his books were likely written in close succession, as noted above. Aaron J. Kleist has narrowed the window for the composition of the poem even further, concluding that "the *Carmen* may be dated to the term of Æthelwold's bishopric and perhaps specifically to Lantfred's residence at Winchester around the years 970–3."[41] In speculating that one of the books whose return Lantfred most desired was Boethius's *Consolation*, this essay offers a slightly more linear order of events, all presumably taking place sometime between 970 and 985, with ca. 1000 as the *terminus ante quem*. First, Lantfred wrote his Boethian verses in Winchester; he then returned to Fleury shortly thereafter, either arriving just before the fire or just after and learning of its destruction only upon his arrival; noting the absence of consolatory reading matter, he quickly dashed off the letter, requesting the return of his copy of the *Consolation*; and finally, he may have made an additional copy shortly thereafter, with MS lat. 6401 preserving either the returned book or the new copy.

If this entire series of events were completed by the close of the 970s, then a Lantfredian *Consolation*—that is, a later manuscript modeled on MS lat. 6401, if not MS lat. 6401 itself—could have returned to England in the possession of Abbo, who sojourned to Ramsey Abbey in 985–87 before becoming abbot of Fleury upon his return to the Continent.[42] At Ramsey, Abbo served as a men-

---

[39] Michael Lapidge, *The Anglo-Saxon Library* (Oxford: Oxford University Press, 2006), 51. See also Lapidge, *Anglo-Latin Literature*, 2:399; and Fritz Saxl and Hans Meier, *Catalogue of Astronomical and Mythological Illuminated Manuscripts*, vol. 1: *Manuscripts in English Libraries*, ed. Harry Bober (London: Warburg Institute, 1953), 157–60.

[40] Papahagi, "Anglo-Saxon Palimpsest," 24.

[41] Kleist, *Striving with Grace*, 127.

[42] Oswald, Archbishop of York (971–72), had only founded Ramsey Abbey in 966, using Fleury, where he had previously spent two years, as a model. Abbo's stay there further cemented the relationship between the two monasteries. For further background on the connections between Fleury and England at this time, see L. Gougaud, "Les relations de l'abbaye de Fleury-sur-Loire avec la Bretagne armoricaine et les îles Britanniques (X et XI siècles)," *Mémoires de la Société d'Histoire et d'Archéologie de Bretagne* 3 (1992): 3–30; and L. Donnat, "Recherches sur l'influence de Fleury au Xe siècle," in *Études ligériennes d'histoire et d'archéologie médiévales: Mémoires et exposés présentés à la*

tor to Byrhtferth (ca. 970–ca. 1020), who himself became an important figure in late Anglo-Saxon letters. Moreover, while teaching and pursuing his own studies there, Abbo must have imported a large number of his own books to supplement the small fenland library, since Ramsey Abbey had only been recently established.[43] Lapidge has demonstrated that one of these books was likely a copy of the *Consolation*, from which Abbo quotes in his *Explanatio in calculo Victorii*, written during those years.[44] In those works produced just before and during his time at Ramsey, Abbo draws from a wide range of Boethius's writings, including, of course, the *Consolation* as well as the *Commentarii in Ciceronis Topica*, *De institutione arithmetica*, *De institutione musica*, *De syllogismo hypothetico*, *In librum Aristotelis Perihermeneias commentarii editio duplex*, *In Porphyrii Isagogen commentorum editio duplex*, and the *Opuscula sacra*.[45]

Abbo was evidently devoted to Boethius's oeuvre, shared some of it with his students, and would have felt the lack of Boethian works in the library at Fleury. Indeed, he likely introduced both his English students, including Byrhtferth, and his Frankish students and subordinates (perhaps including Lantfred, whom he may have taught as a young monk) to the *Consolation*.[46] Lapidge has demonstrated that Byrhtferth himself "shows comprehensive knowledge of Boethius' *De consolatione Philosophiae*, which he quotes throughout his hagiographical and historical writings"—an interest perhaps cultivated by his early teacher, Abbo.[47] Of course Lantfred was heavily invested in the text as well and likely returned to it throughout his life.

Semaine d'études médiévales de Saint-Benoît-sur-Loire du 3 au 10 juillet 1969, ed. R. Loui (Auxerre: 1975), 165–74. For background on Abbo's time at Ramsey, see A.M. Pedan's introduction to his *Abbo of Fleury and Ramsey: Commentary on the Calculus of Victorius of Aquitaine* (Oxford: Oxford University Press, 2003), esp. xi–xv. For a near-contemporary biography, see Aimoinus Floriacensis, *Vita s. Abbonis*, in J.-P. Migne, Patrologia Cursus Completus, Series Latina, 139 (Paris, 1880).

43 For an overview of Abbo's trip to Ramsey, see Mostert, "Le séjour d'Abbon de Fleury à Ramsey," *Bibliothèque de l'École des Chartres* 144 (1986): 199–208.

44 Lapidge, *Anglo-Saxon Library*, 242–43.

45 Lapidge, *Anglo-Saxon Library*, 242–43.

46 Pierre Riché includes Lantfred in a list of Abbo's students in his *Abbon de Fleury: Un moine savant et combatif (vers 950–1004)* (Turnhout: Brepols, 2004), 74–76. For an anlaysis of Boethian influence on an additional student-teacher monastic network, see Ann W. Astell's essay in this volume.

47 Lapidge, *Anglo-Saxon Library*, 125. Lapidge argues that "as authors of the later Anglo-Saxon period such as Byrhtferth begin to attract more scholarly attention, the role played by Abbo of Fleury in the establishment and redirection of scientific learning will come into clearer focus." Lapidge, *Anglo-Saxon Library*, 126.

Warmest thanks to Christopher Baswell, who first introduced me to Boethius's *Consolation*; to Roberta Frank, who taught me that there were two Old English versions; and to Patricia Dailey, who showed me how to read them all.

In short, Boethius's *Consolation* may have arrived in England from the Continent ca. 900, but it did not stop moving—its travels demonstrating not only the interconnectivity of late tenth-century monastic centers in England and on the Continent but also the enduring importance of Boethius's Latin text in the century after it was first translated into English. This brief essay has mapped two potential trajectories of manuscripts crossing and re-crossing the Channel between the sibling houses of Fleury and Winchester, but much of the circulation history remains to be written. Amidst fires and floods, new foundations and moldering old libraries, Boethius's masterpiece continued to circulate and inspire, whether at Winchester, at Fleury, at Ramsey, or beyond.

Consolations of Friendship: The Augustinian Reception of Boethius in Twelfth-Century England

Ann W. Astell

> Vobis tamen etiam illud inspiciendum est, an ex beati Augustini scriptis semina rationum aliquos in nos venientia fructus extulerint.
>
> Boethius, *On the Trinity*[1]

Friends and talk of friendship abound in works in the later Boethian tradition. One might think, for example, of Pandarus's conversations with a languishing Troilus in Chaucer's *Troilus and Criseyde*, or of Ami, the Lover's Friend by name in the *Roman de la Rose*. Friendship is, however, a far from obvious theme in Boethius's *Consolation of Philosophy* itself. Indeed, the Latin vocabulary of *amicitia* does not even appear in Joachim Gruber's index of that work's key terms.[2] Gruber mentions the existence of a "Freundesmotiv" only once, in a brief comment on Book 2, Prose 8, line 6 (2p8.6).[3] How is this discrepancy between source and tradition to be explained?

In this essay I point to three twelfth-century English monks—Lawrence of Durham (1114–54); Lawrence's famous student, Aelred of Rievaulx (1110–66); and Aelred's scribe, friend, and hagiographer, Walter Daniel. Lawrence composed a Boethian prosimetrum entitled *Consolatio de morte amici sui* [*Consolation on the Death of a Friend*] (ca. 1141), and Abbot Aelred composed an influential

[1] Boethius, *De Trinitate*, in *The Theological Tractates*, ed. and trans. H.F. Stewart, E.K. Rand, and S.J. Tester, Loeb Classical Library 74 (Cambridge, MA: Harvard University Press, 1973). "You must however examine whether the seeds of argument sown in my mind by St. Augustine's writings have borne fruit" (Prologue, ll. 31–33).

[2] For the index, see Joachim Gruber, *Kommentar zu Boethius, De Consolatione Philosophiae, Texte und Kommentare* (New York: Walter de Gruyter, 1978), 429–40.

[3] Commenting on 2p8.6 of the *Consolation*: "amicorum . . . fidelium mentes," Gruber, *Kommentar zu Boethius*, notes: "Das Freundesmotiv war bereits 1 m.1, 21 angeklungen" (225).

dialogue, *De spiritali amicitia* [*On Spiritual Friendship*] (1164–65), in which he remembers two departed friends. Aelred laments the death of his friend Simon in *Speculum caritatis* [*The Mirror of Charity*] (ca. 1142), and Walter Daniel offers his own lament for Aelred at the end of his *Vita Aelredi* (1167). Reading Boethius's *Consolation* alongside Saint Augustine's *Confessions*, these writers (I argue) brought to the fore the "Freundesmotiv" latent in the sixth-century dialogue. It is no accident, then, that Jean de Meun (ca. 1240–ca. 1305), the poet of the *Roman de la Rose*, translated both Boethius's *Consolation of Philosophy* (ca. 525) and Aelred of Rievaulx's *De spiritali amicitia* into the vernacular.[4]

Augustine's *Confessions* as Boethian Source

The interweaving of Augustinian and Boethian influences in the medieval Anglo-Latin texts under examination here is complex and admittedly elusive—so much so that my probing of them necessarily replays in a different, analogical key the longstanding scholarly debate about Boethius's own reception of Augustine's *Confessions* in *The Consolation of Philosophy*. Scholars generally agree that Boethius knew Augustine's writings, although (as Seth Lerer notes) "the only clear reference to Augustine by name appears in a theological tractate," in the preface to Boethius's *De Trinitate*.[5] The individual words and phrases in the *Consolation* in which Joachim Gruber, among many others, has heard echoes of Augustine's Neoplatonic doctrine in *Confessions*—Book 7, for instance—may also derive from other sources known to Boethius.[6] Traditional source studies falter, and yet an Augustinian impression remains. When Henry Chadwick at once imagines "Augustine standing behind the . . . shoulder" of Boethius and denies the Christian character of the *Consolation*,[7] he exhibits what Antonio Donato calls a disappointed "Augustinian expectation" of Boethius's work.[8]

---

[4] Jean de Meun, *La consolation de la philosophie de Boéce*, ed. Isabelle Bétemps, Michel Guéret-Laferté, Nicolas Lenoir, et al. (Mont-Saint-Aignan: Presses Universitaires de Rouen, 2004). Jean's translation of Aelred's work is no longer extant, but he mentions it in the letter to Philip VI that prefaces his translation of Boethius.

[5] Seth Lerer, *Boethius and Dialogue: Literary Method in The Consolation of Philosophy* (Princeton: Princeton University Press, 1985), 46.

[6] See, for example, Gruber's note on 3m9.23 (*Kommentar*, 286), where he cites F. Klinger's comparison of Boethius's phrase "da fontem lustrare boni" [grant us to reach that fount of good] both to a hymn of Proclus and to Augustine's *Confessions* 7.10.16: "vidi . . . supra mentem meam lucem incommutabilem" [[I] saw . . . the immutable light higher than my mind].

[7] Henry Chadwick, *The Consolations of Music, Logic, Theology, and Philosophy* (Oxford: Clarendon Press, 1981), 237–38, 248–49, at 249.

[8] Antonio Donato, *Boethius' Consolation of Philosophy as a Product of Late Antiquity* (London: Bloomsbury, 2013), 168.

Donato observes, "When scholars approach the *Consolation*, they unwillingly and unwittingly expect to find in Boethius' text the same fervor and passion towards Christianity that we find in Augustine's *Confessions* and dialogues."[9] Failing to discover that passion, they conclude that Boethius was a "cold scholar,"[10] a classicizing humanist, perhaps even, in his final suffering, an apostate from the Christian faith.

Resisting the mistaken conclusions of affective coldness and apostasy, Donato places Boethius instead within a specifically Late Antique context and social class characterized by a "symbiosis between Greco-Roman culture and Christianity."[11] On that basis, Donato maintains that the *Consolation* is indeed a "Christian work," but one reflective of a specific type of Christian spirituality evident in aristocratic families like the Anicii—a spirituality that sought "to harmonize three quite diverse elements: the attachment to the Roman heritage, the devotion to Christianity and the Pope, and the willingness to co-operate with the barbarians."[12] The difference between Augustine's *Confessions* and Boethius's *Consolation*, Donato maintains, is not that between Christian belief and Platonic philosophy. Rather, the contrast between the two autobiographical works is generational and intensely personal:

> In Augustine's *Confessions* and dialogues we encounter a man who is driven by a passionate search for the truth. On the contrary, in the *Consolation* we find a man who experiences how difficult it is in his present situation to embody the truth by which he was educated and that shaped his way of life until that point.[13]

Difficult indeed. I want to suggest that the *gestalt* of Augustine's *Confessions* specifically as a consolation for a mourner affected what Anna Crabbe has called the "literary design" and "conception" of Boethius's *Consolation*.[14] In *Confessions*, Augustine is twice consoled—first by philosophy in Book 4, when he, still a Manichee, grieves the death of a friend, and then by theology and Ambrosian hymnody in Book 9, when he, newly baptized, deals with the loss of his mother Monica, who has become (in Chadwick's words), Augustine's "supreme friend."[15] Retracing the steps of Augustine's conversion, Boethius strives

---

9 Donato, *Boethius' Consolation of Philosophy*, 168.

10 Donato, *Boethius' Consolation of Philosophy*, 168.

11 Donato, *Boethius' Consolation of Philosophy*, 168.

12 Donato, *Boethius' Consolation of Philosophy*, 19.

13 Donato, *Boethius' Consolation of Philosophy*, 168.

14 Anna Crabbe, "Literary Design in *De Consolatione Philosophiae*," in *Boethius: His Life, Thought, and Influence*, ed. Margaret Gibson (Oxford: Basil Blackwell, 1981), 237–74. Crabbe argues that "Augustine is crucial to the conception of the *Consolation*" (241).

15 Henry Chadwick, *Augustine* (Oxford: Oxford University Press, 1986), 69.

to accomplish his own reconversion.[16] At issue for Boethius in the *Consolation* is not supernatural faith, however, but the recovery of reason itself, that power by which he might seek understanding of the trauma he has suffered, of the death he faces, and of the God before whose face he stands. For Boethius, too, the loss of friends initially figures as but one loss among many others. In both *Confessions* 4 and the *Consolation*, nevertheless, the external loss of a friend or friends may be said to precipitate a philosophical quest, an internal dialogue, that refashions the mourner into a better friend to himself, to others, to God.

Friendly Analogues? Boethius's Sufferer and Augustine's Bereft Friend

This same pattern of bereavement and befriending prevails, *mutatis mutandi*, I argue, in Lawrence of Durham's *Consolatio de morte amici sui* and in the consolatory writings of Aelred and Walter at Rievaulx. In these works, however—unlike in Boethius's *Consolation*—grief at the death of a friend is foregrounded in a way that points unmistakably to Augustine's influence.[17] Translating a likely historical source into an analogue, these monks of England read Boethius in company with Augustine, synthesized their sorrows, and fused their consolations, using Cicero's *De amicitia* as a bridge between them.

Although Boethius uses the word *amicus* [friend] relatively infrequently, the thematic importance of the "Freundesmotiv" should not be overlooked.[18] In 1m1, the prisoner, alone in his cell, apostrophizes his absent friends: "Quid me felicem totiens iactastis, amici? / Qui cecidit, stabili non erat ille gradu" [Why, O my friends, did ye so often puff me up, telling me that I was fortunate? For he

---

[16] See Crabb, "Literary Design," 259: "*Reconversion* is his theme and so he turns to Augustine's masterpiece both to imitate and to challenge." Crabbe likens the sudden appearance of Lady Philosophy to Boethius to that of Lady Continence to Augustine in *Confessions* 8.11.27. See "Literary Design," 254–55.

[17] In *The Prisoner's Philosophy: Life and Death in Boethius's Consolation* (Notre Dame, IN: University of Notre Dame Press, 2007), Joel C. Relihan argues that Boethius's *Consolation* is indeed a consolation, but in the tradition of Mennippean satire. He cites the opinion of Peter von Moos that "Boethius's *Consolation*, insofar as it is a consolation, had only a limited influence in the Middle Ages, for the simple reason that the *Consolation* has little to do with death" (48). Von Moos, however (as Relihan notes), points to Lawrence of Durham's *Consolatio de morte amici sui* as an important exception to that rule. See Peter von Moos, *Consolatio: Studien zur mittellateinischen Trostliteratur über den Tod und zum Problem der christlichen Trauer*, 4 vols. (Munich: Fink, 1971–72), 1:32, C35. I thank Professor Relihan for these references.

[18] As noted above, Gruber, *Kommentar zu Boethius*, observes the existence of the theme (225).

that is fallen low did never firmly stand].[19] Laying bare the wound of his grief to Lady Philosophy, he complains that his bond of friendship with good men ("honestissimorum coetus amicorum") and the innocence of his home life should have put him above any suspicion of treason (1p4). The implicit contrast in these passages between the flattering friends who puffed him up and the honorable *amici* in whose company he pursued philosophy becomes explicit in 2p8, where Lady Philosophy reminds Boethius that his bad fortune has done him a favor in distinguishing between his true and false friends: "Nunc amissas opes querere; quod pretiosissimum diuitiarum genus est, amicos inuenisti" [Cease then to seek the wealth you have lost. You have found your friends, and they are the most precious of all riches, 2p8.7]. The good of friends, "amicorum vero quod sanctissimum quidem genus est" [which is the most honourable and holy [kind] of all, 3p2.9], he learns in Book 3, belongs not to the ever fickle goods of Fortune but to the enduring goods of virtue. "[F]elicitas amicum fecit infortunium faciet inimicum" [The friend gained by good fortune becomes an enemy in ill-fortune, 3p5.13], Lady Philosophy instructs. The tragic fate of Seneca, Nero's *familiaris* [friend], at that emperor's order anticipates Boethius's own execution at the order of Theodoric (3p5.10), even as it distinguishes the false friendship of such an emperor from the true friendship of Boethius's virtuous wife Rusticiana and of Symmachus, Boethius's father-in-law, who was also soon to die under the charge of treason.[20]

Lady Philosophy herself substitutes for and represents these honorable friends, from whom Boethius has been cruelly separated. A true friend, Philosophy presents herself as the sufferer's (Ciceronian) *alter idem* [second self],[21] the self he has forgotten but remembers at her appearance.[22] Perceiving the sufferer's distress, she comes to him, as she says, to bear his burden with him: "Atqui Philosophiae fas non erat incomitatum relinquere iter innocentis" [Surely Philosophy never allowed herself to let the innocent go upon their journey unbefriended, 1p3.5]. In maternal fashion, she soothes, reproves, and instructs until she has led her wayward son to the point of prayer: "Nec frustra sunt in deo positae spes . . .

19 For the Latin text, see *Anicii Manlii Severini Boethii Philosophiae Consolatio*, ed. Ludwig Bieler, CCSL 94 (Turnhout: Brepols, 1957), 1m1.22–23. For translation, see Boethius, *On the Consolation of Philosophy*, trans. W.V. Cooper (Chicago: Regnery Gateway, 1981), 3. Hereafter cited parenthetically.

20 For Philosophy's praise of the virtue of Symmachus and Rusticiana, see 2p4.5–6.

21 See Cicero, *De amicitia*, in *De senectute, De amicitia, De divination*, Loeb Classical Library 154 (Cambridge, MA: Harvard University Press, 1923, repr. 2001), 21.80; and Cicero, *On Friendship*, in *Cicero's Three Books of Offices, Or Moral Duties*, trans. Cyrus R. Edmonds (New York: American Book Company, 1897), 202.

22 "Sui paulisper oblitus est. Recordabitur facile, si quidem nos ante cognouerit" [He has forgotten himself for a moment and will quickly remember, as soon as he recognizes me, 1p2.6].

humiles preces in excelsa porrigite" [Hopes are not vainly put in God . . . Send up on high your prayers from this earth, 5p6.46–47]. Seth Lerer rightly compares the prayerful silence of the *Consolation*'s ending to the "silence of prayer . . . characterized in the *Confessions*,"[23] most famously by Augustine and Monica in their shared mystical ascent at the window in Ostia, shortly before Monica's death.[24]

The theme of friendship proper appears for the first time in *Confessions* 4. Augustine recalls his early years as a young teacher in Thagaste (373–75), when he had a close friend with whom he shared many interests. "Dulcis erat nimis" [It was a very sweet experience], Augustine writes.[25] Within the first year of their bliss, however, Augustine's friend falls mortally ill with a fever, receives baptism in an unconscious state, awakens to rebuke Augustine for his mockery of the sacrament, and then, soon thereafter, dies. "[I]lle abreptus dementiae meae, ut apud te seruaretur consolationi meae" [He was snatched away from my lunacy, so that he might be preserved with you [Lord] for my consolation], Augustine confides.[26]

Wracked by grief, Augustine becomes, as he says, "ipse mihi magna quaestio" [to myself a vast problem].[27] He questions his soul, "quare tristis esset et quare conturbaret me ualde" [Why are you sad, and why are you very distressed?].[28] For the first time he contemplates human mortality: "Mirabar enim ceteros mortales uiuere, quia ille, quem quasi non moriturum dilexeram, mortuus erat" [I was surprised that any other mortals were alive, since he whom I had loved as if he would never die was dead].[29] He wonders at his own desire to go on living: "tantum dolebam et flebam. Miser enim eram et amiseram gaudium meum" [I merely grieved and wept. I was in misery and had lost the source of my joy].[30] Examining his conscience, he accuses himself of having been a selfish, imperfect, nearly ruinous friend to his friend, whose Catholic faith he had derided. He flees Thagaste to go to Carthage, because he cannot bear to be reminded of the friend he has lost.

Confronted by the mutability of earthly things, Augustine ponders the meaning of friendship, beauty, time, and eternity. He takes new pleasure in

---

23 Lerer, *Boethius and Dialogue*, 236.

24 See Augustine, *Confessions* 9.10.23. Throughout I use Augustine, *Confessionum Libri XIII*, ed. Luke Verheijen, *Sancti Augustini Opera*, CCSL 27 (Turnhout: Brepols, 1981); and Augustine, *Confessions*, trans. Henry Chadwick (Oxford: Oxford University Press, 1992, repr. 2008).

25 Augustine, *Confessions* 4.4.7; Chadwick, trans., 56.

26 Augustine, *Confessions* 4.4.8; Chadwick, trans., 57.

27 Augustine, *Confessions* 4.4.9; Chadwick, trans., 57.

28 Augustine, *Confessions* 4.4.9; Chadwick, trans., 58.

29 Augustine, *Confessions* 4.6.11; Chadwick, trans., 59.

30 Augustine, *Confessions* 4.5.10; Chadwick, trans., 58.

the simple comforts of human comradery—those natural joys which belong to what Aelred of Rievaulx, quoting *Confessions* 4, will later call "carnal friendship": namely, "colloqui scilicet et conridere, et uicissim beneuole obsequi; simul legere, simul conferre, simul nugari et simul honestari; dissentire interdum sine odio, tamquam homo sibi, atque ipsa rarissima dissensione, condire consensiones plurimas" [to make conversation, to share a joke, to perform mutual acts of kindness, to read together well-written books, to share in trifling and in serious matters, to disagree though without animosity—just as a person debates with himself—and in the rarity of disagreement to find the salt of normal harmony].[31] Awakened by trauma to philosophy and consoled by it to some extent, Augustine, still in his twenties, writes an aesthetic treatise and reads with understanding the *Ten Categories* of Aristotle, the contents of which he summarizes at the end of *Confessions*, Book 4.[32] He grasps the eternity of God, the transience of all mortal things, and the divine maintenance of the chain of being in its beauty. His consolation of philosophy is incomplete, however. Repeating the question four times, he asks, "quid mihi hoc proderat" [What help was this to me?].[33]

When Augustine becomes a question to himself, the questions he poses to his own soul are not unlike those Lady Philosophy puts to the sufferer in Book 1 of the *Consolation*: "Quid fles, quid lacrimis manas?" [Why do you weep? Wherefore flow your tears? 1p4.1]. "Huncine . . . mundum temerariis agi fortuitis que casibus putas an ullum credis ei regimen inesse rationis?" [Think you that this universe is guided only at random and by mere chance? Or think you there is any rule of reason constituted in it? 1p6.3]. "Sed dic mihi, meministi ne quis sit rerum finis" [But tell me, do you remember what is the aim and end of all things? 1p6.10]. "Atqui scis unde cuncta processerint" [Do you not somehow know whence all things have their source? 1p6.11]. "[H]ominem ne te esse meministi?" [Do you remember that you are a [h]uman? 1p6.14].

Boethius's philosophical dialogue, like Augustine's questioning of himself, is thus tied to the theme of friendship. Lady Philosophy accompanies Boethius as a friend-in-need, personifying his own self-correcting thoughts and directing them higher. A major theme in *Confessions*, friendship is itself a philosophical and theological topic for Augustine,[34] which he traces through a series of experiential forms: the "inimical friendship" of adolescent pear thieves, gangs, and

---

31 Aelred of Rievaulx, *De spiritali amicitia*, in *Opera ascetica*, ed. A. Hoste, CCCM 1 (Turnhout: Brepols, 1971), 3.85; *Spiritual Friendship*, trans. Mary Eugenia Laker (Kalamazoo: Cistercian Publications, 1977), 113; Augustine, *Confessions* 4.8.13; and Chadwick, trans., 60.

32 See Augustine, *Confessions* 4.16.28; Chadwick, trans., 69.

33 Augustine, *Confessions* 4.16.28–31; Chadwick, trans., 69–70.

34 See Marie Aquinas McNamara, *Friends and Friendship in Saint Augustine* (Staten Island, NY: Alba House, 1964); and Richard B. Miller, "Evil, Friendship, and Iconic Realism in Augustine's *Confessions*," *Harvard Theological Review* 104.4 (2011): 387–409.

fraternities (Books 2 and 3); the natural friendships based on common interests and shared pleasures (Book 4); the self-sacrificing friendships of literary exemplars, such as Orestes and Pylades (Book 4); the mutually perfecting friendships of virtuous persons (Book 6); and, finally, the friendships between and among the faithful, who are united in Christ (Book 9). The dynamic, upward spiral of these experiential forms in Augustine's narrative theology will inspire Aelred of Rievaulx's hope (a hope perhaps stronger than Augustine's own) that even false and imperfect friendships may become true.[35]

Augustine's citations of Cicero's *De amicitia* in *Confessions* 4 are obvious and significant. In both works the death of a close friend prompts the question of the proper response to such a loss and opens up a larger discussion about the nature of friendship. The young Augustine's excessive mourning contrasts, however, with the controlled, dry-eyed demeanor of Cicero's Caius Laelius, who applies to himself the consoling "remedy" both of the memory of Scipio's glorious career, his virtuous life, and dignified death and of belief in the soul's immortality, confirmed by Scipio's own dream of Africanus.[36] Cicero's Laelius is careful to explain the qualities of true friendship, which "nisi in bonis amicitiam esse non posse" [cannot exist except among the virtuous],[37] and to distinguish it sharply from the false friendships based on the goods of fortune: riches, health, influence, honor.[38] This Ciceronian distinction, as we have just seen, is also found in Boethius's *Consolation*.

Judging by a different, explicitly Christian standard, Augustine remarks that his first sweet and heart-rending friendship was less than a true friendship, "quia non est uera, nisi cum eam tu agglutinas inter haerentes tibi caritate diffusa in cordibus nostris per spiritum sanctum, qui datus est nobis" [which is not possible unless you, [Lord,] bond together those who cleave to one another by the love which is "poured into our hearts by the Holy Spirit who is given to us" (Rom. 5:5)].[39] Given this standard, as C. Stephen Jaeger remarks, "Friendship fails at every point in Augustine's life prior to the conversion."[40] *Confessions* thus

---

35 See Marsha L. Dutton, "Friendship and the Love of God: Augustine's Teaching in the *Confessions* and Aelred of Rievaulx's Response in *Spiritual Friendship*," *American Benedictine Review* 56 (2005): 3–40. Contrasting Augustine with Aelred, Dutton observes that in Aelred's opinion "even carnal friendship may lead to spiritual friendship and so to God" (31). I am not convinced that Augustine would maintain otherwise.

36 Cicero, *De amicitia* 3.1: "Sed non egeo medicina" [But I am not destitute of a remedy]; *On Friendship*, trans. Edmonds, 173.

37 Cicero, *De amicitia* 5.18; *On Friendship*, trans. Edmonds, 178.

38 See Cicero, *De amicitia* 6.20–22; *On Friendship*, trans. Edmonds, 180–81.

39 Augustine, *Confessions* 4.4.7; Chadwick, trans., 56.

40 C. Stephen Jaeger, "Friendship of Mutual Perfecting in Augustine's *Confessions* and the Failure of Classical *Amicitia*," in *Friendship in the Middle Ages and Early Modern Age: Explorations of a Fundamental Ethical Discourse*, ed. Albrecht Classen and Marilyn Sandidge (Berlin: Walter de Gruyter, 2011), 185–200, at 191. One might add to Jaeger's

challenges the compatibility of Christian *caritas* with classical *amicitia*, even as it holds out the promise (especially in Book 9) of a virtuous, enduring friendship, similar to the one Cicero describes, but transformed by charity and at charity's service. Significantly, the circle of Augustine's friends gathered at Cassiciacum to prepare for baptism includes many of his long-time friends—Alypius, Nebridius, Verecundus—who had shared his interests in philosophy.

An Analogical Imagination: Aelred and the Writings of Rievaulx

As James McEvoy and others have seen,[41] the Prologue to Aelred of Rievaulx's *De spiritali amicitia* is filled with phrases borrowed from Augustine's *Confessions*. Marsha Dutton rightly opines: "*Spiritual Friendship* . . . owes as much to Augustine as to Cicero,"[42] whose *De amicitia* first inspired Aelred's longing to articulate a specifically Christian theology of friendship, "dulcissimi nominis Iesu . . . melle millitum" [sweetened by the honey of the most sweet name of Jesus].[43] Even as the young Augustine benefitted from reading Cicero's *Hortensius*, but found it sadly lacking the "nomen Christi" [name of Christ],[44] Aelred endeavors to supply what is lacking to Cicero's trialogue by proving that friendship "in Christo inchoari, et secundum Christum produci, et a Christo perfici debeat" [begin[s] in Christ, continue[s] in Christ, and [is] perfected in Christ].[45] Indeed, the opening line of Aelred's work evokes Matthew 18:20, "ubi enim sunt duo vel tres congregati in nomine meo ibi sum in medio eorum" [Where two or three are gathered in my name, there am I in the midst of them].[46] Aelred greets his

---

analysis the observation that Aelred of Rievaulx likens his lustful friendships at the court of King David to Augustine's pre-conversion attachments. See Aelred of Rievaulx, *Liber de specvlo caritatis*, in *Opera ascetica*, ed. A. Hoste and C.H. Talbot, CCCM 1 (Turnhout: Brepols, 1971), 1.28.79; and *The Mirror of Charity*, trans. Elizabeth Connor (Kalamazoo: Cistercian Publications, 1990), 134. There Aelred quotes from Augustine: "'Retinebant me, ut ait quidam, nugae nugarum, et uanitas uanitatum antiquae amicae meae'" [My old friends, trifles of trifles and vanities of vanities, held me fast, as [Augustine] said]. See *Confessions* 8.11.26.

41 James McEvoy, "Notes on the Prologue of St. Aelred of Rievaulx's 'De spiritali amicitia,' with a Translation," *Traditio* 37 (1981): 396–411; Brian Noell, "Aelred of Rievaulx's Appropriation of Augustine: A Window on Two Views of Friendship in Monastic Life," *Cistercian Studies Quarterly* 37 (2002): 123–44.

42 Dutton, "Friendship and the Love of God," 5.

43 Aelred of Rievaulx, *De spiritali amicitia*, Prologue, 5; Laker, trans., Prologue, 77.

44 Augustine, *Confessions* 3.4.8; Chadwick, trans., 40.

45 Aelred of Rievaulx, *De spiritali amicitia* 1.9; Laker, trans., 53.

46 Robert Weber and Roger Gryson, eds., *Biblia Sacra: Iuxta Vulgatam Versionem*, 5th edn. (Stuttgart: Deutsche Bibelgesellschaft, 1969, repr. 2007).

first interlocutor, Ivo, with the words: "Ecce ego et tu, et spero quod tertius inter nos Christus sit" [Here we are, you and I, and I hope a third, Christ, is in our midst].[47] Developing the idea of Christ's mediation between friends, Aelred tries to overcome the tension between the natural exclusivity of friendship, on the one hand, and the universality of agapeic love, on the other, by harkening back to a prelapsarian ideal of human sociality,[48] wherein a network of human friendships, in which each would love the friend's friends in ever-widening circles, would exclude no one from a friendship identical, in the end, with charity.[49] In a fallen world, wherein charity can and must be distinguished from friendship,[50] one's friendship with Jesus obliges one, Aelred teaches, to participate in Christ's love for one's enemies.[51]

Aelred uses Cicero's definition of friendship in *De amicitia* 20 as a starting point: "Amicitia est rerum humanarum et diuinarum cum benevolentia et caritate consensio" [Friendship is a mutual harmony in affairs human and divine, coupled with benevolence and charity].[52] Repeating that definition at various points in the course of his conversations, first with Ivo (Book 1) and then with Walter and Gratian (Books 2 and 3),[53] Aelred gradually transforms its meaning from a classical to a Christian sense through paraphrase, scriptural concordance, biblical examples, and Augustinian citation. Even when he follows Cicero most closely, topic by topic, Aelred transforms Cicero's argument.

Most pertinent to our theme of an Augustinian reception of Boethius is the closing of Aelred's *De spiritali amicitia*, where he sings the praises of two deceased friends,[54] even as Laelius concludes Cicero's *De amicitia* with a eulogy in honor of his departed friend, Scipio. Unlike Laelius, whose tearless praise proves the triumph of virtue in friendship, Aelred uses the examples of these two unnamed friends to illustrate his teachings about the twofold basis for the selection of friends (affection and reason) and about the ascending degrees of friendship, leading to a transforming union with God in Christ.[55] Aelred describes these two departed friends, who "tamen uiuunt, semperque uiuent" [nevertheless live

---

[47] Aelred of Rievaulx, *De spiritali amicitia* 1.1; Laker, trans., 51.

[48] Aelred of Rievaulx, *De spiritali amicitia* 1.57; Laker, trans., 63.

[49] Aelred of Rievaulx, *De spiritali amicitia* 1.28–31; Laker, trans., 57–58.

[50] Aelred of Rievaulx, *De spiritali amicitia* 1.32, 1.57–60; Laker, trans., 58, 63–64.

[51] On friendship with Christ, see Aelred of Rievaulx, *De spiritali amicitia* 2.20–21; Laker, trans., 74–75.

[52] Aelred of Rievaulx, *De spiritali amicitia* 1.11; Laker, trans., 53.

[53] Aelred of Rievaulx, *De spiritali amicitia* 1.11, 1.46, 3.8; Laker, trans., 53, 61, 93.

[54] Aelred of Rievaulx, *De spiritali amicitia* 3.119–127; Laker, trans. 126–29.

[55] Aelred's description of noble, natural friendship as "ad Dei delectionem et cognitionem gradus" [a stage toward the love and knowledge of God] (*De spiritali amicitia* 2.18; Laker, trans., 74) recalls Saint Bernard's teaching on the degrees of love in *On Loving God*.

to [him], and always will so live],[56] using language from Cicero's *De amicitia* and Augustine's *Confessions* 4.4 and 7.12. Thus he associates the first friend (whom scholars have identified as Simon, a young monk at Rievaulx) with the friend of Augustine's youth and the second (also unnamed, but identified by Frederick Maurice Powicke as Geoffrey of Dinant)[57] with Augustine's faithful friend and former student Alypius, who was baptized with Augustine and eventually became bishop of Thagaste. As Dutton remarks, "The best evidence of Aelred's familiarity with the *Confessions* is his own writing, full of Augustinian words and phrases, even when apparently characterized by highly personal reminiscences."[58]

In *Spiritual Friendship*, Aelred remembers Simon and Geoffrey warmly, gratefully, without lament. Simon died, however, when Aelred, still a young monk himself and novice-master, was composing the *Speculum caritatis* at the request of Bernard of Clairvaux. Supported by the abbot's own example in lamenting the death of his "intimus affectu" [bosom friend in love],[59] his brother Gerard, Aelred interrupts his instruction in the *Speculum* (as Bernard had interrupted his commentary on the Song of Songs) to give vent to his grief at Simon's death. In their grief, Aelred and Bernard recall Augustine's mourning in *Confessions* 4 and 9.[60] Like Bernard (and unlike Augustine), Aelred fills his passionate speeches to and about Simon with quotations from the Song of Songs. This passionate digression comes at the end of Book 1 of the *Speculum caritatis*, just at the point in his outline when Aelred is to discuss the threefold concupiscence "of the flesh, of the eyes, and the pride of life" (1 John 2:16)—the very topic that is Augustine's recurrent theme in *Confessions*. Tearfully lamenting Simon's death out of his attachment (*affectus*) for his friend, Aelred, ever the teacher, purifies his own "carnal" love,[61] his affection, through writing and thus demonstrates the

[56] Aelred of Rievaulx, *De spiritali amicitia* 3.119; Laker, trans., 126. The phrase echoes Cicero, *De amicitia* 27.102: "Mihi quidem Scipio . . . vivit tamen semperque vivet" [For me, indeed . . . Scipio still lives and will always live].

[57] See F.M. Powicke, *Aelred of Rievaulx and His Biographer Walter Daniel* (Manchester: Longmans Green and Co., 1922), 50.

[58] Dutton, "Friendship and the Love of God," 7.

[59] Bernard of Clairvaux, "Sermon 26: The Blackness of the Bride Compared to the Tents of Kedar: Bernard's Lament for His Brother," in *Sermones super Cantica Canticorum 1–35, Bernardi opera*, vol. 1, ed. J. Leclercq, C.H. Talbot, and H.M. Rochais (Rome: Cistercian Editions, 1957), 26.9; and Bernard of Clairvaux, *On the Song of Songs II*, trans. Kilian Walsh, ocso (Kalamazoo: Cistercian Publications, 1976), 69.

[60] On Bernard's mourning, see Ann W. Astell, *The Song of Songs in the Middle Ages* (Ithaca: Cornell University Press, 1990), 119–35.

[61] Aelred's idea of "carnal" love is in accord with that of Saint Bernard, who affirms the purpose and the necessity of natural affection in the spiritual life. See Bernard of Clairvaux, *On Loving God*, ed. Emero S. Stiegman (Kalamazoo: Cistercian Publications, 1995), 25–27, 98–99.

process of that purification for his readers, whom he invites to recall their own experience of close friendships.

Aelred moves from an address to his readers to an apostrophe to Simon that doubles as a prayer to him, intermingled with prayer to Jesus. In this way, the absent Simon, who has arrived (Aelred believes) at the eternal homeland, becomes a silent interlocutor in a dialogue marked by Christ's presence. Addressing his departed but spiritually present friend, Aelred paraphrases the speech of the suffering Boethius to Lady Philosophy, declaring, "Et certe . . . cernes profecto quam iustus sit dolor meus, quam flenda plaga mea" [You will surely realize how justified is my grief, how worthy of tears my wound].[62] Recalling the grace of conversion and the virtues evident in Simon's life, Aelred becomes calmer: "Ecce qui dolere coeperam, inueni unde gaudeam" [See how I, who began to grieve, have found reason to rejoice].[63] His affection seeks his friend's sweet presence, but his reason does not consent ("sed non acquiescit ratio") to death's reversal.[64] Reason teaches him to desire neither the return of Simon from his heavenly reward nor his own death before the time set by Divine Providence.[65] Resolving to continue to follow the virtuous example set by Simon both in his life and in his manner of dying, Aelred recalls the final words—"Misericordiam, misericordiam, misericordiam" [Mercy! Mercy! Mercy!]—spoken by Simon, who endeavored (it is supposed) "uersiculum illum ex integro psallere: *Misericordiam et iudicium cantabo tibi, Domine*" [to recite in full the verse of the psalm, *mercy and justice shall I sing to you, O Lord*].[66] Significantly, Psalm 100:1 is the same verse with which the household of mourners assembled at the deathbed of Monica responded to the psalmody of Evodius, as Augustine recalls in *Confessions* 9.12.31. The citation of the chanted psalm introduces a prosimetrical element into both Augustine's and Aelred's narratives that calms the sufferer. Like Augustine, who at first restrains his tears and afterwards finds it fitting to cry, Aelred reports that he stood without weeping at Simon's corpse and only later shed overflowing tears. Like Augustine too, Aelred imagines that some might pass judgment against him, "nimis carnalem existimantes amorem meum" [considering [his] love too human].[67] Aelred, however, promises Simon that he will follow him homeward with his tears and his abiding attachment.

---

[62] Aelred of Rievaulx, *De specvlo caritatis* 1.34.99; Connor, trans., 148; Cf. Boethius, *Consolation*, 1p4.1–2.

[63] Aelred of Rievaulx, *De specvlo caritatis* 1.34.104; Connor, trans., 151.

[64] Aelred of Rievaulx, *De specvlo caritatis* 1.34.106; Connor, trans., 152.

[65] Aelred of Rievaulx, *De specvlo caritatis* 1.34.105–106. Connor translates "but my reason does not agree" (152).

[66] Aelred of Rievaulx, *De specvlo caritatis* 1.34.113; Connor, trans., 158.

[67] Aelred of Rievaulx, *De specvlo caritatis* 1.34.112; Connor, trans., 157. Cf. Augustine, *Confessions* 9.12.33; Chadwick, trans., 176.

In his own final illness, Aelred "[m]axime confessiones Augustini manibus portabat assidue, eo quod illos libros quasi quasdam introduciones habebat cum a seculo conuerteretur" [generally had in his hands the *Confessions* of Augustine, for it was these [his hagiographer, Walter Daniel, explains] which had been his guide when he converted from the world].[68] In imitation of Aelred's Augustinian lament for Simon, Walter concludes his *Vita Aelredi* with his own tearful expression of loss at the death of his friend and abbot. In doing so, he says, he applies a physician's "treatment" to his own wound.[69] At first he addresses his own tears, which, like Boethius's, blind his eyes.[70] Finding his tears unable to answer the question "Where is Aelred?" he turns to reason: "With my Reason I shall converse."[71] What follows is a thoroughly Boethian, albeit short, dialogue in which a personified Reason works to cure Walter's "chronic fever" of irrational grief by asking him questions, reminding him of what is proper to his humanity, answering his objections, and recalling him to moderation.[72] When Walter professes his desire "to be brought back to moderation,"[73] Reason speaks, as Lady Philosophy does at the close of the *Consolation*, to close the dialogue in prayer: "Here then I will end your lament with a prayer."[74]

Aelred and his scribe Walter, whom Aelred casts as an interlocutor in *De spiritali amicitia*, certainly knew Boethius's *Consolation of Philosophy*. While Aelred foregrounds Augustine's example in his lament for Simon, and Walter brings Boethius's sufferings readily to mind in the lament for Aelred, both attest to an Augustinian reception of Boethius. Aelred quotes from 5p1.18 of the *Consolation* in a sermon for the Feast of Saint Benedict (Sermon 140), and he paraphrases 3p2.2–4 of the *Consolation* in another sermon (Sermon 54) for that same feast.

Aelred's particular association of Boethius with Benedict of Nursia (480-547), the great father of monasticism, is striking. It suggests that Aelred

[68] Walter Daniel, *The Life of Aelred of Rievaulx and the Letter to Maurice*, trans. F.M. Powicke (Kalamazoo: Cistercian Publications, 1994), 128; *The Life of Ailred of Rievaulx by Walter Daniel*, ed. F.M. Powicke (London: Thomas Nelson, 1950), 50.

[69] Daniel, *Life of Aelred of Rievaulx and the Letter to Maurice*, 141. The text of the lament is not included in Powicke's 1950 facing-page, Latin/English edition of the *Vita Ailredi* (and still no edition of the lament exists). In his edition, Powicke notes the lamentation's presence as a colophon to the *Vita* in Jesus College, Cambridge, MS Q.B.7, fols. 74a–75b. The English translation by Anna Kirkwood and Sr. Jane Patricia Freeland of the "Lament for Aelred" in the 1994 edition is based on their hasty transcription of the manuscript folios. See *Life of Aelred of Rievaulx*, 169, note 147.

[70] Daniel, *Life of Aelred*, 143. Cf. Boethius, *Consolation* 1p1.13.

[71] Daniel, *Life of Aelred*, 143. Lady Philosophy dries Boethius's tears as a preparation for her instruction of him in *Consolation* 1p2.7.

[72] Daniel, *Life of Aelred*, 143–46, at 145.

[73] Daniel, *Life of Aelred*, 146.

[74] Daniel, *Life of Aelred*, 146.

was influenced by the commentary on Boethius's *Consolation* by the Benedictine scholar Remigius of Auxerre (ca. 841–908). In that influential commentary, as Brian FitzGerald has noted,[75] Remigius likens Saint Benedict's nocturnal vision of the whole world in a single ray of light (famously described in Book 2 of Gregory the Great's *Dialogues*)[76] to Lady Philosophy's description of God's providential comprehension of all things "tota simul" [wholly and simultaneously] from eternity.[77] FitzGerald translates the Remigian gloss ("Nam sancti aliquando in hac fragili carne positi fati seriem transcendunt ad tempus. Beatissimus enim Benedictus noster pater quando simul totum mundum conspexit diuino spiritu ultra omnem rerum naturam subleuatus est") as follows: "Sometimes saints placed in this fragile flesh transcend fate's sequence for a time. For blessed Benedict, our father, when he saw the whole world at once, was elevated by the divine spirit beyond all nature of things."[78]

Aelred's Sermon 54 takes for its theme "Beatus vir qui suffert temptationem" [Blessed is the man who endures trial, James 1:12]. Observing that "Itaque in beatitudinis appetite omnes consentiunt; dissident autem in uia qua ad ipsam beatitudinem peruenitur" [all agree in the desire for happiness; they differ in the way by which one might arrive at happiness],[79] Aelred paraphrases *Consolation* 3p2.2-4, where Lady Philosophy teaches concerning happiness: "Hunc . . . diuerso tramite mortales omnes conantur adipisci" [This is the end all men seek to reach, though by different paths, 3p2.4]. Identifying true happiness with the reign of God, Aelred points out that the way to this goal is temptations, tribulations, and persecutions, such as Benedict (and, by implication, Boethius) bore.[80]

[75] For a full discussion, see Brian FitzGerald, "The Medieval 'Vates': Prophecy, History, and the Shaping of Sacred Authority, 1120–1320" (Ph.D. diss., Oxford University, 2013), chap. 4. A revision of this study is now available in his *Inspiration and Authority in the Middle Ages: Prophets and their Critics from Scholasticism to Humanism* (Oxford: Oxford University Press, 2017). I thank Professor FitzGerald for sharing his work with me.

[76] See *The Life and Miracles of St. Benedict (by Pope Gregory the Great)*, trans. Alexius Hoffmann (Collegeville, MN: St. John's University Press, 1925), chaps. 35, 67.

[77] In the *Consolation*, Lady Philosophy defines eternity as "interminabilis uitae tota simul et perfecta possessio" [the simultaneous and complete possession of infinite life, 5p6.4].

[78] For the gloss, see H.F. Stewart, "A Commentary by Remigius Autissiodorensis on the 'De Consolatione Philosophiae' of Boethius," *The Journal of Theological Studies* 17 (1915): 22–42, at 37. I thank Professor Brian FitzGerald for sharing this reference and his translation with me.

[79] Aelred of Rievaulx, Sermon 54, "In Festivitate Beati Benedicti Abbatis," in *Sermones XLVIII–LXXXIV*, ed. Gaetano Raciti, CCCM 2B (Turnhout: Brepols, 2001), 66. Translations of Aelred's sermons are mine.

[80] Aelred of Rievaulx, Sermon 54, 66.

In Sermon 140, also for the Feast of Saint Benedict, Aelred's theme is Isaiah 26:7, "Semita iusti recta est, rectus callis iusti ad ambulandum" [The narrow way of the just is straight; straight is the footpath of the just for walking].[81] Noting the wordplay *recta / rectus*, Aelred observes that one can be just in two ways: by nature (as Christ is), or by grace (as saints, such as Benedict, are). Following Augustine, who in *De trinitate* appropriates Power to the Father, Wisdom to the Son, and Love to the Holy Spirit,[82] Aelred explains corresponding ways of offending God: by weakness (*per fragilitatem*), by ignorance (*per ignorantiam*), and by malice (*per malitiam*). The first two (powerlessness and ignorance) can be remedied easily, according to Aelred, depending on their cause, which is either by chance or by negligence. To explain the former, he quotes Boethius's Lady Philosophy, who defines chance (*casus*) as "inopinatum ex confluentibus causis in his quae ob aliquid geruntur euentum" [an unexpected result from the coincidence of certain causes in matters where there was another purpose, 5p1.18]. (The Boethian example is the case of a man who discovers a buried treasure while cultivating a field, ultimately derived from Matthew 13:44.)

This is not a random citation on Aelred's part. The abbot of Rievaulx has noticed that Book 5 of the *Consolation* begins with Lady Philosophy's stated haste to fulfill her promise to "uiamque tibi qua patriam reueharis aperire" [show you the path by which you may seek your home, 5p1.4], as well as her explicit concern that the sufferer may be too weak, too lacking in power, too tired (*fatigatus*) "ad emetiendum rectum iter" [to complete the straight journey, 5p1.5]. Here Aelred, the Augustinian exegete, dons the robes of Lady Philosophy and joins her teaching not only to Isaiah's biblical prophecy of Christ the Way (John 14:6) as the "semita iusti" [way of the just][83] but also to Saint Benedict's life and Rule (*Regula*) as the homeward way of hermits and monks.[84] The Prologue to the *Rule of Benedict* announces: "Ecce pietate sua demonstrat nobis Dominus viam vitae . . . pergamus itinera eius" [Behold in his loving kindness the Lord shows us the way of life . . . Let us walk in his paths].[85]

In *On Spiritual Friendship*, as we have seen, Aelred interprets this same life and way as the way of friendship that begins, continues, and reaches its perfection in Christ. Even as friends withhold nothing good from one another, being

[81] Aelred of Rievaulx, Sermon 140, "In Festivitate Sancti Benedicti," in *Sermones LXXXV–CLXXXII*, ed. Gaetano Raciti, CCCM 2C (Turnhout: Brepols, 2012), 353–59, at 353.

[82] See Augustine, *De trinitate*, bk. 6.

[83] Aelred, Sermon 140, 356: "Semita iusti Christus est."

[84] Aelred, Sermon 140, 359. Aelred concludes the sermon with citations from Gregory the Great's *Life of St. Benedict*.

[85] *The Rule of Saint Benedict (Latin and English),* trans. Luke Dysinger (Trabuco Canyon, CA: Source Books, 1997, repr. 2003), Prologue, pars. 19 and 21.

bound "dilecionis ac dulcedinis foedere" [by ties of love and sweetness],[86] monks hold all things in common: "Ecce quam bonum et quam iucundum, habitare fratres in unum" [Behold, how good and pleasant it is for brethren to dwell together in unity].[87] The three stages of Aelredian friendship—carnal or affective, rational, spiritual—correspond closely to the philosophical anthropology that the suffering Boethius is challenged, step by step, to recall.[88] Similar to *Spiritual Friendship*, Aelred's *Mirror of Charity* discusses the way of spiritual friendship as a way of charity that fulfills the great commandment to love God and neighbor, and that leads, via ascending stages, to the final Sabbath, the resting in God, with whom one has become "one spirit" (1 Corinthians 6:11).[89] The Apostle John, the beloved disciple, the friend leaning on the bosom of Jesus at the Last Supper (John. 13:21), is, for Aelred, the icon of this Sabbath.[90] As the abbot of Rievaulx teaches, "Haec est uera et aeterna amicitia quae hic inchoatur, ibi perficitur; quae paucorum hic est, ubi pauci boni; ibi omnium, ubi omnes boni" [This is true and eternal friendship, which begins in the life and is perfected in the next, which here belongs to the few where few are good, but there belongs to all where all are good].[91]

Lawrence of Durham's Consolations of Friendship

At about the same time that Aelred wrote the *Mirror of Charity* (ca. 1142), in which he laments the death of his virtuous friend Simon, Aelred's one-time teacher, Lawrence of Durham, composed his *Consolatio de morte amici sui* (ca. 1141), a prosimetrum obviously inspired by Boethius's *Consolation* and (less clearly) by Book 4 of Augustine's *Confessions*. From Augustine, Lawrence draws the courage to cast himself in the role of a bereaved friend, mourning excessively at the death of a Christian friend, the young monk Paganus. From Boethius's dialogue, Lawrence derives a formal structure (sixteen prose sections, with fifteen

[86] Aelred of Rievaulx, *De spiritali amicitia* 1.21; Laker, trans., 55; Cf. Cicero, *De amicitia* 21.81.

[87] Ps. 132:1, quoted by Aelred, *De spiritali amicitia* 3.82; Laker, trans., 112.

[88] See Ann W. Astell, *Job, Boethius, and Epic Truth* (Ithaca: Cornell University Press, 1994), for an interpretation of the three mythological meters in the *Consolation* as corresponding to the threefold definition of human nature as mortal in body, rational in mind, and destined in spirit for eternal life. Boethius's initial definition of the human being as a mortal, rational animal ("rationale animal atque mortale," 1p6.15) is incomplete and leads Philosophia to conclude: "quid ipse sis, nosse desisti" [you have forgotten what you are, 1p6.17].

[89] Aelred of Rievaulx, *De specvlo caritatis* 3.39.109; Connor, trans., 298.

[90] Aelred of Rievaulx, *De specvlo caritatis* 3.39.109; Connor, trans., 299; *De spiritali amicitia* 3.117; Laker, trans., 125.

[91] Aelred of Rievaulx, *De spiritali amicitia* 3.80; Laker, trans., 111.

alternating meters) and many of the arguments used by the unnamed Consoler, who confines himself strictly to rational arguments until the very end, when he postpones until another time the discussion of eschatological matters known only through divine revelation.

Born in Waltham in Essex in 1110, Lawrence became a monk at Durham in 1128, entered the service of Bishop Geoffrey Rufus, and for several years, as A.G. Rigg relates, "divided his time between the court and the cloister."[92] An administrator, chanter, and poet, Lawrence composed a Life of Saint Bridget, which he sent to Aelred[93] when his former student was still in the service of King David I of Scotland, in the years (1130–34) prior to Aelred's conversion of life as a Cistercian. Lawrence's most original work, the *Dialogi*, imagines a series of different, often witty conversations between three friends—a Breton named Peter and Lawrence and Philip—chiefly about the events surrounding the siege of Durham and the subsequent conversion through grace of Bishop William Cummin, who had been excommunicated after forcibly laying claim to the episcopal see at Durham. Like Lawrence's *Hypognosticon*, a biblical epic in nine books of verse (4,684 lines), replete with classical allusions and divided according to the Augustinian Six Ages of history,[94] the *Dialogi* celebrates the miraculous working of divine grace in time, including contemporary lives and events belonging to one's own experience.

This Augustinian perspective on the sheer gratuity of grace points to a personal identification of Lawrence with Augustine. By Lawrence's own admission in the *Dialogi*, he was a highly praised poet who took pride in his verbal talents, beautiful singing voice, and flourishing career until "Hoc mihi me revocans pia gratia verbere prompsit, / Quidve sit hoc quod abit, posse videre dedit" [Kind Grace's blow restored [him] to [himself], / Revealed the nature of this passing world].[95] As a young man, he resembled Augustine in his disdain for the plain style of the Bible.[96] He writes, "Proh dolor! Imberbi mihi plus instare Pla-

---

[92] A.G. Rigg, "Lawrence of Durham: Dialogues and Easter Poem: A Verse Translation," *The Journal of Medieval Latin* 7 (1997): 42–126, at 43. Rigg's translation of the *Dialogi* is based on *Dialogi Laurentii dunelmensis monachi et prioris*, ed. James Raine, Surtees Society 70 (Durham, England: Published for the Society by Andrews and Co., 1880). I use both Raine's text and Rigg's translation.

[93] See Anselm Hoste, "A Survey of the Unedited Work of Laurence of Durham, With an Edition of His Letter to Aelred of Rievaulx," *Sacris Erudiri* 11 (1960): 249–65; and A.G. Rigg, *A History of Anglo-Latin Literature 1066–1422* (Cambridge: Cambridge University Press, 1992), 54–61.

[94] Bede comments on the six days of creation and the six ages of the world in *In Genesim* 1.1093–1224. For a discussion of Bede's patristic sources, see C.W. Jones, "Some Introductory Remarks on Bede's Commentary on Genesis," *Sacris Erudiri* 19 (1970): 119–98, esp. 193–94.

[95] Lawrence of Durham, *Dialogi* 3.515–516; Rigg, trans., 87.

[96] See Augustine, *Confessions* 3.5.9.

toni / Quam Moysi, Senecae quam Josuae cor erat. / Plusque libri Legum quam Regum, plusque poeta / Quam fatuo placuit quisque propheta mihi" [My heart was fixed on Seneca / And Plato, not on Moses, Joshua, / Or Kings: the books of law and poetry / Pleased more my foolish taste than prophets' words].[97] Through Grace, Lawrence confesses, he has come to know "Summum, Petre, bonum, res est Deus optima rerum / . . . Vita beata bonum dabit omne quod omnis amabit, / Est, est namque pius vita beata Deus" [The highest good, the best of all, is God / . . . The blessed life will grant the good that all / Men loved, for 'blessed life' is God, who loves].[98] Sounding a philosophical and ascetical note, Lawrence repeats more than once his desire "scire mori" [to learn to die].[99]

Lawrence voices these somber sentiments in the *Dialogi* as part of a conversation with trusted and witty friends, who intersperse Ciceronian comments about friendship.[100] Peter, for example, declares: "Sed verax, sed continuus, sed ubique fidelis, / Semper amicus amat: sic amo, remque probo. / . . . Sic et amans non ipse levi tua pectora pendo" [A true friend loves forever, without end; My love is true, and I will prove it's so. / . . . Your feelings count a lot with me, your friend].[101] Using a legendary example also employed by Cicero, Augustine, and Aelred, Lawrence calls his friend Philip "Pylades, mihi" [my Pylades], who is sure "immo fide Pyladen vincere promptus" [to outstrip Pylades in loyalty].[102] Philip merrily counters with another classical example of true friends, celebrated in Virgil's *Aeneid*: "sed tibi Nisus adest: / Euryalo tibi Nisus ego; tua signa reclamo; / Te dixisse peto; jussa dedisse puto" [I'll play Nisus' part for you. / You're Euryalus, I'm Nisus, and so / Just state your need; your word is my command].[103]

When Lawrence of Durham imitates Boethius's *Consolation of Philosophy*, he foregrounds the relationships of friendship that bind together the sufferer, Laurentius, his consoler, and the departed Paganus, who has been dear to them both. Udo Kindermann, the editor of the Latin text of Lawrence's *Consolatio* and its translation into German, speculates that when Lawrence in 1141 depicts himself as grieving excessively a young friend's death, he may also be figuring his angry frustration about other matters—in particular, the disfavor and enmity into which he has fallen at the death of his patron, Bishop Rufus, and the rise of his (illegitimate) successor, William Cummin, who forced Lawrence from Dur-

[97] Lawrence of Durham, *Dialogi* 4.479–482; Rigg, trans., 101.

[98] Lawrence of Durham, *Dialogi* 4.521–526; Rigg, trans., 102.

[99] Lawrence of Durham, *Dialogi* 4.45; Rigg, trans., 89.

[100] According to James Raine, "Preface," in *Dialogi* xxxv, Lawrence personally owned a copy of "Tully on Friendship."

[101] Lawrence of Durham, *Dialogi* 1.153–154, 157; Rigg, trans., 48.

[102] Lawrence of Durham, *Dialogi*, 1.169–170; Rigg, trans. 49.

[103] Lawrence of Durham, *Dialogi*, 1.190–192; Rigg, trans., 49.

ham into exile (1143/44): "Die Ungnade steigert sich zur Feindschaft."[104] Lawrence composed his *Consolatio*, after all, during the reign of King Stephen, the terrible time of the Anarchy. Noting the occasional testiness in the exchanges between the sufferer Laurentius and his consoler, Bridget K. Balint opines that this *Consolatio*, unlike Lawrence's *Dialogi*, "cannot function as a model for either pedagogical dialogue or conversation among friends" but instead stands as a "brilliant" representation of "the difficulties and self-contradictions that will arise in any self-interrogation."[105]

Lawrence's Consoler may, in this regard, resemble Walter Daniel's Reason more closely than he does either Aelred's (silently guiding) Simon or Boethius's majestic Lady Philosophy. He names himself insistently, however, the faithful, long-time friend of Laurentius and urges the sufferer on that basis of friendship to disclose the cause of his great grief: "Nichil inter amicos / clam decet esse" [Nothing should be secret between friends].[106]

Mirroring Laurentius's own grief for a friend, the Consoler himself complains and laments the loss of Laurentius's friendship, which has usually been expressed in a confiding to him of Laurentius's troubles. Reading the affective complaints of the first meter of the *Consolatio*, one might, indeed, mistake the Consoler for the sufferer, were it not for the rubric identifying the speaker and the preceding prose section, in which a miserable Laurentius asks, "quam consolationis medicinam admittam" [What medicine of consolation should I take?].[107]

Pleading the rights of a true friend, who is in fact already participating in Laurentius's grief, the Consoler wishes both to console and to be consoled by Laurentius, whom he calls "nostre / maxima pars anime" [the greatest part of our soul],[108] through an intimate sharing of thoughts and feelings, a disclosing of secrets. The Consoler's intense language of friendship, combined with insistent appeals for Laurentius's self-disclosure, effects an uneasy melding of love and besought knowledge. (One is reminded, in fact, of the possibility of a jealous lovers' triangle.) When the supposed Consoler worries aloud about his own moderation of mind,[109] he puts himself at a considerable distance from the towering Lady Philosophy, who sovereignly banishes the theatrical Muses from Boethius's

---

104 Udo Kindermann, ed., *Soll man um Tote trauern? Eine Antwort aus dem Jahre 1141 in der Consolatio des Laurentius von Durham* (Erlangen: Verlag Palm & Enke, 2010), 3.

105 Bridget K. Balint, *Ordering Chaos: The Self and the Cosmos in Twelfth-Century Latin Prosimetrum* (Boston: Brill, 2009), 97. In Appendix III (191–225), Balint provides a complete English translation of Lawrence of Durham's "Consolation on the Death of a Friend," based on Udo Kindermann's edition (cited above) of the Latin text. I use both Kindermann's edition and Balint's translation.

106 Lawrence of Durham, *Consolatio de morte amici sui* m1.21–22; Balint, trans., 192.

107 Lawrence of Durham, *Consolatio de morte amici sui* p1.3; Balint, trans., 191.

108 Lawrence of Durham, *Consolatio de morte amici sui* m1.19–20; Balint, trans., 192.

109 Lawrence of Durham, *Consolatio de morte amici sui* m1.11; Balint, trans., 192.

chamber. As Balint notes, Lawrence and other medieval authors in the Boethian tradition "make significant changes, giving their interlocutors new characteristics and changing the manner in which they interact."[110]

Puzzled that the cause of his grief should somehow be unknown to the Consoler, Laurentius narrates the story of his friendship with the virtuous Paganus, now deceased, whose life in the monastery was a "viva lectio" [living lesson] to him of the cardinal virtues and whose companionship was the source, he claims, of his complete happiness.[111] Through the skillful and strangely invested interrogation of the Consoler, we learn that Laurentius's relationship with his "privatum amicum, immo amorem publicum" [private friend, public love][112] Paganus has aroused not only the envy of others in the house but also Laurentius's own jealousy and fear. Using arguments that echo Lady Philosophy's depiction of perfect happiness, which can only rest in the possession of the eternal good, the Consoler first calls the nature of Laurentius's lost happiness into question. If death could deprive him of it, after all, his happiness cannot really have been perfect: "Sed quia, qui felix semel est, felix manet hicque / nullus id est: gemitus cesset, amice, tuus" [He who is once happy remains happy, and because no one is happy in this world, let your groans cease, my friend].[113]

Lawrence's *Consolatio*, which repeatedly tests Laurentius's experience against the criteria of true friendship, shows the affinity between the *Summum bonum* that is God, on the one hand, and, on the other hand, the highest and most sacred of earthly goods—the good of true friendship—which is to be freely given and received, enjoyed for its own sake, virtuous, never-ending, free from vice, and never simply used to obtain the advantages of wealth, power, and honor. Aelred of Rievaulx emphasizes the potential for a mystical crossing from and with spiritual friends to the God who is "amicitia" [Friendship], because He is Love (1 John 4:16).[114] Lawrence of Durham, by contrast, cautions against the ways in which the very resemblance of these goods may entrap a less-than-true friend into mistaking the temporal joy for the eternal one and suffering the consequences. The Consoler instructs, "Sed imperfectus quilibet ob hoc huiuscemodi infelicitate punitur, quia felicitate corrumpitur. Quantoque maiorem habita conferebat delectationem, tanto ampliorem perdita infert amaritudinem" [Every imperfect man is punished on account of this kind of unhappiness, since he is corrupted by happiness. The more delight conferred by something one is accustomed to, the greater the bitterness its loss brings].[115]

---

110 Balint, *Ordering Chaos*, 8.

111 Lawrence of Durham, *Consolatio de morte amici sui* p3.4; Balint, trans., 194.

112 Lawrence of Durham, *Consolatio de morte amici sui* p4.9; Balint, trans., 197.

113 Lawrence of Durham, *Consolatio de morte amici sui* m4.19–20; Balint, trans., 201.

114 Aelred of Rievaulx, *De spiritali amicitia* 1.69; Laker, trans., 65.

115 Lawrence of Durham, *Consolatio de morte amici sui* p5.11; Balint, trans., 203.

Balint rightly observes, "The conception of humankind that emerges from this text . . . demands asceticism and a true *contemptus mundi* from its students."[116] Ashamed at the Consoler's rebuke, Laurentius admits that, even in the enjoyment of Paganus's friendship, "semper eorum recordatione movebar, que nunquam ei evenire volebam et semper posse sciebam" [I was always disturbed by thoughts of things I wished never to happen, knowing all the while that they could happen].[117] He had wanted Paganus, he says, to outlive him, to be his heir. Only after Laurentius has discovered to what degree he has been a slave of fortune, and has falsely evaluated even the virtuous Paganus as a gift of fortune, is he able to remember and to reclaim what is lasting in their friendship. Still seated in Paganus's immortal soul, Laurentius realizes, is Paganus's kindness toward him ("circa me benevolentiam"), which endures.[118]

The Consoler sets before Laurentius a series of ascetic examples, both Stoic and Christian, of persons so virtuous that they remained dry-eyed at the deaths of sons and husbands. Among these he names the desert mother Melania the Elder, the wealthy fourth-century Roman patroness of Saint Jerome who exchanged the tumult of Rome for the serenity of Jerusalem.[119] He concedes to Laurentius, however: "Quodsi sapientum aliquem suorum exequias amicorum obieceris lacrimis prosecutum, et ego nonnullos hoc idem fecisse concedo, sed nullum ululatibus et lamentis concedo" [But if you object that some wise man followed the exequies of his friends with tears, I myself concede that some have done exactly this; but I concede them no wailings or laments].[120] Since the human soul has two parts, irrational and rational, it follows, he explains, that "Unde et sapiens tangi quidem dolore potest, ceterum vinci non potest" [even a wise man can be touched by sorrow, but he cannot be defeated].[121]

If the excessively grieving mourner at the start of Lawrence's *Consolatio* recalls both Boethius's tear-blinded sufferer and the young Augustine of *Confessions* 4, the now calmer Laurentius, eager to hear about how Paganus "vivit" [lives] and "bene vivit" [lives well] in eternity,[122] resembles those same students at the end of their respective instructions. The Augustine of *Confessions* 9 weeps, finally, after Monica's death, his tears gratefully honoring her many tearful prayers offered on his behalf.[123] Laurentius's Consoler too, we learn, has lapsed "ad lacrimas" [into

116 Balint, *Ordering Chaos*, 96.

117 Lawrence of Durham, *Consolatio de morte amici sui* p7.15; Balint, trans., 207.

118 Lawrence of Durham, *Consolatio de morte amici sui* p15.10; Balint, trans., 221.

119 Lawrence of Durham, *Consolatio de morte amici sui* p13.16; Balint, trans., 217.

120 Lawrence of Durham, *Consolatio de morte amici sui* p13.10; Balint, trans., 216–17.

121 Lawrence of Durham, *Consolatio de morte amici sui* p13.12; Balint, trans., 217.

122 Lawrence of Durham, *Consolatio de morte amici sui* p16.5: "quia quam verum est quod Paganus vivit, tam verum est quod et bene vivit" [just as it is true that Paganus lives, so it is true that he lives well]; Balint, trans., 223.

123 See Augustine, *Confessions* 9.12–13.33–34.

tears] after first repressing them at the passing of Paganus.[124] "Non omnis lacrimas dolor habet" [Pain does not have a monopoly on tears], he insists; there are also tears of joy: "Summo gaudio sepe id patitur natura, quod et dolentibus solet evenire" [In a time of great joy, nature often experiences the same symptoms that occur in suffering people].[125]

Lawrence of Durham's *Consolatio de morte amici sui* is markedly different from Aelred of Rievaulx's nearly contemporaneous lament for his friend Simon—a prayerful lament, saturated with quotations from the Song of Songs, in which the departed friend himself, addressed in second-person, takes the silent part of a sainted consoler in the company of Christ. Ascetical and philosophical, Lawrence's Boethian *Consolatio*, although set in a monastery, harkens back to a Late Antique world, halfway between the passion of Augustine and that of Aelred and distant from their biblical modalities. An earlier student of Boethius, Bovo II, abbot of the Saxon monastery of Corvey (900–16), had warned his monks against the dangers of the sixth-century philosopher, whose Platonic teachings in Book 3 of the *Consolation of Philosophy* were, Bovo held, incompatible with Christian faith.[126] The twelfth-century monks of England studied in this article seem to have protected themselves from any such Boethian danger with an Augustinian remedy, receiving Boethius, together with the bishop of Hippo, as a friend among friends.[127]

[124] Lawrence of Durham, *Consolatio de morte amici sui* p4.13: "Facile michi potest ignosci prolapso ad lacrimas, quas, ne nimie decurrerent, ipse repressi" [I can easily be forgiven for lapsing into tears, which I myself have repressed lest they flow excessively]; Balint, trans., 198.

[125] Lawrence of Durham, *Consolatio de morte amici sui* p4.13; Balint, trans., 198.

[126] See Chadwick, *Consolations of Music, Logic, Theology, and Philosophy*, 247.

[127] For an argument that puts Augustinian consolation at odds with Boethian, see Chad D. Schrock, *Consolation in Medieval Narrative: Augustinian Authority and Open Form* (New York: Palgrave, 2015). For additional explorations of Boethius and Augustine, see Paul E. Szarmach and Hilary Fox's essays in this volume.

Sensible Prose and the Sense of Meter: Boethian Prosimetrics and the Fourteenth Century*

Eleanor Johnson

It is not just contemporary scholars, writers, and readers who strive to defend the humanities; medieval writers, readers, and writer-theorists alike sought ways to justify the writing and studying of literature. As there are now, there were then many possible avenues for defending the production and consumption of literature as, in some way, important to the functioning of an individual's psyche, or to society. Between about 1100 and 1450, in particular, a robust tradition of literary criticism emerged in the form of Latin commentaries; this tradition insisted that literary experience must conduce to moral and ethical learning, if it were to have true value to a reader or to society. Literary works that "pertain to ethics" were to be lauded; those that lacked ethical or moral instruction were merely "lying fictions," to be avoided.[1]

This notion that literature must "pertain to ethics" has a tremendous galvanizing force on the production and theorizing of vernacular literature in the late Middle Ages, but it raises difficult questions: what does it mean, really, for literature to "pertain" to ethics? Must literature *do* ethical work; must it somehow transform its readers into more ethical beings simply by virtue of its being read? If so, how is it supposed to do that?

This underspecification of whether and how literary writing can work ethical transformation for a reader proves generative for late medieval vernacular

* This essay derives from Eleanor Johnson, *Practicing Literary Theory in the Middle Ages: Ethics and the Mixed Form in Chaucer, Gower, Usk, and Hoccleve* (Chicago: University of Chicago Press, 2013).

[1] Commentaries on Avianus, Homer, Arator, Ovid, and Horace claim their authors' works "pertain to ethics." See A.J. Minnis and A.B. Scott, *Medieval Literary Theory and Criticism, 1100–1375: The Commentary Tradition* (Oxford: Clarendon Press, 2001), 16, 17, 19, 20, 33. Conrad of Hirsau says of Aesop's fables: "In that they are made to relate to a moral end, and have been invented to give pleasure, Aesop's fables differ from the lying fictions of Terence, Plautus, and other similar poets" (*Medieval Literary Theory*, 47).

writers, who, in the course of their writing careers, turn into experimental poets and *de facto* literary theorists themselves. In this experimentation, "ethics" is explored through the forms of literature. In modern critical discourse on medieval literature, "ethics" tends, either implicitly or explicitly, to be understood as an intersubjective phenomenon, as the code of prosocial behaviors a person must embody in order to lead a good life.[2] But it is critical to remember that for medieval philosophers, commentators, and poets, the pursuit of individual happiness and fulfillment is itself construed as an ethical pursuit—indeed, the one from which the more "social" forms of ethics emanate.[3] "Ethics," then, as I will discuss it, is not directly concerned with political or interpersonal conduct but is primarily concerned with how to gain deeper understanding of one's own soul and of that soul's relationship to universal truths—for it is in the gaining of such understanding that true happiness consists, and it is *from* such understanding that any and all prosocial, interpersonal, and political ethics becomes possible.[4] By "form" I mean the literary devices, forms, topoi, tropes, and styles by which a work engages with its readers' sense perceptions. The formal power of literary language—its power to make content sensory and hence experiential—is fundamental to late medieval experimentation with ethically transformative writing. In this essay I will explore one particular lineage of using form to do ethics in the literary field.

As will surprise no one who is reading this collection of essays, I contend that this lineage originates in Boethius's sixth-century prosimetrum, *The Consolation of Philosophy*.[5] As scholars have recognized for centuries, the *Consolation* enacts ethical transformation as a spectacle: readers witness Boethius's own psychological renewal in what seems like real-time. In being constructed as a real-time spectacle of psychological transformation, the *Consolation* is designed not only to tell about Boethius's transformation but also to initiate a parallel process

[2] For instance, L.O. Aranye Fradenburg's analysis of desire and its relationship to ethics implicitly understands ethics as relational, contributing to love between people and, in its darker manifestations, to interpersonal violence. See Fradenburg, *Sacrifice your Love: Psychoanalysis, Historicism, Chaucer* (Minneapolis: University of Minnesota Press, 2002).

[3] See Jessica Rosenfeld, *Ethics and Enjoyment in Late Medieval Poetry* (Cambridge: Cambridge University Press, 2011), 1–3. Within an Augustinian framework, ethical action, Rosenfeld notes, is what happens when "the highest goal of the human subject . . . coalesces in one perfected, eternal instance of love for the divine object" (17).

[4] Isidore of Seville, *Etymologiae*, ed. W.M. Lindsay (Oxford: Oxford University Press, 1911), also notes the coincidence of inward- and outward-focused ethics, calling "ethics" equivalent to "morals," as the second part of philosophy. "Altera moralis, quae Graeci Ethica dicatur, in qua de moribus agatur" (2.24.25–6). Throughout this article, I will use "ethics" to refer to both the inward- and outward-focused categories.

[5] For an account of the interconnections of literary form, ethical work, and Boethius's *Consolation* in the earlier Middle Ages, see Susan Irvine and Hilary Fox's essays in this volume.

of transformative consolation for a reader by facilitating identification between that reader and Boethius himself. In this empathic facilitation of learning, the *Consolation* embodies a powerful answer to the mandate that fictive literature should "pertain to ethics." It promises to *do* ethics, and specifically to model the transformation of the soul from self-destructive ideation and affect to self-healing ideation and affect.

In a tremendously consequential move for later medieval literary writers and theorists, the *Consolation* explicitly pins that modeling of ethical transformation to its own mixed-form composition. Throughout, the *Consolation* theorizes prose as the form that embodies rational thought, while it treats meter as the form that embodies sensuality and pleasure. Also throughout, prose is where dialogue—the back-and-forth Socratic conversation between Philosophy and Boethius—takes place. Poetry, in contrast, is where monologic lyricism occurs, where a single speaker—either Boethius or Philosophy—sings a song. The dual formal embodiment of Boethius's learning in dialogic argumentation and monologic lyric is central to the ethically transformative function of the *Consolation*, as is made explicit by Philosophy's own statements. Pervasively, she signals to him *why* she deploys the forms of prose and meter when she does, foregrounding how meter works in a productive synergy with prose—how meter and prose are in fact mutually necessary to ethical reeducation, via their alternating action of argumentation and lyricism. Through Philosophy's signaling, Boethius becomes, in effect, a literary theorist.

To give an instance of this on-the-tarmac literary theorizing of the ethical effects of literary form, early on, after Philosophy sings a song to Boethius, she asks a question that reveals the essential function of metrical poetry in Boethius's process of philosophical learning: "'Sentisne,' inquit, 'haec atque animo illabuntur tuo?'" ["Do you feel these things," she said, "and do they penetrate into your soul?"].[6] This characterization first reveals that Philosophy's healing lyric acts by penetration; song is useful when prose cannot—quite literally—get through to Boethius. Its piercing action breaks through the affective wall of his sorrows. Second, by evoking "sense," Philosophy's characterization suggests that meter penetrates by producing sensory experience. Evidently, Philosophy needs to use the sensual penetration of metrical lyric in order to initiate the process of Boethius's philosophical transformation from despair to hope.

Once Philosophy has "pierced" into Boethius via song, however, she immediately switches to prose, in which she conducts the rational argumentation that is meant to draw Boethius out of his despair. Crucially, the dialogic prose interactions between Philosophy and Boethius are styled to foreground the logical causality that underpins their ideation. A typical prose passage is Book 4, Prose 3, line 8 (4p3.8), which begins with Boethius remembering Philosophy's

[6] *Anicii Manlii Severini Boethii Philosophiae Consolatio*, ed. Ludwig Bieler, CCSL 94 (Turnhout: Brepols, 1957), 1p4.1. Hereafter cited parenthetically.

last point, as in "memento etenim corollarii illius" [For I remember the corollaries to those previous things]. Then, Philosophy turns to explain a number of consequences to Boethius's new understanding. These consequences are marked by a series of causal operators—such as thus, therefore, ergo, for this reason, etc.—that convey a sense of the causal relation among the ideas.[7] These causal operators are interspersed with other rhetorical markers of causality, such as "cui consequens est" [which is a consequence of] and "necesse est" [it is necessary that], so that the prose of a passage is rhetorically designed to foreground the causal relations among ideas through its use of argumentative markers (4p3).

The importance of causality to Philosophy's transformative consolation becomes explicit when she describes how the elegant workings of the universe are bound together by an "indissolubili causarum conexione" [indissoluble connection of causes, 4p6.19]. This causal connection, she explains, emanates from Providence, which calls into being an "indeclinabilem causarum ordinem" [ineluctable order of causes, 4p6.20]. According to Philosophy, nothing emerges from nothing; all events in human life are caused and are foreseen by the unchanging order of the universe. Fortune is thus phantasmatic, a false understanding of the world, based on a failure to understand that mankind is ultimately protected by Providence. The consolation of divine providence is that it secures order and causality in human life, whether human beings see it or not. Causality is part and parcel of Philosophy's consoling teaching; it is part and parcel of Boethian ethical transformation. And it is borne by Boethian prose.

But Philosophy's initial attempts to help Boethius remember the comforts of causality via rational argumentation fail; in response, she switches back into song. To explain why she does so, she deploys a medical metaphor that casts lyric as a poultice or compress that can ease Boethius's psychological pain, to prepare him for the sterner stuff of prose argument. She says:

> Sed quoniam plurimus tibi affectuum tumultus incubuit diversumque te dolor ira maeror distrahunt, uti nunc mentis es, nondum te validiora remedia contingunt. Itaque lenioribus paulisper utemur, ut quae in tumorem perturbationibus influentibus induruerunt ad acrioris vim medicaminis recipiendam tactu blandiore mollescant. (1p5.11–12)
>
> [But since this multiplicity of tumultuous emotions overwhelms you—sorrow, ire, and mourning tear you up . . . stronger remedies cannot yet touch you. So let us use gentler medicines, so that these emotions that have hardened into a cyst may be softened, until it will bear a harsher remedy.]

In this passage the *Consolation* encourages a reader to see lyric as a necessary means of penetrating into one's psyche via one's body, through the action of

[7] See 4p3. Note, for instance, the repetition of *igitur*.

sensuality and palliation. This gentle palliation paves the way for the "stronger remedy" of rational argumentation in prose. Prose is thus cast as the vehicle of serious philosophical interrogation in the *Consolation*, the intellectual substance to which the meter acts as a gentle, penetrating sensory facilitator. Before the end of its first book, *The Consolation of Philosophy* has signaled itself as a metapoetic work, a work of literary theory-in-practice, foregrounding the formal conditions by which it pursues its ethically transformative end and outlining distinct and seemingly innate functionalities for both prose and poetry.[8]

This explicit theory of how the mixed form achieves its transformative function—and, in particular, the notion that prose is somehow more powerful than poetry in the process—is amplified by later medieval commentators on Boethius. William of Conches, for instance, explains that song serves to draw off negative affect and introduce positive affect, while prose is the appropriate space for heavier, more linear, organized logical argumentation.[9] William's commentary notes that Boethian song has a sensual and palliative effect, which then paves the way for the rational argument of prose, in which the substantial work of consolation takes place. As it continues to evolve, the commentary tradition surrounding *The Consolation of Philosophy* constructs prosimetrum as the form of philosophy, the form of consolation, with the poetry playing second fiddle to the rational prose.

But on the Continent in the first two-thirds of the fourteenth century, vernacular poets react to the commentary tradition's quiet demotion of poetry to the status of a second-class ethical citizen, and its concomitant valorization of prose as the form of real rational work. During this period, vernacular poet-theorists on the Continent seek to redeem and even *vaunt* the ethical status of lyrical poetry, relative to prose. For instance, Dante's post-Boethian *Vita nuova* uses prose blocks in two different ways in relation to his lyrical poems. The prose sections that come before his lyrics serve simply to introduce them narratively. The prose sections that follow the lyrics, by contrast, work to unpack his lyrical poems, which, by the glossatorial action of the prose sections, become the implicit ethical and formal core of the entire *Vita nuova*.[10] For Boethius, as he was received and constructed by commentators, poetry was the gentle palliative to the hard-going logic of prose. For Dante, poetry is the hard stuff, where the substantial, transformative work of ethical reeducation takes place; prose becomes the *de facto* ethical, formal, and contextual marginalia of his book, the interpretive aid that guides a reader through the much trickier stuff of poetry.[11] For Guillaume de Machaut, whose mixed-form *Remede de Fortune* contains a mix of different kinds of poetry,

[8] On distinct uses of prose and poetry in Anglo-Saxon England, see Susan Irvine's essay in this volume.

[9] William of Conches, *Glosae super Boetium*, ed. Lodi Nauta, CCCM 158 (Turnhout: Brepols, 1999), p. 6, ll. 61–63.

[10] For elaboration, see Johnson, *Practicing Literary Theory*, 42–54.

[11] See Johnson, *Practicing Literary Theory*, 45–48.

and elides prose form altogether, the statement in defense of poetry's ethical sufficiency is even louder: verse, and verse alone, Guillaume seems to suggest, can do the work of ethical transformation in a post-Boethian literary work.[12]

Crucially, in their revisionist mixed-form works, Guillaume and Dante each explore how the attribution of any specific ethically transformative powers to prose or meter per se is a constructed and conventional literary association that can be reinvented and recast at will. Prose and meter, so carefully delineated in their respective and mutually necessary ethical effects by Boethius and his commentators, become shifting and slippery categories of ethical and formal practice in the hands of these vernacular writers. For them, the mixed form becomes a robust formal engine for literary-theoretical experimentation. Thus, by the time the mixed-form paradigm for ethical writing reaches fourteenth-century England, it has already become a contested zone of literary and literary-theoretical experimentation and a latent zone for promulgating defenses of poetry.

To show what I mean, I will now turn to Chaucer's literary theoretical experimentation in *Troilus and Criseyde* and the *Canterbury Tales*. The Boethianness of the *Troilus* has never been in question: the poem pervasively channels huge swathes of Boethian philosophy, ranging from the conflicts between free will and predestination to the importance of rational argumentation for a process of psychological renewal.[13] Boethian meters, moreover, are occasionally woven into the poem, in the mouths either of main characters or of the narrator.[14] But the *formal* design of the *Troilus* also constitutes a response to Boethius, and to the

---

12 See Johnson, *Practicing Literary Theory*, 48–53.

13 Theodore Stroud, "Boethius' Influence on Chaucer's *Troilus*," *Modern Philology* 49 (1951): 1–9; Bernard Jefferson, *Chaucer and the Consolation of Philosophy of Boethius* (Princeton: Princeton University Press, 1917); Howard Patch, *The Tradition of Boethius: A Study of His Importance in Late Medieval Culture* (Oxford: Oxford University Press, 1935); Howard Patch, "Troilus on Determinism," *Speculum* 6 (1931): 225–43; Charles Owen, "Significance of Chaucer's Revisions to the *Troilus and Criseyde*," *Modern Philology* 55 (1957): 1–5; John Huber, "Troilus' Predestination Soliloquy," *Neuphilologische Mitteilungen* 66 (1965): 120–25; Peter Elbow, "Two Boethian Speeches in *Troilus and Criseyde* and Chaucerian Irony," in *Literary Criticism and Historical Understanding*, ed. Philip Damon (New York: Columbia University Press, 1967), 85–107. Ida Gordon, *The Double Sorrow of Troilus: A Study of Ambiguities in Troilus and Criseyde* (Oxford: Oxford University Press, 1970), 24–60, reads the *Troilus* as an ironic secularization of the thematics of the *Consolation*. John Steadman, *Disembodied Laughter* (Berkeley: University of California Press, 1972), 1–20, sees the end of the *Troilus*, and Troilus's famous ascent into the heavens, as a reworking of and commentary on Boethius's ascent through the spheres. Alice R. Kaminsky, *Chaucer's Troilus and Criseyde and the Critics* (Athens: Ohio University Press, 1980), 41–53, sets out the *Troilus*'s thematic debts to Boethian philosophy and reviews critical assessments of the thematic relation of the *Troilus* to the *Consolation*.

14 As an index of the perceived depth of Chaucer's debt to Boethius, John Fleming, *Classical Imitation and Interpretation in Chaucer's Troilus* (Lincoln: University of Nebraska

mixed form in particular. This may come as a surprising claim, given that the *Troilus* is composed, throughout, in stanzaic verse. But what Chaucer does with the mixed-form mandate of Boethius's work—rather like what Guillaume does in his *Remede de Fortune*—is to devise a two-part *verse* structure for the *Troilus*, consisting, on the one hand, of the historically embedded narrative of the lives of Troilus and Criseyde and, on the other, of the narrator's proems and intermittent lyrical excursuses from the main narrative. In effect, in Chaucer's hands, the historical narrative of the Trojan war, with its intensive emplotment, its constant foregrounding of causality, its incessant insistence on making plain to its audience the order of events and the reasons that they happen, is a versified ethical equivalent of Boethian prose sections, which are, as I have argued, designed to formally render causality itself and help Boethius remember the ineluctable truth of divine providence.[15] At the same time, the narratorial excursuses are, like Boethian meters, affective and sensual commentaries on the main action, which do not connect up with each other but, instead, serve as reprieves and moral signposts for readers.[16] Thus in its structure, the *Troilus* makes a response to the Boethian mixed form and an even stronger response to early medieval Boethian commentators: verse and verse alone, in the *Troilus*, can do the work of both the prose and the meters of the *Consolation*.

This re-vindication of the power of versified poetry gains more momentum and specificity at the very end of the poem. Troilus's post-mortem ascent through the heavenly spheres is established as a revisiting of Boethius's transformative ascent from despair to understanding. Troilus's ascent, though, is not the main Boethian event. Instead, it prepares the reader for the more complete and seemingly "philosophical" transcendence that the narrator undergoes. This narrator, like the narrating Boethius, is transformed by his experience of retelling his tale.[17]

But the narrator's seeming transformation to higher consciousness would have been baffling to a medieval reader steeped in Boethian thematics. From within a Boethian philosophical frame of reference, the narrator's putative turn from worldly tragedy to divine contemplation in the palinode seems anything but warranted. He has not been engaged in a conversation with Philosophy, has not heard her comforting explanations of divine order, and he has not heard her beautiful illustrations of cosmic harmonics. Although there are lengthy Boethian passages stitched into the *Troilus*, they are invariably stitched in with the needle of irony. True, Troilus attacks the Boethian problems of free will and fate in Book 4 of the *Troilus*, but whereas Boethius eventually gleans comfort and un-

---

Press, 1990), 84, calls the *Troilus* a "crooked" translation of the *Consolation*, in apposition with the "straight" translation Chaucer composed in the *Boece*.

[15] For elaboration, see Johnson, *Practicing Literary Theory*, 25–30 and 102–7.

[16] See Johnson, *Practicing Literary Theory*, 107–14.

[17] For more on the transformative power of the *Consolation*, see A. Joseph McMullen's contribution to this volume.

derstanding from his philosophizing, Troilus only works himself into a deeper state of benightedness.[18] Even the narrator himself seems unable to get beyond the idea of Fortune's rampant tyranny in the world—an idea Boethius himself must dispense with quite early on in his own transformative narrative. The poem, then, is crafted in order first to evoke and then to *destabilize* Boethian thematics. And yet, somehow, the narrator seems to attain transformative understanding anyway. He seems, in the end, to free himself from the wheel of Fortune and to find his way to a contemplation of God.

I would suggest that the irony of the narrator's seeming transformation at the end ultimately has its roots in a metapoetic squabble that Chaucer is having with Boethius over the nature and purpose of tragic poetry—a squabble that ties into how and why Chaucer repurposes the mixed form.[19] Perhaps the pinnacle of the narrator's ironic revision of the *Consolation* is that he has been engaged in the one form of poetic activity that Philosophy herself pointedly shuns as deleterious to the health of the soul. In her first appearance, Philosophy realizes Boethius is enmeshed in self-pity, surrounded by the poetic muses—what she further calls the "scenicas meretriculas" or, as Chaucer puts it "comune strompettis of swich a place that men clepen the theatre."[20] These "theatrical" strumpet muses are recognizably the muses of tragedy. Before she even attempts to heal Boethius, Philosophy violently casts out these tragic muses, saying they pierce into him with venomous spines and damage his ability to profit from her teachings. This banishment of tragedy from philosophy's consolation would be familiar to any medieval reader of Boethius and would have made the final turn of the *Troilus*, which the narrator explicitly calls, at that very moment, a "tragedy," a mind-boggling shock.

But shock is precisely the point. The narrator finishes with a renewed conviction in God's eternity and a turn toward prayer. He finishes, that is, in a state of consolation. This ending echoes the transformative end of the *Consolation* itself, but with a literary-theoretical twist. The poem demonstrates that Philosophy's twin consolation can inhere as readily in tragic fiction as it can in philosophical allegory.[21] Chaucer uses Boethius as a literary-theoretical provocation, not just

---

[18] Geoffrey Chaucer, *Troilus and Criseyde*, in *The Riverside Chaucer*, ed. Larry D. Benson, 3rd edn. (Boston: Houghton Mifflin, 1987), 4.954–1078.

[19] For more on Chaucer, Boethius, and the nature of tragedy, see Jonathan Stavsky's essay in this volume.

[20] Cf. 1p1.8; Geoffrey Chaucer, *Boece*, in *The Riverside Chaucer*, ed. Benson, 1p1.49–50.

[21] Thomas Stillinger, *The Song of Troilus: Lyrical Authority in the Medieval Book* (Philadelphia: University of Pennsylvania Press, 1992), too, recognizes the cultivation of empathy as a fundamental part of Chaucer's design, saying, "He writes a book in which it is possible to identify with Troilus or with Criseyde or with the narrator who identifies (in different ways) with both" (216).

for representing his narrator's transformation and modeling one for a reader but also for defending the ethical utility of tragic poetry against the likes of Boethius himself.[22]

More specifically, the *Troilus* demonstrates that its stylistic reinvention of the mixed form, with its formal creation of the experiences of causality and affective catharsis, can produce ethical transformation on its own. The narrator apparently does not need to learn the specific *thematics* of Philosophy's lessons, because the forms and styles—and, specifically, the oscillation between causality and affect—are sufficient to teach him. The poem works, then, as a defense not just of tragic poetry but also of the *formal powers* of tragic poetry to ignite transformative understanding in a reader. It is a work of vernacular literary theory, put into practice. That theory has relied upon Boethian literary theory, but has done so—much as Dante had done in the *Vita nuova* and Guillaume had done in the *Remede*—precisely to re-interrogate and reimagine a formally worked ethical transformation beyond the limit of Boethian literary experimentation.

Now to the *Canterbury Tales*, in which Chaucer revisits a Boethian theorizing of prose and meter's relative ethical status but does so through a far darker lens. Although Boethius's *Consolation* is a theoretical provocation for the *Tales* at a very large scale, I will telescope in for now on Chaucer's own supposed tale-telling performance. In the middle of the *Canterbury Tales*, "the Chaucer-pilgrim" contributes a story to the tale-telling competition among the pilgrims: the tail-rhymed romance the *Tale of Sir Thopas*. This tale, poetically wrought to the point of being tortuous and torturous, and very self-conscious in that wroughtness, narrates, above all else, sensory overload: Thopas's body is described in mind-numbing detail, as are his scents and the scents and sights around him and the cacophony of birdsong that he hears. Harry Bailly, the Host and judge of the Canterbury tale-telling competition, quickly puts the kibosh on this hypersensory tale, telling the Chaucer-pilgrim that his song makes one's "eres aken" [ears ache] and one's mind sluggish.[23] Significantly, the Chaucer-pilgrim's next reflex is to turn from hyper-aesthetic, hyper-ornamented, hyper-songful poetry to the comparatively dull, flat, pale, and insipid *Tale of Melibee*, which is composed in prose. The ethical narrative of this prose tale concerns a female allegorical personification—Prudence—counseling her husband to get over his negative emotions and reconnect with more pro-social values. Prudence achieves this

[22] Here I disagree with Monica McAlpine's reading, which examines the *Troilus*'s generic affiliations with Boethius, reading the *Consolation* as an antitragedy (a demonstration of Boethius's ascent from despair to joy and thus a reversal of the Senecan tragic paradigm by which a man goes from joy to despair) and the *Troilus* as a response to it that reaffirms Boethius's condemnation of tragedy. See McAlpine, *The Genre of Troilus and Criseyde* (Ithaca: Cornell University Press, 1978), 17–19, 30, 52–85, 89, 90, and 120.

[23] Geoffrey Chaucer, *The Canterbury Tales*, in *The Riverside Chaucer*, ed. Benson, VII.923. Hereafter cited parenthetically by fragment and line number.

through the action of carefully constructed and highly causally specific Socratic dialogue—language replete with causal operators, to such an extent that they become a central feature of the tale's design. After this prose argument, the Host Harry Bailly is sufficiently impressed with the tale's ethical lessons to let the Chaucer-pilgrim off the hook, and his performance as a tale-teller ends.

The Consolation of Philosophy pervades this dyad of tales. Throughout the *Consolation*, poetic song is nominated as a mode that works by engaging the hearer's senses and emotions. Thus, diegetically, the narrative that Chaucer's avatar tells about Thopas is, in fact, a thematic exploration of what it would really be like if all that poetry could do was engage the senses and emotions. It is, in a word, a critique of Boethius's theorizations of poetry in the *Consolation*. Moreover, the contents of the *Melibee* thematically reproduce the core dynamics of the *Consolation* as well: a beneficent female personification heals a brain-addled male interlocutor of his sickened perspective on reality, and she does so by the careful enactment of causally sequenced Socratic argumentation. In the *Tales*, the prose form seems to "win" over lyrical poetry as an ethically efficacious form, simply by dint of its not being censured, as *Thopas* was, as a waste of time.[24] Thus, into the mouth of his own self-representation in the *Tales*, Chaucer puts a carefully crafted duo of stories that allow him to comment, however slyly, on the core claims of Boethian literary theory: namely, that song works by engaging the senses, that prose works by engaging reason, and that both are necessary to the ethical transformation of an audience. Chaucer the poet and critic, that is, uses his persona to stage, interrogate, and ultimately undercut a major principle of Late Antique literary form and theory by suggesting that poetry might be ethically inefficacious. An odd and disquieting move for Chaucer—the notional "Father of English poetry"—to make.

In this odd move, Chaucer, a devout Dante scholar and an obsessive reader of Guillaume de Machaut, is responding to their experiments with the ethical power of poetry and their defenses of poetry as a legitimate and efficacious ethical form in its own right. But, whereas they both agitate for an ever greater and more central role for the lyric in a work of ethical literature, Chaucer—again, the notional Father of English poetry—seems here to chip away at its alleged ethical powers. In the Chaucer-pilgrim's performance, lyrical poetry almost seems like a dirty little habit that a truly ethical poet has to overcome before he can move on to the real ethical heavy lifting of prose argumentation, as contained in the *Melibee*.

Chaucer returns to his meditations on the ethical power of the mixed form toward the end of the *Tales*. The end of Chaucer's motley fiction deploys yet another prosimetric contest, though this time it is one in which poetry seems yet more decidedly the loser in the emergent contest between prose and verse. The

[24] "Thy drasty rymyng is nat worth a toord! / Thou doost noght elles but despendest tyme" (VII.930–931).

final three performances in the narrative—the Manciple's poem, the Parson's prose, and the prose of Chaucer himself in the *Retractions*—seem to reinscribe lyrical work yet more deeply as an ethically questionable effort—thus further dismantling the stoutly ethical edifice that Dante and Guillaume had erected as the place of lyrical poetry in their own mixed-form works.

The *Manciple's Tale* begins when the Host urges the Manciple to make peace with the drunken and ethically scurrilous Cook, with whom the Manciple has been fighting. The Manciple does so, ironically, by plying the Cook with yet more liquor. To this the Host responds in a manner that sets up the poetic crisis to follow: "that," he says, "wol turne rancour and disese / T'acord and love, and many a wrong apese. / O Bacus, yblessed be thy name, / That so kanst turnen ernest into game! / Worshipe and thank be to thy deitee!" (IX.97–101). On one level, this assertion, by raising the proverbial glass to Bacchus, recognizes the power of wine to make peace in a community. But, on a second level, the Host introduces a metapoetic problem that will continue to play out over the course of the Manciple's story: the impulse to rely on Bacchanalian modes of persuasion when Apollonian modes of lyrical engagement are not efficacious in improving someone's ethical behavior.[25]

"Phebus" Apollo appears in the first line of the Manciple's actual tale and is both the hero and the victim of the narrative (IX.104). And, significantly, Phoebus is also associated in Boethius's *Consolation* with the salvific power of philosophical song. Through the Manciple's unfolding story, Chaucer situates his "Phebus" even more surely in a Boethian formal and ethical universe. Phoebus has a wife, from whom he wants and expects sexual fidelity; but, as the Manciple notes, by recourse to the second meter of Boethius's third book, no one can constrain a free being:

> Taak any bryd, and put it in a cage,
> And do al thyn entente and thy corage
> To fostre it tendrely with mete and drynke
> . . .
> Although his cage of gold be never so gay,
> Yet hath this brid, by twenty thousand foold,
> Levere in a forest that is rude and coold
> Goon ete wormes and swich wrecchednesse.
> For evere this brid wol doon his bisynesse
> To escape out of his cage, yif he may.
> His libertee this brid desireth ay. (IX.163–174)

---

[25] For a much later but similarly ecstatic yet horrified affirmation of the power of Bacchanalian song, see Friedrich Nietzsche, *The Birth of Tragedy*, trans. Douglas Smith (Oxford: Oxford University Press, 2000).

This passage carefully renders into English a very famous meter from Boethius's *Consolation*, one that concerns the imprisonment of birds, to illustrate the horrible evil of trying to keep any living thing in prison. The Manciple uses this rendering of Boethius's meter not only to make a diegetic point about the futility of trying to "destreyne a thyng" (IX.161) but also to situate Phoebus and his immanent poetic disaster within a larger Boethian frame of reference. He uses it, that is, to mark this tale as in some way itself fettered to Boethius's consoling narrative.

But we quickly see that, like the bird who seeks to escape his cage, the Manciple evokes Boethian thematics only to contradict Boethian literary theory immediately thereafter, through a programmatic figural defrocking of Phoebus himself. Throughout the *Consolation*, Phoebus is associated with poetic healing, relief, and recovery of one's reason. It is Phoebus's penetrating rays that bring light back to Boethius's eyes—in Chaucer's translation, "thanne schyneth Phebus ischaken with sodeyn light and smyteth with his beemes in merveylynge eien."[26] For Boethius, Phoebus is the poetic healer, the musician qua savior who chases the dark clouds of misunderstanding from both mind and heart. In the Manciple's story, by pointed contrast, Phoebus is a profoundly flawed character, a victim of his own passions, who cannot see what is right and what is wrong or distinguish what is true from what is false. When he learns of his wife's infidelity, Phoebus abandons the healing logic of a truly Apollonian poetics altogether and falls back instead on one of the mainstays of Bacchanalianism: violent aggression and cacophony. He murders his wife and strips the crow of his beautiful song—a Chaucerian addition, not present in his Ovidian source—and replaces it with a shrill caw.[27]

Most damaging of all to the idea that Phoebus might, as Boethius says he does, embody a salvific poetics, a poetics of healing harmony, in a passage Chaucer also adds *de novo* to his Ovidian source, Phoebus is shown to be unable to hold back even from destroying his own musical instruments: "For sorwe . . . he brak his mynstralcie, / Bothe harpe, and lute, and gyterne, and sautrie; / And eek he brak his arwes and his bowe" (IX.267–269). Having evoked Boethius, a believer in and advocate for the specific power of Apollonian musical healing, the Manciple depicts a Phoebus not only emotionally frail and vulnerable to deceit but also utterly lacking in self-awareness and subject instead to the whims of passion. Through Phoebus's violent inability to control his passions or to resort to his own healing music as a way out of his suffering, Boethius's vision of a salvific and songful poetics is undermined.

Through this undermining, lyrical poetry's power to provoke generative ethical transformation has once again come under heavy fire in the emergent literary theory and practice of the *Canterbury Tales*. The "transformation" in the *Man-*

---

[26] Chaucer, *Boece*, 1m3.15–17.

[27] *Riverside Chaucer*, ed. Benson, 954, note to ll. 295–296.

ciple's Tale, embodied in the crow, entails mute subordination, not philosophical transcendence. Simultaneously, the ethical transformation that the Manciple recommends extra-diegetically to his readers at the end of his tale is one of paranoid silence, not spiritual renewal. "Kepe wel thy tonge and thenk upon the crowe" [Hold your tongue, and think upon the crow], he repeatedly urges (IX.362).[28] The tale thus ends up being a darkly metapoetic *exemplum*, expressing lyrical poetry's self-destructiveness and susceptibility to ethical unraveling. Consolation is not at all what emerges from this Bacchanalian reboot of Boethius's singing.

Lyrical poetry's power to work ethical transformation comes to seem yet *more* dubious in the *Parson's Prologue*, which appears next in the *Canterbury Tales*. That prologue is in verse but is quickly followed by the Parson's long sermonic piece, which he composes in prose. In combination, these two elements of the Parson's performance—the verse prologue and the prose tale—create another miniature prosimetric contest, after which the prose form decisively wins, forcefully and *permanently* ejecting poetry from the *Canterbury Tales*. This ejection retroactively highlights the banishment of the lyric from Phoebus's home and creates an intertale *prosimetrum* with the Manciple's performance, as well as the intratale one within the Parson's own performance, so that the Parson's sermon creates a prosimetric juncture on two levels—between his own prologue and tale *and* between the Manciple's verse tale and his prose one.

The Parson's rejection of poetry unfurls early and explicitly. When asked to contribute a tale to the competition, he agrees, but says,

> I kan nat geeste [alliterate] "rum, ram, ruf," by lettre,
> Ne, God woot, rym holde I but litel bettre;
> And therfore, if yow list—I wol nat glose [deceive]—
> I wol yow telle a myrie tale in prose. (X.43–46)

By saying he "cannot alliterate, 'rum, ram, ruf,' by letter," nor can he "rhyme any better," the Parson makes a double-voiced assault on poetry. On the one hand, he seems to disavow competency at poetry; he "cannot" achieve its formal intricacies. But, on the other hand, he implies that there is something lying and false about poetry, so that he, a man of the cloth, is not permitted to use it. Since the Parson "will not *glose*, or lie," he "cannot" tell "alliterative poetry" or "rhyme" but must, instead, speak in prose. Thus, at the end of the tale-telling competition, the Parson both affirms the catastrophic conclusion of the *Manciple's Tale* and recurs to the Chaucer-pilgrim's own metapoetic principle from the *Thopas-Melibee* conjunction, suggesting that prose makes a better and more ethically defensible

[28] See similar admonishments at IX.310, 315, 319, and 333. Much of this section of Chaucer's poem derives from Albertano of Brescia's *Tractatus loquendi et tacendi*. See *Riverside Chaucer*, 954, notes to ll. 325–328, 332–333, 338, and 355–356.

use of time than does formally wrought poetry. If Phoebus's lyre is smashed, the Parson seems to say, so much the better: far more worthy speaking, with less *glosing* and more substance, can be accomplished in prose.[29]

When he moves from his versified prologue to his prose sermon, the Parson seems hell-bent on shouting down all forms of fictive literature. As far as he is concerned, any "jangling" or speaking "withouten profit of hym that speketh tho wordes, and eek of hym that herkneth tho wordes" is idleness and sin (X.647–649, 651–652). All speech that does not directly serve Christ—so, by implication, the entire foregoing Canterbury tale-telling contest—merely serves the devil. The Parson, pointedly, embodies his decrying of "jangling" or "ydel speche" in his simple and unornamented prose style. Together, the Parson's denunciation of poetic form in his prologue, his tale's enunciated condemnation of "ydel" fictions, and his formal avoidance of poetic ornamentation in his own prose style read as a metapoetic principle that exiles poetry—both for its songful form and its dubious content—from the Canterbury project.

Indeed, the Parson's puritanical mandates colonize the end of the *Tales*: from the *Parson's Tale* we turn at last to the prose *Retractions*, in which Chaucer admits guilt at feeling that his poetic works, including sections of the *Canterbury Tales*, "sownen into synne" (X.1085). The *Retractions* have long puzzled Chaucerians because their sullen and morose depiction of Chaucer seems discontinuous with the ironic, playful Chaucer of the rest of the *Canterbury Tales*. But there is a reading of the *Retractions* that reveals a Chaucer whose ironic, playful, and experimental sensibility remains intact from the beginning to the end of the *Canterbury Tales*. The *Retractions* should indeed be read in the light of the *Parson's Tale*, but even more in the light of the *Consolation of Philosophy*, as a final Boethian turn in a long arc of imitating, responding to, and reimagining how literary transformation inhabits form. Retroactively, the *Retractions* cast the entire *Tales*—including the verse-canceling performances by the Manciple and Parson—as a vernacular response to Boethius, staging the ethical transformation of the narrating Chaucer through his experience of witnessing the tales of all the foregoing pilgrims.

In this passage, the distance between the authorial Chaucer and the narrating Chaucer-pilgrim protagonist collapses: with no obvious break from the Canterbury narrative, readers are suddenly told that their narrator—the Chaucer-pilgrim—is the same Chaucer who wrote the *Legend of Good Women*, *Troilus and Criseyde*, and, of course, the English translation of *The Consolation of Philosophy*. The collapse of author and narrator draws the *Canterbury Tales* into an ever-closer literary kinship with the *Consolation*: at the very end, we realize that we have been reading a fictional, mixed-form work in which the narrating author Geoffrey Chaucer has also been a main character, whose literary sensibilities had

[29] For a detailed reading of how in particular we might construe Chaucer's meaning in having the Parson call his tale "myrie", see Arvind Thomas, "What's Myrie about the Prose of the Parson's Tale?" *Chaucer Review* 46 (2012): 419–38.

to be formed and re-formed over the course of his literary-philosophical transformation and who finishes that process of literary transformation by transcending fiction and turning his attention to prayer. We realize, that is, that we have been reading a fiction of narratorial transformation, where the transformation in question is from elvish rhymster of "drasty" lyrics (VII.930), as Harry Bailly referred to the song of Thopas, to a supposedly serious author of ethically weighty literary projects.

Once he has collapsed the Chaucer-pilgrim narrator and character with his own authorial identity, and has confessed his sinful works, the author-narrator-protagonist Chaucer disavows almost his entire corpus, excepting works of obvious "moralitee and devocioun" such as the *Consolation* translation (X.1085–1087). In so doing, Chaucer accedes at once to the hard-lined anti-poetic *manifesto* of the Parson and also to Boethian mandates: at the very end of the *Consolation*, Boethius exhorts his audience to eschew vices, to worship and love virtues, and to raise their hearts to righteous hopes and humble prayers.[30] With Boethius's final words in mind, the *Retractions* read as though written as a response to their injunction, filtered through the rigid lens of the Parson's lyric-hating sensibilities. First Chaucer lists his works, acknowledging and revoking those that "sownen into synne." He then prays to God, Jesus, and Mary, "bisekynge hem that they from hennes forth unto my lyves ende . . . graunte me grace of verray penitence, confessioun, and satisfaccioun to doon in this present lyf . . . so that I may been oon of hem at the day of doom that shulle be saved" (X.1089, 1091). The *Retractions* are crafted to reveal Chaucer—as narrator, author, and also *protagonist and hero* of the *Tales*—as, at last, a good student of Boethian literary practice and theory, as well as a good student of his own pilgrims' many tales. He has done it: he has made a mixed-form work that, in the end, enables him to graduate to higher forms of contemplation. Despite, or perhaps because of, his increasing and problematic ejection of lyrical writing from his project, Chaucer has made it; he has become an ethical poetic maker in his own right, and he has done

[30] "Manet etiam spectator desuper cunctorum praescius deus uisionisque eius praesens semper aeternitas cum nostrorum actuum futura qualitate concurrit bonis praemia malis supplicia dispensans. Nec frustra sunt in deo positae spes precesque; quae cum rectae sunt, inefficaces esse non possunt. Aversamini igitur vitia, colite virtutes, ad rectas spes animum sublevate, humiles preces in excelsa porrigite. Magna vobis est, si dissimulare non vultis, necessitas indicta probitatis, cum ante oculos agitis iudicis cuncta cernentis" [For God always remains the constant, foreknowing watcher, and his eternally present vision runs forth with the future quality of our actions, dispensing boons to the good, punishments to the bad. Not in vain are hopes and prayers placed in God; when these are rightful, they cannot but be efficacious. Avoid therefore vices, collect virtues, lift up your soul to righteous hopes, give your humble prayers on high. If you do not choose to lie, a great charge of probity is yours, for you act before the eyes of an all-seeing judge, 5p6.45–48].

so by composing a richly metacritical mixed-form work.[31] In the mixed-form *Canterbury Tales*, Chaucer re-engages with *prosimetrum* as a possible vehicle of ethical change. He shows the mixed form's availability as a foundation on which to build metapoetic explorations of literary experience, culminating with a transformation of its ostensibly humble and bumbling narrator into a fully fledged author of a work of vernacular literary philosophy.

But this reproduction of Boethius's final consolation is revisionist and deliberately thorny in one very consequential way: taken as a whole, the *Canterbury Tales*, although it stages its author-narrator's own eventual turn toward God, does not seek to produce any particular lesson for its *readership*. It does not have a unified didactic goal or message that emerges for a reader gradually and progressively as he or she approaches the end of the work. It does not point clearly or decisively toward a particular vision of divine truth or transcendent contemplation. In this lack of didactic specificity, Chaucer's re-engagement with prosimetric practice and transformative theory marks a pronounced departure from Boethius, who uses prose and meter as vehicles for a carefully sculpted and specific demonstration of divine order. Boethius is not interested in literature's transformative potential per se; he is interested in literature's power to work a particular process of learning, to take its narrator and audience from despair to an awareness of God's supremely ordered goodness. He is interested not just in any consolation but, specifically in Philosophy's consolation—a consolation borne of the feeling of prose and meter but also of the specific lessons that those forms carry when wielded by Philosophy. Instead of being concerned with *what* particular lesson a narrator might learn from a literary work, Chaucer is concerned with *how* and, indeed, *whether* one can learn from literature, with how literary techniques, juxtapositions, and formal interactions can produce transformation in a narrator or model one for an audience. *In toto*, the *Tales* suggest that the spe-

[31] C. David Benson, *Chaucer's Drama of Style: Poetic Variety and Contrast in the* Canterbury Tales (Chapel Hill: University of North Carolina Press, 1986), has also noted the influence of Boethius on the work: "General precedent for the stylistic experiments of the *Canterbury Tales* is provided by Chaucer's favorite philosophical work, Boethius's *Consolation of Philosophy*. Its alternation of prose exposition and soaring poetry (later imitated, though hardly matched, in such works as Alain de Lille's *De Planctu*) may have suggested something of what different kinds of artistries within the same work could accomplish" (23). In a similar vein, Anne Payne, *Chaucer and Menippean Satire* (Madison: University of Wisconsin Press, 1981), has suggested that Chaucer's poem is a deliberate response to the genre of Menippean satire, to which Chaucer was exposed precisely by his readings of Boethius's *Consolation*. Payne, however, focuses primarily on Menippean structures within individual tales—the Knight and the Pardoner, for instance—rather than on how Boethian form might influence the overall construction of the *Tales* as a unified but multiplicitous literary production. Payne suggests that Chaucer used Boethius as a crib for making Menippean satire as a means of destabilizing authority, so that "no answer or position, no matter how authoritative it may seem, can ever provide certainty" (219).

cific lessons of fictive literature are not as important as is an indwelling in the dialectics of meaning and feeling, narration and interruption, linearity and recursion, dialogue and monologue, and prose and meter. Paradoxically, through the *Retractions*, the *Canterbury Tales* offers itself, finally, as a metapoetic defense of literature as a formal mode of doing ethical work, though it leaves the precise formal quiddity of that work titillatingly underdetermined. Chaucer, in the end, like Dante and Guillaume, uses Boethius's relatively rigid formalism as a springboard for supple experimental poetry, literary philosophy, and, in the end, an overall defense of the Literary as a philosophical and ethically transformative category, despite his local engagements of and reflections on the limitations and even dangers of lyrical poetry.

Boethius, Dante, Guillaume, Chaucer, and others together create a convention of what we might think of as critical or theoretical poetics in the late Middle Ages. For the Middle English author writing later in the fourteenth century and into the fifteenth—including John Gower, Thomas Usk, and the inimitable Thomas Hoccleve—the idea that an author could write himself or his audience out of a state of distracted despair and into a state of illuminated hope, combined with the idea that he could do so by intermixing prose with verse, has become an authorizing trope, a mode of situating his own work somewhere on a legible map of literary convention.[32] Post-Boethian prosimetrum has, by the dawn of the fifteenth century, acquired enough cultural-critical mass in England to set off a cascade of complex meditations on the nature of literary experience itself, and on how and whether that experience needed to manifest clear and stable ethical meaning in order to be worth its ink.

What sets off this cascade of meditations on the relationship of form to ethical function, I would argue, is the criticality that has been achieved by earlier experiments with the Boethian mixed form—by Boethius, of course, but also by Dante, Guillaume, and Chaucer. In nature, a "criticality" occurs when a structure or system has achieved its maximum state of some property—mass, density, color, and so on.[33] If even one additional unit of that property is added to the system, the entire system begins to come undone. A cone of sand, for instance, will reach a point of criticality such that the addition of even one single additional grain of sand will cause the structure to begin to crumble. The topos of the mixed-form transformative work has reached, by the fifteenth century, a literary criticality through the experiments of Boethius, Alain, Dante, and Guillaume. At that point, Chaucer starts dropping his poetic grains onto the pile. The whole tropaic structure begins to collapse, and in that collapse, the structure discloses its vulnerabilities as well as its robust compositional strengths. That collapse, far

[32] See especially Anthony G. Cirilla's essay in this volume, on Thomas Usk's consolatory use of Boethius's form.

[33] For the concept of criticality as a metapoetic construct, see Andrew Joron, *The Cry at Zero: Selected Prose* (Denver: Counterpath Press, 2007), 8.

from being destructive, ignites the iconoclastic imagination of writers such as Hoccleve, whose own prosimetric and decisively post-Boethian work, the *Series*, is deliberately rickety in a way that makes its own mixed-form constructedness *felt* as a construction, and thereby encourages readers to think about how, why, and whether any constructed literary encounter might ever prove ethically transformative.[34] And whether it needs to. Thus Boethius's paradigmatic literary work that shows how very deeply literature can "pertain to ethics" becomes a launch site for a later vernacular literary theory that suggests that the literary may not need ethical justification after all. This sharp and decisive *volte face* has its origins not in some thematic squabble vernacular authors have with Boethius but, rather, in their radical, daring, and sometimes hilarious repurposings of his venerated form. Precisely because of the overdetermined and rigid ethical status ascribed to prose and verse in the Boethian commentary tradition, the mixed form becomes wildly productive of a radical, new vernacular literary theory-in-practice, one that insists on the value of literature and literary experience without making too simple a relationship between the literary world and ethical learning. Thus I would conclude by suggesting that, although in very different ways, for post-Boethian vernacular poet-critics such as Chaucer, form is where theory lives.

[34] See Johnson, *Practicing Literary Theory in the Middle Ages*, 202–31.

Nature, Astronomy, and Cosmology in Chaucer's *Boece*

A. Joseph McMullen

The natural world looms large in Boethius's *Consolation of Philosophy*. At times, nature imagery is used to depict a state of being (Boethius's mind is clouded and foggy in Book 1, before the storm clouds are blown away), to portray Fortune's fickleness (e.g., as variable tidal currents in Book 2, Meter 1 (2m1)), or to reveal the inevitability of earthly change (e.g., the seasons in 2m3).[1] The *Consolation* is also filled with astronomical and, more broadly, cosmological knowledge—from notes on the morning and evening stars (1m5) to details about how the elements balance one another in cosmic order (3m9).[2] While the natural world was certainly a significant aspect of the *Consolation*, medieval translations, adaptations, and commentaries commonly took this foundation as a starting point for a vast number of cosmological additions. These works expand on Boethius's references to the natural world, often greatly supplementing information about the elements and the cosmos. For example, several early manuscripts of the *Consolation* containing marginal commentary compare the cosmos to an egg (among a host of other cosmological glosses),[3] the Old English translation of the *Consolation*

[1] See especially Gerard J.P. O'Daly, *The Poetry of Boethius* (Chapel Hill: University of North Carolina Press, 1991), 104–77.

[2] For a good overview, see Stephen C. McCluskey, "Boethius's Astronomy and Cosmology," in *A Companion to Boethius in the Middle Ages*, ed. Noel Harold Kaylor, Jr., and Philip Edward Phillips (Boston: Brill, 2012), 47–74.

[3] This gloss appears in three manuscripts (Einsiedeln, Stiftsbibliotheck, MS 179; Gotha, Forschungsbibliothek, MS M. II 103; and Paris, Bibliothèque nationale de France, MS lat. 13953) beside 3m9.13–14: "mediam animam dicit solem quia inter caelum et terram uidetur spacium trahere. quod totum unum corpus esse asserit. id est caelum. terram. mare. in modum oui quod tribus consistit partibus extremam pro caelo. quod inferius. est. pro aqua. quod infimum pro terra accipiunt" [He calls the sun "soul at the center," for it seems to run its course between heaven and earth. Which is affirmed to be one single body. That is, heaven, earth, and sea in the manner of an egg which consists of three parts. The outer part stands for heaven, that below it is for water, and the lowest for earth]. For the gloss, see Malcolm Godden and Susan Irvine, eds., *The*

produced ca. 890 × 930 has recently been called a "book of nature" due to its large number of additions,[4] and Nicholas Trevet's commentary on 3m9 is twice as long as any other meter (at 7,200 words).[5] It makes sense, then, that Geoffrey Chaucer, author of *A Treatise on the Astrolabe*, possibly the *Equatorie of the Planetis* (a text which describes how to build and use a planetary equatorium), and a great number of other works which draw on astronomical learning (including, among others, *The Miller's Tale* and *Troilus and Criseyde*), would also add cosmological details to his translation of the *Consolation*.[6] Perhaps surprisingly, most of these additions to the *Boece* are not technically "original"—that is, Chaucer very clearly draws from his sources, carefully choosing and adapting his glosses from a wide range of options. This brief article will examine Chaucer's rationale for his cosmological additions and how they fit into his larger translation project, before speculating about why Chaucer supplemented his translation in this way.

Old English Boethius: An Edition of the Old English Versions of Boethius's De Consolatione Philosophiae, 2 vols. (Oxford: Oxford University Press, 2009), 2:511. The translation is based off Peter Dronke's (who uses the gloss in Einsiedeln, Stiftsbibliotheck, MS 179), in *Fabula: Explorations into the Uses of Myth in Medieval Platonism* (Leiden: Brill, 1974), 85. See also Paul E. Szarmach's discussion of the cosmological egg in Meter 20 of the Old English *Boethius* in this volume.

[4] See, by Paul E. Szarmach: "The Old English *Boethius* as a Book of Nature," in *Aspects of Anglo-Saxon and Medieval England*, ed. Michiko Ogura (Frankfurt am Main: Peter Lang, 2014), 69–93; "The *Timaeus* in Old English," in *Lexis and Texts in Early English: Studies Presented to Jane Roberts*, ed. Christian J. Kay and Louise M. Sylvester (Atlanta: Rodopi, 2001), 255–67; and his contribution in this volume. See also John H. Brinegar, "'Books Most Necessary': The Literary and Cultural Contexts of Alfred's *Boethius*" (Ph.D. diss., University of North Carolina at Chapel Hill, 2000), 18–59, for a catalogue of some twenty major astronomical and geographical additions made by author of the *Boethius*.

[5] See Mark J. Gleason, "Clearing the Fields: Towards a Reassessment of Chaucer's Use of Trevet in the *Boece*," in *The Medieval Boethius: Studies in the Vernacular Translations of De Consolatione Philosophiae*, ed. A.J. Minnis (Woodbridge: Boydell and Brewer, 1987), 89–105, at 104.

[6] The authorship of the *Equatorie of the Planetis* is disputed. Derek J. Price, ed., *The Equatorie of the Planetis: Edited from Peterhouse MS. 75.I* (Cambridge: Cambridge University Press, 1955), and Pamela Robinson, "Geoffrey Chaucer and the *Equatorie of the Planetis*: The State of the Problem," *The Chaucer Review* 26 (1991): 17–30, have argued for Chaucer's authorship. A.S.G. Edwards and Linne R. Mooney, "Is the *Equatorie of the Planetis* a Chaucer Holograph?" *Chaucer Review* 26 (1991): 31–42, and Jennifer Arch, "A Case against Chaucer's Authorship of the *Equatorie of the Planets*," *The Chaucer Review* 40.1 (2005): 59–79, meanwhile, argue against Chaucer's authorship. For an overview of Chaucer's astronomical learning and his application of it in his works, see Hamilton Smyser, "A View of Chaucer's Astronomy," *Speculum* 45 (1970): 359–73; J.D. North, *Chaucer's Universe* (Oxford: Clarendon Press, 1988); and Ann W. Astell, *Chaucer and the Universe of Learning* (Ithaca: Cornell University Press, 1996).

Ultimately, Chaucer (via Boethius) may answer this question himself in one of his longest glosses (in 3m11): knowledge of the cosmos gives a greater knowledge of the self.

Unlike other adaptations of the *Consolation*, where sources may remain unknown, critics have confidently identified the texts that Chaucer used to translate the *Boece*. Naturally, Chaucer had a copy of the *Consolation*, but likely the Vulgate version common to fourteenth-century England.[7] His text of the *Consolation* probably contained glosses of the so-called "Remigian" commentary tradition,[8] from which he would draw some twenty-six times.[9] He had Jean de Meun's *Consolation* translation [*Li Livres de confort*] as well, and seems not only to have taken additions from it but also to have used it as an aid (or, more uncharitably, a trot)

---

[7] Tim William Machan, *Textual Criticism and Middle English Texts* (Charlottesville: University Press of Virginia, 1994), explains that the Vulgate *Consolation* "is materially not very different from what Boethius probably wrote in the prison at Pavia, though there are pervasive (if minor) lexical differences: pronouns are inserted, syntax is modernized to that of late medieval Latin, unfamiliar idioms are normalized, and Greek quotations are almost uniformly translated into Latin or garbled beyond intelligibility" (158).

[8] Manuscripts of Boethius's *Consolation* began to contain an ever increasing amount of glosses and *scholia* starting in the ninth century. While this commentary varied greatly from manuscript to manuscript, scholars attributed the glosses in manuscripts before the twelfth century to two early commentary traditions: 1) the "Remigian" commentary, attributed to Remigius of Auxerre (between 902 and 908); and 2) the "St. Gall" commentary, attributed to the abbey of St. Gall (ninth or early tenth century). More recent scholarship has questioned the validity of identifying two distinct traditions, given the great variety among manuscript witnesses, with Malcom Godden, "King Alfred and the Boethius Industry," in *Making Sense: Constructing Meaning in Early English*, ed. Antonette diPaolo Healey and Kevin Kiernan (Toronto: Pontifical Institute of Mediaeval Studies, 2007), 116–38, suggesting that the commentary tradition should be imagined as "highly fluid compilations of glosses and scholia, continually supplemented and adapted over a long period" (121). For background on the commentary tradition, see H.F. Stewart, "A Commentary by Remigius Autissiodorensis on the *De Consolatione Philosophiae* of Boethius," *Journal of Theological Studies* 17 (1916): 22–42; Pierre Courcelle, "Étude critique sur les commentaries de la *Consolation* de Boèce," *Archives d'histoire doctrinale et littéraire du moyen âge* 14 (1939): 5–140; Courcelle, *La Consolation de Philosophie dans la tradition littéraire: Antécedents et posterité de Boèce* (Paris: Études Augustiniennes, 1967); and Fabio Troncarelli, *Tradizione Perdute: La 'Consolatione Philosophiae' nell'Alto Medioevo* (Padua: Editrice Antenore, 1981).

[9] See, by A.J. Minnis: "'Glosynge is a glorious thyng': Chaucer at Work on the *Boece*," in *The Medieval Boethius: Studies in the Vernacular Translations of De Consolatione Philosophiae*, ed. A.J. Minnis (Woodbridge: Boydell and Brewer, 1987), 106–24, at 118; and "Chaucer's Commentator: Nicholas Trevet and the *Boece*," in *Chaucer's Boece and the Medieval Tradition of Boethius*, ed. A.J. Minnis (Cambridge: D.S. Brewer, 1993), 83–166.

for Boethius's most complicated Latin.[10] Chaucer's final source, Trevet's detailed commentary of the *Consolation* [*Expositio super Boetio de consolatione*],[11] is slightly more contested, but A.J. Minnis has had the final word on the issue (while also convincingly proving that Chaucer did not have access to William of Conches's commentary), arguing that Chaucer had most if not all of Trevet's commentary.[12] Generally, Chaucer's use of Trevet's commentary (and Jean's additions) is "restrained,"[13] with passages consciously inserted into the *Boece*. Though these additions have been criticized as unoriginal, the way Chaucer brings them together in the *Boece* was, ultimately, "a product of his own invention."[14]

While the extrapolations, explanatory inserts, and general glossing in the *Boece* were once read as a failure to render precisely or clearly the Latin source text,[15] they have since been considered paradigmatic of late medieval academic translation and indicative of the function of the *Boece*.[16] Over the course of

---

[10] For an edition of *Li Livres de confort*, see V.L. Dedeck-Héry, ed., "Boethius' *De Consolatione* by Jean de Meun," *Mediaeval Studies* 14 (1952): 165–275. See also Tim William Machan, ed., *Sources of the Boece* (Athens: University of Georgia Press, 2005), for a side-by-side edition of the Vulgate *Consolation* and *Li Livres de confort*.

[11] This connection was first noted by Kate O. Petersen, "Chaucer and Trevet," *PMLA* 18.2 (1903): 173–93. For an edition, see Nicholas Trevet, *Expositio super Boetio de consolatione*, ed. E.T. Silk, accessible at <http://minnis.commons.yale.edu>.

[12] Responding to Gleason, "Clearing the Fields," who argued that Chaucer had a full copy of Trevet's *Expositio*, H.A. Kelly, "The Non-Tragedy of Arthur," in *Medieval English Religious and Ethical Literature*, ed. Gregory Kratzmann and James Simpson (Cambridge: D.S. Brewer, 1986), 92–114, asserted that Chaucer only had a partial copy. For Minnis's rejoinder, see "Chaucer's Commentator: Nicholas Trevet and the *Boece*," 89–90; and his "'Glosynge is a glorious thyng,'" 118.

[13] A.J. Minnis and Tim William Machan, "The *Boece* as a Late-Medieval Translation," in *Chaucer's Boece and the Medieval Tradition of Boethius*, ed. A.J. Minnis (Cambridge: D.S. Brewer, 1993), 167–88, at 175.

[14] Tim William Machan, *Techniques of Translation: Chaucer's Boece* (Norman: Pilgrim Books, 1985), 128.

[15] See Hugh Fraser Stewart, *Boethius: An Essay* (London: Blackwood and Sons, 1891), 217; and S.S. Hussey, "The Minor Poems and the Prose," in *The Middle Ages*, ed. Whitney F. Bolton (London: Sphere Books, 1970), 294.

[16] I am making the distinction here between Chaucer's glossatorial additions to the *Boece* (which are considered part of the canonical text) and glosses that are inscribed in the margins of *Consolation* or *Boece* manuscripts. Manuscripts of the *Boece* are also often glossed. Tim William Machan, "Glosses in the Manuscripts of Chaucer's *Boece*," in *The Medieval Boethius: Studies in the Vernacular Translations of* De Consolatione Philosophiae, ed. A.J. Minnis (Woodbridge: Boydell and Brewer, 1987), 124–38, categorizes these glosses into three types: 1) those which gloss philosophical terms; 2) those which aid in the reading of the text (i.e., help with pronouns, answer questions, etc.); and 3) those which gloss unusual English words. Intriguingly, many of these glosses are in Latin. For an overview of late medieval translation practices, see Taylor Cowdery's essay in this volume.

several works, Minnis and Tim William Machan argue that, for Chaucer, translation and glossing were "two aspects of a single activity, *expositio sententiae*."[17] They write:

> For this is translation of the type which routinely incorporates material from the glosses which were the stock-in-trade of the educational system, which had its lexical and semantic parameters largely defined by the grammatical definitions and assumptions which that system enshrined, and which reflects the theory of translation which was channeled by the schools and fed by their interest in semiotics and notions of textual explication (as applied in commentary on the classroom *auctores*).[18]

Chaucer's aim was to open the *sentence* of the *Consolation* by being as faithful to the source text as possible and adding glosses for his audience (well-educated members of both the clergy and laity) where necessary.[19] These glosses, then, must be understood as "integral to Chaucer's translation of his source."[20] Chaucer's extrapolations are inserted into the body of his translation rather than written in the margins, creating a sort of amalgam text or "composite source,"[21] which "confers a certain academic or critical authority on the English text."[22] The glosses on the natural world accord well the intentions of the *Boece*, generally offering further explanation and clarification of the source text. From providing brief notes on the names of winds or stars to making minor revisions of his source text (naming the "day-sterre" in 2m3, for example), Chaucer includes this information to make the *sentence* of the *Consolation* more readily apparent for his audience.[23]

---

[17] Minnis and Machan, "The *Boece* as a Late-Medieval Translation," 173. See also Minnis, "'Glosynge is a glorious thyng'"; and Machan, *Techniques of Translation*.

[18] Minnis and Machan, "The *Boece* as a Late-Medieval Translation," 168.

[19] In this volume, Taylor Cowdery, "Translation for *Sentence* in Middle English Poetry: The Case of John Walton," defines the Middle English concept of *sentence* as "grounded in the material particularities of the letter—events of plot, points of argument, primary characters, and so on—even while it underlies and dictates the local words and sense of that letter. By using either literal or loose techniques to render local meaning, translation for *sentence* thus attempts both to preserve the broader meaning of a text and to realize that meaning in a fuller fashion—to flesh out, as it were, the bones of the source with a new body of words . . . Clearly, *sentence* is not 'sense,' 'menyng,' or 'vndurstonding'; it is rather something greater, something that underlies and dictates local expression."

[20] Minnis and Machan, "The *Boece* as a Late-Medieval Translation," 173.

[21] Minnis and Machan, "The *Boece* as a Late-Medieval Translation," 181.

[22] Rita Copeland, *Rhetoric, Hermeneutics, and Translation in the Middle Ages* (Cambridge: Cambridge University Press, 1991), 143.

[23] One final caveat: Machan, *Techniques of Translation*, has argued that the extant *Boece* likely "had not undergone final revision" and possibly was not intended for the

The simplest of these additions are those which qualify the names of the winds, stars, rivers, etc., used by Boethius in the *Consolation*. While Boethius typically offers only the name itself (i.e., Zephyrus, Lucifer, or the Tigris), Chaucer tends to clarify which natural feature the name signifies. Chaucer generally takes his cue from Jean or Trevet, who also spell out many of these references.[24] Phoebus is often, but not always, glossed as "the sonne" (1m6.3, 3m2.36, 4m1.11, 4m5.28).[25] The Tagus and the Hermus are both glossed as "the ryver" (3m10.12, 14), along with "the same ryverys," the Tigris and the Euphrates (5m1.5–6). Chaucer also glosses the various stars/constellations that make an appearance in the *Boece* with "the sterre": Sirius (1m5.26), Arcturus (1m5.26–7), Boötes (4m5.5, 4m5.7), "the Bere" (4m6.8), and Ursa (which is also "the Bere," 4m6.11). Meanwhile, Hesperus is glossed either as "the sterre" (4m6.15) or "the eve sterre" (1m5.11, 2m8.8), along with Lucifer as either "the sterre" (4m6.17) or "the day-sterre" (3m1.9).[26] The winds are widely glossed by Chaucer, who adds, in most instances, "the wynde that hyghte [is called] . . ." or "the wynd" to the description already found in the *Consolation*: Boreas (1m3.11–12), Aquilon (1m6.11, 2m3.14–15), Auster (1m7.2–3, 2m3.11, 2m4.7), Zephyrus (2m3.10), Eurus (2m4.3–4, 4m3.1), Nothus (3m1.8), and Corus (4m5.24).[27] Occasionally,

public in its present form (114). Nevertheless, and Machan acknowledges this, the *Boece* was circulated in its present form, and we, as critics, can only discuss the text we have.

[24] Trevet, for example, glosses "Auster" in 1m7 with "id est uentus ille" [that is, the wind] and Jean supplies "vens" [wind] in his translation (Chaucer writes "the truble wynd that hyghte Auster," 1m7.2–3). Since Minnis has already compiled the corresponding glosses from Trevet and Jean as they match with the *Boece*, I direct my reader to his much more readable and convenient article than to the individual editions of each text. See "Chaucer's Commentator: Nicholas Trevet and the *Boece*," 104.

[25] All quotes will be cited parenthetically. See Geoffrey Chaucer, *Boece*, in *The Riverside Chaucer*, ed. Larry D. Benson, 3rd edn. (Boston: Houghton Mifflin, 1987). The editors of the *Boece* in the *Riverside Chaucer* follow a tradition of italicizing "clearly extratextual phrases and sentences" (though here only those "not paralleled in either the Latin or the French") (1005). See also Walter W. Skeat, ed., *Boethius and Troilus*, *The Complete Works of Geoffrey Chaucer*, vol. 2 (Oxford: Clarendon Press, 1894); and F.N. Robinson, *The Complete Works of Geoffrey Chaucer* (New York: Houghton Mifflin, 1933), 320–84. Minnis and Machan, "The *Boece* as a Late-Medieval Translation," bemoan this procedure, which "allows to remain the implication that Chaucer's glosses are not integral to his version of the *Consolatio*" (181). I follow the *Riverside Chaucer* in keeping with scholarly convention.

[26] Of course, the morning star and evening star are, technically, neither independent stars nor stars at all (but, rather, Venus).

[27] While the majority of these instances do not have parallels in the *Consolation*, that is not always the case. See, for example, "Boreae spiritus" (probably best translated as "north wind," but "the wind of Boreas") in 1m5. See *Anicii Manlii Severini Boethii Philosophiae Consolatio*, ed. Ludwig Bieler, CCSL 94 (Turnhout: Brepols, 1957), 1m5.19. Hereafter cited parenthetically. Translations are my own unless otherwise noted.

however, Chaucer will add a descriptive adjective, usually following Jean, as in "a swyft wynd that hyghte Chorus" (1m3.7) or "Zephirus, the debonere wynd" (1m5.22). While many of these glosses follow Trevet and Jean—it is outside the scope of this paper to examine every instance—Chaucer is not tied to his sources and will also revise if he sees fit. One example is "ultima Thyle" [the "last" or "furthest" isle Thule, 3m5.7], which Chaucer glosses as "the laste ile in the see that highte Tyle" (3m5.6–7). As Minnis notes, Chaucer seems to draw from both Trevet and Jean in order to come up with his preferred definition of Thule.[28]

While these glosses are primarily functional, Chaucer also adds a series of more explanatory extrapolations on natural phenomena, geography, and astronomy. In a gloss on Euripus (a narrow strait which separates Euboea from Boeotia) that draws on aspects from both Jean and Trevet,[29] Chaucer expands on the meaning of this particular parallel (which Boethius compares to Fortune): "*Euripe is an arm of the see that ebbeth and floweth, and somtyme the streem is on o side, and somtyme on the tothir*" (2m1.4–6). The *Consolation* only provides the allusion to Euripus, but Chaucer, likely understanding the limitations of this example for an English audience, expands the reference to clarify how Fortune ebbs and flows like a tide. Chaucer offers a series of similar glosses in 2m6, in which Nero's rule stretches in all four directions. Boethius describes the vastness of his empire by explaining that his subjects are seen by the sun when it rises and sets, are also seen by cold Ursa Major (i.e., in the north), and are burned by Notus (i.e., the south wind). Chaucer explains the geographical aspect of Boethius's allusions for his reader:

> And natheles yit governed this Nero by septre alle the peples that Phebus, the sonne, may seen, comynge fro his uttreste arysynge til he hide his bemes undir the wawes. (*That is to seyn he governede al the peples by ceptre imperial that the sonne goth aboute from est to west.*) And ek this Nero governyde by ceptre alle the peples that ben undir the colde sterres that highten the septemtryones. (*This is to seyn he governede alle the peples that ben under the partye of the north.*) And eek Nero governede alle the peples that the vyolent wynd Nothus scorklith, and baketh the brennynge sandes by his drye heete (*that is to seyn, al the peples in the south*). (2m6.12–27)

Here too, aspects of these glosses can be found in Jean and Trevet,[30] but Chaucer is himself elaborating on information found there to illuminate Boethius's meaning. Chaucer takes the same approach in two astronomical additions from Book 4. During a discussion of how the heavens (particularly Ursa Major) conform to cosmic order in 4m6, Chaucer supplements "the sterre yclepid the Bere" (4m6.8) with "the same sterre Ursa" (4m6.11)—seemingly to drive home the point that

[28] Minnis, "Chaucer's Commentator," 126.
[29] Minnis, "Chaucer's Commentator," 107.
[30] Minnis, "Chaucer's Commentator," 118.

Ursa is also known as the Bear (Boethius only offers "Ursa"). In another astronomical gloss (on how the stars of Arcturus rotate about the north pole), Chaucer, struggling with his translation of "summo cardine" [the "pole" or "high center" of heaven, 4m5.2] as "the sovereyne centre or poynt," adds the gloss "neyghe to the sovereyne pool of the firmament" (4m5.3–4). Here again, though drawing on Jean and Trevet,[31] Chaucer provides another explanatory gloss to make clearer that this "poynt" is, in fact, the north pole.

Most of Chaucer's other explanatory glosses about the natural world revise the *Consolation*, whether intentionally or not. In 2m8's ode to the mutability of nature, the dimming of the "stella" [literally "star," but probably taken as plural: "stars"] with the rising of the sun is described. While Jean takes "stella" in a plural sense, Chaucer instead opts for the singular "sterre" and, in a gloss following the Remigian commentary tradition, identifies this star as the "day-sterre": "*This to seyn, whan the sonne is rysen, the day-sterre waxeth pale, and leeseth hir lyght for the grete bryghtnesse of the sonne*" (2m3.5–8).[32] Chaucer, then, provides this mostly original gloss to explain which "sterre" is "ydymmed" (2m3.3) for his reader. On several occasions, some problem in transmission has led Chaucer to try to make better sense of his translation with a gloss. In 1m3, when Boethius is comparing how clouds hide the sun and stars to his previous state of mind, Chaucer has trouble with the definition of "glomerantur sidera" (1m3.3). Following Jean (who gives "les estoilles"), he translates the phrase as "the sterres ben clustred" (1m3.5) but should have translated it as "weather gathers" (or "bad weather gathers").[33] In an attempt to clarify this confusion, he adds a gloss "*that is to seyn, whan sterres ben covered with cloudes*" (1m3.5–6), influenced by Trevet's reading.[34] Another translation issue is apparent in 1m7, where the sea—once clear but now stirred up by the wind and muddied—is used as an analogue for obscured truth. Chaucer, rather than following Jean (who provides "l'ordure" [filth]), chooses to translate "aestum" (the substance in the sea stirred up by the wind) as "the heete" (1m7.4).[35] While "heat" is, indeed, a literal translation of "aestum," it is not the

---

[31] Minnis, "Chaucer's Commentator," 144.

[32] Minnis, "Chaucer's Commentator," 110. For greater discussion on this passage, including an identification with the Remigian commentary tradition, see Minnis, "'Glosynge is a glorious thyng,'" 115–16.

[33] Minnis, "Chaucer's Commentator," 96–97.

[34] Trevet offers, "id est nubibus inuoluuntur" (that is, enveloped in the clouds). See Minnis, "Chaucer's Commentator," 96. The full passage is as follows: "And ryght by ensaumple as the sonne is hydd whan the sterres ben clustred (*that is to seyn, whan sterres ben covered with cloudes*) by a swyft wynd that hyghte Chorus, and that the firmament stant dirked with wete plowngy cloudes; and that the sterres nat apeeren upon hevene, so that the nyght semeth sprad upon erth" (1m3.4–11).

[35] Minnis, "Chaucer's Commentator," 104. It also bears mentioning that "aestum" likely read "estum" in Chaucer's version of the *Consolation*. See Machan, *Sources of the Boece*, 50.

most idiomatic translation (which would likely be "surge" or "breaker"), and, furthermore, the connection between wind and sea is unclear (how would the wind heat up the sea?). Thus Chaucer adds a gloss—"*that is to seyn, the boylynge up fro the botme*" (1m7.4–5)—in an attempt to clear up this issue for his reader. In one final, troubled, translation decision, Chaucer distorts the meaning of a passage in 2m8's ode to cosmic harmony. In the *Consolation*, both the sea and the land are kept within fixed bounds. Chaucer, however, keeps "mare" [the sea] the subject into the next clause (about the land), likely because he did not recognize the construction of *licet* plus dative and infinitive ("ne terris liceat . . . tendere" [nor may the land move out, 2m8.11–12]).[36] He then, following Trevet,[37] adds the gloss "that is to seyn, to coveren al the erthe" (2m8.12–13) to explain how cosmic order keeps the sea from overflowing onto land. While these examples highlight mistakes in Chaucer's translation, they also reveal a translator trying to make sense of Boethius's natural philosophy.

Overall, these glosses reveal Chaucer's dedication to making the *sentence* of the *Consolation* clear in his translation, his thoughtful use of sources, and his deep interest in the natural world, astronomy, and cosmology. The question of why Chaucer was so invested in glossing these passages still remains unanswered, however. The best answer, beyond Chaucer's participation in a tradition of late medieval academic translation, comes from Boethius himself: a deep knowledge of nature and the cosmos offers a greater knowledge of the self, truth, and the supreme good.[38] As Gerard J.P. O'Daly writes,

> In an ordered and hierarchical universe the mind can turn to patterns that provide paradigms for behaviour: the natural world informs the moral sphere . . . He [Boethius] appropriates that world, and reads in it the great themes of mental and moral anguish and stability, reflected and symbolized in the change and variety of the natural universe.[39]

A central feature of the *Consolation* is the use of nature to illuminate philosophical arguments, finding parallels in the harmony (and discord) of the macrocosmic natural world which speak to similar issues faced on the microcosmic human level. It seems clear that Chaucer, perhaps inspired by Boethius, felt this way too. In one of his longest glosses in the entire *Boece*, a distinct parallel is made between knowledge of a thing's nature and the natural principles within the human

---

[36] The passage before the gloss is as follows: "that the see, gredy to flowen, constreyneth with a certein eende his floodes, so that it is nat leveful to strecche his brode termes [borders] or bowndes uppon the erthes" (2m8.8–11).

[37] Minnis, "Chaucer's Commentator," 121.

[38] See also Eleanor Johnson's essay in this volume.

[39] O'Daly, *The Poetry of Boethius*, 104–5.

being. Chaucer, who is deeply indebted to Trevet here,[40] greatly expands on Boethius's 3m11, which explains that one must look within to find truth:

> *Whoso wol seke the depe ground of soth in his thought, and wil nat ben disseyvid by false proposiciouns that goon amys fro the trouthe, lat hym wel examine and rolle withynne hymself the nature and the propretes of the thing; and let hym yet eftsones examinen and rollen his thoughtes by good deliberacioun or that he deme, and lat hym techyn his soule that it hath, by naturel principles kyndeliche yhud withynne itself, al the trouthe the whiche he ymagineth to ben in thinges withoute. And thanne al the derknesse of his mysknowynge shall [schewen] more evydently to the sighte of his undirstondynge then the sonne ne semeth to the sighte withoute-forth.* (3m11.13–27)

In the search for truth, one must examine the nature, or the innate characteristics (translating Latin *naturam*), of a thing in order to teach the soul that it has within itself all of the truth that can be found in outside things (i.e., the cosmos). The soul has *naturel principles kyndeliche yhud withynne*, a phrase which could literally be rendered "natural principles naturally hidden within" but which is saturated with meaning due to the semantic range of *nature* and *kinde*. Chaucer continues, again translating Trevet:

> *This to seyn, how schulde men deme the sothe of any thing that were axid, yif ther nere a rote of sothfastnesse that were yploungid and hyd in the naturel principles, the whiche sothfastnesse lyvede within the depnesse of the thought?* (3m11.38–43)

The same root of truthfulness that is hidden in natural principles also dwells in the deepness of thought. The cosmological truths of the universe then can act as the starting point for a deeper knowledge of the self. By providing additional glosses that help explicate these parallels with the natural world, Chaucer is ultimately helping prepare the mind of his reader to explore the "depnesse of the thought."

Indeed, another focal point of the Chaucerian glossing in the *Boece* is on the knowledge that natural science affords. On two occasions, Chaucer is quick to add an explanation to his translation in order make sure his reader does not drastically misunderstand the sense of the text. In 4m1, when Philosophy is describing the flight she and the soul can take through the "heighte of the hevene" (4m1.2), Chaucer pauses at Boethius's notion that the night sky (along with the stars) is "pingitur" [painted, 4m1.13].[41] He then adds the gloss, "*that is to sey, the*

[40] Chaucer is, effectively, translating Trevet's glosses into a unified whole here. See Minnis, "Chaucer's Commentator," 134, but also Petersen, "Chaucer and Trevet," 181–83, for a comparanda table.

[41] The passage before the gloss is as follows, "and thilke soule renneth by the cercle of the sterres in alle the places there as the schynynge nyght is ypainted" (4m1.17–19).

nyght that is cloudeles; for on nyghtes that ben cloudeles it semeth as the hevene were peynted with diverse ymages of sterres," 4m1.19–23). Chaucer, along with Trevet (whom Chaucer follows here), clarifies that while the sky may "semeth . . . peynted," it certainly is not.[42] The ignorance of the "gentes publicus" [common people, 4m5.11] is on display in 4m5, where Boethius alludes to people who would strike bronze objects during a lunar eclipse in fear of the omen. Chaucer, following Jean and Trevet, names these people (the Coribantes, or the attendants of Cybele) and their instruments (drums of different sorts). He next adds a gloss: "*That is to seyn, that ther is a maner peple that hyghte Coribantes, that wenen* [believe] *that whan the mone is in the eclips that it be enchaunted, and therfore for to rescowe the mone thei betyn hir basyns with thikke strokes*" (4m5.18–23). Their ignorance is the "comune errour" (4m5.15), which Chaucer immediately supplies and dispels. In these examples, Chaucer's haste to correct draws attention to the need for knowledge about the heavens.

By supplementing his translation of the *Consolation* with a wide range of glosses on nature, astronomy, and cosmology, Chaucer reveals how important he thinks it is for his readers to understand Boethius's natural philosophy. Chaucer's explanatory extrapolations always seek to render the *sentence* of his source text as clearly as possible for his audience. As Boethius teaches in the *Consolation*, it is through an understanding of the cosmos that one can begin to learn about oneself. Throughout the *Boece*, Chaucer repeatedly indicates the importance he ascribes to understanding the cosmos. By fully opening up the meaning of the *Consolation* through cosmological additions, Chaucer makes this truth easier to access while simultaneously acting in keeping with the functional purpose of his translation.

And, indeed, it may not have been too long before the composition of the *Boece* that Chaucer's own interest in cosmology was first piqued. After explaining one of Chaucer's astronomical errors in the *Boece*, Edgar S. Laird and Donald W. Olson argue that, at this point in his career (in the late 1370s or early 1380s, when he first began translating the *Consolation*), Chaucer probably "lacked the skill" to consult astronomy (though he would later attain that skill).[43] Mahmoud Manzalaoui has noted that the *Consolation* (along with the *Roman de la Rose*, Cicero's *Somnium Scipionis*, and Macrobius's commentary on *Somnium Scipionis*)

[42] Minnis, "Chaucer's Commentator," 138.

[43] Edgar S. Laird and Donald W. Olson, "Boethius, *Boece*, and Boötes: A Note on the Chronology of Chaucer's Astronomical Learning," *Modern Philology* 88.2 (1990): 147–49, at 148. See also Smyser, "A View of Chaucer's Astronomy"; and Roland Smith, Review of *The Equatorie of the Planetis*, ed. D.J. Price, *Journal of English and Germanic Philology* 57 (1958): 533–37, who see a similar trajectory in Chaucer's astronomical expertise.

was "crucial" in Chaucer's scientific development.[44] The *Consolation*, especially, in its synthesis of philosophical and spiritual, "exactly anticipates the Chaucerian use of science at its most meaningful."[45] It is very likely, then, that Chaucer discovered in the *Consolation*, and even more in translating it,[46] his own burgeoning interest in natural philosophy and science. To realize that cultivating this interest could also allow him to contemplate those "naturel principles" which "lyvede within the depnesse of the thought" must have been exhilarating. These cosmological glosses gave Chaucer himself the chance to develop as a natural philosopher.[47] In the examples discussed above, he often consults Jean, Trevet, and possibly Remigian glosses before choosing how to translate (and subsequently gloss) a passage. Though, as I have shown, he is not always right, he is certainly always learning and eager to learn more. These glosses, then, are Chaucer's first true foray into cosmological learning, the beginning of his journey on the path to find "sothfastnesse."

[44] Mahmoud Manzaloui, "Chaucer and Science," in *Geoffrey Chaucer*, ed. Derek Brewer (Athens: Ohio University Press, 1974), 224–61, at 230.

[45] Manzaloui, "Chaucer and Science," 230.

[46] Translation is, after all, the "most intimate act of reading." See Gayatri Chakravorty Spivak, "Translation as Culture," *Parallax* 6.1 (2000): 13–24, at 20.

[47] In this I am following Lodi Nauta, "The 'Glosa' as Instrument for the Development of Natural Philosophy," 3–40, who argues that the evolution of William of Conches's "natural philosophy can be fruitfully seen against the background of the traditional practice of glossing and commentating on ancient texts" (39). Furthermore, "The 'glosa' [here technically something closer to a commentary] was a suitable form for bringing together different ideas and opinions from a variety of sources, thereby itself becoming a sort of encyclopedia from which other commentators in turn could pick out what they wanted" (39).

Tragic Diction in Chaucer's *Boece*, the *Canterbury Tales*, and Hoccleve's *Series*[*]

Jonathan Stavsky

Tragedy in English begins with Chaucer, the first author writing in the language who is known to have used this word.[1] Two of his works—the *Boece* and the *Canterbury Tales*—define it. Two—*Troilus and Criseyde* and the *Monk's Tale*—call themselves a tragedy in the singular or plural. Yet despite his attempts to elucidate, illustrate, and perhaps even popularize this once obscure term, some of Chaucer's fifteenth-century heirs took it for a learned synonym of "book" or "narrative."[2] One such heir concludes an ordinary list of regulations with a rhyme royal envoy modeled on *Troilus and Criseyde*, V.1786–1792, where he labels the fruit of his labor a "litel tragedie."[3] As this loose usage suggests, generic taxonomies are a prominent but not always rigorously observed element in the universe of Chaucerian tragedy, which instead comprises a broad set of literary commonplaces drawn from the *Boece*, the *Monk's Prologue* and *Tale*, the *Nun's Priest's Prologue*, and *Troilus and Criseyde*.

Though Chaucer is hardly the originator of this discourse, the part he played in shaping it has not been sufficiently delineated. In the best treatment of the subject to date, Henry Ansgar Kelly argues that Chaucer lit upon a definition of tragedy in a commentary on *The Consolation of Philosophy* and mistakenly

* A significant part of this essay was written during the author's stay as a Fulbright Postdoctoral Fellow at the University of Pennsylvania in 2013–14. The rest was completed during his appointment as Mandel Postdoctoral Fellow at the Hebrew University of Jerusalem.

1 *The Middle English Dictionary*, <http://quod.lib.umich.edu/m/med/>, s.v. "trağedī(e, (n.)," sense a; s.v. "trağēdien, (n.)."

2 Examples of this usage are given in Henry Ansgar Kelly, *Chaucerian Tragedy* (Cambridge: D.S. Brewer, 1997), 40–43. Kelly proceeds to list other peculiar conceptions of tragedy.

3 Kelly, *Chaucerian Tragedy*, 41-42. Citations of Chaucer's works follow *The Riverside Chaucer*, ed. Larry D. Benson, 3rd edn. (Boston: Houghton Mifflin, 1987). Hereafter cited parenthetically, with the *Canterbury Tales* cited by fragment and line number.

assumed that it was "an existent literary form."[4] Since his understanding of tragedy is otherwise derivative, maintains Kelly, the revival of the genre in England is no more than an "unconscious contribution" by a passive reader and slavish translator of Boethius.[5] A fresh look at the *Boece* and the *Canterbury Tales* indicates that Chaucer engaged with and revised the idea of tragedy found in the commentary tradition.[6] In so doing, he fashioned a rich yet distinct tragic idiom whose artistic potential consists of the range of attitudes it enables both to itself as a genre and to its Boethian intertext. Unlike the Aristotelian model, where plot is the "first principle" and "soul of tragedy," and diction is fourth in order of importance,[7] its Chaucerian counterpart has a stronger discursive component than previous scholarship has recognized.

To flesh out the significance of Chaucer's tragic diction, the last section of this essay will explore its role in the *Series* (ca. 1419–21) by Thomas Hoccleve (ca. 1367–1426), the self-styled disciple who was instrumental in securing his master's place in the canon.[8] Though Hoccleve does not classify any of his poems as a tragedy—and is consequently absent from histories of the genre in England—his last work repeatedly draws on the Monk's recasting of Boethius when narrating the downfall of various characters, himself included. At the same time, whereas the Monk exemplifies the vicissitudes of Fortune but fails to explain how one is to face them, Hoccleve employs the language of tragedy as part of his quest for greater awareness.

---

[4] Kelly, *Chaucerian Tragedy*, 260; cf. 40.

[5] Kelly, *Chaucerian Tragedy*, 260; cf. 40.

[6] For another approach to translations of Boethius as they intersect with contemporary ideas of genre, see Susan Irvine's essay in this volume, which reads the reception of the Old English *Boethius* within the generic conventions of the *opus geminatum*.

[7] Aristotle, *Poetics*, ed. and trans. Stephen Halliwell, in *Aristotle: Poetics; Longinus: On the Sublime; Demetrius: On Style*, Loeb Classical Library 199 (Cambridge, MA: Harvard University Press, 1995), 1–141, at 6.1450a.38–39.

[8] As demonstrated in Ethan Knapp, *The Bureaucratic Muse: Thomas Hoccleve and the Literature of Late Medieval England* (University Park: Pennsylvania State University Press, 2001), 93–106, Hoccleve's other major work, the *Regiment of Princes*, also makes sophisticated use of the *Consolation*. According to Nicholas Perkins, "Haunted Hoccleve? *The Regiment of Princes*, the Troilean Intertext, and Conversations with the Dead," *The Chaucer Review* 43 (2008): 103–39, it does so via the mediation of *Troilus and Criseyde*. More research is needed to determine whether Chaucer's other Boethian works fulfill an intermediary function in this earlier text.

The *Boece* on Tragedy

Given the rarity of the word *tragedy* in the Middle Ages, Kelly argues that its meaning at various junctures depends entirely on the reception history of the few texts in which it occurs, such as the *Consolation* and its commentaries. To understand Chaucerian tragedy, one should be able to retrace the line of transmission leading from Boethius to Chaucer while bracketing off all other ideas of the genre.[9] Having charted this nexus, Kelly extends it to fifteenth-century authors such as Lydgate and Henryson, whose conception of tragedy derives from Chaucer. Despite his attempt to avoid anachronism, Kelly labors under a different kind of modern assumption: He mistakes the purview of his philological method for the confines of the phenomena it aims to examine. The fact that Chaucer encountered Boethius's reference to tragedy in a particular set of textual circumstances does not preclude sustained engagement with the imagery, tenets, and values of the *Consolation* as a whole. Nor can his understanding of the genre be abstracted into a discrete and "nonqualitative"[10] definition the length of a manuscript gloss. Instead, such definitions form part of a broader textual economy with which they interact on various levels, ranging from the propositional to the figurative. By discounting Chaucer's intellectual agency, Kelly overlooks some important evidence about the reception and reformulation of the Boethian tradition in Chaucer's works.

Closer examination suggests, first, that Chaucer offers several competing definitions of tragedy, each of which implies a different reading of Boethius; and, second, that his final recension of the *Monk's Prologue* and *Tale* ironizes this pilgrim's appropriation of the *Boece*.[11] As Ruth Morse has put it, "[s]ince one of

[9] Like Kelly, I do not deal with Chaucer's reception of Dantean tragedy or the question of his acquaintance with, and reaction to, other Italian theorists and writers of tragedy such as Albertino Mussato and Antonio Loschi. For studies of the former literary relationship, see, e.g., Piero Boitani, "The *Monk's Tale*: Dante and Boccaccio," *Medium Ævum* 45 (1976): 50–69; and Winthrop Wetherbee, "Chaucer and the Tragic Vision of Life," *Poetica* 55 (2001): 39–53. For the latter, see Renate Haas, "Chaucer's *Monk's Tale*: An Ingenious Criticism of Early Humanist Conceptions of Tragedy," *Humanistica Lovaniensia* 36 (1987): 44–70. Kelly, *Chaucerian Tragedy*, 78n155, finds fault with Haas for neglecting to specify "where these humanist ideas of tragedy were to be found and how Chaucer and his audience could have learned about them." She actually does point out significant parallels between the *Monk's Prologue* and *Tale* and humanist discourse on this genre, though such correspondences may be due to a common source.

[10] Kelly, *Chaucerian Tragedy*, 77. Tellingly, Kelly defines his own methodology against "qualitative" approaches (141).

[11] My analysis does not consider the early recensions of the Monk's discourse on tragedy but, rather, considers the form it eventually took. For a summary of the "four chronological stages in the composition of the *Monk's Tale* and its links," see Kelly, *Chaucerian Tragedy*, 65–68. Larry Scanlon, *Narrative, Authority, and Power: The Medieval*

Chaucer's great innovations was the exploration of misunderstanding, there is room to explore not 'what he meant by "tragedy,"' but the range of meaning . . . he might have played with, deferred to, and differed from."[12] The result of this process is a discourse that cuts across the Chaucerian oeuvre and is deeply concerned with the ability of literature either to provide or to preclude enlightenment in the wake of catastrophe. To write tragedies or to employ tragic diction after Chaucer therefore entails negotiating these points of reference, often by means of complex allusions whose significance is liable to elude modern readers.

Let us begin with the genre as treated in Chaucer's translation of the *Consolation* before comparing it with the Monk's adaptation:

> What other thynge bywaylen the cryinges of tragedyes but oonly the dedes of Fortune, that with an unwar strook overturneth the realmes of greet nobleye? (*Glose. Tragedye is to seyn a dite of a prosperite for a tyme, that endeth in wrecchidnesse.*) (Book 2, Prose 2, lines 67–72 [2p2.67–72])

> But glorie, how deceyvable and how foul is it ofte! For which thyng nat unskilfully a tragedien (*that is to seyn, a makere of dytees that highten tragedies*) cride and seide: "O glorie, glorie," quod he, "thow nart nothyng elles to thousandes of folk but a greet swellere of eres!" (3p6.1–6)

Whereas Nicholas Trevet's *Expositio super librum Boecii de consolatione* defines tragedy as "carmen de magnis iniquitatibus a prosperitate incipiens et in aduersitate terminans" [a song about great iniquities beginning in prosperity and ending in adversity], the *Boece* gloss omits the mention of "great iniquities."[13] Rather than credit Chaucer with having realized that "the idea of tragedy as dealing with vicious protagonists whose misdeeds deserved and invited their downfall is quite foreign to the Boethian context," Kelly insists that a mere "stroke of good Fortune" accounts for this modification.[14] Chaucer's Latin text happened to be equipped with an abridged version of Trevet's commentary in the form of glosses such as those found in Cambridge, Cambridge University Library, MS Ii.3.21 (known as the Croucher manuscript after its fifteenth-century owner), which

---

Exemplum and the Chaucerian Tradition (Cambridge: Cambridge University Press, 1994), rejects the hypothesis that Chaucer wrote it before the Canterbury period as being a "clear case of aesthetic preference masquerading as a judgment of philological fact" (217–18). If Chaucer did indeed subscribe to its worldview at some point, its final phase may be read as a palinode.

[12] Ruth Morse, "Absolute Tragedy: Allusions and Avoidances," *Poetica* 38 (1993): 1–17, at 8.

[13] Trevet's discussion of 2p2.37 may be found in *Exposicio fratris Nicolai Trevethi anglici ordinis predicatorum super Boecio de consolacione*, ed. Edmund T. Silk, in an unpublished typescript, at p. 200; quoted in Kelly, *Chaucerian Tragedy*, 51.

[14] Kelly, *Chaucerian Tragedy*, 51–52.

also contains one of the two best witnesses of the *Boece*. Since the latter version calls tragedy "carmen de prosperitate incipiens et in aduersitate terminans," Kelly infers that "Chaucer's explanation is a direct translation of this gloss."[15]

While contesting an earlier study by Alastair Minnis, who suggests that Chaucer worked primarily with the complete version of Trevet's commentary, Kelly acknowledges that several glosses in the *Boece* are directly derived from it.[16] Nevertheless, he rules out the possibility that Chaucer and the Croucher scribe omitted the mention of "great iniquities" from Trevet's definition for different reasons, or with different implications.[17] The one might have deleted the words *magnis iniquitatibus a* for the sake of concision, thereby producing the shorter though not quite Latinate phrase "carmen de prosperitate incipiens." The other conceivably arrived at the same conclusion as Kelly about the irrelevance of "great iniquities" to Boethius's philosophy, whatever the source on which he relied.

A second discrepancy between the *Boece* and both the Trevet and Croucher glosses increases the probability that Chaucer's definition of tragedy was partly shaped by independent study of the *Consolation*. Whereas his predecessors have "a" or "de prosperitate *incipiens* et in aduersitate terminans," Chaucer stresses "prosperite *for a tyme*, that endeth in wrecchidnesse" (emphasis added). The former phrase implies a clear movement from prosperity to adversity. The latter foregrounds an unexpected transition, in better accord with Boethian philosophy, which holds that Fortune's dealings are never schematic or easy to predict. It is "with an *unwar strook*" that she "overturneth the realmes of greet nobleye" (emphasis added). The swiftness of her maneuvers is also evident in the poem that precedes this discussion: "Thus sche pleyeth, and thus sche prooeveth hir strengthes, and scheweth a greet wonder to alle hir servauntz yif that a wyght is seyn weleful and overthrowe in an houre" (2m1.14–18). Chaucer's first divergence from Trevet may therefore be similarly deliberate and significant.

15 Kelly, *Chaucerian Tragedy*, 52.

16 Henry Ansgar Kelly, "The Evolution of *The Monk's Tale*: Tragical to Farcical," *Studies in the Age of Chaucer* 22 (2000): 407–14, at 408–9, responding to A.J. Minnis, "Chaucer's Commentator: Nicholas Trevet and the *Boece*," in *Chaucer's Boece and the Medieval Tradition of Boethius*, ed. A.J. Minnis (Cambridge: D.S. Brewer, 1993), 83–166, at 87–89, 108, 124–25.

17 Kelly, *Chaucerian Tragedy*, 53.

Tragedy in the *Canterbury Tales*

The Monk's discourse on tragedy is often taken to be a straightforward if uninspired versification of the relevant passages from the *Boece*. Kelly praises one of his definitions for its "concision,"[18] the same quality he ascribes to Chaucer's gloss. In fact, the Monk draws extensively on the *Boece* yet remains true to it neither in letter nor in spirit. While his narration is replete with snippets of Boethian wisdom,[19] its faulty generic framework prevents them from cohering into a meaningful and transformative process:

> Tragedie is to seyn a certeyn storie,
> As olde bookes maken us memorie,
> Of hym that stood in greet prosperitee,
> And is yfallen out of heigh degree
> Into myserie, and endeth wrecchedly.
> And they ben versified communely
> Of six feet, which men clepen *exametron*.
> In prose eek been endited many oon,
> And eek in meetre in many a sondry wyse. (VII.1973–1981)

Even as it reproduces the Chaucerian gloss, this passage from the *Monk's Prologue* amplifies what, originally, was brief and to the point. In so doing, it produces various details that conflict with the *Boece*. For example, its definition of tragedy's form—"a certeyn storie"—is more restrictive than Chaucer's term *dite*,[20] especially if the latter is taken in the sense of "[a]ny literary composition in verse or prose."[21] More importantly, the Monk believes that it is the tragic protagonist who "endeth wrecchedly," whereas the *Boece* allows for either the "dite" or

[18] Henry Ansgar Kelly, *Ideas and Forms of Tragedy from Aristotle to the Middle Ages* (Cambridge: Cambridge University Press, 1993), 172.

[19] Scholars who believe the Monk is a sound expositor of the *Boece* typically rely on such excerpts without taking into sufficient account the artistic context in which they appear. See, for example, Douglas L. Lepley, "The Monk's Boethian Tale," *The Chaucer Review* 12 (1978): 162–70, which argues that the Monk's tragedies fit the perspective of Books II–IV of the *Consolation*.

[20] By contrast, Trevet and the Croucher glossator limit the sense of *tragedia* to "carmen." Ill at ease with this disparity, Kelly, *Chaucerian Tragedy*, 61, mentions "William of Conches's more general term, *scriptum*." Nevertheless, when faced with the possibility that Chaucer might have consulted more than one commentary on Boethius, he again endeavors to justify his belief that the *Boece* gloss on tragedy was translated word for word from the Croucher Manuscript (81).

[21] *The Middle English Dictionary*, s.v. "dītē, (n.)," sense 1a. The *MED* quotes the *Boece* gloss under sense 1c, "a drama; esp., a tragedy." However, with the possible exception of a quotation from the anonymous fifteenth-century translation of Higden's *Polychronicon*, none of the examples it provides has any theatrical resonances.

"prosperite" to conclude "in wrecchidnesse." Trevet and the Croucher manuscript have tragedy end "in aduersitate." This shift of emphasis has several implications. First, since the protagonists' fortunes are over when tragedy comes to a close, their irreversible ruin becomes central to all but one of the Monk's narratives. Second, emotion is brought to the fore of tragedy, which now involves a fall from "greet prosperitee" and "heigh degree" into "myserie" so as to highlight its psychological effects. Whereas plots may be reversed and kingdoms refounded, the death of a protagonist completes his or her "aventures" upon this earth and rules out the possibility of learning from one's personal misfortune.

The same dialectic is observable in the Monk's second definition of tragedy, offered at the beginning of his *Tale*:

> I wol biwaille in manere of tragedie
> The harm of hem that stoode in heigh degree,
> And fillen so that ther nas no remedie
> To brynge hem out of hir adversitee.
> For certein, whan that Fortune list to flee,
> Ther may no man the cours of hire withholde.
> Lat no man truste on blynd prosperitee;
> Be war by thise ensamples trewe and olde. (VII.1991–1998)

The Monk seems to follow the *Boece* more closely here than he does in the previous instance. Like any tragedian, he will bewail the fickleness of Fortune and the fall of those who count on her blessings. If Fortune's strokes are "unwar," his audience is to be made "war."[22] Yet, in one crucial detail, he both emulates and contradicts his Boethian source: the protagonists' helplessness once Fortune "list to flee"—that is, the lack of a "remedie / To bring hem out of hir adversitee." To be sure, this is the sentiment with which Boethius begins his narrative in the *Boece*: "'Allas! I wepynge, am constreyned to bygynnen vers of sorwful matere,'" he cries, mourning the loss of his "weleful" youth now that "eelde is comyn unwarly[23] uppon [him]" and longing for death to release him from "Fortune . . . cloudy," which "hath chaunged hir deceyvable chere" (1m1.1–28). In response, he blames his friends for having "avaunted" him "to be weleful," because "he that hath fallen stood noght in stedefast degre" (1m1.30–32). Before long, however, Philosophy recognizes that Boethius is a "sike man," rids him of the "poetical muses," who "nat oonly ne asswagen noght his sorwes with none remedies, but thei wolden fedyn and noryssen hym with sweete venym," and bids them suffer

[22] For the double meaning of *unwar* (both undiscerning and indiscernible) in 2p2, see Kelly, *Chaucerian Tragedy*, 52. The final section of the present study examines the role of the latter sense in Hoccleve's *Series*.

[23] Chaucer directly translates the Latin "inopina" (1m1.9), rejecting Jean de Meun's paraphrase "plus tost que je ne cuidoie" (1m1.9). I quote from *Sources of the Boece*, ed. Tim William Machan (Athens: University of Georgia Press, 2005).

him "to ben cured and heeled" by her own "muses" (1p1.48–72). From then on the purpose of the *Boece* is neither to mourn nor, in the last analysis, to admonish but to heal. As Monica McAlpine has argued, the "whole of the *Consolation* can be understood as the working out of [an] alternative interpretation of the Muses' song."[24]

This alternative finds no expression in the *Monk's Tale*. Rather than reread 1m1 in the light of the argument that follows, the Monk casts the latter in line with the former. His delivery oscillates between wailing and lambasting, both of which stunt the growth of his worldview.[25] For instance, having observed that "hym that folweth al this world of prees [turmoil] / Er he be war is ofte yleyd [laid] ful lowe," he cautions his audience: "Ful wys is he that kan hymselven knowe!" (VII.2136–3218).[26] Though "ensamples trewe and olde" may teach us something about the general manifestations of Fortune, they do not clarify how we may get to know ourselves if we are unaware of its effect on us in particular.[27] His litany of downfalls brings him further and further away from Boethian philosophy until, for the last time in his *Tale*, the Monk provides another definition of the genre:

Tragediës noon oother maner thyng
Ne kan in syngyng crie ne biwaille
But that Fortune alwey wole assaille
With unwar strook the regnes that been proude;
For whan men trusteth hire, thanne wol she faille,
And covere hire brighte face with a clowde. (VII.2761–2766)

Thus, the Monk's travesty culminates in the final image of his *Tale*, a paraphrase on the lines "Fortune cloudy hath chaunged hir deceyvable chere to meward," drawn from the very poem impugned by Philosophy, who proceeds to banish those responsible for it. Returning to the *Boece*, one discovers the full signifi-

---

[24] Monica E. McAlpine, *The Genre of Troilus and Criseyde* (Ithaca: Cornell University Press, 1978), 52. For additional discussion of McAlpine and the expulsion of the Muses, see Eleanor Johnson's essay in this volume.

[25] For the dulling effect of the Monk's narration, see Jahan Ramazani, "Chaucer's Monk: The Poetics of Abbreviation, Aggression, and Tragedy," *The Chaucer Review* 27 (1993): 260–76. His lamentation is criticized in Kurt Olsson, "Grammar, Manhood, and Tears: The Curiosity of Chaucer's Monk," *Modern Philology* 76 (1979): 1–17.

[26] The futility of line VII.2138 is pointed out in R.E. Kaske, "The Knight's Interruption of the *Monk's Tale*," *English Literary History* 24 (1957): 249–68, at 265.

[27] See, however, Jodi Grimes, "Knowing Fortune: The Limits of Boethian Knowledge in *The Monk's Tale*," *Carmina Philosophiae* 19 (2010): 49–68, who argues that Philosophy's failure to explain how we are to become aware of the workings of Providence is reflected in, and responsible for, the limitations of the *Monk's Tale*, which dramatizes the perspective of the prisoner Boethius.

cance of Chaucer's decision to have the Monk conclude where his source begins. Boethius's next reference to clouds occurs when Philosophy "wipe[s] a litil" the prisoner's "eien that ben dirked by the cloude of mortel thynges" (1p2.25–26). Changing the meaning of this image, Boethius explains: "Ryght so and noon other wise, the cloudes of sorwe dissolved and doon awey, I took hevene, and resceyved mynde to knowe the face of my fisycien" (1p3.1–4). In this and most further occurrences, clouds stand no longer for inscrutable Fortune but for the muddled minds of human beings, symbolized by the prisoner's "eien, that weren fulle of the wawes of wepynges" (1p2.29).[28]

Not only does the Monk persist in maintaining that humanity's path to enlightenment is hampered by external rather than internal obstacles but also, by employing the word *face* from 1p3—rather than *chere* from 1m1—in the line "And covere hire brighte face with a clowde," he also conflates Philosophy with the deity she undertakes to deconstruct.[29] This is the ultimate affront to Boethius's interlocutrix, who—in the poem that I have suggested is relevant to the *Boece* gloss on tragedy—distinguishes herself from his apparent nemesis by stressing that while "Fortune . . . desceyvable . . . enhaunceth up the humble chere of hym that is discounfited," she actually "neither heereth ne rekketh of wrecchide wepynges" (2m1.7–11). Hence there is little use in simply bewailing her assaults, for she remains untouched by the lamentation that her rival Philosophy seeks to cure.

From the perspective of reception history, the most significant product of the disparity between Chaucer's engagement with the *Consolation* and that of the Monk is the multiple responses the Monk elicits—as many as three in the context of the *Canterbury Tales* alone: the Knight's and Host's criticism and the *Nun's Priest's Tale*, which is commissioned in order to answer it. The first two are typically frowned upon by modern scholars. Larry Scanlon calls the Knight's wish for a "gladsome" (VII. 2778) antidote to monkish "hevynesse" (VII.2769) a case of "Pollyannaish special pleading."[30] Derek Pearsall dismisses the Host's preference for "desport" and "game" (VII. 2791) as "naive escapism . . . a reminder that there are views of existence even more inadequate than the Monk's."[31] In fact, both pilgrims employ Boethian resonances in order to correct the faulty reading of the *Consolation* to which they have been exposed.

---

[28] See *Boece*, 1m7.1, 3m9.44, 3m11.10, 4m1.20–21, 5p2.37, 5m2.11, and 5m3.43. Two possible exceptions are 2m3.11 and 4m1.6.

[29] The original distinction made in the *Consolation* between "vultus" ("chere") and "facies" ("face") in this sequence is also observed by Jean de Meun, whose translation has "voult" and "face" respectively.

[30] Scanlon, *Narrative, Authority, and Power*, 226.

[31] Derek Pearsall, ed., *A Variorum Edition of the Works of Geoffrey Chaucer: The Nun's Priest's Tale* (Norman: University of Oklahoma Press, 1984), 129.

As Robert Kaske once argued, the Knight's ideal plotline satisfies both popular conceptions of good and bad fortune and the doctrine that all fortune is good.[32] By insisting that "of swich thyng were goodly for to telle" (VII.2779), this pilgrim reasserts and develops the aesthetic criterion demanding "[t]ales of best sentence and moost solaas" (I.789), which the Host likewise paraphrases just before the Monk begins to speak (VII.1964). The philosophical significance of pleasure gains further depth the moment one realizes that the Knight is echoing key words from Theseus's classic expression of Boethian "wysdom" (I.3041),[33] which contrasts the "gladder" (I.3051) attitude of the enlightened with the "hevynesse" (I.3058) of willful grouching (I.3045, 3057–3058, 3062). Although the Knight is more reflective in his *Tale* than in this intervention, there are enough parallels between them to suggest that Chaucer had the former in mind when composing the latter.

Despite the Host's claim to have nearly "fallen doun for sleep" into a "slough" while Daun Piers was turning out tragedies (VII.2797–2798), he was obviously alert enough to register and redeploy the specialized vocabulary the Monk had used to codify his misreading of the *Boece*: the cloud of Fortune (VII.2782), the no-remedy situation (VII.2784), and the undue emphasis on lamentation (VII.2785), which Harry Bailly joins the Knight in terming "hevynesse" (VII.2787). More philosophically informed remarks, such as "Anhanged was Cresus, the proude kyng; / His roial trone myghte hym nat availle" (VII.2759–2760), are passed over in silence. Though on the personal level the Monk has made the Host less "war," the latter's *ad rem* criticism remains sound.

The confines of the present essay do not permit a detailed examination of the Boethian elements in the *Nun's Priest's Tale*.[34] However, it should be noted that its narrator "quits" both the previous tale and the responses that follow it. Common to Boethius, the Monk, the Knight, and the Host is the premise that wisdom is a sufficient safeguard against misfortune; the differences among them

[32] Kaske, "The Knight's Interruption," 262–64, 266–67. Cf. *Boece*, 4p7.48–52.

[33] For a reading of this speech in relation to the *Monk's Tale* and Chaucerian tragedy in general, see John F. Mahoney, "Chaucerian Tragedy and the Christian Tradition," *Annuale Mediaevale* 3 (1962): 81–99, at 92–93. For a view of the *Knight's Tale* as "profoundly un-Boethian," see Terry Jones, "*The Monk's Tale*," *Studies in the Age of Chaucer* 22 (2000): 387–97, at 389. According to Jones, "the Monk doesn't get the chance to develop the positive side of Boethius's argument because the Knight interrupts him" (393). Although Jones is right in questioning those who perceive the Knight only as "verray," "parfit," and "gentil" (I.72)—he would rather see him as false, corrupt, and despotic—his argument that the Monk not only succeeds in "quitting" the Knight (387) but also in preaching the true philosophy of Boethius, should by now appear suspect.

[34] A more extensive discussion of the *Nun's Priest's Tale* in the philosophical context of Boethius and in the dramatic context of the *Monk's Prologue* and *Tale* is offered by Nancy Dean, "Chaucerian Attitudes toward Joy with Particular Consideration of the *Nun's Priest's Tale*," *Medium Ævum* 44 (1975): 1–13.

consist in how these concepts are understood and expressed. The Nun's Priest issues a reminder that even the learned are capable of making fatal errors of judgment caused by the inherent flaws of human (or gallinaceous) nature after the Fall. Like the Monk, Chauntecleer recounts a series of tragic *exempla* in order to advise caution.[35] He then remembers his love for Pertelote, mistakes it for divine grace, and loses track of his argument. Echoing the Knight, he is moved to exclaim, "I am so ful of joye and of solas" (VII.3170) and "Ful is myn herte of revel and solas!" (VII.3204). His fortunes immediately turn, however:

> But sodeynly hym fil a sorweful cas,
> For evere the latter end of joye is wo.
> God woot that worldly joye is soone ago;
> And if a rethor koude faire endite,
> He in a cronycle saufly myghte it write
> As for sovereyn notabilitee.
> Now every wys man, lat him herkne me[.] (VII.3205–3211)

These high-flown remarks are calculated to cast doubt on the feasibility of both the Monk's call for caution—for bearing other people's downfalls in mind—and the Knight's belief in the possibility of philosophical happiness. Nevertheless, fond as the Nun's Priest is of mimicking the former pilgrim's tragic idiom (see VII.3338–3341), he satisfies the latter by allowing Chauntecleer to outwit Don Russell with the aid of "wys God" (VII.3408). In other words, the narrator fulfills the terms of his commission even as he challenges its underlying assumption that one may resist tragedy simply by espousing a better worldview—or by employing a more effective literary genre. Only the benevolent intervention of Providence can put the misguided back on the right path and open their eyes: a Christian belief that is nearly absent from the universe of Chaucerian tragedy and Boethian philosophy.

Hoccleve's Chaucerian Tragedies

Let us now turn to the reception of the Monk's Boethian definitions of tragedy in the works of Chaucer's followers. Contrary to Lydgate, who uses the word *tragedy* in several of his writings,[36] Hoccleve does not seem to have set much store by this novel term. Nevertheless, as in the case of the Knight, Host, and Nun's Priest, there are other ways in which he signals his debt to, and contention with,

[35] Especially reminiscent of the *Monk's Tale* is the exemplum of Croesus (VII.3138–3140; cf. VII.2727–2760). On this point, see Charles S. Watson, "The Relationship of the *Monk's Tale* and the *Nun's Priest's Tale*," *Studies in Short Fiction* 1 (1964): 277–88, at 279.

[36] Six occurrences are quoted in *The Middle English Dictionary*, s.v. "tragedī(e, (n.)," sense a.

the Monk's appropriation of Boethius. The intertextual relationship he establishes in the *Series* has two aspects: structural and lexical. These diverse poems and prose pieces are united by the repeated downfalls they relate or interpret: of the mentally ill and subsequently ostracized author, the betrayed Roman empress, the dying youth whom death caught unawares, and, finally, the gullible Jonathas who is repeatedly tricked by his mistress Fellicula.

At the same time, Hoccleve answers the Knight's and Host's objections by placing equal stress on recovery, as each of these characters learns to cope with misfortune. Surprisingly, this feature also has its precedent in the Monk's storytelling. His sole tragedy with a happy ending, an episode based on Daniel 4, tells how King Nebuchadnezzar turned into a beast in punishment for his pride (VII.2143–2182).[37] In keeping with the biblical account, the monarch's "wit" is eventually restored (VII.2178), and he spends the rest of his days praising God.[38] This narrative is of particular interest to Hoccleve, who alludes to it when describing his own metaphorical transformation into a "wilde steer," at least in the eyes of his surroundings.[39]

These large-scale correspondences provide a framework for readers to make sense of the resonances of the *Monk's Prologue* and *Tale* interspersed throughout the *Series*. A further distinction may be drawn here: between passages that employ tragic diction for the sake of reflection and those which do so in order to admonish. The latter function resembles the Monk's futile fulminations. Railing against the accomplices of coin clippers, Hoccleve exclaims "Nowe, maintenours, biwar nowe of a fal" yet immediately adds "I speke of no persone in special."[40] His reluctance or inability to cite the ruin of a particular offender undercuts the urgency of his polemic, leaving him with more sound than fury. There is an element of self-parody in this passage, as Hoccleve's *Regiment of Princes* often exhorts various groups of people to beware: "Thow art nat seur what that thee shal befalle," says the middle-aged Hoccleve to fickle benefactors, "Welthe is ful slipir; be waar lest thow falle."[41]

On another occasion, the *Series* borrows a few lines from the Monk's tragedy of Nebuchadnezzar while obscuring its theological perspective. Condemn-

[37] See especially *Canterbury Tales*, VII.2172; and Daniel 4:22, 29–30.

[38] By singling out the Monk's rewriting of Daniel 4 as his most enlightened narrative, I do so only in comparison with his other tragedies. For a more critical view of this episode, see Douglas J. Wurtele, "Chaucer's Monk: An Errant Exegete," *Journal of Literature and Theology* 1 (1987): 191–209, at 195–98.

[39] "Men seiden I loked as a wilde steer" (*Series: 1, My Compleinte*, l. 120). Consisting of five parts, *The Series* appears in Thomas Hoccleve, *"My Compleinte" and Other Poems*, ed. Roger Ellis (Exeter: University of Exeter Press, 2001), 113–260.

[40] Hoccleve, *Series: 2, A Dialogue*, l. 159.

[41] Hoccleve, *The Regiment of Princes*, ed. Charles R. Blyth (Kalamazoo: Medieval Institute Publications, 1999), 902–3.

ing the misrule of the emperor's brother in the *Tale of Jereslaus's Wife*, Hoccleve writes that his "herte was so eleuat / And so prowd þat by wight ne sette he noon. / Himself forgat he for his hy estat."[42] In the *Monk's Tale*, the end-rhymes similarly allude to the Persian monarch's pride just before his fall: "This kyng of kynges proud was and elaat; / He wende that God, that sit in magestee, / Ne myghte hym nat bireve of his estaat" (VII.2167–2169). The latter is contemptuous of the God who is about to change his fortune; the former, conversely, despises humanity and therefore fails to understand himself in relation to others.

While this social conception of sin gives a new slant to an old story, it hardly anticipates the divine punishment that is meted out to the emperor's brother and the other villains who betray the empress. Without a full-blown doctrinal scheme in the verse part of *Jereslaus's Wife*, one cannot know for sure whether their repentance is as genuine as Nebuchadnezzar's. Instead, the narrator urges male readers "whos vsage is, women to greeue" to "[l]et Goddes wreches . . . miroure"[43] them, but there is no guarantee that his tale will make them more aware of the workings of Providence.[44] For once, the contrast between the *Series* and the *Monk's Tale* increases the uncertainty hovering over Hoccleve's work. That he creates this impression by recasting the most discerning episode of his Chaucerian intertext is a poetic feat in and of itself.

The ironic uses to which monkish bombast is put in the *Series* call into question the efficacy of scolding. As previously suggested, the Monk misinterprets the *Consolation* when he draws on it for the purpose of dispensing reproaches. Whether or not Hoccleve registered the distance between Chaucer and his faulty reader of Boethius, achieving such an effect is one means by which the *Series* endeavors to break free of the admonitory mode frequently employed in the *Regiment of Princes*. Another, of course, is offering an alternative to it: the quest for self-knowledge in an uncertain world. Tragic diction plays a role here as well. A case in point is the adjective *unwar*,[45] whose range of meanings Chaucer had expanded at least partly under the influence of the *Boece* translation project. According to the *Middle English Dictionary* (*MED*), the first documented occurrence of the sense "[u]nexpected, unforeseen; unpredictable, unforeseeable; sudden" is the phrase "unwar strook" in the *Monk's Tale*, which, of course, is traceable

[42] Hoccleve, *Series: 3, Fabula de Quadam Imperatrice Romana*, ll. 65–67.

[43] Hoccleve, *Series: 3, Fabula de Quadam Imperatrice Romana*, ll. 722 and 727.

[44] In Jonathan Stavsky, "Hoccleve's Take on Chaucer and Christine de Pizan: Gender, Authorship, and Intertextuality in the *Epistre au dieu d'Amours*, the *Letter of Cupid*, and the *Series*," *Philological Quarterly* 93 (2014): 435–60, I consider the possibility that Hoccleve's *Series* recants the antifeminism of his previous writings, beginning with the *Letter of Cupid*. However, for all the seriousness of this endeavor, its contribution to raising awareness of God's role in human affairs remains unclearly defined.

[45] The closest the *Regiment* comes to employing this word is by negating its antonym in "Allas, I nothyng was waar of the wo / That folwed me" (ll. 656–657).

to the *Boece* gloss.[46] The *MED* lists two further examples from Chaucer, one from Trevisa, one from the Stonor letters, and six from Lydgate. Hitherto unnoticed, Hoccleve also shows an interest in this usage and is arguably the first writer after Chaucer to have employed it with reference to an unexpected downfall:

> And now, as fisshes been with hookes kaght,
> And as þat briddes been take in a snare,
> Deth hath me hent. Eschape may Y naght.
> This vnwaar woful hour me makith bare
> Of my custumed ioie and my welfare.
> The tyme is past. The tyme is goon for ay.
> No man reuoke or call ageyn it may.[47]

The source for this part of the *Series*, Henry Suso's *Horologium sapientiae*, II.2, has no equivalent for the adjective *vnwaar.* Instead, the original Latin for lines 246–249a, a first-person recasting of Ecclesiastes 9:12, contains the Vulgate adverb *extemplo*, which Hoccleve could have easily rendered as "sodeyn" without disturbing the metrical scheme of this line.[48] In an earlier passage, he similarly translates "cum extemplo mors supervenit"[49] as "whan vnwaarly deeth / Vpon hem fallith."[50] Though previously attested in this uncommon sense in one early Middle English text, the adverb *vnwaarly* may likewise have been perceived by fifteenth-century readers as having a Chaucerian, or Boethian, ring.

As we have seen, a comparable sentiment is expressed in Boethius's lament, at the beginning of the *Boece*, over the "eelde" that "is comyn unwarly uppon [him]" (1m1.13). Like Boethius, Hoccleve begins his trajectory by complaining that "sithin [he] with siknesse last / Was scourgid, cloudy hath bene þe fauour / That shoon on [him] ful briȝt in times past."[51] Elsewhere he moans, again echoing 1m1, "Sithen my good fortune hath chaungid hir chere, / Hie tyme is me to crepe into my graue."[52] The verbal correspondences among the complaints appearing in the *Boece*, *My Compleinte*, and *Lerne to Dye* point to an important difference between the Monk and Hoccleve. Whereas the former always presents tragedy as extrinsic to himself, the latter recounts both his and others' downfalls and, in some cases at least, emphasizes their similarities. Consequently, while he occasionally approximates the Monk's vision of a life shrouded in clouds where

---

46 *The Middle English Dictionary*, s.v. "unwā̆r(e, (adj.)," sense 2a.

47 Hoccleve, *Series: 4, Ars Utillissima Sciendi Mori* ("*Lerne to Dye*"), ll. 246–252.

48 Henry Suso, *Horologium sapientiae*, in *Heinrich Seuses Horologium sapientiae*, ed. Pius Künzle and Dominikus Planzer (Freiburg: Universitätsverlag Freiburg Schweiz, 1977), II.2 (530.17–19).

49 Suso, *Horologium*, II.2 (527.23–24).

50 Hoccleve, *Series: 4, Ars Utillissima Sciendi Mori* ("*Lerne to Dye*"), ll. 65–66.

51 Hoccleve, *Series: 1, My Compleinte*, ll. 22–24.

52 Hoccleve, *Series: 1, My Compleinte*, ll. 260–261.

self-knowledge is at once necessary for survival and impossible to acquire, the author of the *Series* must advance beyond it because his own welfare is at stake. Yet, in the absence of a unifying figure of authority, his path to understanding is not charted as clearly as Boethius's. Rather, Hoccleve sharpens our awareness by raising the problem of its attainment in different contexts where tragic diction is used before or after a downfall.

A fuller analysis of the influence of the *Consolation* on the *Series* would dwell on their shared concern with spiritual healing, their mixed forms, the Boethianism of Hoccleve's other sources, and his possible reliance on tragic diction as developed in *Troilus and Criseyde*; however, further pursuit of these avenues falls outside the purview of the present investigation.[53] My purpose has been to point out the Monk's contribution to fashioning a literary idiom that would allow future writers to engage the *Boece* in new, complex, and meaningful ways. For all his shortcomings, one can no longer argue that his "*Tale* suggests by inversion what the nature of authentic Chaucerian tragedy . . . might be."[54] Only by taking account of its diverse manifestations and distinct vocabulary can we understand the appeal Chaucer's conception of tragedy held for the coterie that gathered around his works.

[53] They are considered from different perspectives in Penelope B.R. Doob, *Nebuchadnezzar's Children: Conventions of Madness in Middle English Literature* (New Haven: Yale University Press, 1974), 208–31; Perkins, "Haunted Hoccleve"; Eleanor Johnson, "Sensible Prose and the Sense of Meter: Boethian Prosimetrics and the Fourteenth Century," in this volume; and, more fully, in Johnson, *Practicing Literary Theory in the Middle Ages: Ethics and the Mixed Form in Chaucer, Gower, Usk, and Hoccleve* (Chicago: University of Chicago Press, 2013), 202–31. None of these studies reads Hoccleve in the light of the *Monk's Prologue* and *Tale*, however.

[54] McAlpine, *The Genre*, 31.

The Potages of Foryetfulness: Thomas Usk, Lady Love, and the Boethian Rhetoric of Personification

Anthony G. Cirilla

> I saw, stondynge aboven the heghte of myn heved, a woman of ful greet reverence by semblaunt, hir eien brennynge and cleer-seynge over the comune myghte of men; with a lifly colour and with swich vigour and strengthe that it ne myghte nat ben emptid.
>
> Chaucer, *Boece*[1]

> Right so with ferdenesse myn herte was caught. And, I sodainly astonyed [astonished], there entred into the place there I was lodged a lady, the semelyest and moste goodly to my syght that ever toforne apered to any creature, and trewly in the blustrynge of her looke she yaue gladnesse and comforte sodaynely to al my wyttes, and ryght so she dothe to euery wyght that cometh in her presence.
>
> Thomas Usk, *The Testament of Love*[2]

---

[1] Geoffrey Chaucer, *Boece*, in *The Riverside Chaucer*, ed. Larry D. Benson, 3rd edn. (Boston: Houghton Mifflin, 1987), 1p1.3–9. Here Chaucer is translating "astitisse mihi supra uerticem uisa est mulier reuerendi admodum uultus, oculis ardentibus et ultra commune hominum ualentiam perspicacibus, colore uiuido atque inexhausti uigoris" [I became aware of a woman standing over me. She was of awe-inspiring appearance, her eyes burning and keen beyond the usual power of men. She was so full of years that I could hardly think of her as of my own generation, and yet she possessed a vivid colour and undiminished vigour]. For the Latin source, see *Anicii Manlii Severini Boethii Philosophiae Consolatio*, ed. Ludwig Bieler, CCSL 94 (Turnhout: Brepols, 1957), 1p1.1. For a modern English translation, see Boethius, *The Consolation of Philosophy*, trans. Victor Watt (New York: Penguin, 1999).

[2] Thomas Usk, *The Testament of Love*, ed. R. Allen Shoaf (Kalamazoo: Medieval Institute Publications, 1998), 1.2.113–116.

The Testament of Love was composed by Thomas Usk while he was imprisoned for his political involvement, and his narrative depicts a Lady Love who shocks Usk's imprisoned narrator out of his depressed torpor in order to educate him about the source of true happiness. As can readily be seen, Boethius's narrative use of the rhetorical device of personification is not merely alluded to in Usk's *Testament* but also pervades the structure of Usk's own narrative. Indeed, one can oftentimes read the *Testament* in moments such as the appearance of Lady Love as a reading of the portrayal of Philosophy in the *Consolation*: here the astonishing impact of Lady Philosophy's countenance is written directly into the narrative voice of the *Testament* as we are introduced to Lady Love. Although he was certainly familiar with Boethius's Latin, Usk's primary model in the *Testament* seems to have been Chaucer's *Boece*, and as a result his text is entirely in prose rather than in the prosimetric style.[3] Methods of reading brought to bear upon Boethius's *Consolation* (and Chaucer's *Boece*) therefore have a necessarily profound impact upon readings of Thomas Usk's *Testament*, especially in regards to a textual feature as essential to both texts as personification clearly is. I propose that a misreading—or, rather, an over-simplified reading—of Boethius's employment of personification has led directly to an insufficient understanding of the aesthetic aims of Usk's *Testament* as a Boethian personification narrative. From C.S. Lewis to Jennifer Arch, Usk's conversation with Lady Love has often been reduced to a sort of allegorical psychomachia. Arch, assessing Lady Philosophy as a "temporarily suppressed aspect" of Boethius's mind, extends her reading of Boethian personification to argue that Lady Love is a thinly veiled metaphor for Usk's "educational needs."[4] This is not to take away the recuperative efforts that Lewis and Arch made on Usk's behalf but to illustrate the ease with which even critics favorable

[3] Eleanor Johnson, *Practicing Literary Theory in the Middle Ages: Ethics and the Mixed Form in Chaucer, Gower, Usk and Hoccleve* (Chicago: University of Chicago Press, 2013), writes persuasively on Usk's attempt to fashion, instead of prosimetrum, an alternating series of what one might call prosaic prose versus songful prose in the *Testament*: "Because of its apologetic ambitions, the *Testament* seeks to promote an image of its author-narrator as a good person, deserving of sympathy. It does so not only narratively, by insisting on Usk's good service, but also through its formal choices, especially its inclusion of extremely artificed, songful prose passages . . . Usk may claim 'rude' lack of ornament for his writing, but what he actually produces is often a rather conspicuously songful mode of prose . . . Thus, the *Testament* is very much in the experimental tradition of Chaucer's *Boece*, exploring and exploiting the logic and limits of prose style to produce a transformative work" (176–78). This is, to date, the strongest analysis of Usk's structural aesthetic that I have encountered.

[4] Jennifer Arch, "The Boethian *Testament of Love*," *Studies in Philology* 105.4 (2008): 448–62, at 450–51. I am not disputing that Philosophy and Love are temporarily suppressed aspects of their authors' minds, but I assert that focusing on this fact circumvents the rhetorical power of the figures in question. It is, in some sense, to read the last paragraph of a story first.

toward Usk have, in my view, somewhat hastily assessed the narrative function of Usk's Boethian personification, especially in regards to personification as a cue for some measure of allegorical reading.

Some critics, however, have recently moved away from allegory in favor of investigating how Boethian literary methods address personal experiences of suffering on the literal level.[5] In the present discussion, I further this critical trend by proposing that a rhetorical appraisal of Lady Philosophy's status as a personification provides a better foundation for understanding the role of personification narratives modeled after Boethius's *Consolation*. Of course, "allegoria," or the device of using one mode of expression to signify another, is rhetorical in the general sense that it uses a linguistic device to persuade audiences. But analysis of any text's rhetorical value must begin at as well as culminate in the literal level of that text, because rhetoric as a discipline is concerned with the persuasion generated by specific words present in the text, whereas allegorical interpretation aims ultimately to discover how the text "speaks other" than what it says.[6] The poststructuralist approach to allegory, seen in the work of Paul de Man, Carolyn Van Dyke, and numerous others in recent years, has shown how truly muddy the process of allegory can be, but the persistent goal of allegory to reach past the literal level (however skeptically treated or complicated) serves nonetheless to weaken attempts to appreciate the literal level of any text lost to the label of allegory. Personification narratives are especially vulnerable to having their literal levels diminished by contemporary critics, for the apparently sensible reason that personifications are not literal persons. But the rhetorical value of personifications, their value as speaking figures who produce persuasion in their audiences (whether a textual, imagined audience such as the "I" of the text

[5] I am especially indebted to the work of Elizabeth Elliott, *Remembering Boethius: Writing Aristocratic Identity in Late Medieval French and English Literature* (Burlington: Ashgate, 2012), and Johnson, *Practicing Literary Theory*, who have both argued, from different perspectives, for heeding carefully the literal level of Boethian narratives. See also Johnson's essay in this volume.

[6] Rhetoric and its relationship to allegory is an incredibly complicated subject, especially in the Middle Ages. Rita Copeland and Ineke Sluiter, eds., *Medieval Grammar and Rhetoric: Language Arts and Literary Theory, AD 300–1475* (Oxford: Oxford University Press, 2009), have recently contributed to our understanding that "Grammar and rhetoric, the language disciplines," not only "formed the basis of any medieval education" but also were together implicated in the process of medieval literary analysis (1–2). Grammar, because its emphasis is on correct use of language to signify, approaches textual features such as personifications allegorically because, treated technically, personification (as well as most tropes) is an "incorrect" use of language that is corrected through interpretation into a coherent "sententia," an accurately stated meaning that is signified by the trope. However, because rhetoric as a discipline is more concerned with the suasory impact of language over audiences, it does not necessarily share the same allegorical impetus.

or the actual reader), is inescapably in the language which communicates these personified figures as literal presences in their narratives.

To the end of recovering or emphasizing the literal value of personification for Boethius (and so for Chaucer and Usk), I use the rhetorical term *ethopoeia*, or the making of a secondary *ethos*, to describe the persuasive impact of Philosophia, and *ethopoetics* to describe the narrative aesthetics based on this rhetorical device. To illustrate the utility of this mode of reading personifications in the Boethian tradition, I focus here upon Lady Love in Usk's Boethian *Testament*, with hopes of underscoring the aesthetic power she brings to the text in ways that previous critics have failed to fully appreciate. By learning to experience Philosophia rhetorically, as full of years, vigor, and color, and extending this hermeneutic to her personified progeny, exampled here in Lady Love as a figure seemly to look upon and comforting to behold, I believe we can correct the misreading of personification as a merely mechanical narrative device and reclaim it as a rhetorical means of personalizing truths necessary for private consolation.

Reading *The Testament of Love*

Misreading is inscribed into the history of Usk's *Testament*; highlighting the history of this misreading contextualizes the rereading of personification in Usk here proposed. Indeed, part of Usk's motivation in writing his Boethian text was to defend his shift of allegiance from the rebellious John Northampton to King Richard II and prevent it from being misread as mere political posturing rather than a sincere change of heart.[7] Worse, Usk is afraid that his mysterious benefactress, Margarite, will believe the lies he imagines his political enemies were spreading about him and that his efforts for civic good and for her love

[7] See, as an example of the discussion of politics, David Carlson, "Chaucer's Boethius and Thomas Usk's Testament of Love: Politics and Love in the Chaucerian Tradition," in *The Centre and its Compass: Studies in Medieval Literature in Honor of Professor John Leyerle* (Kalamazoo: Medieval Institute Publications, 1993): 29–70. Carlson sees Usk's use of Chaucer "as a literary source and model" as "mercenary above all" (34), reformulating Boethian love in a Chaucerian way and employing a Chaucerian subordination of politics to personal pleasure (36). By collapsing Lady Philosophy and Lady Fortune together in the figure of Lady Love, in Carlson's view, Love becomes a more effective, more persuasive figure than either, providing a unique reading in two ways: first, one which is unusually enthusiastic about Usk's aesthetics; and second, one which pays careful attention to how Lady Love produces aesthetic effects: "Where Chaucer made a narrative of it, Usk personified and allegorized this common conception [of love], returning it to the setting of Boethian fiction, of philosophical dialogue between a sapiential figure and an imprisoned man" (68).

have been in vain—the concern of misreading which informs the whole text.[8] It is this concern for which Lady Love descends into Usk's prison cell to engage him throughout the *Testament* in an extended philosophical dialogue about how virtuous love is its own reward. Whatever his contemporaries thought of the *Testament* (of which we know almost nothing), Usk's sole literary production was misread as an autobiography of Geoffrey Chaucer by William Thynne in the early sixteenth century, and it was misprinted with quires of the manuscript out of order. As discussed by Anne Middleton, once nineteenth-century scholarship rejected the *Testament* from Chaucer's canon, almost more because of distaste for the text than any scholarly observation, it was discovered by Walter William Skeat that, in the proper order, the first letter of all thirty chapters formed the acrostic, *MARGARETE OF VIRTW, HAVE MERCI ON THIN USK.*[9] This allowed a correctly ordered reading of the text for the first time in three hundred years. Significantly, in addition to being an acrostic, this plea is also an apostrophe, a rhetorical appeal to an absent audience. The persona of Margarite is imagined for the audience as virtuous, merciful, and powerful (not to mention intelligent, or at least detail-oriented if we are intended to infer that she might adduce this riddle herself). Apostrophe shares with personification a fashioning of *ethos*, the persuasion of character, where *ethos* is otherwise absent—Margarite did not write this text, and the actual "Lady Love" never appeared in any jail cell. But both have two concomitant rhetorical results: Usk is persuaded by them, and he shapes his readers' attitudes towards him by invoking them.

The *Testament of Love* remained mostly maligned as a politically obsequious and aesthetically overwrought failure, however, until C.S. Lewis attempted a more charitable view of the text. Lewis attributes some of the *Testament*'s aesthetic imperfections to Usk's models, since Usk was working with Chaucer's uncharacteristically scholarly, even at points slavish, translation of the *Consolation* and with the difficult Latin of Anselm's *De concordia.*[10] Lewis writes:

> His interweaving of divine and human love, if sometimes confusing, has an original turn, and gives rise to great beauties of sentiment, and in his styles, while the faults are largely those of the models, the merits are

[8] See Lewis Lucy, "The Identity of Margaret in Thomas Usk's Testament of Love," *Medium Aevum* 68.1 (1999): 63–72, for an example of the speculation on the identity of the historical Margaret.

[9] Anne Middleton, "Thomas Usk's 'Perdurable Letters': The *Testament of Love* from Script to Print," *Studies in Bibliography* 51 (1998): 63–116, is the single most important discussion of the material transmission and textuality of the Testament, especially as regards the corrected reading of the text (81).

[10] For a discussion of Chaucer's translation practice in the *Boece*, see A. Joseph McMullen's essay in this volume.

> his own. He would have been happy if he had kept clear of politics and moderated his philosophical ambition.[11]

Scholars have since developed Lewis' conciliatory remarks about Usk's talents into apologies for his aesthetics or at least appeals to understand them more fairly. Marion Turner has explored how Boethian morality and Chaucerian irony, two powerful and related influences on Usk, produce challenging tensions for any writer to navigate. Stephen Medcalf, perhaps the most vigorous endorser of Uskian aesthetics, points out how elaborately Usk has layered the concepts held in his prose and how subtly he improves the Boethian arguments taken from Anselm's *De concordia*.[12]

Recently and powerfully, Elizabeth Elliott and Eleanor Johnson, in separate monographs on the medieval influence of Boethius, have discussed how Usk draws on Boethian notions of the *sensorium*, memory, and a mixed style of songful prose, along with an acute sense of personal failure, to create a sense of poetic identity and a source of discursive authority. For Elliot, Usk uses the *Consolation* "as a model for conceptualizing experience . . . self construction coincides with the formulation of an ideology of public service, as Usk recasts personal history in Boethian terms."[13] The result of the rhetorical awareness of "the particular value of the perceptible, material forms as a stimulus to human cognition, the role of the senses in conceiving an ineffable God," causes Usk to use memory devices of the embodied—the tree, the knot in the heart, clothing, violence, and so forth.[14] In a similar vein, expanding on Lewis's point that "Usk is trying to write prose which shall have wings like verse,"[15] Eleanor Johnson writes that "the *Testament* also evokes Boethian theories of how the process of ethical transformation feels—sensorily—to the transformee."[16] By sublimating Boethian prosimetric to songful prose, Johnson argues,

> The *Testament* is very much in the experimental tradition of Chaucer's *Boece*, exploring and exploiting the logic and limits of prose style to produce a transformative work . . . In Usk's hands . . . the mixed form paradigm for apologetic consolation becomes not just a protreptic for an everyman

[11] C.S. Lewis, *The Allegory of Love* (Oxford: Oxford University Press, 1936), 231.

[12] See Stephen Medcalf, "Transposition: Thomas Usk's *Testament of Love*," in *The Medieval Translator: The Theory and Practice of Translation in the Middle Ages*, ed. Roger Ellis (Woodbridge: D.S. Brewer, 1989), 181–95, which develops George Sanderlin's discussion in "Usk's *Testament of Love* and Saint Anselm," *Speculum* 17.1 (1942): 69–73, into a vision of the Testament of a dialectic between Anselmian and Chaucerian approaches to Boethius.

[13] Elliott, *Remembering Boethius*, 98.

[14] Elliott, *Remembering Boethius*, 106.

[15] Lewis, *The Allegory of Love*, 223.

[16] Johnson, *Practicing Literary Theory*, 167.

> reader but also a slyly encrypted manual for right rule, a vernacular mirror for princes.[17]

The observation that *The Testament of Love* operates with a deep and pervasive indebtedness to the *Consolation*, especially for its structure of a sorrowful, imprisoned persona in dialogue with a personification, is thus well known to readers and critics of Usk. Nonetheless, Lady Love remains an almost invisible center of *The Testament of Love*, a transparency encouraged by an allegorical reading of her narrative function.

The allegorical approach to Boethius, and subsequently to personification narratives such as Usk's, can be seen in Jennifer Arch's 2008 article, "The Boethian *Testament of Love*."[18] There Arch questions previous critics who have regarded Usk as distorting Boethian philosophy to support political activism for Usk's own purposes. Arch effectively shows that Boethius can be read, without doing violence to his text, as supporting political efforts, provided those efforts are engaged by a virtuously ordered will. Usk may prioritize this argument more than the *Consolation* does, but a shift in emphasis is not necessarily a misreading. I agree with Arch's essential argument, but, in passing, she makes this comment:

> Because Philosophy claims Boethius as her own, in effect he is conversing with himself. It is essential that the process of education be self-education, geared towards the intellectual and emotional state of the learner. Philosophy is exactly the physician the prisoner Boethius requires in his state of self-pity, because she is a temporarily suppressed aspect of his own mind.[19]

She extends this reading to Usk, where she writes that Usk's "Choice of Love demonstrates an awareness of the opportunity the *Consolation* affords him as well as a clear understanding of his own educational needs."[20] Though it is not Arch's intention, this allegorical strategy allows for a strong emphasis on reading the *Testament* as political polemic, because it circumvents the textual narrator's

---

[17] Johnson, *Practicing Literary Theory*, 178, 183. While I cannot disagree with Johnson's conclusion, that the *Testament* is "not just a protreptic for an everyman reader but also a slyly encrypted manual for right rule, a vernacular mirror for princes" (183), this conclusion slips away from a reading of the text's potentially personal relevance for the concrete individual who wrote (and concrete, sub- or para-political persons who read) the *Testament*. This aspect is not dismissed by Johnson, but the invocation of an "everyman reader" suggests expected readings of allegorical texts (i.e., *Everyman*) that have the tendency to turn texts into pronouncements rather than confessions or consolations.

[18] Jennifer Arch, "The Boethian *Testament of Love*," *Studies in Philology* 105.4 (2008): 448–62.

[19] Arch, "The Boethian *Testament of Love*," 450.

[20] Arch, "The Boethian *Testament of Love*," 451.

response to the presence of Lady Love and translates that response into a literary trick with an almost purely partisan agenda.[21] I believe that this interpretation, while part of the real purpose of the *Testament* to be sure, reduces too much the sincere concerns and personal gratitude Usk seems to have for Love's teachings and her presence. The allegorical reading of Lady Love's conversation with the narrator arranges the text into an almost exclusively outward-facing posture that deceptively imitates personal confidence between the interlocutors, a literary performance affecting intimacy but expediently written for any sympathetic and potentially useful eavesdropper. Allegorical personification in a text such as the *Testament* thus lends itself nicely, for example, to Paul Strohm's reading of the *Testament* as a highly polemical piece:

> Staged within the consolatory form of the Testament is therefore a subversive counterargument . . . many of the familiar devices of the consolatory allegory are invaded or bent to new use . . . The voice of Love . . . is suddenly and unpredictably bent toward purposes of factional vindication . . . Love, we find, is a factionalist herself . . . Usk's highly self-interested and precipitate personal choices seem consistent with his attempt to bend literary form to personal purposes of immediate advancement.[22]

Strohm here of course means politically personal purposes rather than emotionally or spiritually personal purposes, and there is no denying, of course, the deeply political motivations behind Usk's *Testament.* Even so, Strohm's reading of Usk may get at the underlying distaste for the text, in addition to perceptions of it as an aesthetic failure, which has marked its critical discourse since the nineteenth century. Read as personification allegory, the *Testament* seems to stray over the line from having a moral meaning to being a didactically partisan treatise—from being politically conscious to being mere political propaganda (not an entirely unfair assessment, given Usk's involvement with Northampton as a professional propagandist). My hope here is not to refute Lady Love's literary role in expressing Usk's political motivations but to expand her into the affective, sensory, and personal reading provided by Johnson, by reorienting Lady Love's place in the history of Boethian personification.

---

[21] Such an emphasis comes out strongly in Joanna Summer's chapter on Usk from her book, *Late Medieval Prison Writing and the Politics of Autobiography* (Oxford: Oxford University Press, 2004), entitled simply, "Thomas Usk and the *Testament of Love.*" My intention is not to dismiss the political motivations of the *Testament*, which are clearly there, but simply to balance them against the more individual-centered motivations, which can also be detected in the text.

[22] Paul Strohm, "Politics and Poetics: Usk and Chaucer in the 1380s," in *Literary Practice and Social Change in Britain, 1380–1530*, ed. Lee Patterson (Berkeley: University of California Press, 1990), 103–12.

In short, the received method of interpreting personifications allegorically has allowed a misreading of *The Testament of Love*, or at least an over-reading, concerning the relationship of Lady Love to Usk's social and political goals in composing a Boethian narrative. Joel Relihan wrote recently that *The Consolation of Philosophy* is "both over-familiar and under-read; it is the modern reception of the text, and the expectations raised in readers because of this reception, that must be countered."[23] In my view, this is especially applicable to Lady Philosophy's status as a personification, and thus to Usk's Lady Love as well. James Paxson wrote in *The Poetics of Personification* that "fewer and fewer thinkers today believe in the old axiomatic association between personification and allegory,"[24] and yet this association continues to pervade, if implicitly, much scholarship aimed at Boethius's literary reception history. In contrast, the conceptual relationship of personification to allegory as a narrative mode is not found anywhere in the rhetorical handbooks of antiquity or the Middle Ages.[25] This is not to say personification allegories did not exist—that would be an absurd position—but it does strongly suggest that personification and allegory were not, at least at the level of rhetorical theory, considered inseparably linked. This linking was articulated in the eighteenth century and was only solidified by the Romantics, who introduced an unhistorical distinction between personification and *prosopopoeia*, at the expense of the former. Personification was explicitly tied to imbuing personhood to abstractions and *prosopopoeia* to granting personhood to physical objects, whether animate or inanimate. Personification thus became inherently more polemical and ephemeral, and less artistic, than *prosopopoeia*. This long-standing trajectory of interpreting personification with a pejorative valence has thus understandably left Usk somewhat out in the cold as regards critical assess-

[23] Joel C. Relihan, *The Prisoner's Philosophy: Life and Death in Boethius's Consolation* (Notre Dame, IN: University of Notre Dame Press, 2007), 9. Although Relihan goes too far in ironizing Greco-Roman philosophy in Boethius's *Consolation*, in my view at least, his reading nonetheless reinvigorates the attention a reader of the text must pay to the reactions of the prisoner in a powerful way that helps to revive the rhetorical nature of the text, in addition to its allegorical and philosophical components.

[24] James Paxson, *The Poetics of Personification* (New York: Cambridge University Press, 1994), 5. In one of the few book-length studies that treats the rhetorical device holistically, Paxson presents one of the most important histories of personification ever composed, one which has informed my thinking on the subject more thoroughly than any number of footnotes could impress upon the reader.

[25] This discussion is in part a condensation of "A History of Personification Theory," 8–34, taken from Paxson's *Poetics of Personification*, but it also is informed by Copeland and Sluiter, eds., *Medieval Grammar and Rhetoric*, a diachronic anthology of ancient and medieval grammatical and rhetorical handbooks; and Joseph M. Miller, Michael H. Prosser, and Thomas W. Benson, eds., *Readings in Medieval Rhetoric* (Bloomington: Indiana University Press, 1973).

ment, because a different response to personification has since developed than the one Usk most probably had in his own time.

Personification as *Ethopoesis* in Boethius and Usk

Unlike the eighteenth- and nineteenth-century differentiations, anthropomorphism and personification were both covered under the heading of *prosopopoeia* in antiquity and the Middle Ages, as early as the writing of Emporius the Orator, an approximate contemporary of Boethius. Emporius, in fact, provides a rhetorical understanding of *prosopopoeia* that is helpful to understanding Boethius's use of personification, as well as later personifications influenced by Boethius. In a brief tract, Emporius defines *prosopopoeia* as the fourth branch of *ethopoeia*, the construction of another speaker's characteristics, voice, and general *ethos* within one's own rhetorical composition, whether aural or written. Itself entitled *On ethopoeia*, Emporius heralds the device as central to the orator, so that as a type of *ethopoeia*, *prosopopoeia* is to be regarded as a persuasive conjuration of *another* speaker's *ethos*, distinct from that of the actual orator, in the audience's imagination. Emporius writes:

> Etsi adlocutio non est officii oratorum plena matieres, est tamen vel materiae portio vel omnium praeparatio. Adfectus etinim inesse omnibus orationibus debet, cuius imitandi prima hic exercitatio datur. Denique a nonnullis haec materia ethopoeia nominatur, quod ethos, id est adfectum dicentis effingat.
>
> [Although impersonation is not the whole substance of the orator's duty, still it is a major part of the material and is necessary in the preparation of all the material. Attitudes are, after all, essential to all orations, and major attention must be given to the art of reproducing them.][26]

It is not simply the presentation of the absent speaker's thoughts but also, primarily through language, an attempt to give the audience the capacity to imagine the sensory presence and likeness of what the imagined someone brings to her utterance. Concerning *prosopopoeia*, in the same tract Emporius writes:

> Est et illud quartum genus adlocutionis, quod ab oratoribus magnis in causis gravioribus et tragicis frequenter adsumitur, cum mutis damus verba et fingitur persona quae non est, sicuti M. Tullius verba provinciae Siciliae vel rei publicae loquentis inducit: id prosopopoeia nominatur.

[26] Karl Halm, ed., *Rhetores Latini minores* (Leipzig: B.G. Teubner 1863), 561; Emporius the Orator, "Concerning Ethopoeia," trans. Joseph Miller, in *Readings in Medieval Rhetoric*, 33.

> [There is a fourth kind of impersonation, which is frequently adopted by great orators in especially serious or tragic cases; it involves giving words to the dumb and creating a person who does not really exist, as when M. Tullius [Cicero] attributes words to the province of Sicily or represents the republic as speaking; this is called *prosopopoeia*.][27]

Prosopopoeia is therefore a more specific form of *ethopoeia*, which attempts to translate the persuasive potential of things or ideas into *ethos*, so that the audience can experience the impersonal through an imaginative construction of the sensible qualities of the human figure. Unlike allegorical personification, which invites a hermeneutics of removal, that is, of stripping away the integument or covering, *ethopoeic* personification would resist such decoding and instead invite application, imbuement, or incorporation of the audience's sensory imagination into the linguistically constructed ethos. This does not mean that such personifications cannot be usefully read allegorically—often they can and have been so read extensively by numerous critics. But, I contend, this circumventing or deconstructive approach to the personification tends to miss the affective experience involved when *ethopoeic* personification is present in the text. Therefore, I present here textual justification for an *ethopoeic* reading of Boethius's personification of Lady Philosophy, and discuss how Usk deepens this type of personification by calling upon the Catholic notion of sacramentality in his rhetorical presentation of Lady Love.

First, the dynamic description of how both personifications emerge suddenly into the imprisoned life-worlds of both figures, while reducible to allegory, presents aesthetically pleasing imagery that invites imagination over analysis. After a grief-saturated poem, the prisoner of the *Consolation* narrates:

> In the mene while that I, stille, recorded these thynges with myself and merkid my weply compleynte with office of poyntel, I saw, stondynge aboven the heghte of myn heved, a woman of ful greet reverence by semblaunt, hir eien brennynge and cleer-seynge over the comune myghte of men; with a lifly coloure and with swich vigour and strengthe that it ne myghte nat ben emptid . . . I sette myne eien on hir and fastned my lookynge, I byholde my noryce, Philosophie, in whoos houses I hadde conversed and hauntyd fro my youthe; and I seide thus: "O thou maystresse of all vertues, descended from the sovereyne sete, whi arttow comen into this solitarie place of myn exil? Artow comen for thou art maad coupable with me of false blames?"[28]

---

[27] Halm, *Rhetores Latini minores*, 562; Emporius, "Concerning Ethopoeia," 35.

[28] Chaucer, *Boece*, 1p1.1–9, 1p3.4–12. Here Chaucer is translating "Haec dum mecum tacitus ipse reputarem querimoniamque lacrimabilem stili officio signarem astitisse mihi supra uerticem uisa est mulier reuerendi admodum uultus, oculis ardentibus et ultra communem hominum ualentiam perspicacibus, colore uiuido atque inexhausti uigoris . . . Itaque ubi in eam deduxi oculos intuitumque defixi, respicio nutricem meam, cuius ab

The situational parallels invite recognition—like Boethius, Usk is interrupted from his indulgent grief by a striking, sudden apparition:

> Rehersynge these thynges and many other without tyme or moment of rest me semed for anguysshe of disease that al togyder I was rauysshed, I can not tel howe; but holy al my passyons and felynges weren loste as it semed for the tyme and sodainly a maner of drede light in me al at ones . . . Right so with ferdenesse myn herte was caught. And, I sodainly astonyed, there entred into the place there I was lodged a lady, the semelyest and moste goodly to my sight that ever toforne apered to any creature, and trewly in the blustrynge of her looke she yave gladnesse and comforte sodaynely to al my wyttes, and ryght so she dothe to every wyght that cometh in her presence . . . but yet with a quakynge voyce as I durste, I salved her and enquired what she was, and why she, so worthy to sight, dayned to entre into so foule a dungeon.[29]

The passage is characteristic of how careful and responsive a reader of Boethius Usk is—he detects the potential of Lady Philosophy's imposing appearance to inspire both fear and reverence and makes this awe an explicit part of his description because it is central to his theme of the simultaneous Daunger and Joy that Lady Love inspires.[30] Like Boethius, Usk experiences a visceral dissonance between the noble presence of his mentor and his wretched environment, the dismal dungeon. In addition, the presence of these figures inspires in Boethius and

---

adulescentia laribus obuersatus fueram, Philosophiam. Et quid, inquam, tu in has exsilii nostri solitudines, o omnium magistra uirtutum, supero cardine delapsa uenisti? An ut tu quoque mecum rea falsis criminationibus agiteris?" [While I was quietly thinking these thoughts over to myself and giving and vent to my sorrow with the help of my pen, I became aware of a woman standing over me. She was of awe-inspiring appearance, her eyes burning and keen beyond the usual power of men. She was so full of years that I could hardly think of her as of my own generation, and yet she possessed a vivid colour and undiminished vigour . . . I turned my eyes and fixed my gaze upon her, and I saw that it was my nurse in whose house I had been cared for since my youth—Philosophy. I asked her why she had come down from the heights of heaven to my lonely place of banishment, 1p1.1, p3.2–4].

[29] Usk, *Testament*, 1.2.101–119.

[30] The commonplace of personifying Daunger and Joy, of course, has its roots in the poetic love tradition surrounding *The Romance of the Rose*, Daunger and Joy being the personified attendants of the beloved, typically ornamental figures rather than *ethopoeic* as discussed here. The theme illustrates the intertwining happy thoughts and worried imaginings of the prospective lover: "blysse of my ioye that ofte me murthed is turned in to galle to thynke on thing that may not at my wyl in armes me hent" (1.1.32–36). So, for example, Usk's narrator protests that "sir Daunger laced me in stockes" and is concerned that Lady Love "wol not maken by your might the virtue in mercy of the Margaryte on me for to stretche" (1.3.341–343).

Usk a power to break the silence of their depressed thoughts, to hear their own voices and the voices of their interlocutors, within the imaginative landscape of their writing. The allegorical possibilities of these details present themselves, but the cognitive confusion of physically dire circumstances and the dazzling, inspiring interlocutors are as much a matter of how the imagination and the senses are activated by the personifications as they are a matter of rational analysis. As we know from Book 5 of the *Consolation*, intellect, the highest mode of thought, does not solely rely on reason but incorporates the epistemic power of both the senses and their interaction with the imagination.

Vivid *ethopoeia* is woven into the presence of these personifications immediately, with a force that echoes throughout both texts in their entirety, discouraging a removal of the allegorical "integument" often referred to by medieval theorists.[31] In fact, the discussion of clothing, the most frequent metaphor for an allegory's illusory surface, is used by Lady Philosophy and Lady Love in ways which seem to resist an allegorical approach. Relating the anecdote of the pseudo-philosophers, Lady Philosophy says:

> The heritage of whiche Socrates . . . whan that the peple of Epycuriens and Stoyciens and manye othere enforceden hem to gon ravyssche everyche man for his part . . . they as in partye of hir preye todrowen me, cryinge and debatyng ther-ayens, and korven and torente my clothes that I hadde woven with myn hands; and with tho cloutes that thei hadden arased out of my clothes thei wenten awey wenynge that I hadde gon with hem every del.[32]

[31] An excellent foundational discussion of the allegorical "integument" is Theresa M. Kelley, *Reinventing Allegory* (Cambridge: Cambridge University Press, 1997). Also see Carolyn Van Dyke's seminal work on the subject, *The Fiction of Truth: Structures of Meaning in Narrative and Dramatic Allegory* (Ithaca: Cornell University Press, 1985).

[32] Chaucer, *Boece*, 1p3.28–44. Here Chaucer is translating "Cuius hereditatem cum deinceps Epicureum uulgus ac Stoicum ceterique pro sua quisque parte raptum ire molirentur meque reclamantem renitentemque uelut in partem praedae traherent, uestem quam meis texueram minibus disciderunt abreptisque ab ea panniculis totam me sibi cessisse credentes abiere" [After that the mobs of Epicureans and Stoics and the others each did all they could to seize for themselves the inheritance of wisdom that he left. As part of their plunder they tried to carry me off, but I fought and struggled, and in the fight the robe was torn which I had woven with my own hands. They tore off little pieces from it and went away in the fond belief that they had obtained the whole of philosophy, 1p3.7]. It bears pointing out that Marshall McLuhan, *The Classical Trivium: The Place of Thomas Nashe in the Learning of His Time*, ed. W. Terrence Gordon (Corte Madera: Gingko Press, 2006), explains that Stoics and Epicureans were known as bad pedagogues because they devalued the third branch of the *trivium*, rhetoric, in favor of logic and grammar. In a sense, then, by disapproving of these groups, Lady Philosophy could be understood as reaffirming her rhetorical nature. Lady Philosophy, who recites the vast majority of poems in the *Consolation*, is thus rejecting not grammar when she rejects the

Like the tyrants of Book 4 of the *Consolation*, the pseudo-philosophers are deprived in their intellectual appropriation of the whole of philosophical truth when they regard Lady Philosophy as an impersonal object to be dissected instead of a personal whole. Clothing implies the dignity of a presence, which has voice, "an individual substance of a rational nature," as Boethius the theologian defines personhood.[33] In a related vein, Love speaks not of her own clothing but of imparting clothing to Thomas Usk through his service to Margarite:

> If any man yeue to another wight . . . a garnement or a cote, though he were the cote or else thilke clothing, it is not to putte to him that was naked the cause of his clothinge, but only to him that was yeuer of the garnement. Wherfore I saye, thou that were naked of loue and of thyselfe non have mightiest, it is not to putte thyne owne persone, sithen thy loue cam thorow thy Margaryte-perle.[34]

Even as she describes Margarite's love as imparting virtue the way one man grants another his cloak, Love is, in a manner similar to Philosophy, creating self-identification—putting on, rather than taking off, is how she is to be understood. Being naked of Love is a poor state that one has no power to rectify—Margarite has made possible not only a self-clothing but also a self-consoling by granting the *persona* of Love to his imagination. This act, which is inspired by Lady Philosophy's use of clothing to delineate her own value, is now used by Lady Love to impart value to Usk, which is essentially what it means to personalize someone, the aim of Boethian *ethopoetic* rhetoric.

The Healing Rhetoric of *Ethopoetic* Personification

Clothing as ornament that cannot be separated from the thing ornamented conceptually echoes the Catholic notion of sacramentality, a sacrament being an efficacious sign that represents the grace which it simultaneously dispenses, and its primary function of healing some aspect of the individual's spirituality.[35] Indeed,

---

Muses but a similar disciplinary tyrannical impulse in poetry, which can also be found in some sects of philosophy.

[33] This comes from Boethius's tracts on Trinitarian philosophy, where he labors to create a conception of personhood that can be reconciled to the Christian monotheistic view of the Father, Son, and Holy Spirit.

[34] Usk, *Testament*, 3.6.888–894.

[35] It should be pointed out that this argument is something of a challenge to Lewis's distinction between allegory and sacramentalism posited in the second chapter of *The Allegory of Love*, where he writes that the one "leaves the given—his own passions—to talk of that which is confessedly less real, which is a fiction. The symbolist leaves the given to find that which is more real" (45). Allegorical readings of personifications

the faint reference Lady Philosophy makes to the sacrament of confession is expanded by Lady Love, who compares rhetoric to the sacrament of communion. Lady Philosophy asks Boethius, "First wiltow suffer me to touche and assaye th'estat of thi thought by a fewe demaundes, so that I may understand what be the manere of thi curacioun?"[36] Finding his subsequent answers deficient, she says:

> "I nas nat desseyved . . . that ther ne faileth somewhat, by whiche the maladye of perturbacion is crept into thi thought, so as by the strengthe of the palys chynynge and open. But sey me this: remembrestow what is the ende of thynges, and whider that the entencion of alle kende tendeth?" "I have herd tolde it somtyme," quod I, "but drerynesse hath dulled my memorie."[37]

Boethius has committed the Platonic sin of forgetting what one ought to remember, and Lady Love transfers this sin to an act with anti-Eucharistic implications:

> "O where haste thou be so longe commensal that hast so mykel eaten of the potages of foryetfulnesse and drunken so of ignorance that the old soukyng whiche thou haddest of me arne amaystred and lorn fro al maner of knowing? O this is a worthy person to helpe other that can not counsayle him selfe." And with these words for pure and stronge shame I woxe al reed.[38]

Boethius self-diagnoses as having been afflicted with spiritual amnesia, but Usk merely blushes, an inherently ambiguous act that does not so clearly explicate

emphasize their fictional status; sacramental, and thus implicitly rhetorical, readings use personification to bring the individual closer to the real experience of holding ideas. In presenting a challenge to Lewis's model, however, I likewise underscore its continued importance in the contemporary discourse surrounding allegory.

36 Chaucer, *Boece*, 1p6.1–4. Here Chaucer is translating "Primum igitur paterisne me pauculis rogationibus statum tuae mentis attingere atque temptare, ut qui modus sit tuae curationis intellegam?" [Will you first then let me discover your state of mind and test it with a few simple questions? That way I can discover the best method of curing you, 1p6.1].

37 Chaucer, *Boece*, 1p6.33–39. Here Chaucer is translating "Num me, inquit, fefellit abesse aliquid, per quod uelut hiante ualli robore in animum tuum perturbationum morbus inrepserit? Sed dic mihi, meministine quis sit rerum finis quoue totius naturae tendat intention? Audieram, inquam, sed memoriam maeror hebetauit" ["I was right, then . . . in thinking that something was missing. Your defenses have been breached and your mind has been infiltrated by the fever of emotional distraction. So tell me, do you remember what is the end and purpose of things and the goal to which the whole of Nature is directed?" "I did hear it once," I said, "but my memory has been blunted by grief," 1p6.9–10].

38 Usk, *Testament*, 1.4.375–379.

self-knowledge (even if it suggests some). The blush could refer to shame of having eaten the "potages of foryetfulnesse and drunken so of ignorance," or his failure to continue to partake of the old sustenance which he had before from Lady Love, or the indictment that he is unworthy to help others because he cannot counsel himself—or, most likely, all of these together. Usk's narrator had earlier compared the experience of internalizing rhetoric to that of eating food, a visceral construction of identity that emphasizes his own embodied reality and that of the one who feeds him. With recognition of such an embodied self comes an awareness of personal vulnerability, surely the general significance of any blush, however ambiguous in detail. This embarrassment over betraying improper rhetorical influence is especially involved in the self-consciousness of writing in such a conspicuous literary tradition as Boethian and Chaucerian identity performance. Of his predecessors Usk writes, "al the grettest clerkes han had ynough . . . and made therof great rekes and nobles ful of al plentyes to fede me and many another."[39] As with Boethius, Usk needs a treatment that cares for his whole experience of self, not merely his capacity to understand logic. Usk's decision to compose in the vernacular, in addition to being a result of his admiration for Chaucer (including Chaucer's philosophical poetry as well as his *Boece*) is, in spite of other political and personal motivations (such as, perhaps, a lack of confidence in composing in Latin, professed by Usk himself in the prologue of the *Testament*) also a means to reduce the alienation between himself and his Boethian counsel. As Walter Ong has argued, there is an inherent intimacy associated with the mother tongue, especially when there is a strong presence of a learned, "official language," as with learned Latin "[f]irst languages especially are associated with feeding . . . It is by 'eating,' psychologically chewing, swallowing, digesting, assimilating from within, rather than by mere visual imaging that the written word becomes truly oral and thereby alive and real, entering into the human consciousness and living there."[40] I do not hold it as merely fortuitous, therefore, that this is precisely what Lady Love, Usk's vernacular Lady Philosophy, will do at the end of the text—that is, take up residence in Usk's heart to reinforce the healing impact of her rhetorical ministrations. She does not simply educate Usk's mind but uses her utterances to provide sustenance for his soul.

Both Lady Philosophy and Lady Love subsequently begin to treat their patients with the penance-inducing power of Rhetorica and her sister from the quadrivial arts, Musica. At the opening of Book 2, Philosophia tells the prisoner:

> But now is tyme that thou drynke and ataste some softe and delitable thynges, so that whanne thei ben entred withynne the, it mowe maken wey to strengere drynkes of medycines. Com now forth, therefore, the suasyoun

---

39 Usk, *Testament*, Prologue, 69–73.

40 Walter J. Ong, *Interfaces of the Word: Studies in the Evolution of Consciousness and Culture* (Ithaca: Cornell University Press), 24.

> of swetnesse rethorien, whiche that goth oonly the righte wey while sche forsaketh nat myn estatutz. And with Rethorice com forth Musice, a damoysele of our hous, that syngeth now lightere moedes or prolacions, now hevyere.[41]

Unlike Boethius, Usk does not relay the poetry recited by Love, perhaps because, although the audience needs to know that poetic rhetoric matters, the audience of his writing is not the sole purpose of his meditation. He leaves the audience out of perhaps the most intimate communications between himself and his interlocutor, but does so to convey rather than conceal the importance of that heard utterance. Again to quote Ong, "Sound exists only when it is going out of existence: in uttering the word 'existence,' by the time I get to the '-tence,' the 'exis' is gone and has to be gone."[42] Usk highlights the difficulty of relating the experience of rhetorical persuasion and musical affect by relaying Lady Love's song at a remove, forcing the reader to imagine his prose as a translation of a non-existent poem:

> In this meane whyle this comfortable lady ganne synge a wonder mater of enditynge in Latyn. But trewly the noble colours in rethorik wyse knytte were so craftily that my connyng wol not stretche to remember; but the sentence I trowe somdele have I in mynde. Certes, they were wonder swete of sowne, and they were touched al in lamentacion wyse and by no werbles of myrthe. Lo, thus ganne she synge in Latyn, as I may constrewe it in our Englysshe tongue: ". . . but in the churche at matins he is behynde, for yvel disposycion of his stomake; therefore, he shulde eate beane breed, and so dyd his syre his estate ther with to strengthen."[43]

The intuitive, numinous influence of rhetoric's persuasive power and music's wordless, stirring language share the capacity to communicate an experience which cannot be reduced to words—which cannot be summarized, though it can be pointed to, by the allegorical reading, the "kernel." As opposed to eating the "potages of foryetfulness," rhetoric which leads to the Boethian transgression of

---

[41] Chaucer, *Boece*, 2p1.37–47. Here Chaucer is translating "Sed tempus est haurire te aliquid ac degustare molle atque iucundum, quod ad interior transmissum ualidioribus haustibus uiam fecerit. Adsit igitur rhetoricae suadela dulcedinis, quae tum tantum recta calle procedit, cum nostra institute non deserit cumque hac musica laris nostri uernacula nunc leuiores nunc grauiores modos succinat" [It is time, then, for you to take a little mild and pleasant nourishment which by being absorbed into your body will prepare the way for something stronger. Let us bring to bear the persuasive powers of sweet tongued-rhetoric, powers which soon go astray from the true path unless they follow my instructions. And let us have as well Music, the maid-servant of my house, to sing us melodies of varying mood, 2p1.7–8].

[42] Ong, *Interfaces of the Word*, 20.

[43] Usk, *Testament*, 2.2.97–102, 136–138.

self-forgetfulness, and writing which is not reintegrated into a sound-emphasized epistemology that remembers the nature of the self, the "noble colours in rhethorik" produce a memory of meaning even if the individual is not capable of reconstructing the details which transformed that meaning into sustenance for the listener. "Beane breed," a simple diet of necessity, is not anti-rhetorical but, instead, rhetorically mindful of what the individual needs in order to stay in tune with himself and with God. The lesson comes from Lady Love's *ethos* as well as her *sentence*, and to achieve it she too engages in the construction of *ethopoeia*—the ethos of a man of the cloth who eats what keeps him healthy both physically and spiritually. This rhetoric of nourishment achieves its harmony through the voice of the personification, a voice we are asked to imagine as truly voiced—tied to a temporal actuality that writing destroys—through Usk's *ethopoetic* rhetoric of sacramentality.

Conclusion: Lady Love's *Ethopoetic* Rhetoric of Sacramental Harmony

The function of sacraments such as baptism and the Eucharist, as has been discussed by Sarah Beckwith, is to symbolize while also enacting the communal wholeness made possible by Christ.[44] Beckwith's understanding of the sacraments is crucial for her understanding of medieval theater, because "everything onstage is a sign," and so theater "is not so much inimical to the sacramental disclosure of God as the perfectly consonant form for the religion of incarnation."[45] Rhetoric, like theatrics, is performative language that uses ornamentation to disclose rather than to hide meaning. Personification, which imbues ideas about the world with the sensory persona of human figuration, in this way can be said to perform a sacrament of rhetoric for both Boethius and Usk: Love of Wisdom and Love themselves are permitted to speak when words have otherwise failed to preserve the socio-theological unity in which both Boethius and Usk believe. Lady Philosophy teaches a harmony of thought and reality, which resists easy allegorical dichotomizing on a cosmic level:

> That the world with stable feyth varieth accordable chaungynges . . . al this accordaunce [and] ordenaunce of thynges is bounde with love, that governeth erthe and see, and hath also comandement to the hevene. And yif this love slaked the bridelis, alle thynges that now loven hem togidres wolden make batayle contynuely, and striven to fordo the fassoun of this

[44] See Sarah Beckwith, *Signifying God: Social Relation and Symbolic Act in the York Corpus Christi Plays* (Chicago: University of Chicago Press, 2001). As Beckwith explains it, in medieval sacraments, "signs participate in their reality" (61).

[45] Beckwith, *Signifying God*, 29.

> world, the which they now leden in accordable faith by fayre moevynges. This love halt togidres peples joined with an holy bond, and knytteth sacrament of mariages of chaste loves; and love enditeth laws to trewe felawes. O weleful were mankynde, yif thilke love that governeth hevene governed yowr corages.[46]

It is worthy of note that Lady Philosophy, "Love of Wisdom," refers to herself not as the source of harmony but only as a means of accessing understanding and vision of that harmony. Her injunction for Boethius to turn to God and pray suggests that Love is, therefore, something more than Love of Wisdom, even if they are not mutually exclusive. Usk's change of personifications emphasizes even more than Boethius does the aspects of persuasion that go beyond *logos*, by choosing as his central *ethos* that which Lady Philosophy herself praised so ardently. Lady Love, through her ubiquitous use of the elusive imagery of the "knot in the herte," brings this harmony of philosophical truth and embodiedness even more directly into the individual:

> "O," quod she, "there is a melodye in heven whiche clerkes clepen 'armony,' but that is not in brekynge of voyce, but it is a maner swete thing of kyndely werchyng [behaving according to a principle of nature] that causeth joye out of nombre to recken, and that is joined by reason and by wysdome in a quantyte of proporcion of knyttyng, God made al thing in reason, and in wytte of proporcion of melody we mowe not suffyse to shewe . . . But of suche hevenly melody mokel travayle wol bringe out in knowing right lytel. Sweteness of this paradise hath you ravished . . . Blysse of two hertes in ful love knytte may not aright byn ymagyned. Ever is their contemplacion in ful of thought studye to plesaunce, mater in bringynge, comforte everyche to other . . . This blysse is a maner of sowne delicious in a queynte [curious, attention-drawing] voyce touched and no dynne of notes . . . This armony, this melody, this perdurable joye may nat be in doynge, but between hevens and elementes or twey kindly hertes ful knyt in trouth of naturel

46 Chaucer, *Boece*, 2p8.1–7. Here Chaucer is translating "Quod mundus stabili fide / concordes uariat uices . . . hanc rerum seriem ligat / terras ac pelagus regens / et caelo imperitans amor. / Hic si frena remiserit, / quicquid nunc amat inuicem / bellum continuo geret / et quam nunc social fide / pulchris motibus incitant / certent soluere machinam. / Hic sancto populous quoque / iunctos foedere continent, / hic et coniugii sacrum castis nectit amoribus, / hic fidis etiam sua / dictat iura sodalibus. / O felix hominum genus, / si uestros animos amor / quo caelum regitur regat!" [The world in constant change maintains a harmony . . . And all this chain of things in earth and sea and sky One ruler holds in hand: If Love relaxed the reins all things that now keep peace would wage continual war and wreck the great machine which unity maintains with motions beautiful. Love, too, holds peoples joined by sacred bond of treaty, and weaves the holy knot of marriage's pure love. Love promulgates the laws for friendship's faithful bond. O happy race of men, if Love who rules the sky could rule your hearts as well, 2m8.1–30].

> understondyng, withouten wenynge and disceit as hevens and planettes, whiche thynges continually for kyndly acordaunces foryeteth al contrarious mevynges that into passive diseases may sowne."[47]

Cosmic and personal harmony cannot be written, because harmony is by nature heard and not seen, and even when it is written, we are called to remember it as "sowne delicious in a queynte voice." Harmony can be remembered in writing, but it can only be felt within the secret places of the individual's interiority, a place uniquely heard, as Ong would have it, rather than seen. The impact of this sacramental experience of the *ethopoetic* personification's rhetoric is that the cosmic unity of God's good plan becomes at least imaginable, if not immediately perceivable, in spite of the experience of true suffering.

Lady Philosophy and her progeny, Lady Love, can be read as allegorical in spite of the sentiments they relate, and this capacity should not be forgotten in the process of understanding either figure. However, Usk went to his execution by thirty strokes of the sword still holding fast to the ideas he had written in the *Testament*, and, like Boethius, he called upon personification to give him the personal strength required to maintain his convictions in the face of the direst of consequences. The contemporary association of allegory with a purely cerebral experience of a text, albeit undercut by much recent scholarship, must be nuanced to appreciate the value these texts could have for their writers in real, lived experience. The sense that Usk failed to achieve a mental ascent away from his worldly problems where his model, Boethius, succeeded, is first based in a misreading of Boethius, one which regards the personified status of Lady Philosophy (and thus the process of imagining her with presence and voice) as unessential to her meaning and asserts that this use of personification is employed by Usk—which I have argued is insufficient for both writers. Second, and related, it is a misreading to encounter these personifications through chirographical or (more likely, in our post-print bias) typographical silence, a silence encouraged by allegory, where personifications such as Lady Philosophy and Lady Love are "seen through" as translucent codes instead of listened to as valued voices. It is a third misreading, based on the previous two, to think that Usk held Love as undifferentiated in *ethos* and thus was unaware of her different persuasive presence, from Philosophy (Love of Wisdom). Lady Philosophy tells her pupil that in order for his mind to comprehend her teachings, they must be clothed with the feathers of philosophy. Reflecting instead on the presence of Lady Love inscribed in his own heart rather than leaving new qualities in his mind, Usk responds to her not by attributing her to a facet of his own psychology but as a force simultaneously transcendent and immanent to his interiority.

In this manner, which can be termed sacramental, Love retains the *ethopoeic* status of a person he has both imagined and encountered imaginatively, a harmonized

[47] Usk, *Testament*, 2.9.817–845.

duality which allows him to perceive the sacramental nature of what she has taught him about the merits of service to Love. Reflecting on this, Usk writes,

> Howe was it that syghtful Manna in deserte to children of Israel was spirytuel meate. Bodily also it was, for mennes bodies it norissheth. And yet neverthelater, Christ it signyfyed . . . If breed thorowe virtue is made holy flesshe, what is that our God saythe? It is the spyrite that yeveth lyfe; the flesshe of nothing it profyteth.[48]

Through sacramental symbolism, the physicality of bread becomes an embodiment of spirituality, not an allegory for it. Likewise, an allegorical reading of personification, ironically enough, is not the spiritual reading of personification but the literal one — the "letter of the law" is that personifications are abstractions only pretended to have voice and presence. The "spirit of the law" fills personification with the personal *sensorium* of Usk's imagination:

> Trewly, the ilke wyl whiche that the Lady of Love me lerned "affectyon of wyl" to nempne, whiche is in wyllyng of profitable thynges, yvel is it not but whan to fleshly lustes it consenteth ayenst reason of soule . . . this is the grace and the frute that I long have desired: it dothe me good the savour to smell.[49]

In the same way that understanding Lady Philosophy as an *ethopoeic* personification allows her visible and audible nature to contribute to the prisoner's understanding that God's omniscience ensures rather than limits free will, so Lady Love's voice and presence activates Usk's sensory imagination to remember that human love, even unrequited, presents the human will with an opportunity to experience the grace of God and to see again the sacramental harmony of temporal suffering with eternal bliss. Restoring the *ethopoeic* quality of Usk's central personification therefore corrects a misreading of the *Testament* as reducible to only a political face-saving gesture, and it allows for a complementary reading of it as having real personal significance for its author. This may not make the text more palatable to all modern audiences, but it may help us to more effectively access the aesthetic persuasiveness a fourteenth-century English intellectual might have found in personification's capacity to at once represent and create an intimate rhetoric of consolation.

---

[48] Usk, *Testament*, 3.9.305. "How was it that manna, lovely to behold, in the desert to children of Israel was spiritual meat. Bodily also it was, for men's bodies it nourishes. And yet nonetheless, Christ it signified . . . If bread through virtue is made holy flesh, what is that our God said? It is the spirit that gives life; the flesh of nothing it profits."

[49] Usk, *Testament*, 3.9.1068–1088. "Truly, the same will which that the Lady of Love taught to me, 'affection of will' by name, which is in willing of profitable things, evil is it not but when to fleshly lusts it consents against reason of the soul . . . This is the grace and the fruit that I long have desired: it does me good the savor to smell."

Translation for *Sentence* in Middle English Poetry: The Case of John Walton

Taylor Cowdery

In the prologue to his Middle English translation of Boethius's *Consolation of Philosophy*, John Walton defines the object of his translation by recourse to a common, if ambiguous, term.[1] Praying for inspiration, he asks that God fill him with wisdom—so that, he says,

> As fro þe text þat I ne vary noght
> But kepe þe sentence in hys trewe entent,
> And wordes eke als neigh as may be broght
> Where lawe of metir is noght resistent[2]

What does Walton mean by *sentence*, and what is the relationship of this *sentence* both to the words of his source and to their ultimate translation into fifteenth-century Middle English verse? The primary aim of this essay is to define *sentence* against the other critical terms used in the vernacular literary theory of Walton's time. Its secondary aim is to chart the course of a greater trend, within late medieval letters, towards what I will call "translation for sentence": literary translation, in other words, which takes as its object the *sentence* of a source text.

Though, as a phrase, "translation for sentence" might suggest an exotic set of literary practices, the term *sentence* was ubiquitous in later Middle English writing. From Chaucer's claim that the *sentence* of the four gospels is "al oon" to the Wycliffite Bible Prologue's notion that "best translating is . . . to translate aftir þe

[1] Walton was an Augustinian canon of Osney; he completed his translation ca. 1410. For more on his biography and for the patron of his text, Elisabeth Berkeley, see Ian Johnson, "Making the *Consolatio* in Middle English," in *A Companion to Boethius in the Middle Ages*, ed. Noel Harold Kaylor, Jr., and Philip Edward Phillips (Leiden: Brill, 2012), 423–24; and Brian Donaghey, Irma Taavitsainen, and Erik Miller, "Walton's Boethius: From Manuscript to Print," *English Studies* 80 (1999): 398–407, at 401–3.

[2] John Walton, trans., *De Consolatione Philosophiae*, ed. Mark Science, EETS o.s. 170 (London: Oxford University Press, 1927), 3.1–4. All subsequent references to Walton's translation will be given parenthetically by stanza and line number.

sentense and not oneli aftir þe wordis," the term appears often in theoretical discussions of language, meaning, and translation.[3] Its use appears to have spiked in the later fourteenth and early fifteenth centuries—compare its abundance in Chaucer with its absence in Langland and scarcity in Gower—and thus its rise would seem to parallel the rise both of vernacular manuscript production and of vernacular translation in fifteenth-century England.[4] Whether or not it is the case, as Margaret Connolly has suggested, that the explosion of translation at the end of the fourteenth century was a response to an increased demand for new literary works, "translacioun" as a literary practice—and with it, translation for *sentence*—would seem to have come into new prominence under the Lancastrians, with poets such as John Lydgate, Thomas Hoccleve, and Osbern Bokenham all identifying aspects of their work in such terms.[5]

---

[3] Geoffrey Chaucer, *The Canterbury Tales*, in *The Riverside Chaucer*, ed. Larry D. Benson, 3rd edn. (Boston: Houghton Mifflin, 1987), VI.952. *Prologue to the Wycliffite Bible*, in *The Earliest Advocates of the English Bible*, ed. Mary Dove (Exeter: University of Exeter Press, 2010), ll. 2812–2813, p. 81.

[4] There are no instances of *centens*, *sentens*, or *sentence* in the Katherine or Wooing Groups, most early Middle English romance, or the *Pearl* Poet. There are three instances of *sense* in Langland, but no instances of *sentence* or its variants, while in Gower's *Confessio* there are eleven total instances of *sentence*. In Chaucer, by contrast, there are 103 instances of *sentence* and one instance of *sens*. See, respectively, *Concordances to the Katherine Group and the Wooing Group*, ed. Lorna Stevenson and Jocelyn Wogan-Browne (Cambridge: D.S. Brewer, 2000), 80, 446, 803, and 905; *A Concordance to Middle English Metrical Romances*, ed. Toshio Saito and Mitsunori Imai, 2 vols. (Frankfurt: Peter Lang, 1988), 1:84, 1:370, 2:87, 2:353; *A Concordance to Five Middle English Poems*, ed. Barnet Kottler and Alan M. Markman (Pittsburgh: University of Pittsburgh Press, 1966), 88 and 508; *Piers Plowman: Concordance*, ed. Joseph S. Wittig (London: The Athlone Press, 2001), 120 and 575 (col. 2); *A Concordance to John Gower's Confessio amantis*, ed. J.D. Pickles and J.L. Dawson (Cambridge: D.S. Brewer, 1987), 92 and 540 (col. 2); and *A Glossarial Concordance to the Riverside Chaucer*, ed. Larry D. Benson, 2 vols. (New York: Garland Publishing, 1993), 1:116, 1:755 (cols. 1–2), 2:23, and 2:121 (col. 2). For the upsurge in fifteenth-century translation, see Richard Firth Green, *Poets and Princepleasers: Literature and the English Court in the Late Middle Ages* (Toronto: University of Toronto Press, 1980), 149–61. For the increase in vernacular manuscript production ca. 1400, see A.S.G. Edwards and Derek Pearsall, "The Manuscripts of the Major English Poetic Texts," in *Book Production and Publishing in Britain, 1375–1475*, ed. Jeremy Griffiths and Derek Pearsall (Cambridge: Cambridge University Press, 1989), 257.

[5] See Margaret Connolly, "Compiling the Book," in *The Production of Books in England 1350–1500*, ed. Alexandra Gillespie and Daniel Wakelin (Cambridge: Cambridge University Press, 2011), 133–34. See, for instance, John Lydgate, *Fall of Princes*, ed. Henry Bergen, EETS e.s. 121–24 (London: Oxford University Press, 1924–27): "I shal procede in this translacioun" (438); Thomas Hoccleve, *Regiment of Princes*, ed. Charles R. Blyth (Kalamazoo: Medieval Institute Publications, 1999): "of Gyles of Regiment / Of Princes, plotmeel thynke I to translate" (2052–2053); and Osbern

In much scholarship on medieval translation theory, *sentence* has been taken to be synonymous with *sense*, an immaterial or even universal type of linguistic meaning.[6] Located beyond the accidents and particularities of earthly language, *sense* is understood to be that property of meaning which remains stable, in spite of both historical "chaunge[s]" in human "forme[s] of speche" and local differences in syntax and lexis.[7] In other words, even when the words change, this *sense* remains the same. Such an Hieronymian vision of "sense," which dreams of possible equivalences between texts ancient and modern, foreign and native, also dreams of a kind of translation that would, as Walter Benjamin puts it, make "both the original and the translation recognizable as fragments of a greater language," allowing "pure language, as though reinforced by its own medium, to shine upon the original all the more fully."[8] But while this understanding of translation would seem to hold in certain contexts—the allegoresis of the *Ovide moralisé*, for instance, or the Middle English *Lives of Christ*—it does not hold when translation for *sentence* is considered.[9] Most simply, this is because *sense* is not the same thing as *sentence*, and so it is a contradiction in terms to assume that translation for *sentence* is exclusively literal or loose. Something rather like the bones, or skeleton, of a text, I argue that *sentence* is in fact grounded in the particularities of the letter—particular events of plot, points of argument, primary characters, and so on—even while it underlies and dictates both the local words and local sense of that letter. It refers not to the universal sense of the text, that is, but to its particular structure. Via the use of either literal or loose techniques to render local meaning, translation for *sentence* thus attempts both to preserve the broader meaning of a text and to realize that meaning in a fuller fashion—to flesh out, as it were, the bones of the source with a new body of words.[10]

Bokenham, *Legendys of Hooly Wummen*, ed. Humphrey Milford, EETS o.s. 206 (Oxford: Oxford University Press, 1938): "mercyful inclyne / Thy petous erys on-to the translatour / þi legend compylyd" (3125–3127). For the way in which these and other poets invoke "sentence," see my discussion in section two below.

[6] See Rita Copeland, *Rhetoric, Hermeneutics, and Translation* (Cambridge: Cambridge University Press, 1991), 57 and 225. See also Ian Johnson, *The Middle English Life of Christ* (Turnhout: Brepols, 2013), 155.

[7] Chaucer, *Troilus and Criseyde*, in *Riverside Chaucer*, ed. Benson, 2.22.

[8] Walter Benjamin, "The Task of the Translator," trans. Harry Zohn, in *Illuminations*, ed. Hannah Arendt (New York: Schocken Books, 1968), 78–79. Compare Andrew Cole, "Chaucer's English Lesson," *Speculum* 77.4 (2002): 1128–67, at 1131–32.

[9] For medieval translations of Ovid, see Vincent Gillespie, "The Study of Classical Authors: From the Twelfth Century to c. 1450," in *The Cambridge History of Literary Criticism*, vol. 2: *The Middle Ages*, ed. Alastair Minnis and Ian Johnson (Cambridge: Cambridge University Press, 2005), 200–206. For Middle English *Lives of Christ*, see Johnson, *Middle English Life of Christ*, 154–55.

[10] Tim William Machan and Alastair Minnis, for instance, view Chaucer's *Boece* as a highly literal, but expanded, translation of the "sentence" of Boethius. By contrast,

As a result, while translation for *sentence* does attempt to produce correspondence between the *sentence* of source and the *sentence* of target, it does not aim for equivalence between the local words, sense, or style of the two. Source and target may correspond in bone structure, but they often differ greatly in the flesh. It is in this regard that, as I argue below, late medieval translation might well be characterized as a "horizontal activity," one that was much more Trevisan than it was Hieronymian.[11] In a textual culture in which "artists buil[t] on to artefacts from the past accretively," a single *sentence* could and did produce multiple realized translations for use in tandem.[12] Translation within this culture thus had "none of the appropriative or imperial flavor of translation in the classical Roman period."[13] It viewed translation as a collaborative construction of meaning rather than the singular appropriation of it. Jerome and Benjamin might have dreamt of equivalence, but during a period when Vulgate Latin was less reliable than Wycliffite English, their fifteenth-century successors seem to have been more practical-minded.[14] Why trust one translation, they seem to ask, when you could compare two, or four, or eight?

---

poetic translation for *sentence* can be extremely loose—almost a "continuous gloss," as Roger Ellis puts it—with several lines added to each stanza to fill out rhyme and meter where needed. See Tim William Machan and Alastair Minnis, "The *Boece* as a Late-Medieval Translation," in *Chaucer's Boece and the Medieval Tradition of Boethius*, ed. A.J. Minnis (Cambridge: D.S. Brewer, 1993), 172–73; Tim William Machan, *Techniques of Translation: Chaucer's Boece* (Norman: Pilgrim Books, 1985), 107; and Roger Ellis, "The Choices of the Translator in the Late Middle English Period," in *The Medieval Mystical Tradition in England: Papers Read at Darlington Hall, July 1982*, ed. Marion Glasscoe (Exeter: University of Exeter Press, 1982), 18–46, at 36.

[11] The phrase is from Nicholas Watson, "Theories of Translation," in *The Oxford History of Literary Translation*, ed. Roger Ellis (Oxford: Oxford University Press, 2008), 86.

[12] James Simpson, *Reform and Cultural Revolution* (Oxford: Oxford University Press, 2002), 64. Alastair Minnis and Tim William Machan document evidence for the way in which translators used, and publicized their use of, multiple source texts and translations; see Minnis and Machan, "The *Boece* as a Late-Medieval Translation," 178–79.

[13] Vincent Gillespie, "Religious Writing," in *The Oxford History of Literary Translation*, ed. Roger Ellis (Oxford: Oxford University Press, 2008), 234–83, at 234. But see Copeland, *Rhetoric, Hermeneutics, and Translation*: "Translation is always, in one way or another, an act of appropriation" (186); and Ralph Hanna, "The Difficulty of Ricardian Prose Translation," *Modern Language Quarterly* 51.3 (1990): 319–40: "Translation ultimately concerns rights of control" (340).

[14] See the *Prologue to the Wycliffite Bible*: "þe comyne Latyn biblis han more nede to be corrected, as many as I haue seyn in my liyf, þan haþ þe Englisch Bible late translatid" (ll. 2850–2851; p. 82). Compare Ralph Hanna, Tony Hunt, R.G. Keightley, Alastair Minnis, and Nigel F. Palmer, "Latin Commentary Tradition and Vernacular Literature," in *The Cambridge History of Literary Criticism, vol. 2: The Middle Ages*, ed. Alastair Minnis and Ian Johnson (Cambridge: Cambridge University Press, 2005), 393.

Sentence in Theory

In Middle English theory, *sentence* is an ubiquitous term. Often it is designated as the object of translation—as that which a given translator hopes to preserve or follow in his source. Walton, for instance, claims that he will "saue" the "sentence" of Boethius in his translation (3–4); his claim finds echoes in similar formulations in the work of Peter Idley and John Lydgate.[15] Osbern Bokenham, in turn, suggests that he has followed his source "fro sentence to sentence," and Gilbert Banester claims to translate "aftir þe sentence" of his original.[16] Much of the term's difficulty is due to its ambiguous scope of reference. In Capgrave and Bokenham, for instance, *sentence* can refer either to a single aphorism or to stanzas upon stanzas of poetry, and it is for this reason that translation for *sentence* might at first appear a variation on Jerome's theory of translation *per cola et commata*, or "sense unit."[17] Such a neat definition of *sentence* falls apart, however, when we consider the often playful, and sometimes maddening, polysemy of the term in fifteenth-century verse. At one point in John Metham's *Amoryus and Cleopes*, for instance, Palemedon reads the "ful sentens" of a letter; the "sentens of this bille," he says, declares that the citizens must attend the consecration of a temple. In response,

> the bariunnis that were in hys presens
> Alowyd hys sentens and seyd yt was for the best
> To enclyne that tyme to the pepillys sentens.[18]

---

[15] Lydgate, *Fall of Princes*, Prol.448. Peter Idley, *Instructions to his Son*, ed. Charlotte D'Evelyn (Boston: D.C. Heath and Company, 1935), 2.i.34.

[16] Bokenham, *Legendys*, l. 4715. Gilbert Banester, "The Tale of Guiscardo and Ghismonda," in *Early English Versions of the Tales of Guiscardo and Ghismonda and Titus and Gisippus from the Decameron*, ed. Herbert G. Wright, EETS o.s. 205 (London: Oxford University Press, 1937), l. 625.

[17] For translation *per cola et commata*, see Karen Pratt, "Medieval Attitudes to Translation and Adaptation: The Rhetorical Theory and the Poetic Practice," in *The Medieval Translator II*, ed. Roger Ellis (London: University of London, Centre for Medieval Studies, 1991), 1–27, at 1–3; and Louis Kelly, *The True Interpreter* (Oxford: Basil Blackwell, 1979), 121–22. For examples of *sentence* denoting large blocks of text, see, e.g., John Capgrave, *The Life of St. Katherine*, ed. Karen A. Winstead (Kalamazoo: Medieval Institute Publications, 1999), 1.1027 (referring to forty-three lines of poetry), 4.239 (thirty lines), 4.351 (thirty-five lines); or Bokenham, *Legendys*, l. 4305 (forty-four lines) and l. 6552 (twenty-one lines).

[18] John Metham, *Amoryus and Cleopes*, in *The Works of John Metham*, ed. Hardin Craig, EETS o.s. 132 (London: Kegan Paul, Trench, Trübner & Co., 1916), ll. 195, 203, 204–206.

Here, "sentens" is obviously ambiguous, denoting as much the opinion and judgment of the barons as it does the content of the "bille." Metham's passage thus plays upon the many possible meanings of the term: it can denote "judgment," "doctrine," "opinion," even "allegorical meaning"—and, indeed, in fifteenth-century poetry, *sentence* means all of these things.[19]

The causes of this polysemy can be traced, in part, to the etymological roots of *sentence* in the Latin term *sententia*, which is often found alongside two other terms, *sensus* and *verbum*, in classical discussions of translation. *Sensus* and *verbum* are most familiar from a series of *dicta*, originally in Cicero but passed on to the Middle Ages through Jerome, which hold that "sense-for-sense" is better than "word-for-word" translation.[20] While the legacy of Jerome's position has received much critical attention, what has gone largely unnoticed is the role that *sententia* plays in his theories as a distinct third term. In his preface to Eusebius's *Chronicle*, for instance, Jerome says that in translating, he sometimes finds that

> Significatum est aliquid unius uerbi proprietate: non habeo meum quo id efferam, et dum quaero implere sententiam, longo ambitu uix breuis uiae spatia consummo [. . .] Si ad uerbum interpraetor absurde resonat; si ob necessitatem aliquid in ordine, in sermone mutauero, ab interpraetis uidebor officio recessisse.
>
> [Some word has forcibly expressed a given thought; I have no word of my own to convey the meaning; and while I am seeking to satisfy the sense I may go a long way round and accomplish but a small distance of my journey . . . A literal translation sounds absurd; if, on the other hand, I am obliged

---

[19] For *sentence* as "judgment" in a legal or moral sense (*MED* sense 3), see, e.g., Bokenham, *Legendys*, 815–819, 3755–3777, 7174, or Idley, *Instructions*, 2.i.1609–1610 and 2.ii.503–504. For *sentence* as "doctrine" (*MED* sense 2), see, e.g., Walton, *Boethius*, 564.6-8, or Hoccleve, *Regiment*, ll. 2038–2041. For *sentence* as "opinion" (*MED* sense 1), see, e.g., Lydgate, *Fall*, 2.781, or Idley, *Instructions*, 2.i.1882–1886. For *sentence* as "allegorical meaning" (*MED* sense 5f), see, e.g., Capgrave, *Life of Katherine*, 4.687–699 and 4.1380–1393.

[20] See Jerome, *Letter* 57, section 5, trans. W.H. Fremantle, in *The Principal Works of St. Jerome*, ed. Philip Schaff and Henry Wace (Grand Rapids: Eerdmans, 1954): "For I myself not only admit but freely proclaim . . . I render sense for sense and not word for word [*non uerbum e uerbo, sed sensum exprimere de sensu*]." Cf. *Epistle* 57, in *Epistulae*, ed. I. Hilberg, CSEL 54 (Vienna: F. Tempsky, 1910). For discussion, see Copeland, *Rhetoric, Hermeneutics, and Translation*, 42–54; Ruth Morse, *Truth and Convention in the Middle Ages* (Cambridge: Cambridge University Press, 1991), 186–88; Werner Schwartz, "The Meaning of *Fidus Interpres* in Medieval Translation," *Journal of Theological Studies* 45 (1944): 73–78, at 74–75; and Samuel Workman, *Fifteenth Century Translation as an Influence on English Prose* (Princeton: Princeton University Press, 1940), 74–80.

> to change either the order or the words themselves, I shall appear to have forsaken the duty of a translator.][21]

Jerome then lists a number of extant Greek translations of Scripture—Aquila's hyper-literal version, the close translation of Theodotion, and the looser paraphrase of Symmachus—before suggesting that the "fifth, sixth, and seventh" scriptural translations preserved in Origen's *Hexapla* "exhibit so pleasing a variety of their own that, in spite of their being anonymous, they have won an authoritative position."[22] Rather than a binary structure, Jerome's scheme of translation is a spectrum, with full sense meaning (the *sententia* of the source) on one end and pure literalism (the *verbum* of that source) on the other; *sensus*, in turn, is located somewhere between *sententia* and *verbum*. Multiple translations are "pleasing" in their variety, as Jerome says, because each "fill[s] in the sentence" (*sententiam implere*) in its own way.

While the later Middle Ages received Jerome in a complex fashion, his distinction between *sensus* and *sententia* seems to have been transmitted relatively intact.[23] In the Latin tradition, Augustine echoes Jerome when he uses *sententia* to refer to the general meaning of a passage or clause and *sensus* to denote the local sense of words in this passage or clause. As he writes in *De doctrina christiana*,

> et ex ambiguo linguae praecedentis plerumque interpres fallitur, cui non bene nota sententia est, et eam significationem transfert, quae a sensu scriptoris penitus aliena est.
>
> [Ambiguity in the original language often misleads a translator unfamiliar with the general sense of a passage, who may import a meaning which is quite unrelated to the writer's meaning.][24]

[21] Jerome, "Preface to the Chronicle of Eusebius," in *The Principal Works of St. Jerome*, 483 (col. 2). Cf. Jerome, *Prefatio*, in *Evsebii Pamphili Chronici*, ed. John Knight Fotheringham (London: Humphrey Milford, 1923), 1 (col. 2).

[22] Jerome, "Preface to Eusebius," 284 (col. 1). Cf. Jerome, *Prefatio*, in *Evsebii Pamphili Chronici*, ed. Fotheringham, 2 (cols. 1–2). For a brief discussion of Aquila, Symmachus, and Theodotion, see Timothy Michael Law, *When God Spoke Greek* (Oxford: Oxford University Press, 2013), 78–79.

[23] For the evolution of *sententia* from the twelfth to the fourteenth centuries, see Johnson, *Life of Christ*, 42–43; Minnis and Machan, "The *Boece* as Late-Medieval Translation," 169–70; and, more generally, Marjorie Curry Woods, "In a Nutshell: *Verba* and *Sententia* and Matter and Form in Medieval Composition Theory," in *The Uses of Manuscripts in Literary Studies*, ed. Charlotte Cook Morse, Penelope Reed Doob, and Marjorie Curry Woods (Kalamazoo: Medieval Institute Publications, 1992), 19–37.

[24] Augustine, *De doctrina christiana*, trans. R.P.H. Green (Oxford: Oxford University Press, 1999), 2.12. See also Augustine, *De doctrina christiana*, ed. Joseph Martin, CCSL 32 (Turnhout: Brepols, 1962), 2.12.

Sententia is thus distinct both from the *significatio* of a word and the slightly more general *sensus* of a word or a phrase, a distinction that is echoed elsewhere in Augustine's text.[25] In the ninth, tenth, and eleventh centuries, Anglo-Saxon scholars such as Alfred and Ælfric also seem to have noted ambiguity in the relationship between *sensus* and *verbum*—Alfred happily strikes a middle route in translating "hwilum word be worde, hwilum andgit of andgite" [sometimes word by word, sometimes sense for sense][26]—and Hugh of Saint Victor, in the twelfth century, opted for a tripartite distinction between three terms—*littera*, *sensus*, and *sententia*—in his discussion of scriptural interpretation.[27] Finally, in the fourteenth and fifteenth centuries, Middle English theory would seem to follow these earlier theories by marking out a difference between local signification (*sense*, *undurstonding*, *menyng*) on the one hand and general meaning (*sentence*) on the other.[28] The *Prologue to the Wycliffite Bible*, for instance, stresses these distinctions in its translation of the very same passage of Augustine cited above.

> [I]n translating of wordis equyuoke, þat is, þat han many signeficaciouns vndur o lettre, mai liȝtli be perel, for Austin seiþ in þe secounde book of

[25] Augustine, *De doctrina christiana*, trans. Green: "[I]f not just one meaning but two or more meanings [*duo uel plura*] are perceived [*sentiuntur*] in the same words of scripture . . . the person examining the divine utterances . . . may reach that meaning or carve out from the words another meaning [*aliam sententiam . . . exsculpat*] which does not run counter to the faith, using the evidence of any other passage of the divine utterances" (3.27). See also Augustine, *De doctrina christiana*, ed. Martin, 3.27.

[26] See *Sweet's Anglo-Saxon Reader in Prose and Verse*, 15th edn., rev. Dorothy Whitelock (Oxford: Clarendon Press, 1967), 7, ll. 71–72. For discussion of Ælfric's musings on the relationship between "word" and "andgit," and for an assessment of Alfred's adaptation of Jerome's formula in the Prefaces to the *Cura Pastoralis* and the Old English *Boethius*, see Robert Stanton, *The Culture of Translation in Anglo-Saxon England* (Cambridge: D.S. Brewer, 2002), 82–84. On the Old English *Boethius* and Alfredian translation, see also the first five essays in this volume.

[27] Hugh of St. Victor, *Didascalicon*, trans. Jerome Taylor (New York: Columbia University Press, 1991), "Exposition includes three things: the letter, the sense, and the inner meaning [*litteram, sensum, sententiam*]" (3.8). See also Hugh, *Didascalicon*, ed. Charles Buttimer (Washington: Catholic University Press, 1939), 3.8. For discussion of the Middle English distinction between "sense" and "sentence," see Burnley, "Late Medieval English Translation," 50–51.

[28] The "Second Prologue" to the *Myroure of Oure Ladye*, for instance, distinguishes between the "dyverse vnderstondynges," or senses, of a single word and the broader "sentence" in accordance with which these words should be translated, or "turnyd." The fifteenth-century poet George Ashby likewise suggests that the "true menyng formal," or local sense, ought to be kept in accord with broader, "sentenciall" meaning. See John Henry Blunt, ed., *The Myroure of Oure Ladye*, EETS e.s. 19 (London: N. Trübner & Co., 1873), 7–8; and George Ashby, *Active Policy of a Prince*, in *George Ashby's Poems*, ed. Mary Bateson, EETS e.s. 76 (London: Kegan Paul, Trench, Trübner & Co., 1899), ll. 50–54.

> *Cristen Techyng* þat if equyuok wordis be not translatid [in]to þe *sense or vndurstondyng* of þe autour it is errour . . . þerfor a translatour haþ greet nede to studie wel þe *sentence* boþe bifore and aftir, and loke þat sich equyuoke wordis acorde wel wiþ þe *sentence.*[29]

As in Augustine, the "sentence," or broader meaning, must guide the translator's rendering of the local "sense or vndurstondyng" of his text's "wordis." Clearly, "sentence" is not "sense," "menyng," or "vndurstonding"; it is rather something greater, something that underlies and dictates local expression. "Sense" can be "equyuoke," but "sentence" is rooted in firmer stuff.

With these distinctions in mind, I would like to return now to *sentence* and its polysemy. Although, as I noted above, *sentence* can and does take on a wide variety of meanings, it is persistently associated in literary contexts with a second term: *substaunce.* As critics have noted, *sentence* and *substaunce* are often linked, sometimes in doublet form, in fifteenth-century discussions of translation practice.[30] Writers such as George Ashby, Peter Idley, and the anonymous author of the *Life of St. Elizabeth of Spalbec* all suggest that there is a distinction between what the *Spalbec* author calls "þe substaunce of þe story" and the local "sens" of its words.[31] But it is John Lydgate who most prominently, and insistently, links *sentence* with *substaunce.* In the prologue to the *Siege of Thebes*, for example, Lydgate praises Chaucer for "keping in substaunce / The sentence" of the words of his Canterbury pilgrims,[32] while in the *Fall of Princes* he designates as his target the "substaunce & sentence" of his source.[33] The *Danse Machabré* and the *Troy Book* offer even blunter conflations of *substaunce* and *sentence* when they insist that Lydgate has translated his sources "not worde be worde but folwyng the

---

[29] *Prologue to the Wycliffite Bible*, ll. 2947–2957, p. 84. For a discussion of this passage, see David Lawton, "The Bible," in *The Oxford History of Literary Translation*, ed. Roger Ellis (Oxford: Oxford University Press, 2008), 199–200.

[30] Watson, "Theories of Translation," 89–90; and Workman, *Fifteenth Century Translation as an Influence on English Prose*, 80–81. Daniel Wakelin, *Scribal Correction and Literary Craft: English Manuscripts 1375–1510* (Cambridge: Cambridge University Press, 2014), suggests that the two words are "interchangable in meaning" and notes a number of instances in which scribes have corrected or replaced one with the other (220).

[31] *The Life of St. Elizabeth of Spalbec*, in Carl Horstmann, ed., "Prosalegenden: die Legenden des MS Douce 114," *Anglia* 8 (1885): 102–96, at 107. Compare Ashby, *Active Policy*, l. 34, 39 (who refers to "thentent and substance" and the "intential substance" of his source); and Idley, *Instructions*, 2.i.671–674 (who discusses the "substaunce" of a story he once heard).

[32] Lydgate, *Siege of Thebes*, ed. Robert R. Edwards (Kalamazoo: Medieval Institute Publications, 2001), ll. 53–54.

[33] Lydgate, *Fall of Princes*, 2.157–161: "As I coude, I gan my penne auaunce, / Albe I was bareyn off eloquence, / Folwyng myn auctour in substaunce & sentence: / For it suffised, pleynli, onto me, / So that my lord my makyng took at gre."

substaunce," or that he "leue[s] þe wordis and folwe[s] þe sentence," having kept the meaning of his translation equivalent "in substaunce" to that of his source.[34] The words may have changed, but the "substaunce" of the story, Lydgate suggests, has remained the same.

Two conclusions regarding *sentence* are now possible. First, when it is used in conjunction with other critical terms in Middle English theory—namely, *sense*, *undurstonding*, and *menyng*—the term *sentence* refers to a kind and quality of meaning that is not limited to the local signification of individual words or groups of words. Second, when *sentence* is considered in relation to *substaunce*, its occasional doublet partner, the term would seem to refer to the structure or core of a source text: the events of a story, the major characters of that story, the key points in a philosophical tract, the short aphorism that might be distilled from a complex argument. This *sentence* is a skeleton of meaning, the bones that are distinct from and opposed to the flesh of rhetorical and narrative elaboration. As such, "sentence" is not the whole of a source text but, rather, the "essential part" or "gist" of that source.[35] Naturally enough, Middle English writers differ in their assessments of what the "gist" of a given source might be, but most concur that it ought to be preserved—to be "saue[d]," in Walton's phrase. But saved from what, we might ask, and to what purpose?

Sentence in Practice

From the very start of his translation, Walton worries about the difficult matter of his source. To an extent that outruns even fifteenth-century professions of inadequacy, he repeatedly invokes his lack of "cunnyng and of wit" (1.1), insisting that the depth and power of his source text lies beyond his comprehension.[36] "This subtile matere of boecius," "this mater wiche þat is so excellent," he says, will surely exceed the abilities of one who has "tasted wonder lyte / As of the welles of calliope" (2.2, 3.5, 8.1–2).

Walton's consolation in the face of this worry is twofold: first, the aid of other translations and commentaries—in this case, Chaucer's *Boece* and Nicholas Trevet's *Expositio super Boetio*—and second, a marked theoretical distinction between the *sentence* of his source and its words, or "eloquence."[37] Like many

---

[34] Lydgate, *Dance of Death*, ed. Beatrice White, EETS o.s. 181 (London: Oxford University Press), l. 666; Lydgate, *Troy Book*, ed. Henry Bergen, EETS e.s. 97–126 (London: K. Paul, Trench, Trübner & Co., 1906–35), 2.180, 190.

[35] The *MED* gives one definition of *sentence* as "the gist, essential part" (sense 5d).

[36] For an overview of fifteenth-century professions of inadequacy, see David Lawton, "Dullness and the Fifteenth Century," *English Literary History* 54.4 (1987): 761–99.

[37] Ian Johnson has demonstrated that Walton relies heavily on both Chaucer and Trevet; see Johnson, "Walton's Sapient Orpheus," in *The Medieval Boethius: Studies in the*

of the writers discussed above, Walton does indeed use *sentence* to refer to the gist or core of his source matter—its "sothfast sentence" or "trewe . . . sentence" (150.5, 825.1)—and he frequently employs it to designate the aphorisms of other authors, such as Plato or Euripides, as pithy and true.[38] "Saving" the *sentence* is thus the preservation of content, not of eloquence, for local words may be merely incidental to the greater *sentence* of a text; and in this regard, it is perhaps unsurprising that Walton's most telling use of the term comes at a moment of Christian revelation. As many will recall, in the discussion immediately following Book 3, Meter 9 (3m9) ("O qui perpetua"), Boethius grapples with Philosophy's idea that different types of happiness—"souereign myght, and souereign suffisaunce, / Lust, honour, fame" (492.6–7)—are simply expressions of a single good, which is God.[39] These types of happiness, she argues, might differ in form, but "[i]n substaunce ben þey oo þing and no moo, / And verraily þe same þing expresse" (501.3–4). After Boethius agrees that these types all share in a single "substaunce" of divine good, Philosophy declares victory—

> "Than may I," quod sche, "well and sikerly
> Þe *sentence* and þe som of this matere
> Lo þus concluden full and fynally:
> Lo þat þe substance of oure god on hy
> Is set and founded in none oþer place
> Bot in þe same good eternally." (502.2–7; my emphasis)

An interpolation, Walton's use of *sentence* here finds itself obviously paired with "þe som of this matere" and placed in close proximity to the "substaunce of oure god on hy."[40] As is suggested by his own commentary to the text, Walton has

---

Vernacular Translations of De Consolatione Philosophiae, ed. A.J. Minnis (Cambridge: D.S. Brewer, 1987), 144–54. See also Johnson, "Making the *Consolatio* in Middle English," 423–24, for an overview. For similar observations on Chaucer's *Boece*, compare Machan, *Techniques of Translation: Chaucer's Boece*, 6–7 and 127–30. I have cross-referenced both Chaucer's *Boece* and Trevet's *Expositio*, where relevant, to contextualize Walton's choices of translation.

[38] The first two instances translate, respectively, "veram . . . sententiam" and "vera sententia"; in each, Walton echoes Chaucer, who has "the sothe sentence" and "this sentence is verray and soth." See *Anicii Manlii Severini Boethii philosophiae consolatio*, ed. Ludwig Bieler (Turnhout: Brepols, 1984): 1p6.44, 5p1.22; and Chaucer, *Boece*, in *The Riverside Chaucer*, ed. Benson, 1p6.87–88 and 5p1.42–43. For Walton's use of "sentence" to designate a pithy maxim, see 77.5, 416.5–6, 564.6.

[39] For further disucssion of 3m9, see Nicole Guenther Discenza and Paul E. Szarmach's essays in this volume.

[40] Walton follows the Latin in rendering *substantiam* as "substance"; cf. *Consolatio*, ed. Bieler, 3p10.122. Walton eschews any immediate echo of Chaucer but may follow his earlier statement, "sovereyn good the somme and cause of al," or perhaps Trevet's gloss: "bonum est summa et causa omnium [the Good is the sum and cause of all]". Cf. Chaucer,

here co-opted Philosophy's words.[41] The "sentence and þe som"—not only of the subject under discussion but of the *Consolation* in general—has become the Christian good, identical with the Christian God.

Here Walton's choices raise important questions about the Boethian *sentence* that he claims to save. If the particular words of a source are incidental to the *sentence* of that source—if, like the many forms of earthly happiness, they may be subordinated to a single form of the good—then the translator's decision to omit or alter those words is defensible so long as it can be justified in the name of preserving this *sentence*. As two prominent medieval dictionaries had it, translation is the *expositio sententie*, or the exposition of *sentence*, and indeed there are many instances in which Walton's rendering of *sentence* takes on a character closer to that of exegetical analysis or rhetorical exposition than to what we might now consider translation.[42] Sometimes these expositions define or specify ambiguous matter in his source, as when he glosses *fama* [renown] by clarifying its application both to people and to places, or when he expands Boethius's *morbus animorum* [disease of the mind] into rather more words than necessary.[43] At other moments, these expositions "open" the sense of his source.

Boece, 3p10.215–16, and Nicholas Trevet, *Expositio super Boetio de consolatione*, ed. E.T. Silk, accessed 24 November 2014, <http://minnis.commons.yale.edu>, 3p10 §125, p. 444.

[41] Walton's commentary on his translation, preserved in Copenhagen, Kongelige Bibliotek, MS Thott 304 2°, and reproduced in a print edition of 1525, has only recently been attributed to Walton; see Alastair Minnis, *Translations of Authority in Medieval English Literature: Valuing the Vernacular* (Cambridge: Cambridge University Press, 2009), 24; and Donaghey, Taavitsainen, and Miller, "Walton's Boethius," 401. I cite from Mark Science's edition of Walton's *Boethius*, which reproduces the commentary as an appendix (see 364–79), but because the Copenhagen manuscript, and the print edition on which it is based, is acaudal and acephalous, this text may well be incomplete. For Walton's Christianization of this section of the *Consolation*, and in particular of 3m9, see Science, ed., *Consolation*, 367–71. For a digitized copy of the Thott MS, see <http://www.kb.dk/permalink/2006/manus/627/eng/>

[42] The *Catholicon* of Joannes Januensis, cited in Johnson, *Life of Christ*, 15. Machan notes that the fifteenth-century *Medulla grammatice* also defines translation as the "ouyrberynge et expositio sentencie." See Machan, "Chaucer as Translator," in *The Medieval Translator*, ed. Ellis, 61.

[43] For *fama*: "Noght only mennes names singulerly / The wiche þat ben renomed glorius, / But citees been vnknowen vtterly / Wiche þat now ben ful worschipful to vs" (293.1–4). For *morbus animorum*: "[W]e schulle not demen skilfullye / Hym worthy hate þat seek is bodelye, / Bot rewe rathire on his peynes sore, / Then gostly langour schulde vs greuen more" (708.4–7). Cf. *Consolatio*, ed. Bieler, 2p7.21 and 4p4.132. In both cases, Walton departs from or expands upon Chaucer, and in neither does he seem to echo Trevet; cf. Chaucer, *Boece*, 2p7.57–59 and 4p5.293–296; and Trevet, *Expositio*, 2p7 §§24–30, pp. 278–79; 4p5 §149, pp. 589–90.

> Thow vnderstondest noght perauenture,
> Now what þe purpose of my menyng isse.
> Lo a full wonder þyng, I the ensure,
> I purpose for to tellen the expresse,
> So þat vnnethe I can my wordes dresse
> In open sentence for to make it clere. (315.1–6)

Walton clarifies the sense of the Latin—*quid loquar* [what I say] becomes "þe purpose of my menyng" and *verbis explicare vix queo* [it is difficult to explain in words] becomes "my wordes dresse / In open sentence for to make it clere"—just as Philosophy promises to clarify her own philosophical terms.[44]

The most notable symptom of Walton's expansion and interpretation of his source's *sentence*, however, can be seen in his broader attempt to Christianize its teaching.[45] Minor examples of this impulse abound. Walton translates *mens* as "soule," for instance, and he adds, in his translation of 1m5 ("O stelliferi conditor"), the idea that humans were created "after þe forme of þe," where "þe" refers implicitly to the Christian God.[46] His most daring interpolation onto Boethius's text, however, occurs in his translation of 5m3 ("Quaenam discors foedera rerum"), in which he manages to read St. Paul into Boethius's musings over the problems of human knowledge. Beginning with an echo of 1 Corinthians 13:12—"When þat þe soule is soole and separate / Beholdyng on þat souereigne þoght onely, / Than may sche seen þat now ne may sche nate" (881.1–3)—Walton

[44] Cf. *Consolatio*, ed. Bieler, 2p8.4. Walton interpolates the idea of "openness" here, departing both from Chaucer, who has "unnethe may I unplyten my sentence with wordes," and from Trevet, who makes no relevant comment. Cf. Chaucer, *Boece*, 2p8.7–11 and Trevet, *Expositio*, 2p8 §§5–6, p. 291. For the idea of the "open" sense, see Cole, "Chaucer's English Lesson," 1141–47 and 1162–63; and Rita Copeland, *Pedagogy, Intellectuals, and Dissent in the Later Middle Ages: Lollardy and Ideas of Learning* (Cambridge: Cambridge University Press, 2004), 124–39.

[45] Compare Ian Johnson, "Walton's Heavenly *Boece* and the Devout Translation of Transcendence," in *The Medieval Mystical Tradition in England: Exeter Symposium VIII*, ed. E.A. Jones (Cambridge: D.S. Brewer, 2013), 162–75.

[46] "For-why þe corps þat haþ the soule oppressed" (538.1), and "For of þy werk we ben a porcioun, / Noght foule bot faire after þe forme of þe" (123.1–2). Cf. *Consolatio*, ed. Bieler, 3m11.9–10 and 1m5.44–45. In both cases, Walton departs from Chaucer, who has "the body, bryngynge the weighte of foryetynge" and "noght a foul partie, but a fair partie of so greet a werk"; cf. Chaucer, *Boece*, 3m11.28–29 and 1m5.52–53. Trevet glosses *obliviosam* [forgetfulness] as *grauedinem* [catarrh] and makes no local reference to the idea that men are made after the "form" of God, choosing to gloss *non uilis* [not the worst (part)] as *immo ualde nobilis pars* [indeed, the most noble part] instead. Cf. Trevet, *Expositio*, 3m11 §9, p. 474 and 1m5 §45, p. 148.

refracts Boethius through a theological lens until, finally, he concludes with an explicit invocation of Paul's *speculum in enigmate*, or "mirror darkly."[47]

> Þis sume than whiche sche holdeþ here
> So in here þoght remembrynge ofte ageyn,
> Sche sekeþ in *þat souereyn merour clere*
> Where euery sothe may singulerly be seyn
> Enforsyng here wiþ labour and wiþ peyn,
> Forgeten þing, if þat sche may it fynde,
> To put it to þe tresour of hire mynde. (883.1–7; my emphasis)

Þis "souereyn merour clere"—which, if it is not simply a Pauline interpolation, seems loosely to approximate Boethius's *consulit alte visa* [watches over us from the heights]—recurs in the prose discussion that follows the meter, this time as "Þe myrrour of the hyhe eternite."[48] Þe *sentence* of these passages, it would seem, is rooted in their latent Christian meaning as much as in their literal sense.[49]

Walton's extensive Christianization of Boethius has led some critics to conclude that, for him, *sentence* is rooted not so much in the letter of the text as in a universal, and transhistorical, religious meaning.[50] To a certain extent, this reading seems plausible. Walton works as much from Trevet and Chaucer as from Boethius's Latin, and he is more than happy, as I have shown above, to resort to interpolation if the greater *sentence* he perceives is not bolstered by the local words of his source. But this reading, which would class the object of Walton's translation, and *sentence* more generally, as something transhistorical and universal—something, as one critic puts it, "well-nigh inexhaustible" and simply "there to be discovered" by the translator—cannot account for the recurrent anx-

[47] Þere seem to be no relevant antecedents for Walton's interpolations in Chaucer, who refers to "derked lookynge" and "the heye thought (that is to seyn, God)" but makes no mention of a mirror; cf. *Boece*, 5m3.14 and 5m3.39–40. Walton likewise seems to have departed from Trevet, who glosses the meter extensively but neither discusses Paul nor mentions a *speculum*; see *Expositio*, 5m3, esp. §§20–21, p. 713, and §§25–29, pp. 714–15.

[48] See Walton: "he behaldeth in þat exsaumplere / Þe myrrour of the hyhe eternite, / Þe fourme of man in his simplicite" (908.3-5). Þe phrase appears to be an interpolation; cf. *Consolatio*, ed. Bieler, 5p4.83. Þe interpolation also lacks a basis in Chaucer—who has "the eighe of intelligence is heyere, for it surmountith the universite, and loketh over that bi pure subtilte of thought"—and Trevet, who refers rather to Aristotle's *Metaphysics*, Book 12, for an understanding of the passage. Cf. Chaucer, *Boece*, 5p4.162–165, and Trevet, *Expositio*, 5p4 §§88–91, pp. 737–38.

[49] My reading is confirmed by Walton's commentary to his text, which twice discusses Paul's *speculum* in relation to Boethius; see Science, ed., *Consolation*, 364, 379.

[50] Copeland, *Rhetoric, Hermeneutics, and Translation*, 147; Johnson, "Walton's Heavenly *Boece*," 162; Johnson, "Making the *Consolatio*," 427.

iety that Walton feels towards his source.[51] If "sentence" is really transhistorical, immaterial, and immutable, then why would he despair of "sau[ing]" it?

One clue might be found in Walton's prologue. Just before announcing his intention to "kepe þe sentence" of Boethius, Walton introduces an intriguing challenge to his project: the problem of what he calls "corrupcioun."

> This subtile matere of boecius
> Heere in þis book of consolacioun
> So hye it is, so hard and curious
> Ful fair abouen myn estimacioun,
> Þat it be noght be my translacioun
> Defouled ne corrupt to god I praye. (2.1–6)

To worry that one's translation might "defoule" or "corrupt" one's source is hardly unusual, but what is unusual is the degree to which Walton obsesses over this idea throughout the rest of his text. Sometimes, "corrupcioun" appears in frightening images of the body gone wrong. We hear of the "wiȝte" of "corrupcioun" in the flesh, of tumors that are filled with "attre and corrupcioun," of the "coruptible cors" that imprisons the spirit (538.2, 372.8, 272.3). At other times, "corrupcioun" is used in relation to metaphysical things, as when the song of the muses is called a "swete venym of corrupcioun," or when it is said that the soul does not "torneþ to corrupcioun" (45.2, 225.8).

Of the many instances of "corrupcioun" in Walton's text, the group that stands out in greatest relief can be found in Philosophy's discussion of the lives, and deaths, of earthly things. Throughout his treatment of the passage, Walton interpolates "corrupcioun" many times. The dead body, he writes, is "careyn torned to corrupcioun," and things that "faileþ on" are "to corrupcioun i-broght" in death (514.8, 516.4-5).[52] Stones are treated as almost magical objects for their ability to withstand decay, for the tenacity with which their parts cling together:

---

[51] So argues Alastair Minnis: "[T]extual authority in general, like authoritative textual meaning in particular (*sensus*, *sententia*, whatever the term), was regarded as well-nigh inexhaustible, there to be discovered, inscribed, transmitted." See *Translations of Authority*, 11. Compare Johnson, "Making the *Consolatio*," 432.

[52] Both instances are interpolations; cf. *Consolatio*, ed. Bieler, 3p11.27. Walton here departs both from Chaucer, who makes no mention of corruption (see *Boece*, 3p11.56–73), and from Trevet, who makes no mention of corruption in his gloss (see *Expositio*, 3p11 §§30–45, pp. 455–56). Walton may pick up the idea from Trevet's comments on the meter immediately preceding, however: "Item habitus anime separate cognitiuus corrumpi non potest per obliuionem . . . sed habitus cognitiuus anime coniuncte corrumpi potest per obliuionem" [Also it is known that the soul, in its condition of being separated (from the body), cannot be corrupted by forgetfulness . . . but it is (also) known that the soul, in its condition of being conjoined (to the body), can (indeed) be corrupted by forgetfulness]. See Trevet, *Expositio*, 3m11 §9, pp. 473–74.

"How þei wiþstonde theire particioun, / And clyngen faste as euery man may seen / To saue þe partes fro corrupcioun!" (526.2–4).[53] In each case, "corrupcioun" is understood to be a force of dissolution—as that which breaks the whole into parts.[54] It is this conception of the term that Walton ultimately imposes upon Philosophy's concluding statements:

> Forwhy þe souereyn goddes purveaunce
> Haþ ȝeuen þis as cause effectuele
> To þinges þat ben of his ordinaunce,
> And be a verray kyndely gouernaunce
> Thei schol desiren all-wey for to be
> As longe as nature haþ þat suffisaunce
> To kepe þe parties in theire vnite.
>
> There is noght why þou schuldest doute in þis,
> Þat alle þing ne coueiteþ kyndely
> To kepe it-self in ferme and stabilnesse,
> And be corrupt þei loþen vtterly. (530.2–531.4)[55]

It is hardly a leap to connect this vision of matter in decay—in which all things long by nature to "kepe þe parties in theire vnite" and "loþen vtterly" to "be corrupt"—with Walton's anxiety in his prologue. What if the process of translation, he seems to wonder, will serve to speed rather than slow the advent of decay? What if his "insuffishaunce of cunning and of wit / Defaut of langage and of eloquence" (1.1–2) are simply too great to be withstood—no matter his desire, good intentions, and prayers to God?

One thing is clear in any case: Walton believes his text, and its *sentence*, to be subject to the forces of both material and linguistic "corrupcioun." Like Capgrave, who recounts a bizarre dream in which a writer is forced to consume the decayed text of his exemplar—"with bredys rotyn, levys dusty and rent"—be-

---

[53] There is no mention of corruption in the Latin; cf. Bieler, *Consolatio*, 3p11.70. While Trevet has nothing about corruption for this passage (see *Expositio*, 3p11 §80, p. 460), Walton may pick up the idea from Chaucer, who writes here of the manner in which "every thing kepeth thilke that is accordynge and propre to hym, ryght as thinges that ben contrarious and enemys corrumpen hem" (3p11.138–42).

[54] Walton's commentary echoes the idea that "corrupcioun" is a force of dissolution and division: "of nature euerything vvythstandeth in that it may / hys ovvne corruption and diuision of hys partes." See Science, ed., *Consolation*, 379, and cf. 370–71.

[55] Again the Latin has nothing about corruption, though it does mention the desire of all things *devitare perniciem* [to avoid destruction]; cf. *Consolatio*, ed. Bieler, 3p11.85–86. Walton differs both from Chaucer, who writes that all things desire "eschuynge of destruccioun," and from Trevet, who offers an extensive analysis of the desire of all things for their own preservation (see §§103–21, pp. 464–70) but does not mention corruption. See Chaucer, *Boece*, 3p11.86–87; and Trevet, *Expositio*, 3p11 (esp. §§97–102, p. 464).

fore he can begin to translate it, Walton sees the preservation of *sentence* as both a physical and a metaphysical task.[56] Like Lydgate and Gower before him, Walton hopes to preserve the books "of hem that writen ous tofore."[57] As a result, he is keenly sensitive to the deterioration of human knowledge over time—the way in which rotting books, language shifts, and historical change work towards its dissolution, bit by bit. *Sentence*, for Walton, is hardly universal or "well-nigh inexhaustible." It is a physical thing, one rooted in the particular structure that underlies the letter of a text.

Translation for *Sentence* in Fifteenth-Century England

With this more material understanding of *sentence* in mind, I would now like to reconsider fifteenth-century translation theory in relation to the Benjaminian "dream" of language equivalence. As I suggested in my introduction, Benjamin's desire for equivalence of meaning—and his concomitant desire for a kind of translation that would allow "pure language" to "shine upon the original all the more fully"[58]—do not characterize translation for *sentence*, either in practice or in theory. Ironically enough, this is partly because Benjamin's auratic ideal is ill suited to a manuscript culture. In a land of scribal variants and decayed exemplars, the linguistic, temporal, and physical distance between the "original" and its copies could be enormous. Fifteenth-century poets were highly aware of this distance and often took it up as a theme in their poetry. In his *Life of St. Katherine*, for instance, Capgrave outlines a convoluted *stemma* for his own source text: a "parsone of Sent Pancras" finds a Latin translation of Katherine's *vita* "fer up in Grece i-beryed in the grownde."[59] After bringing the translation back to England, the parson translates its Latin, itself a translation from Greek, into English prose, but it is so hard to understand, so full of the "straungenesse" of the parson's "derk langage," that Capgrave must translate it yet again, this time into English verse.[60] Just as there is a "grete distauns" between England and the grave of Katherine "in Arabie," so too is there a great historical, spatial, and linguistic distance

[56] Capgrave, *The Life of St. Katherine*, Prol.86.

[57] See Gower's prologue to the *Confessio amantis*, in *The English Works of John Gower*, ed. G.C. Macaulay, EETS e.s. 81–82 (London: Kegan Paul, Trench, Trübner, 1900–01): "Of hem that writen ous tofore / The bokes duelle, and we therfore / Ben tawht of that was write tho: / Forthi good is that we also / In oure tyme among ous hiere / Do wryte of newe som matiere / Essampled of these olde wyse" (1–7). Cf. Lydgate's prologue to his *Fall of Princes*, 1–28, for a fifteenth-century variation on this idea.

[58] Benjamin, "Task of the Translator," 78-79, and see my introduction above.

[59] *The Life of St. Katherine*, Prol.227, 50–51.

[60] *The Life of St. Katherine*, Prol.176–186, 62.

between the book in our hands and the "original" account of Katherine's life.[61] Other poets echo Capgrave by expressing similar interest in the *stemmae* of their source texts: Bokenham describes the circumstances under which he physically carries, or "translates," the *Life of St. Margaret* from Rome to England, while Walton, in an odd but important aside, notes the location of Boethius's grave: "In Pavie been his boones sikerlye" (26.8).[62]

Given the interest that fifteenth-century writers took in the literal and conceptual distance between themselves and their sources, it is possible that Benjamin's ideal of language equivalence might have seemed to them not merely implausible but even frightening or monstrous. At one point in Capgrave's *Life of St. Norbert*, Norbert agrees to perform an exorcism on a young woman under the control of a demon. As he chants above her, demanding that the demon leave in peace, she abruptly opens her mouth,

> And eke forth anoon, witȝouten ony more,
> The deuel gan speke and no þing rore;
>
> But seide oute in Latyn al þat ilk book,
> Whech we Cantica Canticorum calle.
> Euery man gan sterten, waytyn and look,
> For þus þei seide at þat tyme alle,
> Thei herd neuyr no wondir so sodeynly falle.
> For first þe maydin in Latyn al þis book spak,
> And aftir þat a exposicioun, witȝouten ony lak,
>
> Rehersed sche þerto; and ȝet aftir this
> In hir owne langage, in Teutony tunge,
> Opened sche þese wordes witȝouten mys.[63]

The act of double translation recounted here—first, an "exposicioun," either in Latin or the vernacular, and then an "open" translation "in Teutony tunge"—serves, I think, as an implicit comment on Capgrave's own practice of translation. The spectacle of a demon translating the Song of Songs perfectly, "witȝouten ony lak, witȝouten mys," is understandably frightening, particularly given Capgrave's note that the possessed woman was "not lerned but hir sauter only."[64] Perfect translation is here recast as demonic—as a marvel to be regarded with fear rather than adulation.

---

[61] *The Life of St. Katherine*, 5.1948, 5.1933.

[62] Bokenham, *Legendys*, ll. 97–122.

[63] John Capgrave, *The Life of St. Norbert*, ed. Cyril Lawrence Smetana (Toronto: Pontifical Institute of Mediaeval Studies, 1977), ll. 1070–1081.

[64] Capgrave, *Life of St. Norbert*, l. 1084.

I would suggest that the episode Capgrave describes throws into doubt Benjamin's assumption that, in translation, the equivalence of source with target is desirable above all else. Indeed, if Walton's project of translation is in line with other projects of literary compilation, like Gower's *Confessio amantis* or Lydgate's *Fall of Princes*, then it aims not for equivalence between source and target but for correspondence between them. It is an attempt, in other words, to pass on the *sentence* of Boethius in a suitable, but admittedly different, linguistic form. Walton understands this goal of correspondence, I suggest, in terms of what he calls "suffishaunce," or sufficiency—sufficiency in terms of the correspondence of his text's *sentence* with the *sentence* of Boethius, and in terms of the role that his translation will play in relation to other translations extant during his time.

> I haue herd speke and sumwhat haue i-seyne
> Of diuerse men þat wondir subtillye,
> In metir sum and sum in prose pleyne,
> This book translated haue *suffyshauntlye*
> Into Englisshe tonge, word for word, wel neye;
> Bot I most use þe wittes þat I haue;
> Þogh I may noght do so, yit noght-for-thye,
> With help of god þe sentence schal I saue. (4.1–8; my emphasis)

The reference to Chaucer, and perhaps also to other, now lost, English versions of the *Consolation* ("diuerse men þat . . . This book translated haue"), might seem to be hubris masked as humility: Chaucer translated "word-for-word," while Walton will translate, as is proper, "sense-for-sense."[65] But when it is recalled that Walton invoked "suffisaunce" in relation to the desire of all things to persist—as long as they have "suffishaunce" by nature, they desire "to kepe þe parties in theire vnite" (530.8)—the tone of the passage shifts.[66] *Suffisaunce*, as a term, seems to mean something like "the ability to make do," or "the ability to do well enough." If this is correct, it is unlikely that Walton would use it in a backhanded assertion of superiority to Chaucer. Moreover, in contrast to the stated "suffishaunce" of others, Walton also declares his own insufficiency twice: first, at the start of his prologue, and second, at its very end:

---

[65] Walton acknowledges Chaucer's translation in the next stanza (5). On the superiority of "sense-for-sense" over "word-for-word" translation, for which Jerome advocated, see Copeland, *Rhetoric, Hermeneutics, and Translation*, 45–51. Chaucer's *Boece* was in fact a rather literal, or "word-for-word," translation. See Machan, *Techniques of Translation*, 107; and Minnis and Machan, "The *Boece* as Late-Medieval Translation," 179, 182–83. See also A. Joseph McMullan's essay in this volume.

[66] *Suffishaunce* or its variants does not occur in Chaucer's translation, nor does Trevet mention the idea. See Chaucer, *Boece*, 3p11.168–187; Trevet, *Expositio*, 3p11, §§97–102, p. 464; and also above.

And euery lord or lady what ȝe be
Or clerk þat likeþ for to rede þis,
Besekyng lawly wiþ humylite
Supporte where I haue seyde amys;
Correcteþ only þere þat nedful is,
If word or sentence be noght as it scholde.
My-self I am vnsuffishuant I-wys
For if I couthe have bettre done I wolde. (31.1–8)

Although stating a desire for correction from one's patron is conventional during this time, I think that Walton rather oversteps the humility *topos* in this case.[67] Referring not merely to the unnamed patron of his text, he asks for the help of all readers—"euery lord or lady what ȝe be / Or clerk þat likeþ for to rede þis"—in the service of his greater project: the preservation of *The Consolation of Philosophy*. If you find "word or sentence" out of place, Walton suggests, take your pen in hand, and correct my manuscript.

In place of a standard of equivalence, then, Walton would seem to adopt a standard of sufficiency for his translation practice. An equivalent translation, following Benjamin, attempts to produce within itself "the echo of the original." Identical to that original save superficial differences of diction and syntax, it proposes, like that demonic echo of the Song of Songs, no essential difference between itself and its source.[68] A sufficient translation, by contrast, attempts only to reproduce, in its own manner, an integral part of the original: its *sentence*. It does not pretend to totality. As it happens, other fifteenth-century poets invoke just such a standard of "suffisaunce" for their work.[69] As I noted above, Lydgate suggests that to follow his source "in substaunce & sentence . . . suffise[s]" for his purposes.[70] Metham apologizes for his lack of poetic style by stating that, even if he were in possession of high rhetorical powers, "the tyme suffyse noght them to combyne" in the translation of his source.[71] Bokenham uses the term widely

---

[67] On the conventional desire for correction in fifteenth-century vernacular literature, see Ruth Evans, Andrew Taylor, Nicholas Watson, and Jocelyn Wogan-Browne, "The Notion of Vernacular Theory," in *The Idea of the Vernacular: An Anthology of Middle English Literary Theory*, ed. Wogan-Browne, Watson, Taylor, and Evans (University Park: Pennsylvania State University Press, 1999), 320–21. Compare Lawton, "Dullness and the Fifteenth Century," 762–70.

[68] Benjamin, "Task of the Translator," 76.

[69] For a discussion of "suffishaunce" in Middle English writing, see Ruth Evans, Andrew Taylor, Nicholas Watson, and Jocelyn Wogan-Browne, "Authorizing Text and Writer," in *The Idea of the Vernacular: An Anthology of Middle English Literary Theory*, ed. Wogan-Browne, Watson, Taylor, and Evans (University Park: Pennsylvania State University Press, 1999), 8–10.

[70] Lydgate, *Fall of Princes*, 2.159–160. See also above.

[71] Metham, *Amoryus and Cleopes*, l. 1777

and, like Walton, invokes it as an explicit standard of translation.[72] Saying that he is too old to learn how to "craft up" the "centens" of his source with "colours / of rhetorical speche both to & fro," Bokenham asks instead:

That I kunnyng may han suffycyently
To seruyn þe deocyoun of my lady
Aftyr hyr entent, þat is to seyne,
That I may translate in wurdys pleyne
In-to our langwage oute of latyn
The lyf of blyssyd Mare Mawdelyn.[73]

No replacement for the Latin *vita*, Bokenham's translation hopes merely to make accessible, in English "wurdys pleyne," the "sentence" of Mary's life for those who would read it.

Translation for *sentence* is thus a partial and contingent process, one that tries to accomplish enough without trying to accomplish everything. Because *sentence* is a physical thing—properly, the skeletal structure underlying a source text, a structure that, like the text, is susceptible to corruption—it is at once integral to and only a single part of that source. It is incomplete, and requires fleshing out in translation. As a result, where multiple translations may correspond in *sentence*, they will necessarily differ in terms of language, style, genre, structure, and length.[74] This is why Walton, Bokenham, and Capgrave all refer the reader to other translations in the course of their own texts.[75] Different translations, they suggest, may give the same, partial *sentence*, but no one translation will provide a fully "suffishaunt" realization of it. Even in the case of the Wycliffite Bible, the

[72] He says, for instance, that, while he could recount many "exaunplys" of vice, the story of "þis Quyncyan / As to oure purpoos ys suffycyent," and he notes that, while his translation of Elizabeth's *vita* is less "copyously" made than those of Gower and Lydgate, it does tell of "her merytys suffycyently." See Bokenham, *Legendys*, ll. 8883–8885 and 10530–10535.

[73] Bokenham, *Legendys*, ll. 5234–5239 and 5249–5254.

[74] Several critics have noted that late medieval English translation has a character of "correspondence" rather than "equivalence." See, for instance, J.D. Burnley, "Late Medieval English Translation: Types and Reflections," in *The Medieval Translator: The Theory and Practice of Translation in the Middle Ages*, ed. Roger Ellis (Cambridge: D.S. Brewer, 1989), 37–53, at 44; Ellis, "Choices of the Translator," 36; and David Lawton, "The Destruction of Troy as a Translation from Prose," *Studia Neophilologica* 52.2 (1980): 259–70, at 266–70.

[75] Bokenham, in his *Legendys*, refers the reader to Lydgate's *Lyfe of Oure Ladye* and Capgrave's *Life of St. Katherine* (2005–2007, 6354–6360). Capgrave, in his *Life of St. Katherine*, sends the reader to Philo, *Machabees*, and Apollonius of Tyre (1.106–112; 1.617–637).

belief that a single authoritative translation could be "suffishaunt" does not seem to have held.[76]

It is in this sense that, as I suggested above, late medieval translation might be considered more Trevisan than Hieronymian. When Trevisa insists that multiple translations of a source are not only acceptable but even desirable—"no synfol man," he writes, "doþ so wel þat he ne myȝte do betre, noþer makeþ so good a translacyon þat he ne myȝte make a betre"—he gives voice to a literary culture that rejected Jerome's dream of equivalence in translation.[77] His argument suggests, in turn, that fifteenth-century translation ought to be theorized not as the appropriation of source text into target text but, rather, as the collaboration of source with target—a claim that manuscript evidence would seem to support.[78] When Walton refers to Boethius's bones, he stresses, like Trevisa, the temporal and spatial differences between his source and his text. Like these bones, the *sentence* of Boethius can persist in translation across great lengths of space and time. It will remain, however, only a partial, skeletal echo of its original—one whose very emptiness permits, or even encourages, a multiplicity of interpretations.

[76] Evidence suggests that the Wycliffite translators saw their text as a complement to—but not a replacement for—Jerome's vulgate. See Hanna et al., "Latin Commentary Tradition," 394 and 392–400 generally. Compare Lawton, "The Bible," 201, 220.

[77] Trevisa, *Dialogus inter dominum et clericum*, in Ronald Waldron, "Trevisa's Original Prefaces on Translation," in *Medieval English Studies Presented to George Kane*, ed. Edward Donald Kennedy, Ronald Waldron, and Joseph S. Wittig (Woodbridge: D.S. Brewer, 1988), 293. For Trevisa's influence on Middle English translation, see, e.g., Copeland, *Rhetoric, Hermeneutics, and Translation*, 226; and Johnson, *Life of Christ*, 156.

[78] Several fifteenth-century copies of Jean de Meun's *Li Livres de confort*, Chaucer's *Boece*, and Walton's *Boethius* feature the Latin and vernacular texts in a collaborative arrangement, in a side-by-side, intercalated, or double column format: 1) Cambridge, Saint John's College, MS G.29 (Walton's *Boethius*); 2) London, British Library, MS Harley 43 (Walton's *Boethius*); 3) Chicago, Newberry Library, MS f36, ff. 78–204 (Walton's *Boethius*, with Latin and English interspersed); 4) Columbia, University of Missouri, MS Fragmenta Manuscripta 150 (a fragment of Chaucer's *Boece*, 2m7–2p8, with Latin and English on opposing pages); 5) Cambridge, Cambridge University Library, MS Ii.III.21 (Chaucer's *Boece*, the base for Machan's edition and discussed by Machan, *Techniques of Translation: Chaucer's Boece*, 122); 6) Paris, Bibliothèque de l'Arsenal, MSS 732 and 733 (French and Latin parallel texts); and 7) New York, Morgan Library, MS 332 (French main text surrounded by Latin text and Latin glosses). For further discussion, see Daniel Wakelin, *Humanism, Reading, and English Literature 1430–1530* (Oxford: Oxford University Press, 2007), 12–13; and Alastair Minnis, "Chaucer's Commentator: Nicholas Trevet and the *Boece*," in *Chaucer's Boece*, ed. Minnis, 91.

Contributors

Ann W. Astell is Professor of Theology at the University of Notre Dame, where she was appointed in 2007, after serving as Professor of English and chair of Medieval Studies at Purdue University. Her research focuses on medieval literature and spirituality, and she is the author of six books, including *The Song of Songs in the Middle Ages* (1990), *Job, Boethius, and Epic Truth* (1994), *Chaucer and the Universe of Learning* (1996), *Political Allegory in Late Medieval England* (1999), and *Joan of Arc and Sacrificial Authorship* (2003). The writing of her most recent book, *Eating Beauty: The Eucharist and the Spiritual Arts of the Middle Ages* (2006) was supported by a John Simon Guggenheim Memorial Fellowship (2001–2002).

Anthony G. Cirilla is Assistant Professor of English at College of the Ozarks in Branson, MO. He defended with distinction his dissertation, *Trivial Persons: The Trivium, Personification, and Identity in Medieval Literature, ca. 400–1400*, through the English Department of Saint Louis University in 2016, and for the past three years he has taught at his undergraduate institution, Niagara University, as well as another college in the Western NY region, Villa Maria. His academic focus is on the thought, aesthetics, and influence of Boethius's *Consolation of Philosophy*, with special interest in Chaucer and the Chaucerians, Arthuriana, allegory, and the liberal arts..

Taylor Cowdery is Assistant Professor of English at the University of North Carolina at Chapel Hill. His current book project investigates theories of matter and form in late medieval poetry, philosophy, and science—or, in brief, what medieval poets thought literature was made of. He has held academic fellowships from the Deutscher Akademischer Austauschdienst and at the Medieval Institute at Notre Dame, and his most recent article appears in the 2016 issue of *Studies in the Age of Chaucer*. He received his Ph.D. from Harvard University in 2016.

Nicole Guenther Discenza is Professor of English at the University of South Florida, where she teaches Old and Middle English and History of the English Language. Her publications include *Inhabited Spaces: Anglo-Saxon Constructions of Place* (University of Toronto Press, 2017) and *The King's English: Strategies* *of Translation in the Old English Boethius* (State University of New York Press, 2005). With Paul E. Szarmach, she co-edited *A Companion to Alfred the Great* (Brill, 2015).

Hilary Fox is Assistant Professor of English at Wayne State University in Detroit, Michigan. Her work on identity, ethics, and exemplarity in Anglo-Saxon writing has appeared in *The Journal of English and Germanic Philology*, *Medium Ævum*, and *Review of English Studies*. She is a former Harper-Schmidt Fellow in the Humanities Division at the University of Chicago.

Susan Irvine is Quain Professor of English Language and Literature at University College London. She is author of *Old English Homilies from MS Bodley 343* (1993) and *The Anglo-Saxon Chronicle MS E* (2004), and co-author (with Malcolm Godden) of *The Old English Boethius* (2009) (awarded the International Society of Anglo-Saxonists 2011 'Best Edition' Prize) and *The Old English Boethius with Verse Prologues and Epilogues* (2012). She is currently editing the prologues and epilogues to Alfredian writings.

Eleanor Johnson is Associate Professor of English and Comparative Literature at Columbia University. Her first book, *Practicing Literary Theory in the Middle Ages: Ethics and the Mixed Form in Chaucer, Gower, Usk, and Hoccleve*, was published by Chicago in 2013, and her second book, entitled *Staging Contemplation: Participatory Theology in Middle English Prose, Verse, and Drama*, is forthcoming from Chicago in Summer of 2018.

A. Joseph McMullen is Assistant Professor of English at Centenary University. He received a PhD in English and Celtic Literatures and Languages from Harvard University in 2015. His work is broadly concerned with medieval literary landscapes and connections between Anglo-Saxon England and early medieval Ireland. He recently co-edited, with Georgia Henley, *Gerald of Wales: New Perspectives on a Medieval Writer and Critic* (University of Wales Press, 2017).

Haruko Momma is the Angus Cameron Professor of Old English Language and Literature, the Chief Editor of the Dictionary of Old English, and Professor of Medieval Studies and English at the University of Toronto. She is the author of *The Composition of Old English Poetry* (Cambridge, 1997) and *From Philology to English Studies: Language and Culture in the Nineteenth Century* (Cambridge, 2012). She also co-edited *A Companion to the History of the English Language* (Wiley-Blackwell, 2008), the special issue *Old English across the Curriculum* for *Studies in Medieval and Renaissance Teaching* (2015), and the special issue *The Study of Old English in Nineteenth-Century Europe* for *Poetica* (2017).

Jonathan Stavsky is Senior Lecturer of English at Tel Aviv University and Alon Early Career Fellow. A graduate of the Hebrew University of Jerusalem and previous recipient of the Fulbright and Mandel postdoctoral fellowships, he has published on the fifteenth-century reception of Chaucer's poetry and on late-medieval configurations of the story of Susanna and the Elders. His critical edition, translation, and study of the romance *Le Bone Florence of Rome* was published by the University of Wales Press in 2017.

Paul E. Szarmach is Emeritus Professor of English and Medieval Studies at Western Michigan University, where he directed the Medieval Institute (1995–2007) and served as Distinguished Faculty Scholar. He is currently Research Associate in English at UC-Berkeley. His primary interest is Old English prose with special reference to Latin backgrounds. He was elected a Fellow of the Medieval Academy in 2006, when he also received the Robert L. Kindrick Service Award from Centers and Regional Associations, a Standing Committee of the Medieval Academy.

Erica Weaver is Assistant Professor of English at the University of California, Los Angeles. Her current book project traces the role of distraction in the development of early medieval literature and literary theory, particularly during the tenth-century Benedictine Reform movement. She received her PhD in English from Harvard University in 2018, and her article on the Old English *Boethius* (in *Anglo-Saxon England* 45) was awarded the Paul E. Szarmach Prize for an outstanding first article in the field of Anglo-Saxon studies.

Index

Abbo of Fleury, x, xxxi, 90n6, 91n9, 100–101
Explanatio in calculo Victorii, 101
agency, xxxi, 33, 74–75, 97, 157.
Aimoin of Fleury, 89–90, 101n42
Miracula Sancti Benedicti, 89–90
Alain of Lille, 140n31, 141
Alcuin of York, xiii, 4n12, 4n13, 11, 42n32, 93–94, 98n34
Aldhelm of Malmesbury, 4n12, 4n13, 11–12
Alfred the Great, ix, xiv–xviii, 7–10, 12, 21n7, 53–54, 72–73, 76, 94, 200
Alfredian translation program, ix–x, xivn14, xv, 2, 21n7, 51–52, 53–54, 76, 94–95
allegory, ix, xxvi, xxxii, 22, 63, 83, 132–34, 172–74, 177–91, 195, 198
angels, 21–22, 25–26, 32–34, 48–50
angelic understanding, 33, 49
rebel angels, 25–26, 34
Anglo-Latin, xi, xxxi, 4, 7, 96n26, 97–101, 103–24
Anselm of Canterbury, 175–76
De Concordia, 175–76
Aquinas, ix, 37n11.
Aristotle, 48, 109, 156, 206n48
Metaphysics, 206n48
Poetics, 156
Physics, 48
Ten Categories, 109
Ashby, George, xxviii–xxix, 200n28, 201
A Prisoner's Reflections, xxviii–xxix
Active Policy of a Prince, 200n28, 201n31
Asser, xxn41, 12, 52, 76
Vita Ælfredi, 12, 76
astronomy, x, xxxi–xxxii, 143–54
audience, xv–xvi, xxx, 6–11, 17, 20, 25–29, 46–49, 52, 59, 73–75, 131–41, 147–53, 161–62, 173–75, 180–81, 187–92
Augustine, xivn14, xv, 31–32, 36, 49–52, 53–54, 62, 75–76, 78–79, 103n1, 104–24, 199–201
Confessiones, 75–76, 104–15, 118–24
De doctrina Christiana, 78–79, 199–201
De trinitate, 117
Enarrationes in Psalmos, 62
Soliloquia, xivn14, 31, 36, 43, 46, 49–52, 53–54
authorship, xvii, xxii, 1–11, 16, 21n7, 35, 43, 50, 144n6
Ælfric of Eynsham, xvii, 3, 37, 75, 94, 96, 200
Ælred of Rievaulx, x, xxxi, 103–4, 106, 109–24
De spiritali amicitia, 104, 109n31, 111–18, 122n114
Speculum caritatis, 104, 113
Æthelweard, xvii, 94
Chronicon, xvii, 94
Æthelwold, Bishop of Winchester, 95–96, 99–100

Banester, Gilbert, 197
Bede, 11, 79, 119n94
De natura rerum, 41n30
Historia ecclesiastica, xivn14, 11–12, 79
In Genesim, 119n94
Old English translation of, 12, 95n24
opus geminatum [twinned work], and the, 11–12

Vitae S. Cuthberti, 4n13
Benedict of Nursia, 89–91, 115–17
Benedictine Reform, 91, 94–96
Benjamin, Walter, 77, 195–96, 209–12
Beowulf, 44–45
bispell [parable] 46, 63, 85. See also *exemplum*
Boethius, Anicius Manlius Severinus (as a historical figure), ix
Commentarii in Ciceronis Topica, 101
De institutione arithmetica, 98n36, 101
De institutione musica, ixn2, 101
De syllogismo hypothetico, 101
De trinitate, 103, 104, 117
In librum Aristotelis Perihermeneias commentarii editio duplex, 101
In Porphyrii Isagogen commentorum editio duplex, 101
Opuscula sacra, ixn2, 101
See also *Consolation of Philosophy*, specific passages
Boke of Coumfort of Bois, The, xxviii
Bokenham, Osbern, 194, 197–98, 210, 212–14
Life of St. Margaret, 210
Boniface, 94
Bovo II of Corvey, 40, 45n41, 124
Byrhtferth of Ramsey, xv, xxi, 101

Caelius Sedulius, 10–13, 15–16
Carmen paschale, 10–13, 15–16
Capgrave, John, 197–98, 208–11, 213
Life of St. Katherine, 217, 209–10, 213n75
Life of St. Norbert, 210
Carolingian background of the *Consolation*, xiii, 2, 15, 52, 90–95
cart image/cartwheel, xxx, 45–48, 55, 62–65, 67
Cassian, John, 86
Charlemagne, ix
Chaucer, Geoffrey, ix–xiii, xxiii–xxix, xxxi–xxxii, 130–65, 167–69, 171–72, 174–76, 181n28, 183n32, 185nn36–37, 186, 187n41, 189n46, 193–94, 195–96n10, 201–2, 203nn37–38, 203n40, 204n43, 205n46, 206, 207n52, 208n53, 208n55, 211
Boece, x–xiii, xxiii–xxviii, xxxi–xxxii, 131n14, 136, 143–64, 167–69, 171–72, 175–76, 181n28, 183n32, 185nn36–37, 186, 187n41, 189n46, 195–96n10, 202, 203n37, 203n40, 204n43, 205n44, 205n46, 206nn47–48, 207n52, 208n55, 211nn65–66, 214n78
"Boethian lyrics," xxv–xxvi
Book of the Duchess, The, xxv
Canterbury Tales, The, xxv, xxxi, 130, 133, 136–38, 140–41, 155–56, 160–65
Host, the; Harry Bailly, 133–35, 163–66
House of Fame, The, xxv
Knight's Tale, The, xxv, 164n33
Legend of Good Women, The, xxv, 138
Manciple's Tale, The, xxv, 135–38
Miller's Tale, The, xxxii, 144
Monk's Tale, The, xxv, xxxii, 155–69
Nun's Priest's Tale, The, xxv, 155, 163–65
Parliament of Fowls, The, xxv
Parson's Prologue and Tale, The, xxv, 135, 137–39
Retractions, xxv, 135, 138–39, 140
Tale of Melibee, The, xxv, 133–34, 137
Tale of Sir Thopas, The, xxv, 133–34, 137, 139
Treatise on the Astrolabe, xxxii, 144
Troilus and Criseyde, xi, xxv–xxvii, xxxi, 103, 130–33, 138, 144, 155, 156n8, 169, 195
Wife of Bath's Tale, The, xxv
Christianization, 92n13, 204n41, 206
Cicero, 9, 48, 85, 107, 110–12, 120, 181, 198
De amicitia, 106–7, 110–13, 118n86
Somnium Scipionis, 153
cloud (image), 136, 143, 150, 153, 161–63
commentary, x, xii, xix–xxiv, xxvii–xxix, xxxii, 16, 35, 39–40, 45, 46n43, 54, 72, 80, 92n13, 98, 113, 116, 129, 130n13, 142, 143–47, 150, 153,

154n47, 155–56, 158–59, 160n20, 203, 204n41, 206n49, 208n54
Consolation of Philosophy, specific passages
1m5, 22, 143, 148–49, 205
1p5, 23, 128–29
2p6, 80–81
3m9, xxx, 26, 31, 38n14, 39–45, 104n6, 143–44, 163n28, 203
3m11, 32, 145, 152, 163n28, 205n46, 207n52
3m12, 6
3p12, 25–27
4p4, 55, 58–62, 65–66, 204n43
4p6, 9n25, 32, 55, 59, 62–63, 97, 128
5p3, 32–33, 98
5p6, 20, 33, 98, 108, 116n77, 139n30
cosmology, xii, xxii, xxx–xxxii, 19–24, 31, 42–47, 143–54
curiosity (intellectual), 29–31.

Daniel, Walter, xxxi, 103–4, 115, 121
Vita Aelredi, 104, 115
Dante, 129–35, 141, 157n9
Vita nuova, 129–33
Deor, 44
Diogenes Laertius, 81
Lives of Eminent Philosophers, 81
disobedience, 22–32
Dunstan, Archbishop of Canterbury, xxxi, 90, 95, 97–98
Durham, 119

earth-as-egg metaphor, xviii, 42–43, 143
ecocriticism, xii
Emporius the Orator, 180–81
On ethopoeia, 180–81
eternity, 20–21, 33–34, 49–50, 56–61, 65, 69, 75, 108–9, 116–18, 132, 139, 206
ethics, xxii, 37–38, 55–62, 76–80, 125–43
ethopoeia, xxxii, 174, 180–88
exemplum, xxix, xxxi, 26–28, 67, 72–77, 80–88, 110, 137, 158n11, 165. See also *bispell*

false tales, 27–29
fate, xxviii, xxx, 5, 23, 32, 43–48, 56–69, 71, 84, 116, 131–32
Fleury, xxxi, 89–93, 95–102
foreknowledge, divine, xxvi, xxx, 20–22, 32, 45, 68, 97, 139n30
forgetfulness, 71, 84, 185–88, 205n46, 207n52
form, literary, ix–xiii, xxv, xxx, 1–17, 40, 47, 50, 125–42, 156, 157n11, 160, 169, 172n3, 176, 178. See also prosimetrum and *opus geminatum*
Fortune, xxvi, xxviii–xxix, 22–23, 47, 71, 84, 107, 110, 128, 132, 143, 149, 156, 158–59, 161–68, 174n7
Fortune's wheel, ix
Foucault, Michel, 72–73, 86–87
"technologies of the self," xxxi, 72–73, 86–87
free will, xxvi, xxx, 20–21, 23, 26, 32–33, 68, 93, 97, 130–31, 191
freedom, 21–22, 48, 67–68, 75, 81, 87
friendship, 51, 98, 103–15, 117–24, 161, 189n46
amicitia, 103, 110–12, 118, 122

geography, 149
giants, xxx, 26–29, 32, 34
glosses, x, xix–xxiv, xxviii, 11, 25n14, 32, 35, 39, 83, 116, 129, 143–54, 157–60, 163, 168, 196n10, 203n40, 204, 205n46, 206n47, 207n52, 214n78
Gower, John, 141, 194, 209, 213n72
Confessio amantis, 209n57, 211
Gregory, xv, 10n28, 86
Dialogues, xivn14, 10n28, 116
Life of St. Benedict, 117n84
Pastoral Care, xivn14, 53
Grimbald of St. Bertin, 52
Guillaume de Machaut, 129–31, 133–35, 141
Remède, 129–31

Haidu, Peter, 73–74
Henryson, Robert, xxviii–xxix, 157
Orpheus and Eurydice, xxviii–xxix
Hercules, xixn33, 45, 55, 67–69, 81, 87, 88n48
killing of Bosiris, 87

history, use of, 72–75, 77–80
Hoccleve, Thomas, xi–xiii, xxvi–xxviii, 141–42, 156, 165–69, 194
  Regiment of Princes, xxvi, 156n8, 166–67, 194n5, 198n19
  Series, xxvii, xxxii, 142, 156, 161n22, 166–69

Idley, Peter, 197, 198n19, 201
Isidore of Seville, 36–37, 52, 79, 126n4
  De natura rerum, 41n30
  Etymologiae, xxx, 36–37, 79, 126n4

James I of Scotland, xxviii–xxix
  Kingis Quair, xxviii
Jean de Meun, xxiv, xxvii, 104, 145–46, 148–50, 153–54, 161n23, 163n29
  Li Livres de confort, xxiv, 145–46, 148–50, 153–54, 161n23, 163n29, 214n78
  Roman de la Rose, 103–4, 153
Jerome, 123, 195–99, 200n26, 211n65, 214
John the Old Saxon, 52
John the Scot, 51
John Walton, x, xxiii, xxvii–xxviii, xxix, xxxii, 193, 197–98, 202–14
Johnson, Samuel, ix–x, xxvii
Jove, xxx, 26, 27–29, 32, 34
judgment, xxx, 50, 55, 59, 66, 77, 87, 114, 158n11, 198
Junius, Francis, 3

Kelly, Henry Ansgar, 146n12, 155–59, 160, 161n22
kingship, 10, 33, 48, 54, 72–73, 87–88, 97

Lantfred of Fleury, 90, 95–101
  Carmen de libero arbitrio, 93, 96–98, 100
  Translatio et miracula S. Swithuni, 95–96, 98
Lawrence of Durham, xxxi, 103, 118–24
  Consolatio de morte amici sui, 103, 106, 118, 121–24
  Dialogi, 119–21
leoð [poetry], 7–8
Lerer, Seth, 39, 66n21, 68n25, 104, 108
Lewis, C.S., x, 172, 175, 176n11
Liberius, xxxi, 72, 77, 80, 82–87
Life of St. Elizabeth of Spalbec, 201
Lydgate, John, 157, 165, 168, 194, 197, 201–2, 209, 212
  Danse Machabré, 201
  Fall of Princes, 201, 209n57, 211, 212
  Siege of Thebes, 201
  Troy Book, 201–2

manuscripts
  Cambridge, Cambridge Univ. Lib. Ii.3.21 ("the Croucher manuscript"), 158–61
  Cambridge, Corpus Christi College, MS 173, 12
  Copenhagen, Kongelige Bibliotek, MS Thott 304 2, xxiii, 204n41
  London, British Library, MS Cotton Otho A.vi, xvi, 3, 82n40
  London, British Library, MS Cotton Tiberius A.xv, 98
  London, British Library, MS Harley 2506, 99
  Orléans, Bibliothèque municipale, MS 127 (105) ("the Winchcombe Sacramentary"), 92
  Oxford, Bodleian Library, MS AUCT.F.3.5, xxviii
  Oxford, Bodleian Library, MS Bodley 180, xvi, 3, 82n40
  Paris, Bibliothèque nationale de France, MS lat. 987 ("the Winchester Benedictional"), 92
  Paris, Bibliothèque nationale de France, MS lat. 6401, 92–93, 98–100
Marenbon, John, 10n5, 22n50, 20n4, 20n5, 38–40
Martianus Capella
  De nuptiis Philologiae et Mercurii, 9, 14–15
mercy, 56, 57, 62, 65, 114, 182
Metham, John, 197–98, 212

Amoryus and Cleopes, 197, 212
mind, xvi, xviiin31, 13, 24, 32–33, 37, 46, 48–49, 56, 61, 64, 67, 72, 74–75, 81–87, 103n1, 104n6, 118n88, 121, 133, 136, 143, 150–52, 163, 172, 177, 185n36, 186, 190, 204
mod, xvi, 9, 13, 24, 37, 46, 49, 56, 64, 66–67, 71, 75, 82–84, 85n42, 86–88
moderation, 115, 121
"the middle way," 68–69
monasticism, xxviii, 87, 91–95, 115, 122–24
Monica, mother of Augustine, 108, 114
mourning/bereavement, 110, 113, 118, 128, 161, 31, 106
music, ixn2, xiii, 139, 187

nature, xxxi–xxxii, 24–25, 30–31, 37, 39, 41–43, 75, 124, 143–54, 208
Nebuchadnezzar, 166–67
Neoplatonism, xiii, xxi, xxx, 40–43, 46, 53, 104
Nicholas Trevet, xxii–xxiv, xxvii, xxix, xxxii, 46n43, 144, 146, 148–50, 151–54, 158–61, 206, 207n52, 208n53
Expositio super librum Boecii de consolatione, xxii, 146, 158, 202, 203n37, 204n40, 204n43, 205n44, 205n46, 206n47-48, 207n52, 208n53, 208n55, 211n66
Nimrod, 31, 34

Old English *Boethius*, xi–xxi, xxx–xxxi, 1–11, 13–17, 19–69, 71–76, 80–88, 93–94, 96n27, 143–44, 200n26
Meter 20 (see also *Consolation of Philosophy* 3m9), xxx, 38–43, 144n3
Meter 23 (see also *Consolation of Philosophy* 3m12), 6
Old English *Genesis,* 30
Old English *Heptateuch,* 30
Ong, Walter J., 186, 190
opus geminatum [twinned work], xii, 2, 4, 6–7, 10–13, 15–16, 96, 156n6
Orpheus, xxix
Osgar, Abbot of Abingdon, 95–96, 98
Ovide moralisé, 195

Paul, 205–6
performance, 88, 134, 178
personification, xiii, xxxii, xxxii, 134, 172–75, 177–80, 181–84, 185n35, 190–91
philosopher (as a figure in Anglo-Saxon England), 36–37, 40–41, 47, 65–69, 82
Plato, 9, 30, 31, 32, 37n11, 39
Timaeus, 39
prayer, 20, 21, 33–34, 40, 41, 107–8, 114–15, 123–24, 132, 139, 208
prefaces, Old English, xivn14, xv, xvii, xxx, 1–4, 7–11, 13–17, 50n48, 53–54
prison, xxiv, xxix, 15, 81, 136, 145n7, 175
prosimetrum, xvi, xxx, 9, 16, 98, 103, 118, 126, 129, 137, 140–41, 172n3
prosopopoeia, 179–81
providence, divine, 20, 43n34, 45, 47–48, 59, 63, 97, 114, 128, 131, 162n27, 165, 167
psychology, xxx–xxxi, 74–76, 126–30, 161, 186, 190
punishment, xxx, 20, 33, 55, 56–58, 60–62, 65, 67, 97, 139n30, 166–67
purgatory, xxx, 55–62, 65

Elizabeth I, Queen, x

Ramsey, xv, xxxi, 100–102
rebellion, xxx, 22, 26, 27, 28, 34
Remigius of Auxerre, xx, 15, 116, 145
Richard II, 174
Ricoeur, Paul, 75, 77
Rusticiana, wife of Boethius, 107

sacramentality, 181, 184, 188
Scholasticism, 37
Seafarer, The, 74, 88
self-knowledge, ix, xxxi, 71–77, 83–88, 145, 151–52, 167–69, 185–86

sentence [sense or understanding], xxiii, xxvii, xxxii, 147, 151, 153, 164, 187–88, 193–214
Solomon and Saturn I, 77–78
soul, xviiin31, xxv, 24, 31–32, 39–40, 42–43, 50–51, 53, 55–62, 64–66, 73–75, 84–85, 108–10, 121, 123, 126–27, 132, 139n30, 143n3, 152, 156, 186, 191, 205, 207
  sawol, 74–75
  ternary organization of postmortem souls, 57–58, 64–65
speculative philosophy, xiii, xxx, 37, 54n6
Stoicism, 67, 87, 123, 183
strangeness, 6, 207
subjectivity, xxxi, 73–74, 88
Suso, Henry, 168
  Horologium sapientiae, 168
Symmachus, Quintus Aurelius Memmius, 107n20, 199

Theodoric, 81, 107
Theodulf of Orléans, xiii, 93
Thynne, William, 175
Tower of Babel, xxx, 29–32, 34
tragedy, xxxii, 16n49, 131–32, 133n22, 155–69
translation theory, xi, xii–xviii, xxiii–xxviii, xxxii, 2–6, 17, 21n7, 34, 41–43, 50n18, 51–55, 78n28, 143–44, 146–47, 151–54, 187–88, 193–202, 204, 206, 209–14
Trevisa, John, 168, 196, 214
tyranny, 87, 132

unwar [both undiscerning and indiscernible], 158–59, 161–62, 168
Usk, Thomas, xi–xii, xxii, xxiiin57, xxvi, xxviii, xxix, xxxii, 141, 171–92
  Testament of Love, xxiiin57, xxvi, 171–92

vernacular, x, xii–xiii, xivn14, xv, xix, xxi, xxiii, xxviii, xxix–xxx, 1–2, 5, 6, 9–10, 12, 16–17, 38, 41, 43, 52–54, 104, 125, 129–30, 133, 138, 140, 142, 177, 186, 193–94, 210, 212n67, 214n78
Vita Boethii, 14

Wanderer, The, 44
Wærferth of Worcester, 52
William of Conches, xxii, 129, 146, 154n47
William of Malmesbury, xvii
Winchester, xxxi, 12, 92–93, 95–102
Wulfstan Cantor, 96
Wycliffite Bible, 193
wyrd, 5, 23, 43–45, 47–48, 63, 68–69, 71, 82

Zeno of Elea, 80–83, 88